Organizational Behaviour and Work: A Critical Introduction

Fiona M. Wilson

Professor of Organizational
Behaviour, Department of Business and
Management, University of Glasgow

OXFORD
UNIVERSITY PRESS

OXFORD
UNIVERSITY PRESS

Great Clarendon Street, Oxford OX2 6DP

Oxford University Press is a department of the University of Oxford.
It furthers the University's objective of excellence in research, scholarship,
and education by publishing worldwide in

Oxford New York

Auckland Bangkok Buenos Aires Cape Town Chennai
Dar es Salaam Delhi Hong Kong Istanbul Karachi Kolkata
Kuala Lumpur Madrid Melbourne Mexico City Mumbai Nairobi
São Paulo Shanghai Taipei Tokyo Toronto

Oxford is a registered trade mark of Oxford University Press
in the UK and in certain other countries

Published in the United States
by Oxford University Press Inc., New York

A Catalogue record of this book is available from British Library

Library of Congress Cataloging in Publication Data
Data available
ISBN 0-19-926141-5

Typeset by SNP Best-set Typesetter Ltd., Hong Kong
Printed in Great Britain by
Antony Rowe, Chippenham, Wiltshire

DEDICATION

For my closest relatives and friends on whose love and support I depend.

■ ACKNOWLEDGEMENTS

Thanks must be extended to Stewart Clegg who was instrumental and inspirational in helping design the original course from which this book has developed. The first set of reviewers, Chris Grey and David Wilson provided much support and enthusiasm at the proposal and later stages of the book that motivated me in the writing. For the second edition six new anonymous reviewers have provided the most positive and constructive feedback a prospective author could wish for—many thanks to them.

■ CONTENTS

INTRODUCTION

Work occupies a substantial proportion of most of our lives. It can be a symbol of personal value, provide status, economic reward, and a potential. It can also be regarded as a punishment. Work and employment structure our lives and shape inequalities of condition and opportunity.

Work can be divided into four types. The first is recognized and rewarded work which is paid. This takes the individual into a labour market to sell their skills, time, and energy to an employer like a university, a private or public company, or their family, if they work in their family business. The second type is reproductive labour and concerns the efforts involved in raising one or more children to adulthood. A third type of work is maintenance labour, the chores necessary to maintain yourself and other members of your family by cooking, paying the bills, food shopping, gardening, laundry, and so on. The fourth type is unpaid work, voluntary work for charities, churches and other religious groups, hospitals, and political parties. Levels of voluntary activity are high and there has been a rapid growth in the number of charities (Halfpenny and Reid 2002).

Women still take the major share of housework and childcare even when both partners work (Gershuny 1997; Mihill 1997, Bianchi et al. 1999). Women on average do about 70 per cent of household work (Baxter 2000). They do the lion's share of domestic work even when husbands are retired or unemployed. Husbands' household labour is 'remarkably unresponsive' to decreases in their overall working hours, to increases in their wives' working hours, and to the fact that their wife is a high earner (Kynaston 1996). Men's lives 'continue to be consistently enhanced by their appropriation of female labour' (Kynaston 1996: 233). Little mention is made of this in books on work or organizational behaviour. The context in which work is defined as men's or women's work must be considered. The all-pervasive influence of culture and social structure on organizational behaviour needs to be explored.

The book is designed to challenge what constitutes organizational behaviour (OB). The meaning of the term is far from clear. Is it behaviour that occurs in some specified place and not in others or behaviour controlled by an organization (Weick 1969: 25)? Should we only be interested in behaviour that happens within organizations? What happens within organizations affects what happens outside and vice versa. Organizational behaviour is seen here chiefly as being about the particular ways that individuals' dispositions are expressed in an organizational setting and about the effects of this expression. While at work there is rest and play. What happens in rest and play, both inside and outside the organization, impacts on organizational life.

We also can gain insight into organizational behaviour by looking at less organized work, like work 'on the fiddle', which has been examined by both psychologists and social anthropologists, and what work means to the unemployed. This book would ask you to question what organizational behaviour is and how it is influenced. What are the common characteristics to be found in organizations and what behaviour draws our attention? For you is it all about work, or do rest and play have a part too?

Textbooks on organizational behaviour usually include chapters on perception, personality, motivation, job satisfaction, job design, leadership, learning, and socialization. We seem to have accepted the litany of topics which fall under the heading of OB. This litany does not reflect the much wider range of issues and topics under discussion in management and OB journals. Nor are these topics usually dealt with from a critical perspective, examining for example the weaknesses in the research from the 'gurus' like Herzberg and Belbin. Organizational or occupational psychology has mainly informed the discipline that is cited in textbooks, yet is only one small part of what currently is recognized as constituting OB. The psychology approach has a 'scientific' view, a mission to construct and validate theories that can explain and predict organizational behaviour. Science provides a justification for believing there is no problem with the status of knowledge. Knowledge produced through scientific methods is unproblematically true and scientists are potentially neutral agents in the process (Hollway 1991). The individual is usually the unit of analysis. Theory construction in organizational psychology is based on a highly analytic and experiment-based form of science, rooted in the natural sciences. There has, in the past, been an unwillingness to reflect on and critique the discipline (Steffy and Grimes 1992), though there are now books which treat psychology critically (e.g. Fox and Prilleltensky 1997; Trew and Kremer 1998). The bulk of the research in organizational psychology does not focus on dynamic issues like organizational power, conflict, class, politics, and ideology. As a result there is a very tidy and sanitized view of what goes on in organizations, yet we all know that work issues and behaviour in organizations are much more than this. There is uncertainty, chaos, and confusion in organizing. There is control and resistance, work being degraded and deskilled too. Workplaces are not peopled by high-performing, highly committed individuals bound together in a common cause by a corporate mission enshrined within a strong organizational culture (Noon and Blyton 2002). Workplaces are sites of inequalities, divided by class, levels of education, race, and gender. Workplaces are places where romance takes place, where people find others they develop relationships with, outside work. They are also places where harassment, bullying, and other behaviours take place. We need then a critical approach, taking a critical or radical view of contemporary behaviour in organizations, an approach that considers fun, exploitation, repression, unfairness, and unequal power relations. Sociology must inform what Organizational Behaviour is in textbooks too.

Much of what we read in textbooks about work is about men and their work, how they are motivated, how they gain job satisfaction, are stressed, and so on. As Crompton (1989: 129) too has noted, much of the empirical research and theorizing on work, particularly in sociology, is derived from outdated studies of predominantly white male production workers. The theory of organizations and work is mainly a chronology of men's writings, research, and theory. Female management theorists, like Mary Parker Follett (Graham 1995), Joan Woodward (Tancred-Sheriff and Campbell 1992), and Simone Weil (Grey 1996) have been written out of, or marginalized from, the history and development of management ideas. Classical theory comes from the intellectual 'fathers' like Weber and Taylor. The fathers' ideas formed the foundation for the theory and research methods of organizational behaviour. Women's experiences are conspicuously absent from theory, methods, and data. Practically all organizational behaviour, analysis, and theory is about the male world. The topics that preoccupy it are topics which preoccupy men—power, leadership, technology, stress, the world of the (mainly male) manager and the work he does, and so on, with women only as adjuncts to men. If women are dealt with it is usually in a chapter thrown in as an extra, almost as beside the point rather than as an intrinsic component of behaviour in organizations. Half the population of organizations is left at the edge or just tagged onto OB texts (Wilson 1996). Very little in organizational behaviour texts deals with the nature, structure, and functioning of female-dominated jobs. Despite the fact that authors such as Richard Brown (1976) and Janet Wolff (1977) argued nearly three decades ago that gender should figure more largely in organizational analysis, little progress has been made (Wilson 2003). A great deal of research focuses on men with no reference at all to women but when research is focused on women, it is almost always with reference to men. If comparisons are not made with men, the research is viewed as incomplete (Bernard 1998). Research on women in their own right is not worthy of male attention.

A PERSONAL EXPERIENCE

A Ph.D. student had an experience where this view became a reality for her. She presented her research proposal and methodology—on women entrepreneurs (women who own and manage bed and breakfast establishments) to a group of academics and found that they did not think that she should limit her study to women. What about men who own and manage bed and breakfast establishments, they asked? Would the same question have been asked if she had designed her research on male managers or male entrepreneurs?

I published a book *Organizational Behaviour and Gender* (in 1995 and 2003) to try to begin to redress the balance. Gender is not just about women, but also about men. Gender is more than an individual trait or set of roles. The differences between women and men are not essential to either sex. This book is written, as others like Grint (1998) and Noon and Blyton (2002) have begun to do, to discuss women's work in balance with men's, to think about the implications of unpaid domestic work, to consider issues of ethnicity as well as gender. (If, when reading this book you think there is too much on women and work, ask yourself why this is the case when about half the population of organizations is female.) Gender is systematically and inextricably tied to other inequality issues like race, sexual orientation, and class.

The issues of the racial and ethical foundations of organizational power and control are only just beginning to emerge in the literature (Reed 1996). Race, like gender, offers itself as a kind of performance, a set of practices, and language. If we were to 'colour' organizational studies, we would need to think more about what colour means and take apart the grammars of race (black/white, African/American/Asian American, native/indigenous) to track racial identity and search ideological commitments (Ferguson 1994: 93).

Another area from which OB could profitably draw is emotion and feeling. As Fineman (1996) notes, a scan of the indexes of textbooks on organizational behaviour and theory reveals few, if any, entries under emotions or feelings. Yet gripes, joy, drudgery, anger, anxiety, frustrations, glee, embarrassment, and tedium are part of the social creation and personal expression of work and organizational life. Activities like recruiting, firing, negotiating, and persuading are felt and shaped by feelings. Emotion emerges as an issue in many of the chapters here; you are asked to consider the place of emotion in organizations.

This book also asks you to look outside what are normally thought of as organizations and how we usually think of work. What can be learnt from 'deviant' work, work in the sex industry, like prostitution, for example? Everett Hughes, a sociologist, encouraged his students to look at 'dirty' or deviant types of occupations. These occupations are interesting in their own right and can help highlight factors of general relevance to work experience which we might not notice in conventional work where we too easily take them for granted (Watson 1997). Why is there so little mention of sex, violence, pain, and power in organizational life (Burrell 1997: 52)? Gibson Burrell would say that organization studies tend to ignore or hide that which is thought to be unacceptable in polite company and management writers have acted like funeral directors or morticians, using cosmetics and 'rouge of excellence' to cover 'necrotic collapse' of organizational structures. There is plenty of research which reveals the difficulties, problems, and realities of organizational life, and plenty from outside organizations that could help inform our understanding about what happens in organizations, but so far little of it has appeared in mainstream management textbooks.

The book has been written as an alternative to the standard introductory texts in management. The purpose was to provide a fresh critical look at management and organizations, to uncover the issues and assumptions underlying the world of management and subject them to scrutiny. The emphasis here has been on exposing and discussing deep-seated features of organizational life like inequality, conflict, domination, subordination, and manipulation. It was written particularly for those people who acknowledge that there are few certainties about how to manage and many difficulties, uncertain tensions, irrationalities, and dilemmas to face in the mundane realities of work.

This book is designed to offer an introduction to a view of organizational behaviour that has a long history but, as yet, has not been included in many of the introductory texts. The style of writing is deliberately simple and straightforward in order to encourage students to grasp the basic ideas, arguments, and controversies before moving on to more complex levels of analysis and explanatory theory. Some of the chapters are longer than others; for example the chapter on meaning of work is short while the one on culture is long. This should not lead students to assume that the longer the chapter, the more important the subject. Shorter chapters may occur as there is less research currently on the topic or if there is much more which is closely related; for example in the case of meaning of work there are close links with the view from below and unemployment chapters.

Lecturers who want to use this book as a basis of their course design have some choices to make. They could lecture, using some of the sources here or from elsewhere, having the book as mandatory or supplementary reading, using the questions for further research (now simply called 'questions') and reading for tutorials, assignments, and exam questions. Or they could abandon the lecture/tutorial mode of teaching in favour of using the book as essential reading and the questions for further research as a basis for student projects for class, assignment, and exam. What was lecture time could be used for exercises like stress testing, or for excerpts from films or video as a means of getting attention for the subject. You choose.

■ QUESTIONS

1. Where does student work fit in? What category would you need to add? Why isn't the work you do as a student defined as 'work'? Look at the contents pages of other management and organizational behaviour texts and see what kind of work is typically discussed.

2. How do Organizational Behaviour books usually treat behaviour. Whose approach is being used? Is it useful to a practising manager? If you were a practising manager, what would you want to know?

■ SUGGESTIONS FOR FURTHER READING

There are other textbooks that encourage critical thinking in management, for example L. Fulop and S. Linstead (1999), *Management: A Critical Introduction*, Houndmills: Macmillan and A. B. Thomas (2003), *Controversies in Management: Issues, Debates, Answers*, London: Routledge. Similarly P. Thompson and D. McHugh (2002), *Work Organizations*, Houndmills: Palgrave and T. Watson (2002), *Organising and Managing Work*, Harlow: Pearson Education Ltd., and J. Barry et al. (2000), *Organization and Management: A Critical Text*, London: Thomson Learning help develop a more critical approach to the realities of work organization.

■ REFERENCES

Baxter, J. (2000), 'The Joys and Justice of Housework', *Sociology*, 34/4: 609–31.

Bernard, J. (1998), 'My Four Revolutions: An Autobiographical History of the ASA', in K. A. Myers, C. D. Anderson, and B. J. Risman (eds.), *Feminist Foundations: Towards Transforming Sociology*, London: Sage, ch. 1.

Bianchi, S., Robinson, J. P., Sayer, L., and Milkie, M. (1999), 'Is Anyone Cleaning the Bathroom? Trends in Gender Differentials in Housework', paper presented at the American Sociological Association Meetings, Chicago, August.

Brown, R. (1976), 'Women as Employees: Some Comments on Research in Industrial Sociology', ch. 2 in D. L. Barker and S. Allen (eds.), *Dependence and Exploitation in Work and Marriage*, Harlow: Longman.

Burrell, G. (1997), *Pandemonium: Towards a Retro-Organizational Theory*, London: Sage.

Crompton, R. (1989), Review of Y. Gabriel (1988), *Working Lives in Catering*, in *Work, Employment and Society*, 3/1: 129–30.

Ferguson, K. (1994), 'On Bringing More Theory, More Voices, More Politics to the Study of Organization', *Organization*, 1/1: 81–100.

Fineman, S. (1996), 'Emotion and Organizing', in S. R. Clegg, C. Hardy, and W. R. Nord (eds.), *Handbook of Organization Studies*. London: Sage Publications, ch. 3.3.

Fox, D., and Prilleltensky, I. (1997), *Critical Psychology: An Introduction*, London: Sage Publications.

Gershuny, J. (1997), 'The Changing Nature of Work', press release, ESRC Research Centre on Micro-Social Change, University of Essex.

Graham, P. (1995), (ed.), *Mary Parker Follett: Prophet of Management*, Boston, Mass.: Harvard Business School Press.

Grey, C. (1996), 'Towards a Critique of Managerialism: The Contribution of Simone Weil', *Journal of Management Studies*, 33/5: 591–611.

Grint, K. (1998), *The Sociology of Work: An Introduction* (2nd edn.), Cambridge: Polity.

Halfpenny, P., and Reid, M. (2002), 'Research on the Voluntary Sector: An Overview', *Policy and Politics*, 30/4: 533–50.

Hollway, W. (1991), *Work Psychology and Organizational Behaviour: Managing the Individual at Work*, London: Sage.

Kynaston, C. (1996), 'The Everyday Exploitation of Women: Housework and the Patriarchal Mode of Production', *Women's Studies International Forum*, 19/3: 228, 232–3.

Mihill, C. (1997), 'New Man is Shunning Equal Shares of Chores', *Guardian*, 8 Sep.

Noon, M., and Blyton, P. (2002), *The Realities of Work* (2nd edn.), Basingstoke: Palgrave Macmillan Press.

Reed, M. (1996), 'Organizational Theorizing: A Historically Contested Terrain', in S. R. Clegg, C. Hardy, and W. R. Nord (eds.), *Handbook of Organization Studies*. London: Sage. ch. 1.1.

Steffy, B. D., and Grimes, A. J. (1992), 'Personnel/Organizational Psychology: A Critique of the Discipline', in M. Alvesson and H. Wilmott (eds.), *Critical Management Studies*, London: Sage, ch. 9.

Tancred-Sheriff, P., and Campbell, E. J. (1992), 'Room for Women: A Case Study in the Sociology of Organizations', ch. 2 in A. J. Mills and P. Tancred, *Gendering Organizational Analysis*, London: Sage.

Trew, K., and Kremer, J. (1998), (eds.), *Gender and Psychology*, London: Arnold Publishers.

Watson, T. J. (1997), *Sociology, Work and Industry*, London: Routledge.

Weick, K. E. (1969), *The Social Psychology of Organizing*, Reading, Mass.: Addison-Wesley Publishing Company.

Wilson, F. M. (2003), *Organizational Behaviour and Gender* (2nd edn.), Aldershot: Ashgate.

——(1996), 'Research Note: Organizational Theory. Blind and Deaf to Gender?', *Organization Studies*, 17/5: 825–42.

Wolff, J. (1977), 'Women in Organizations', in S. Clegg and D. Dunkerley (eds.), *Critical issues in Organizations*, London: Routledge & Kegan Paul, pp. 7–20.

1 Scene Setting

This chapter aims to provide a context for understanding behaviour in organizations. While other textbooks might wish to describe the environment in which organizations operate in terms of finance, stakeholders, and other influences or constraints on organizational behaviour, this chapter aims to describe key facts about people and work in order to set the scene for the rest of the book. It wants you to think about what information would be useful to you when you are a manager.

Chapters on the business environment in management textbooks tend to concentrate on background information on how to analyse the general business environment and identifying environmental influences—the political, legal, economic, socio-cultural, and technological influences. The examples given are usually of manufacturing organizations. Rarely do examples include the farming industry, service organizations, or charities.

If you work for a charity, you will want to know about how to boost donations against a backdrop of statistics that suggest that individual giving is lower now than it was ten years ago (NCVO 2001). Further it might be useful to know that the worse off give proportionately more than the better off. The richest 20 per cent of households give less than 1 per cent of their household expenditure to charities. Seven hundred thousand top-rate taxpayers gave nothing to charity in 2001 (*Observer*, 5 May 2002). The poorest give 3 per cent (Banks and Tanner 1997). Some research demonstrates a larger discrepancy (Egan 2001). The reasons for lack of giving by the rich are explored by Edwards (2002). If you are a manager in the Department of Social Security, you might need to know that there is an increase in the numbers of those in poverty despite the national minimum wage and the working families tax credit (*Guardian* 2001).

The farming industry receives a lot of media attention but virtually no attention in mainstream management texts. Farming is increasingly being dominated by large corporations who have an interest, for example, in promoting genetically modified (GM) crops. Interesting questions for managers are 'Could better management reduce the reality of hunger for over 800 million people in the world?' 'Will GM crops stop hundreds of millions going without enough to eat?' If you manage a charity like Christian Aid, this is a crucial question. Christian Aid believes that GM crops are irrelevant to ending hunger (Christian Aid Reports 2000: 2). One way it is managing its campaign is by gaining the support of over forty organizations ranging from the Iceland Foods retail chain to the

Townswomen's Guilds. Famine could be a management problem. In 1995 India exported 5 million tonnes of rice and $625 million worth of wheat and flour. At the same time, more than one in five Indians went hungry (Christian Aid Reports 2000: 6). There is more food available but more people are going hungry. For example the food available to each person in Latin America increased by 8 per cent between 1970 and 1990 but the number of those going hungry increased by 19 per cent (Christian Aid Reports 2000: 6). Is this a situation that could be managed? Has the promise of globalization, which was to lift underdeveloped economies onto a level playing field with the developed ones, failed?

Globalization

This is a term originally used to describe the gradual connection between different societies. Globalization now usually refers to the global presence and expansion of organizations like Christan Dior, McDonald's, or Exxon and products like Coke as well as global production methods like Just in Time, Total Quality, and Lean Production. Coupled with the increasing role of worldwide telecommunications and e-commerce, there is an unprecedented rate of internationalization happening. This is the case with new ventures as well as old (Oviatt and McDougall 1995).

Many scholars make the mistake of equating large organizations with globalization. For example, while Walmart (who operate Asda in Britain) is the biggest company in the world, as measured by sales, it is not a global company; it is primarily a North American business with only 9.6 per cent of its stores being outside its home region. Similarly Carrefour of France has 9,200 stores but only 19 per cent of Carrefour's revenues originate from outside Europe so it cannot be called a global company (Rugman and Girod 2003).

Globalization is a strongly contested concept, one reason being that there is no consensus as to its meaning and significance. It is thought, for example by Steeten (2001) to lead not to bland sameness across countries, but to sharpened social-spatial inequalities. Sociologists are concerned that national and regional cultures may be submerged by a common global capitalist culture and that globalization will increase existing inequalities as well as the pace of growth of individualism (Herriot and Scott-Jackson 2002). So much for the global situation but what would you need to know about the working population in Britain?

The Working Population in Britain

As the general population in Britain is gradually rising so the number of those of working age is increasing. The population is expected to rise from 59.2 million in 1998 to over 63.5 million by 2021 and to peak around 2036, then gradually fall. With the increase in the state retirement age of women from 60 to 65 (expected between the years 2010 and 2020) the working age population will further rise in numbers (Population Trends 2000). The prevalence of disability increases with age. Currently 19 per cent of the working age population are long-term disabled (Labour Force Survey 2001). The number of children parents have is also changing; instead of the average family having 2.5 children it is expected that they will have 1.8. (Evandrou and Falkingham 2000). Data on ethnic origin of the population in the UK show that 92 per cent are white. Only 3.5 per cent are Asian or Asian British while 2 per cent are black or black British. Chinese make up just 0.3 per cent (Labour Force Survey 2001).

STOP

Thinking about Cloning and the Reproduction of Sameness

Essed and Goldberg (2002) provocatively ask who, in the future, will be biologically cloned? It seems likely that in the biological cloning of humans the preference will be for male, white, able-bodied, heterosexual, and highly intelligent beings. Whilst biological cloning is still to be realized, cultural cloning brings exclusion into focus. The preference for reproducing white (Euro) masculine privileges in terms of race, ethnicity, gender, or profession is not contested with the same force of indignation as might be found in the case of biological cloning. The exclusiveness of the whiteness of the highest European echelons remains silenced. Thirty years of equal opportunities has done little to change the reproduction of sameness (see also Special Report on Race in the Boardroom 2002). Preferences for sameness are also embedded in our allegiance to copy culture, mass produce, consumerism, and the promise of eternal growth (Schwarz 1996; Klein 1999).

The working population is ageing so will today's youth have to support an increasingly large elderly population? Is age discrimination stopping older workers supporting themselves? These are all questions that are regularly raised in the media. There have been some alarmist projections of demographic 'time-bombs' in Britain arising from population ageing and declining fertility. There are more older people in our society; in 1901 nearly one in seven were aged over 50 but by 1997 this had doubled to one in three (ONS 1999). The state retirement age for women is going to be increased from 60 to 65; this is going be phased in by 2020 so the size of the female working age population will increase. The older population is heterogeneous with substantial differences in socio-economic status, employment patterns and stability, education, ethnicity, and gender (Bernard et al. 1995; Elman and O'Rand 1998; Phillipson 1998).

The working population is gradually becoming older. By 2008 it is expected that the population of pensionable age will exceed the number of children (Shaw 2000). One reason for this is increased life expectancy, which is expected to rise from 74.9 years for men to 78.5 and from 79.7 years to 82.7 for women by 2020. As people live longer and medical advances help older people lead active lives, they may want to work longer or may welcome early retirement as a time to establish their own business and a means of gaining control over their lives. Will the increase in pensioners bring increased pressure on health and social services or will tomorrow's older population be wealthier and healthier? Research indicates that as life expectancy increases there will be a rise in the proportion of people experiencing light to moderate disabilities but a fall in those with severe disabilities (Evandrou and Falkingham 2000).

The alarmist projections were fuelled by a growing trend of older people, particularly older men (over 50 years old) leaving their jobs prematurely. Early exit from employment accelerated during the 1980s and 1990s. The early exit phenomenon has been described as 'one of the most dramatic economic transformations of labour markets in modern industrial economies' (Rein and Jacobs 1993: 53). It entails a number of routes out of employment including early retirement, voluntary or compulsory redundancy, dismissal and retirement on grounds of ill health. Early exit in most cases proves permanent (Duncan 2003); it is widespread across both the public and private sectors, in growth industries as well as those experiencing employment decline (Campbell 1999). At one stage it was thought that this trend would create jobs for the young and reduce official rates of unemployment. In fact it was discovered that older workers should be persuaded to stay at work in order to offset the impending shortage of young workers (House of Commons 1989). Early exit is now seen as a phenomenon derived from age prejudice.

The issue of age prejudice and age discrimination remains under-researched. The definition of who is an older worker is ambiguous and contingent. It varies with industry, occupation, and gender. For example women report experiencing age discrimination or being considered too old for employment at earlier ages than men (Encel and Studencki 1997; Ginn and Arber 1995; Onyx 1998).

Ageism

The term 'ageism' came into existence around the same time as 'sexism', in the late 1960s in the USA but only entered public discourse in Britain in the 1980s. It refers to the systematic stereotyping of, and discrimination against, people because they are old (Loretto et al. 2000). Research has clearly shown that older workers experience ageism.

Recent research for the Department for Education and Employment finds widespread evidence of discrimination against older workers (DfEE 2001b). Around one in four older workers report experiencing age discrimination in relation to job applications. One in twenty report experiencing age discrimination with respect to promotions, training, and development as well as compulsory retirement. Employers dispense with workers aged 50 and over through voluntary or compulsory redundancy on grounds of age or costs (Parsons and Mayle 1996). Studies of performance appraisal show older workers receiving lower performance ratings than their younger counterparts (e.g. Saks and Waldman 1998) and pay discrimination when compared with younger colleagues (Barnum et al. 1995). Career progression is also limited (Cox and Nkomo 1992).

Attempts to counter ageism have been made by the British government, who set up an Advisory Forum on Older Workers in 1992. An Employers' Forum on Age followed this in 1996, aimed at persuading employers to jettison ageist practices. These initiatives have tried to discourage discrimination in terms of exit, recruitment, training, and promotion practices. The way the argument has developed is that discrimination on the grounds of age is only ageist if guided by irrational prejudice and mistaken beliefs rather than by commercial criteria (Campbell 1999). Employers, it has been found, think that older workers are less productive and have less relevant skills. They think they are resistant to change and new technology, are less trainable, leave employment sooner so that training them has a lower rate of return, and are more prone to absenteeism and ill health (Taylor and Walker 1993, 1995). Older workers are less likely to undergo training and less likely to be offered training by employers (Taylor and Urwin 2001). Yet age has been found to be a poor proxy for performance (Grimley Evans et al. 1992). Discrimination against older workers can lead to sub-optimal use of human resources and a narrow pool of talent on which to draw. Early exit due to discrimination has resulted in skill shortages, a loss of 'collective memory', and the good relations, coupled with an understanding of the ageing market, generated by ageing workers with ageing customers.

It is not just those in the older age groups who are discriminated against in employment. A quarter of those between 16 and 24 claimed to have experienced age discrimination in employment (Age Concern 1998). Upper age bars in some recruitment advertisements for professional posts are set as low as 30 and training and promotion opportunities tend to diminish rapidly after 40 years of age (Trinder et al. 1992). A survey of workplaces found that 40 per cent have formal written equal opportunities policies that included reference to age (Culley et al. 1998: 13).

STOP

An Example of Ageism

Generation Xers—those born in the 1970s and 1980s are seen as fickle. They are stereotyped as inexperienced, lacking in responsibility and dependability, disloyal, and more interested in their social lives than work. Half of those under 25 say they have been discriminated against because of their age, claims a survey by the Chartered Institute of Personnel Development (Hilpern 2003). If you are 'youthful' is this your experience?

The Ageing Population and Business Ownership

Recent government initiatives have encouraged older people to remain economically active. Initiatives aimed at getting people back into employment, promoting self-employment and business ownership amongst older people include PRIME, New Deal 50+ scheme, and the Employment Zones initiative (DfEE 2001b). Of those aged 65 or over, who are economically active, a quarter are self-employed (Tilsey 1995). Older people seem to run successful businesses. Cressy and Storey (1995) found that only 19 per cent of start-ups survived after six years, but 70 per cent of the businesses, with owner managers over 55, were still in business. Older people are more likely to have the experience and assets for business ownership than younger age groups (Fry 1997). One would expect older people's motivation for setting up a business to be a strong desire for independence and control. Maybe it is because they face discrimination in employment, but there is a dearth of research on motivation to set up a business amongst the older group.

The Growth of the Enterprise Economy

Small and medium sized-businesses (those with less than 250 employees) account for 99 per cent of all businesses in the UK (Department of Trade and Industry 1997). While the importance of new firms to economic growth and competitiveness has been widely recognized (Hay and Kamshad 1994) and the encouragement of enterprise has been central to the economic strategies of successive governments, the success of the 'enterprise economy' depends on a flow of individuals willing and able to start up in business. There has been a substantial increase in the number of mid-life small business start-ups (Fuller 1994). Widowed women have been found to exhibit higher entrepreneurial rates than any other category (Goffee and Scase 1985). Many individuals invest redundancy payments or occupational pensions providing themselves with a business that they envisage will provide them with stable employment until the end of their working life (Fuller 1994).

Unemployment, Employment, and Race

Since 1997 unemployment has continued to fall. One of the reasons for this has been changes made to the benefit system (Nickell and Quintini 2002). Unemployment benefits have declined and the whole benefit system has become more focused on getting the unemployed back into work.

When the male partner in a couple becomes unemployed, you might expect that the female partner will find a job to supplement the household income. However research has indicated the opposite (McGinnity 2002). In Britain the employment rate of the wives of unemployed men is considerably lower than the employment rate of the wives of employed men. There has been a rise in both 'work rich' households and 'work poor' (Gregg and Wadsworth 1999). This may be because both partners lack education or that the leisure times of husbands and wives complement each other and so the couple may prefer to spend time together rather than the wife working when the man is unemployed. Alternatively it may be that they negatively view the prospect of the woman becoming the breadwinner.

Despite legislation to combat racial discrimination, Britain's non-white ethnic minority do not appear to face a level playing field in the labour market. Within this group unemployment is higher for Pakistani, Bangladeshi, African, and Afro-Caribbean women and men (Sly 1996); the lowest rates are for Chinese men and women (Bhavnani 1994). Their relative position does not appear to have improved since the 1970s. Native ethnic minorities appear to be faring little better than their parents (Blackaby et al. 2002). National figures for unemployment show high rates for those from ethnic minorities. For example 21 per cent of Pakistani and Bangladeshi women are registered as unemployed compared to 4.9 per cent for white women (Dale et al. 2002a). Even with higher-level qualifications Pakistani and Bangladeshi women experience considerable barriers to employment and have high levels of unemployment. There are major differences in the employment of Indian women and those from Pakistan and Bangladesh. Women of Pakistani and Bangladeshi origin have low levels of economic activity, particularly married women and women with dependent children. By contrast Indian women have much higher levels of economic activity, similar to that of white women. Differences in employment patterns are related to migration, level of education, language ability, local labour markets, and employment opportunities (Dale et al. 2002*b*).

Even when black and ethnic minority women are skilled and experienced, they are twice as likely to be unemployed or work longer hours, in poorer conditions, for lower pay than white women (Roberts 1994). Pakistani and Bangladeshi women are five times more likely to be unemployed than white women, the gap being greatest in recessionary periods. Ethnic women work through financial necessity, due to higher rates of black male unemployment, larger family size, lower household incomes, and the necessity of working longer hours to bring home a living wage (Phizacklea and Wolkowitz 1995). The rate of unemployment among young black men stands at three times that of young white men (Sly 1995).

Black women (from African-Caribbean descent) are continually concentrated in specific occupations and sectors of the labour market. In the early post-migration years black women were concentrated in nursing or semi-skilled manual work like catering. Today most black women are employed in public administration (central and local government), retail, and distribution (Bhavnani 1994). Within these occupations black women are over-represented in the lower-paid and lower-status jobs. Their presence as senior managers is virtually negligible (Modood 1997). Black women continue to work in settings in which sexism and racism are everyday aspects of paid work (Reynolds 2001).

STOP

An Example of how to Counter Racism?

Black police officers in the Metropolitan police in London are four times more likely to leave in the first two years than their white counterparts. The 'Met' need to increase the number of minority officers because they are failing to hit Home Office recruitment targets. In order to help counter its public image of being racist, the Met created a 'refer a friend' scheme which would have paid black officers a £350 'bounty' for every minority recruit they attracted. However the staff felt that it evoked images of slavery and the idea that you could buy a black person. The Black Police Association felt it demeaning and warned that officers keen to make money could abuse it (Muir 2003).

Part-Time Working

Another change that has come about is a change in the number of part-time jobs. Part-time working is mainly found in restaurants, hotels, and retail establishments and other sectors of the 'leisure' industry. As employment levels have recovered following recessions, most job growth is in part-time work and the bulk of the new jobs have been taken by women, though some part-time work has gone to men. Although the employed labour force grew by nearly 2.5 million between 1984 and 1986, for example, male full-time work fell by 2 per cent while male part-time work grew fivefold (Convery 1997). You might ask what is wrong with part-time work and more women working? While the majority of part-timers choose to work fewer hours than full-timers, a significant minority do not. In 1984 about 420,000 people were doing part-time work because they could not get a full-time job. By 1996 this had risen to 800,000 'involuntary' part-time workers (Convery 1997). Part-time jobs are worse than full-time jobs in skill levels, wage rate, and promotion prospects. While part-time work is not associated with job insecurity and unemployment, it constitutes a trap which lowers women's lifetime employment prospects and earnings (Tam 1997).

Many believe that part-time work offers flexibility and choice, particularly in terms of time that can be spent with the family. However part-time working is difficult to obtain in some jobs, like management where only 6 per cent of managers and senior officials are employed part-time. There are still far too few opportunities for flexible working at senior levels in organizations (Equal Opportunities Commission 2002). Part-time work, splitting a job between two people (job sharing), or working from home could be considered by employers as a way of sharing heavy management responsibilities.

Women and Employment

One of the more important social and economic changes in the last thirty years has been the increase in women's employment, particularly that of mothers. More women in the UK are either seeking work or in work than was the case in the past. While only a half of women were in or seeking any sort of work in 1971, this proportion had grown to two-thirds by 1983 and almost three-quarters by 1999 (British Social Attitudes 2000). However women in the labour force face inequality. Women still lag behind men in terms of income (Rake 2000). While the average gross annual earnings for men in Britain is £24,298, females only earn £11,811 (48.6 per cent of men's earnings). In management women fare better. The average gross weekly earnings for male managers and administrators are £668.90, while for females the figure is £468.80 (70 per cent) (New Earnings Survey 2000). Surveys regularly uncover pay gaps for managers. For example the *Guardian* uncovered an average pay gap of more than £9,000 between male and female chief executives in the public service. Men can earn as much as £25,000 more than women doing comparable jobs (Parker and Weaver 2002).

Men's and Women's Jobs

Jobs tend to be seen as either male or female jobs. Men dominate some jobs like taxi driving and chauffeur work (93 per cent male), security guard (92 per cent male), software professionals (84 per cent male) while women dominate jobs such as receptionist (95 per cent female), care assistants (90 per cent female), nursing (90 per cent female) and hair-dressing (88 per cent female) (EOC analysis of Labour Force Survey 2001).

Educational qualifications have a crucial impact on employment prospects and earn-ings potential. While the qualification levels of women and men under the age of 25 are now very similar, currently a higher percentage of males have qualifications (Equal Opportunities Commission 2003). Qualifications and the presence of dependent children influence the very different patterns of employment of men and women. Following the birth of their children some women are able to return to full-time work, many work part-time, and others withdraw from the labour market altogether. During the past 25 years there has been an increase in the poverty of mothers, particularly lone mothers (who head 90 per cent of one-parent families) (EOC 2003).

Men, Women, and Management

More than 2.6 million men and 1.1 million women were employed as managers and sen-ior officials in Britain in spring 2001 (EOC 2002). The managerial occupational group accounts for 14 per cent of total employment in Britain (18 per cent for male but only 9 per cent for female) and is the largest of nine major occupational groupings. Men out-number women in nine out of the eleven managerial groups, accounting for example for 94 per cent of production managers and 90 per cent of managers in construction. Managerial jobs remain strongly gender segregated.

The 213,000 ethnic minority managers account for 6 per cent of all managers. The fig-ure is slightly higher for men (6 per cent) than for women (5 per cent). They form an above average proportion of managers and proprietors in hospitality and leisure services (13 per cent) and in other service industries. Only 3 per cent of production managers are from ethnic minorities.

There has been a growth in the numbers of women in management in the last three decades. The proportion of women taking MBA courses has risen from around 10 per cent a decade ago to nearly 40 per cent today (*Guardian*, 5 November 2001). How-ever as Table 1-1 shows, women in the UK hold just 24 per cent of all management

Table 1.1 Percentage of female executives by responsibility level

Responsibility level	1974	1990	1995	2000	2001
Director	0.6	1.6	3.0	9.6	9.9
Function head	0.4	4.2	5.8	15	15.8
Department head	2.1	7.2	9.7	19	25.5
Section leader	2.4	11	14.2	26.5	28.9
Whole sample	1.8	7.9	10.7	22.1	24.1

Source: Institute of Management and Remuneration Economics (2001).

positions and 9.9 per cent of directorships (Institute of Management and Remuneration Economics 2001).

The 'glass ceiling', the situation where women can see but not reach higher-level jobs and so are prevented from progressing in their careers, appears still to exist in many organizations. Only one woman made it to CEO in the FTSE 100 list and she was the only female in that list paid more than £1 m in 1999 (Singh et al. 2001). Similar figures are found in the USA, where women still only occupy 11.2 per cent of the top CEO positions in the private sector, and in Australia, a paltry 2.9 per cent (Cassella 2001).

Despite thirty years of equal opportunities legislation designed to eradicate discrimination, less than one in five public service organizations in Britain are run by women (Parker and Weaver 2002). The situation for women in public services in other countries appears to be no better or worse (for example see Zafarullah 2000, who discusses the brick wall and glass ceiling that women in the civil service in Bangladesh face). While there are signs of positive trends in increasing numbers of women in managerial and administrative posts, the jobs taken by women are mostly in low-paid service sector jobs, for example in the hotel sector (Wilson 1994; Rubery and Fagan 1994). In this sector women earn below the average of all women's earnings. There is a tendency for some types of management jobs to be associated with either women or men. Men still predominate in production and Information Technology jobs.

Mothers and Fathers' Attitudes to Work and Family

Whilst the volume of research on fathers has increased, discussion about work and family life still tends to be focused on working mothers. Rarely do we hear of working fathers. A majority of mothers make significant changes to their working lives to accommodate children. They are likely to take prime responsibility for childcare because of the pay gap, the fact that they tend to earn less than their partner, and high childcare costs (Hatten et al. 2002). Mothers are more likely than fathers to take time off work when children are sick (O'Brien and Shemilt 2003).

Men want to work and few men want to reduce their hours or stop work altogether, yet British fathers continue to work long hours. Some fathers work longer hours when children are born, feeling a greater pressure to provide financially. Others compress their work into fewer hours so that they can get home earlier. Just a small minority of fathers make major changes that enable them to be more involved in family life (Hatten et al. 2002). Time spent by fathers with children accounts for about one-third of parental childcare time. Fathers' use of flexible working practices is low. Flexitime, part-time/reduced hours, and job sharing are used by 20 per cent, 6 per cent, and 2 per cent of fathers respectively (O'Brien and Shemilt 2003).

New parental rights at work came into force in 2003. Maternity leave rose from 18 to 26 weeks. For the first time men have the right of two weeks' paid paternity leave and parents can request flexible working hours. It is expected though that men may be reluctant to take up their rights as a man who works long hours is valued in our society.

STOP Men want to use work as an excuse not to do work (at home) that they perceive as low status and unpaid (Cary Cooper, quoted in Sweet 2003). Is this true? What evidence can you produce to support or refute this statement?

Male professional workers appear to be caught in their own time bind and cultural stereotypes so are unlikely to lower barriers to flexible working. There seems to be an 'executive hourglass' created by a club of workaholics addicted to working long hours which sets the performance standard for themselves and those seeking promotion. A survey of male professional workers (Knell and Savage 1999) found that while 84 per cent believed that organizations should offer flexible working and over half indicated they would like greater flexibility at work, they displayed a clear preference for full-time working. The majority did not want to work part-time and were not prepared to work shorter hours for less money. The male workers felt that flexible working practices would be abused and that being flexible would lead to 'career death' in terms of lack of promotional opportunities. Ninety per cent thought that senior roles require more commitment than a 9–5 working day. The authors of the report, Knell and Savage, conclude that if entrenched attitudes like this are left unchecked and unchallenged, it will continue to prove difficult for individuals to balance a serious working career with their life responsibilities. It will be hard for those who do work flexibly to reach senior management positions unless they work at the same pace as their colleagues.

Homeworking

Working at home is a global phenomenon (Felstead and Jewson 2000). Official statistics on homeworking can be found for the USA, Canada, Australia, New Zealand, the European Union, Japan, India, Hong Kong, as well as some developing nations; it appears to be a growing phenomenon, particularly in the USA, Australia, Canada, and Europe. The extent of homeworking in the UK has increased dramatically in the past two decades. While it is difficult to measure the exact numbers of homeworkers (and difficult to gain access, Phizacklea and Wolkowitz 1995) it has been estimated that they grew in number over the period 1981 to 1998 from 1.5 per cent of the workforce to 2.5 per cent (Felstead et al. 2000). Ethnic minorities are over-represented among those working at home in manual occupations. It is thought that nearly half of all homeworkers are from ethnic minorities and that over a third are of Pakistani, Indian, or Bangladeshi origin (Low Pay Commission 1998). Asian women continue to experience greater difficulties in finding employment outside the home than equivalent white women (Dale et al. 2002a). Those working from home rank among the lowest paid in the labour market but white homeworkers fare better than non-white (Felstead and Jewson 2000).

Other Scene-Setting Issues

Chapters in texts on Organizational Behaviour, particularly those on organizational culture, usually fail to acknowledge that those seeking to be recruited have often considered the values and culture of the organization to which they have applied. For example if you are against testing on animals, you are unlikely to apply for a job at Huntingdon Life Sciences near Cambridge, England. If you are concerned about the welfare of babies in developing countries, you may be affected by the news that Nestlé is accused of violating the World Health Organization's code of marketing of breast milk substitutes (Yamey 2000). If you are against genetically modified food, you may not want to take a job as a manager in Monsanto. If you are considering joining the army, and do not approve of the fur trade industry, you might like to know that the British Army needs 65 bears, 42 rabbits, 40 sheep, and at least two foxes each year to ensure their soldiers look their best on the parade ground (Brady 2003). What scene-setting issues would you need to know about? Having looked at the context in which work is organized, and set the scene in this chapter, the next chapters will begin looking at the rationale behind how jobs are designed and how people are fitted into jobs. The book will then go on to look at the realities of work experience, in particular what work means.

■ SUGGESTIONS FOR FURTHER READING

1. Curran, J., and Blackburn, R. A. (2001), *Researching the Small Enterprise*, London: Sage. Small and medium sized businesses are clearly important to the economy and this book is a good introduction to the subject area.

2. Publications from the Office for National Statistics or from the government offices in your country that give you a context for behaviour that you then see in organizations.

3. Publications from charities like Joseph Rowntree Foundation and others to give you knowledge about a broad range of organizations and how they might function.

4. Newspapers have on-line search facilities so you can search by key word for the topical organizational issues of the day.

5. Grint, K. (2000), *Work and Society: A Reader*, Cambridge: Polity Press. Chapter 3 on Child Labour, Chapter 5 on Domestic Work, and Chapter 9 on Race, Ethnicity and Employment.

6. Felstead, A., and Jewson, N. (2000), *In Work, at Home*, London: Routledge. This book compiles evidence from around the world on home-located production.

■ WEB LINKS

The Department of Trade and Industry (**www.dti.gov.uk**) is a government web site that gives details of new employment law, for example the new laws that affect working parents. The Equal Opportunities Commission web site is also very useful for information on employment law and research reports (**www.eoc.org.uk**)

The Daycare Trust (**www.daycaretrust.org.uk**) is a national childcare charity that promotes affordable childcare and provides information on childcare issues. Age Concern (**www.ageconcern.org.uk**) is a national network of more than 400 independent charities, providing services such as day care and information for people aged over 50. They campaign on issues like age discrimination and pensions, and work to influence public opinion and government policy about older people. Humanitarian organizations like Christian Aid (**www.christian-aid.org.uk**) and Actionaid (**www.actionaid.org**) provide useful information on the campaigns that they run on clean water, injustice, and other humanitarian issues.

■ **QUESTIONS**

1. How affordable is childcare for working parents? The Daycare Trust, a charity, found in 2001 that the typical cost of a nursery place for 2-year-olds is £5,700 a year (£7,000 in London). This is more than the average household spends each year on either food or housing. A quarter of all mothers of pre-school children are not able to access the type of childcare they would prefer (Gaber 2003). How accessible and affordable is childcare for working parents?

2. Research has suggested that women may be choosing self-employment as a flexible form of work that allows them to combine motherhood and a career. How much research evidence supports this view?

3. A Conservative Cabinet minister has argued that charity chief executives should be paid higher salaries so that their pay matches that earned by top managers. He said 'If we are to attract and retain the very best of leadership, and the sector deserved nothing less, then we have to be prepared to compete almost on an equal footing with the rest of the market' (*Guardian*, Wednesday, 23 October 2002). The chief executive of Cancer Research UK was paid £140,000 in 2001–2. Should chief executives and managers of charities be paid wages that match those found in other organizations? Would those who give to charity be 'put off' knowing how much goes towards manager's salaries?

4. Often when you begin to read about management, the achievements of managers throughout history are heralded. The building of the pyramids is often used as an example of such an achievement. Never is the lack of achievement discussed though some of the weaknesses in management systems, say appraisal systems, might be discussed. Why, for example, do we not hear that world production of grain is enough to feed everyone in the world but around 1.2 billion do not have enough to eat? Clean water is one of life's essentials but over one billion people continue to live without it. It is estimated that 2 million people die every year from diseases related to a lack of safe, clean drinking water (Actionaid leaflet 2002). Everyday 25,000 people die of hunger and poverty (see Actionaid's web site). Is this due to a failure of management?

5. Did the introduction of technology into the home (washing machines, vacuum cleaners, etc.) reduce the amount of time spent on housework? (See Vanek 1974; Sullivan 1997.)

6. Has the time men and women spend working decreased or increased in the last four decades? (See Sullivan and Gershuny 2001.)

7. Actionaid is a humanitarian organization whose mission is to work with poor and marginalized people to eradicate poverty by overcoming the injustice and inequity that cause it. As an organization, they say they work by the following values: mutual respect, equity and justice,

honesty and transparency, solidarity with poor and marginalized people, courage of conviction, humility. Is it only humanitarian organizations that deal with injustice and inequity? Are these issues that should concern all organizations? If not, why not?

◼ GROUP EXERCISE

Widowed women have been found to exhibit higher entrepreneurial rates than any other category. What are the main categories of those who set up businesses and how many are in each group? Is this what you would expect?

◼ REFERENCES

Age Concern (1998), 'Age Discrimination: Make it a Thing of the Past', *Age Concern*, London.

Ainsworth, S. (2002), 'The "Feminine Advantage": A Discursive Analysis of the Invisibility of Older Women Workers', *Gender, Work and Organization*, 9/5: 579–601.

Banks, J., and Tanner, S. (1997), *The State of Donation: Household Gifts to Charity 1974–96*, London: The Institute for Fiscal Studies.

Barnum, P., Liden, R., and Ditomaso, N. (1995), 'Double Jeopardy for Women and Minorities: Pay Differences with Age', *Academy of Management Journal*, 38/3: 863–80.

Bernard, M., Itzin, C., Phillipson, C., and Skucha, J. (1995), 'Gendered Work, Gendered Retirement', in S. Arber and J. Ginn (eds.), *Connecting Gender and Ageing: A Sociological Approach*, Buckingham: Open University Press.

Bhavnani, R. (1994), *Black Women in the Labour Market: A Research Review*, London: Equal Opportunities Commission.

Blackaby, D. H., Leslie, D. G., Murphy, P. D., and O'Leary, N. C. (2002), 'White/Ethnic Minority Earnings and Employment Differentials in Britain: Evidence from the LFS', *Oxford Economic Papers*, 54/270–97.

Brady, B. (2003), 'Army Battle to Hold on to their Bear Necessities', *Scotland on Sunday*, 11 May, p. 8.

British Social Attitudes (2000), *Women's Attitudes to Combining Paid Work and Family Life*, London: Women's Unit of the Cabinet Office.

Campbell, N. (1999), 'The Decline of Employment among Older People in Britain', CASE paper 19, Centre of Analysis of Social Exclusion, London.

Cassella, N. (2001), 'Women in Fight to Reach Top Roles', *Sunday Times* (Perth), 11 July.

Christian Aid Reports (2000), http://www.christianaid.org.uk/indepth/9905suic/suicide2.htm

Convery, P. (1997), 'Unemployment', in A. Walker and C. Walker (eds.), *Britain Divided: The Growth of Social Exclusion in the 1980s and 1990s*, London: Child Poverty Action Group.

Cox, T., and Nkomo, S. (1992), Candidate Age as a Factor in Promotability Ratings, *Public Personnel Management*, 21/2: 197–210.

Cressy, R., and Storey, D. (1995), 'New Firms and their Banks', Centre of Small and Medium Sized Enterprise, Warwick University Business School and NatWest Bank, Warwick and London, December.

Cully, M., O'Reilly, A., Millward, N., Forth, J., Woodland, S., Dix, G., and Bryson, A. (1998), *The 1998 Workplace Employee Relations Survey: First Findings*, London: Department of Trade and Industry.

Dale, A., Shaheen, N., Fieldhouse, E., and Kalra, V. (2002*a*), 'The Labour Market Prospects for Pakistani and Bangladeshi Women', *Work, Employment and Society*, 16/1: 5–25.

———Kalra, V., and Fieldhouse, E. (2002*b*), 'Routes into Education and Employment for Young Pakistani and Bangladeshi Women in the UK', *Ethnic and Racial Studies*, 25/6: 942–68.

Department of Trade and Industry (1997), *Small and Medium Enterprise (SME) Statistics for the UK 1996*, Statistical Press Release P/99/662 August.

DfEE (2001*a*), *Age Diversity: Summary of Research Findings*, London: Stationery Office.

——(2001*b*), *Action on Age: Report on the Consultation on Age Discrimination in Employment*, March, London: Stationery Office.

Duncan, C. (2003), 'Assessing Anti-ageism Routes to Older Worker Re-engagement', *Work, Employment and Society*, 17/1: 101–20.

Edwards, L. (2002), *A Bit Rich? What the Wealthy Think about Giving*, London: Institute for Public Policy Research.

Egan, B. (2001), *The Widow's Might: How Charities Depend on the Poor*, London: Social Market Foundation.

Elman, C., and O'Rand, A. M. (1998), 'Midlife Work Pathways and Educational Entry', *Research on Ageing*, 20/4: 475–505.

Encel, S., and Studencki, H. (1997), '*Gendered Ageism: Job Search Experiences of Older Women*', NSW Committee on Ageism and the Department for Women (NSW), Sydney (cited in Ainsworth 2002).

Equal Opportunities Commission (2001), *EOC Analysis of Labour Force Survey*, Spring, London: Office for National Statistics.

——(2002), *Women and Men in Britain: Management*, Manchester: EOC.

——(2003), *The Lifecycle of Inequality*, Manchester: EOC.

Essed, P., and Goldberg, D. T. (2002), 'Cloning Cultures: The Social Injustices of Sameness', *Ethnic and Racial Studies*, 25/6: 1066–82.

Evandrou, M., and Falkingham, J. (2000), 'Looking Back to Look Forward: Lessons from Four Birth Cohorts for Ageing in the 21st Century', *Population Trends*, 99: 27–36, London: The Stationery Office, ISBN 0 11 621176 8.

Felstead, A., and Jewson, N. (2000), *In Work, at Home: Towards an Understanding of Homeworking*, London: Routledge.

———Phizacklea, A., and Walters, S. (2000), 'A Statistical Portrait of Working at Home in the UK: Evidence from the Labour Force Survey', ESRC Future of Work Programme Paper Series, ESRC, Swindon.

Fry, A. (1997), 'Shades of Grey', *Marketing*, 24 Apr.

Fuller, T. (1994) (ed.), *Small Business Trends 1994–1998*, Durham: Durham University Business School.

Gaber, I. (2003), 'Childcare still failing', *Society*, 16 Apr.

Ginn, J., and Arber, S. (1995), ' "Only Connect": Gender Relations and Ageing', in S. Arber and J. Ginn (eds.), *Connection Gender and Ageing: A Sociological Approach*, Buckingham: Open University Press.

Goffee, R., and Scase, R. (1985), *Women in Charge: The Experience of Female Entrepreneurs*, London: Allen & Unwin.

Gregg, P., and Wadsworth, J. (eds.), *The State of Working Britain*, Manchester: Manchester University Press.

——Hansen, K., and Wadsworth, J. (1999), 'The Rise of the Workless Household', in Gregg and Wadsworth (1999).

Grimley Evans, J., Goldacre, M. J., Hodkinson, M., Lamb, S., and Savory, M. (1992), 'Health: Abilities and Well Being in the Third Age', The Carnegie Inquiry into the Third Age, Research Paper 9, The Carnegie Trust, Dunfermline.

Guardian (2001), 'Anti-Poverty Policy: A Bit Rich?' http://society.guardian.co.uk/20001budget/comment/0,8416,449248,00.html

Hatten, W., Vinter, L., and Williams, R. (2002), 'Dads on Dads: Needs and Expectations at Home and at Work', Mori Social Research Institute, Research Discussion Series, Manchester: Equal Opportunities Commission.

Hay, M., and Kamshad, K. (1994), 'Small Firm Growth: Intentions, Implementation and Impediments', *Business Strategy Review*, 5/3: 49–68.

Herriot, P., and Scott-Jackson, W. (2002), 'Globalization, Social Identities and Employment', *British Journal of Management*, 13: 249–57.

Hilpern, K. (2003), 'Office Hours: Ageism in Reverse', *Guardian*, 14 Apr., story found on infoweb.newsbank.com.

House of Commons (1989), *The Employment Patterns of the Over-50s*, vol. i, Employment Committee Session 1998–9, London: HMSO.

Institute of Management and Remuneration Economics (2001), *UK National Management Survey*, London: Institute of Management.

Klein, N. (1999), *No Logo*, New York: Picador.

Knell, J., and Savage, C. (1999), 'Flexible Working and Male Professionals: Can't Change, Won't Change', *Industrial Society*, London: The Resource Connection.

Labour Force Survey (2001), Office for National Statistics, London. See web page at www.data-archive.ac.uk/findingData/lfsAbstract.asp

Loretto, W., Duncan, C., and White, P. (2000), 'Ageism and Employment: Controversies and Ambiguities and Younger People's Perceptions', *Ageing and Society*, 20: 279–302.

Low Pay Commission (1998), *The National Minimum Wage: First Report of the Low Pay Commission*, London: The Stationery Office.

McGinnity, F. (2002), 'The Labour-Force Participation of the Wives of Unemployed Men: Comparing Britain and West Germany Using Longitudinal Data', *European Sociological Review*, 18/4: 473–88.

Modood, T. (1997), *Ethnic Minorities in Britain*, London: PSI.

Muir, H. (2003), 'Met's "Black Bounty" Recruitment Plan Shelved', *Guardian*, 20 May, story found at infoweb.newsbank.com.

New Earnings Survey (2000), Tables A6.1 and A10.1, National Statistics Publication, London: Office for National Statistics.

Nickell, S., and Quintini, G. (2002), 'The Recent Performance of the UK Labour Market', *Oxford Review of Economic Policy*, 18/2: 202–20.

NVCO (2001), 'Charitable Giving: The Tide Has Turned: The Fall and Rise of Charitable Giving 1995–2000', *Research Quarterly*, 13.

O'Brien, M., and Shemilt, I. (2003), *Working Fathers: Earning and Caring*, Manchester: EOC.

ONS (1999), *Social Focus on Older People*, London: HMSO for the Office of National Statistics.

Onyx, J. (1998), Older Women Workers: A Double Jeopardy', in M. Patrickson and L. Harmann (eds.), *Managing an Ageing Workforce*, Warriewood, NSW: Woodlane.

Oviatt, B., and McDougall, P. (1995), 'Global Start Ups: Entrepreneurs on a Worldwide Stage', *Academy of Management Executive*, 9/2: 30–44.

Parker, S., and Weaver, M. (2002), 'Women Continue to Trail Behind in Pay Terms', http://societyguardian.co.uk/salarysurvey/story/0,12406,798028,00.html.

Parsons, D., and Mayle, L. (1996), 'Ageism and Work in the EU: A Comparative Review of Corporate Innovation and Practice', working paper, Cranfield, Cranfield University.

Phillipson, C. (1998), *Reconstructing Old Age: New Agendas in Social Theory and Practice*, London: Sage.

Phizacklea, A., and Wolkowitz, C. (1995), *Homeworking Women: Gender, Racism and Class at Work*, London: Sage.

Population Trends (2000), Office for National Statistics, London: Stationery Office.

Rake, K. (2000) (ed.), *Women's Incomes over the Lifetime*, London: The Stationary Office.

Rein, M., and Jacobs, K. (1993), 'Ageing and Employment Trends: A Comparative Analysis for OECD Countries', in P. Johnson and K. Zimmerman (eds.), *Labour Markets in an Ageing Europe*, Cambridge: Cambridge University Press, pp. 53–76.

Reynolds, T. (2001), 'Black Mothering, Paid Work and Identity', *Ethnic and Racial Studies*, 24/6: 1046–64.

Roberts, B. (1994), *Minority Ethnic Women: Work, Unemployment and Education*. Manchester: Commission for Racial Equality.

Rubery, J., and Fagan, C. (1994), 'Occupational Segregation: Plus ca change', in R. Lindley (ed.), *Labour Market Structures and Prospects for Women*, Institute for Employment Research, University of Warwick/Equal Opportunities.

Rugman, A., and Girod, S. (2003), 'Retail Multinationals and Globalization: The Evidence is Regional', *European Management Journal*, 21/1: 24–37.

Saks, A., and Waldman, D. (1998), 'The Relationship between Age and Job Performance Evaluations for Entry Level Professionals', *Journal of Organizational Behavior*, 19/4: 409–19.

Schwartz, H. (1996), *The Culture of Copy: Striking Likeness, Unreasonable Facsimiles*, New York: Zone Books.

Shaw, C. (2000), '1998-based National Population Projections for the United Kingdom and Constituent Countries', Office for National Statistics, *Population Trends* (Spring), London: The Stationery Office.

Singh, V., Vinnicombe, S., and Johnson, P. (2001), 'Women Directors on Top UK Boards', *Corporate Governance: An International Review*, 9, forthcoming.

Sly, F. (1995), 'Ethnic Groups and the Labour Market: Analyses from the Spring 1994 Labour Force Survey', *Employment Gazette*, June (Dept. of Employment, HMSO): 251–62.

——(1996), 'Ethnic Minority Participation in the Labour Market: Trends for the Labour Force Survey 1984–1995', *Labour Market Trends* (HMSO), 104/6: 259–70.

Special Report on Race in the Boardroom, 18 February, 2002 cited in Essed and Goldberg 2002.

Steeten, P. (2001), *Globalisation: Threat or Opportunity?*, Copenhagen: Copenhagen Business School Press.

Sullivan, O. (1997), 'Time Waits for No (Wo)man: An Investigation of the Gendered Experience of Domestic Time', *Sociology*, 31/2: 221–39.

——and Gershuny, J. (2001), 'Cross-national Changes in Time-Use: Some Sociological (Hi)stories Re-examined', *British Journal of Sociology*, 52/2: 331–47.

Sweet, C. (2003), 'Will It Change Your Life?', *Guardian*, 12 May, found at www.guardian.co.uk/women/story/0,3604,931092,00.html

Tam, M. (1997), *Part-Time Employment: A Bridge or a Trap?* Aldershot: Avebury.

Taylor, P., and Urwin, P. (2001), 'Age and Participation in Vocational Education', *Work, Employment and Society*, 15/4: 763–79.

——and Walker, A. (1993), 'Employers and Older Workers', *Employment Gazette*, 101/8: 371–8.

————(1995), 'Utilising Older Workers', *Employment Gazette*, 103/4: 141–5.

Tilsey, C. (1995), 'Older Workers: Findings from the 1994 Labour Force Survey', *Employment Gazette* (Apr.), 133–40.

Trinder, C., Hulme, G., and McCarthy, U. (1992), 'Employment: The Role of Work in the Third Age', The Carnegie Inquiry into the Third Age, Research Paper 1, Dunfermline: The Carnegie UK Trust.

Vanek, J. (1974), 'Time Spent in Housework', *Scientific American*, 231 (Nov.), 116–20.

Wilson, R. (1994), 'Sectoral and Occupational Change: Prospects for Women's Employment', in R. Lindley (ed.), *Labour Market Structures and Prospects for Women*, Institute for Employment Research, University of Warwick/Equal Opportunities Commission, Manchester.

Yamey, G. (2000), 'Nestle Violates International Marketing Code, Says Audit', *British Medical Journal*, 321/8 (1 July).

Zafarullah, H. (2000), 'Through the Brick Wall and the Glass Ceiling: Women in the Civil Service in Bangladesh', *Gender, Work and Employment*, 7/3: 197–209.

2 Rationality: From Founding Fathers to Eugenics. Is it all about Fitting Workers to Jobs?

Employers and managers seek to extract the best performance from employees; they seek to devise methods that ensure individuals act in the organization's interest. Organizations depend on people for their competitive advantage. People possess skills, experience, and knowledge that have economic value to organizations. Demand is placed on employees to add value by helping to lower costs or provide greater output. How have they tried to do this? As we shall see in this chapter, at first the emphasis was on finding the best way to manage the human resource through scientific and mechanical means. Frederick Taylor and Henry Ford were looking to make labour more efficient. Fitting workers to jobs was the aim. The Human Relations movement counteracted some of the worst features of Taylorism, stressing the importance of an understanding of employee's social, rather than simply economic, needs. This chapter asks you to question the rationality behind Taylorism, Fordism, and Human Relations; what were they trying to achieve. Is the rationality all about better fitting workers with jobs? Using knowledge from psychology, intelligence and psychometric testing, it could be argued that workers are better aligned with the goals of the job.

Early management thinkers or theorists (Babbage 1989; Taylor 1911; Ure 1835) sought to apply 'rational' scientific practices to organization with the view of improving its performance. They mainly thought of organizations as machines while people were seen as too variable and unreliable. According to Ure (1835), for example, 'science now promises to rescue . . . business from handicraft caprice, and to place it . . . under the safeguard of automatic mechanism'. For Ure there were 'right mechanisms' for managing; one 'mechanism' would be for the manager to remove jobs which require dexterity from the workman, who cannot be relied upon, and place these jobs in the safe hands of mechanization so simple a child could supervise. Similar views can be found in both Babbage's and Taylor's writings. Frederick Winslow Taylor (1856–1915) believed that the best management was true science 'resting upon clearly defined laws, rules and principles' (1911: 7). The problems of production lay in the hands of management because they lacked knowledge on how to maximize production, the workers had a rationale for restricting output (the fear of underpayment or redundancy), and payment systems lacked sufficient incentive. Applying the principles of scientific management could solve all these problems. For Taylor it was the manager's job to gather together all the traditional knowledge, which in the past was possessed by the workmen, and then classify, tabulate, and reduce this knowledge to rules, laws, and formulae which became a science.

'Experiments in Scientific Management'

The Spanish–American War in 1898 gave Taylor the opportunity to try his first experiment in scientific management at the Bethlehem Steel Company. With the war came an increase in the price of pig iron (iron from the smelting furnace). The pig iron was in a field adjoining the works and needed to be moved inside to the furnaces. A railway was laid out to the field, an inclined plank placed against the side of the railroad 'car'. Each man was required to pick up a 'pig of iron' weighing about 92 lbs, walk up the inclined plank, and drop it in the car. About 12.5 tons per man per day could be loaded by an average man, but it was found that the first-class men could handle between 47 and 48 tons. Four of the best pig iron handlers were picked from seventy-five. Then one was chosen to start the experiment, a man Taylor called 'Schmidt' and described as 'of the mentally sluggish type'. (Schmidt was in fact called Henry Knolle (Johnson and Gill 1993) and had recently built his own house.)

This man was offered $1.85 per hour instead of $1.25 if he followed another man's instructions on when to pick up the iron, when to walk, and when to rest; he managed to load 47.5 tons of iron a day. He never failed to work at this pace and do the task set him during the three years Taylor was at Bethlehem. This 'science' being developed amounted 'to so much that the man who is suited to pig iron cannot possibly understand it, nor even work in accordance with the laws of this science, without the help of those who are over him' (1911: 48). A fit pig iron handler should be 'so stupid and so phlegmatic that he more nearly resembles in his mental make-up the ox than any other type . . . He is so stupid that the word "percentage" has no meaning to him . . .' (1911: 59). In this way the man was selected, trained, and supervised. Seven out of eight pig iron handlers were thrown out of their jobs, but we are assured that they were given other jobs with the Bethlehem Steel Company.

Similar treatment is to be found in the second experiment to develop a science of shovelling. A first-class shoveller was found to do his biggest day's work with a shovel load of about 21 lbs. Eight or ten different kinds of shovels were provided at the Bethlehem Steel Company, one for each type of material depending on the weight of that material, for example a small one for ore (a heavy material) and a large one for ashes (a light material). Providing the different shovels prevented the shoveller, who previously owned their own shovel, from going from shovelling ore with a load of about 30 lbs per shovel to handling rice coal with a load, on the same shovel, of less than 4 lbs. Every day the shoveller would be given and would implement instructions for doing each new job; he would also be given feedback on his performance the previous day. Clerks planned the work the shovellers did. This time the work of 400 and 600 yard labourers was reduced to the work of 140.

Four duties emerge for the managers in developing the science. First they develop a science for each element of work which replaces the old rule of thumb. (The rule of thumb was based on experience or practice, not on measurement and calculation.) Secondly they scientifically select, then train the worker. Thirdly they cooperate to ensure that all the work is being done in accordance with the principles laid down, and fourthly they have an almost equal division of work and responsibility between manager and worker. The management takes over all the work for which they are better fitted than the worker. They plan out the work at least one day in advance and each worker should receive a set of written instructions describing in detail the task they have to accomplish, the time it should take, as well as the means by which it should be done. When the workers have done the work right, within the specified time limit, they should receive an addition to their ordinary wages of between 30 and 100 per cent. Workers should never be asked, if the job has been scientifically studied, to work at a pace that could injure their health. With the scheme in place it was found that the workers and manager could profit considerably. The system was not designed to provide satisfying work but to maximize rewards and increase the division of labour.

Similarly Frank Gilbreth studied bricklaying, analysing the movement, speed, and tiring rate of the bricklayer (see Taylor 1911). He developed the exact positions that the feet of the bricklayer should occupy in relation to the wall, the mortar box, and pile of bricks. He studied the best height for the mortar box and brick pile then designed an adjustable scaffold to hold the materials. He asked that the bricks be sorted and packed in an orderly pile before being brought to the bricklayers, so that they were placed with their best edge up on a simple wooden frame; each brick could be lifted in the quickest time in the most advantageous position. He was thus able to reduce the motions of bricklayers from eighteen per brick to five. He also taught the bricklayers to pick up bricks with the left hand while at the same time taking a trowel full of mortar with the right hand. In this way 350 bricks per person per hour could be laid rather than the previous 120 bricks per hour. For this the standards and cooperation have to be enforced; the duty of enforcement lies with management. If the workforce agree to this enforcement, they receive higher pay.

While Taylor's 'men' were being scientifically selected and trained, 'girls' were working ten-and-a-half-hour days inspecting ball bearings for bicycles in another plant. Gradually their hours were shortened to ten, nine and a half, nine, then eight-and-a-half-hour days for the same pay. With each shortening of the day came an increase in output. The best workers were selected; some of the most intelligent, hardest working, and trustworthy girls were laid off because they did not perceive the fault and discard defective ball bearings fast, or accurately, enough. The honesty and accuracy of those remaining inspectors was checked. Senior inspectors checked one anonymous lot. The chief inspector, in turn, checked the work of the senior inspectors. The inspectors were also kept in check by another method. Every two or three days a lot of balls was prepared by a foreman so it contained a definite number of perfect and defective balls; this was given to an inspector for checking and the inspector's accuracy was recorded. An accurate and daily record was kept of the quantity and quality of all the work. Temptation to slight (neglect) the work or make false returns was, Taylor claimed, removed. The inspectors' ambition was 'stirred' by increasing the wages of those who turned out a large quantity of good quality while those who did indifferent work found their wages were lowered. Those who were slow or careless were discharged. The inspectors were seated so far apart that they could not conveniently talk whilst at work, but were given ten-minute breaks each hour and a half so they could leave their seats, walk around, and talk. This was found to be the best way to gain steady work without overexertion. Taylor believed that feedback on performance was needed at regular intervals, like every hour. Profit sharing would only be mildly effective (1911: 94). As a result of these changes, 35 'girls' did the work formerly done by 120. The accuracy of the work at higher speed was two-thirds greater than at the former slow speed. In return the women's average wage was 80 to 100 per cent higher with an eight-and-a-half-hour day and a half-day holiday on a Saturday.

A psychologist might explain the roots of Taylor's thinking in terms of his upbringing. His youth was preoccupied with order, control, and parsimony, clearly rooted in the puritanical strictures of his family. Fastidious analysis was made of his sporting activities, country walks, sleeping position, and even his dancing (Fineman 2000). (In dancing he would make an advanced list of the unattractive and attractive girls expected to attend and then compute the time he would spend with each on a precisely equal basis!) It also has to be noted though that Taylor emerged in a particular climate and time of thinking about how to apply rational scientific practices to organization to increase performance.

From a job design perspective, Taylor's scheme rests upon the principle of the division of mental and manual labour. It also involved: (*a*) a general principle of the maximum decomposition, breaking up of tasks; (*b*) the divorce of direct and indirect (setting up, preparation, maintenance) labour; (*c*) the minimization of skill requirements leading to minimum job-learning time (Littler 1985). These were the principles of job design accepted in the USA and, more slowly, in Britain. But not all economies accepted Taylor's ideas. A different pattern is to be found in Japan where factories depended on a tradition of work teams incorporating managerial and maintenance functions and few staff specialists, which allowed for considerable job flexibility. However according to Dore (1973) Taylor's time and motion studies were introduced there for a period around the First World War.

Taylor's work was carried out in union-free or weakly unionized plants, while the American Federation of Labour (AFL) initiated an anti-scientific management campaign (Grint 1991). Within weeks of its first major implementation, a strike broke out in Watertown Arsenal. A full investigation by the House of Representatives (a government assembly) found widespread malpractices and so Taylorist methods were banned from all arsenals, navy yards, and for 1916–49, from all government-funded operations (Noble 1974). The Society of Mechanical Engineers (despite Taylor being president) refused to publish the Principles of Scientific Management on the grounds that it was not scientific. Taylor was himself appalled at the strong hostility he witnessed amongst rank-and-file workers in response to his design of industrial organization (Stearns 1989). Workers' feelings of anger, disaffection, humiliation, can breach organizational controls (Fineman 1996).

Despite the problems inherent in Taylor's work design, Henry Ford adopted the principles of Taylorism for his car plants, having seen the system of mass disassembly (taking animal carcasses to pieces) in the Chicago meat packing plants before the First World War (Ackroyd and Crowdy 1990; Burrell 1997: 138). Ford had the wit to appreciate that the process of disassembly of animal carcasses in principle could be applied in reverse to the construction of complex products like cars. Here is an illustration of how the principles of mass assembly production were begun. He began with the little pieces and found that one man took twenty minutes to produce an electrical alternator. When the process was spread over twenty-nine operations, assembly time was decreased to thirteen minutes. Raising the height of the assembly line by 8 inches reduced this to seven minutes, while further rationalization cut it to five minutes (Sims et al. 1993). The closely monitored, machine-paced, short-cycle, and unremitting tasks were combined with an authoritarian work regime.

Ford was aware that some of the jobs were monotonous. They were 'so monotonous that it seems scarcely possible that any man would care to continue long at the same job' (Ford 1923: 106). However Ford's research showed that no man's mind had been twisted or deadened by the work and if a person did not like the repetitive work they did not have to stay in it (Ford 1923). While the jobs were repetitious, the workers also had to devote themselves to a system of harsh discipline both at work and outside the factory gates. Ford had a missionary zeal to change the behaviour of men as well as make automobiles. He was passionately opposed to gambling, drinking alcohol, smoking, and sex outside marriage so insisted that any employee who was found to be indulging in any of these activities be expelled from the prosperity-sharing, five dollar a day pay scheme. Fifty investigators were employed to monitor the behaviour of employees. Midnight raids on employees' homes were not uncommon (Corbett 1994: Case 27).

> **STOP** A report in the *New York Times* (8 January 1928) described Henry Ford as the 'Mussolini of Detroit'. Is this a fair description of the man? (See Corbett 1994: Case 27.)

In the early 1920s Ford's share of the car market was two-thirds. Fifteen years later, it had fallen to 20 per cent. According to Drucker (1989) Henry Ford tried to run his billion-dollar business without managers. Henry Ford ran a one-man tyranny where he employed secret police that spied on Ford executives and informed him of any attempt on the part of executives to make decisions. When they seemed to acquire managerial authority or responsibility they were generally fired. Henry Ford demoted first-line supervisors regularly every few years so they would not become 'uppity' and forget they owed their job to him. Drucker believes that it was this absence of management that caused the fall of the Ford Motor Company. After the Second World War, Henry Ford's grandson (Henry Ford II) took over the company; he rebuilt management, though he had no business experience at all. He took most of his concepts of management and organization, along with his top managers, from his big competitor, General Motors.

Why would you pay a highly skilled worker to do a job from start to finish when you could split the job into component parts, assign each task to minimally qualified workers, and so reduce costs and increase output? Designing jobs so that each worker repeatedly performs a limited number of tasks in accordance with instructions provided by management increases efficiency, results in uniform products, and gives management increased control. Management have no need to rely on the cooperation of workers to tell them how long a task takes, how many people are required to do a job, how much work can be completed in one shift. With less skilled jobs comes management's power to dictate wages, hours, and working conditions and greater interchangeability of workers. The logic of routinization of work is simple, elegant, and compelling (Leidner 1993). Routinization and detailed division of labour does, however, increase the possibility of a few people potentially disrupting a whole production process.

This routinization, deskilling, of work began in manufacturing industry. As clerical work grew, the principles were applied there so the thinking work was removed, leaving jobs lacking in variety and opportunities for decision making (Braverman 1974). For Braverman there were three principles of Taylorism:

1. the dissociation of the labour process from the skills of the workers;

2. the separation of conception (the thinking about how work is done) from the execution (doing) of the work;

3. the managerial use of the monopoly of this knowledge to control each step of the labour process and its mode of execution.

Following Marx, Braverman says that work under capitalism is geared to the creation of profit rather than the satisfaction of human needs, thus there is a conflict of interests between labour and capital. In these antagonistic conditions it is necessary for managers to secure maximum possible control over the labour process. (The labour process, as defined by Marx, has three elements—purposeful human activity directed to work, the materials on which work is performed, and the instruments of work.) Braverman argues that the consequence of the extension of scientific management is degradation of the labour process, with jobs becoming increasingly specialized and routine. (For a critique of Braverman see Edwards 1978; Grint 1991: 190–5.)

The effect on workers is well documented. Routinized jobs lack variety, job satisfaction, and meaning. A process of deskilling is complemented by the application of technology to the labour process.

Managements did not always get their own way, however, as studies by Noble (1979), Buchanan (1985), Zeitlin (1983), and Wilson (1987) illustrated in the engineering industry. Taylorism could never be a universal set of specific practices. There was a defence from the 'doers' of work from the developing trade union movement, as well as scepticism

---

AN EXAMPLE OF DESKILLING AND DEGRADATION OF WORK

Watanabe (1990) describes how labour was deskilled and degraded in the Japanese banking sector. Labour control was intensified and labour conditions deteriorated. The computer systems had book-keeping skills, for example, so the work of a large mass of employees became routine and monotonous, punching computer terminal keys and so on. The work of middle management was also simplified as functions requiring judgement and discretion became almost unnecessary. Branch managers were placed under the unified and centralized control of head office by the use of computers so their authority was reduced and accountability increased. A polarization of labour occurred, a separation of mental and physical labour. Mental labour was concentrated in fewer employees such as top managers and systems analysts.

from some of the employers worried about labour unrest. Taylorism was never a universal practice and is inappropriate in some industries, like machine tools manufacture (Broadbent et al. 1997: 4). But it does inform a management philosophy that managers have a right to manage and allows a 'scientific' rationale for professional status and autonomy of managers.

STOP When marking essays, lecturers often notice that students talk about Taylor and Taylorism as if it is history, some management idea that existed in the past, and is now outdated and old-fashioned. It is easy to see why—Taylor was writing and practising management at the start of the twentieth century. But his ideas are alive and well today. What examples can you think of that demonstrate that Taylorism is still of relevance and is in use today?

Numerous scholars have documented the unintended and unfortunate consequences of the trend towards work simplification (e.g. Argyris 1964; Blauner 1964; Herzberg et al. 1959; Walker and Guest 1952). Routine non-challenging jobs often led to high employee dissatisfaction, increased absenteeism and turnover, and substantial difficulties in effectively managing employees who worked on simplified jobs (Hackman and Lawler 1971). Researchers experimented with job enlargement and redesign to make jobs more meaningful and challenging. However, support for job redesign was hard to substantiate empirically. A major evaluative study of job redesign studies suggested missionary zeal, the publication of positive results only, and the employment of poor research designs (Blacker and Brown 1978).

An understanding of job design requires recognition of the strategic choices open to managers (Child 1972; Monanari 1979). Management, for example, has choices about the techno-structural arrangements, or the sort of technology in which to invest, and on the type of structures used to manage the organization. Despite the wide variety of choices available, job designers use a common set of criteria (Davis et al. 1955; Taylor 1979). They typically opt for a technology which minimizes the time required to perform the job, the skill level needed, the necessary training time, and the individual's contribution to the whole process. The choices usually made, then, seek to minimize immediate costs through specialization and routine. Management also has choices over the pattern of local control. When information processing requirements are low, then job holders are usually subjected to a relatively direct form of control (Clegg 1984; Friedman 1977). Economic and psychological values underpin the choices. The economic ones are Taylorist and include ease of training and replacing staff and the reduction of direct labour costs resulting from deskilling. The psychological value rests in the belief that individuals need close external control; the worker is seen as naturally lazy and unreliable (McGregor 1960). These economic and psychological views may be widely held by both key decision-makers and job holders and represent a strong pressure for and expectation of the design of relatively simple, closely supervised jobs. Employing easily replaced people in

AN EXAMPLE OF TAYLORISM IN PRACTICE

United Parcel Service employ industrial engineering managers who, for example, stipulate how fast their drivers walk; they are expected to walk at a pace of 3 ft per second. Until recently drivers were instructed in how to move in an effort to maximize efficiency. Packages were to be carried under the left arm and the driver stepped into the van with the right foot while holding the van's keys on the middle finger of the right hand. The rules about personal appearance include beards being forbidden, moustaches must not extend beyond the corner of the mouth, and the hair must not grow so long that it covers the top of the collar or the ear lobes. While this does not increase efficiency it does ensure, in the company's view, that employees look neat and clean (*Financial Times*, 16–17 August 1997, p. 7).

technologically simple jobs which are highly constrained and directly supervised goes a considerable way towards meeting the needs of managers to make their operations predictable and to maintain direct control over events. Scientific management can best be identified by its most prominent features—time and motion studies and incentive payments (Taska 1995). However it can also be seen as bolstering middle-class professionals' social and political struggle for legitimacy, giving them a role in influencing the training given to workers (Taska 1995).

Despite the limitations of Tayloristic job design and its negative effects, there are many benefits to be gained by the employer. Taylorism can bring about efficient working; efficiency was Taylor's guiding obsession. Taylor's scientific management is very much in practice in many organizations.

Neat and clean jobs may be found in the parcel delivery service but Taylor's principles are also found applied in less clean jobs, such as those to be found in a chicken factory. Here too work can be segmented into simple repetitive operations. Packing the chicken, for example, involves four people doing one of four tasks: inserting the giblets and tucking the legs in, bagging the chicken, weighing it, and securing the top of the bag. An employee in a chicken factory was found to be checking over 2,000 chickens an hour, 14,000 chickens a day. This involved checking that no chickens had been left with livers, hearts, or similar organs. In the words of the employee this meant, 'putting your hand in the backside of a chicken, feeling around then bringing anything out, dropping it in the bin, and then going on to the next' (see Noon and Blyton 2002: 148). The employees found the work hard.

While scientific management has long been associated with behavioural problems at work, it has more recently become associated with inefficiencies arising from inflexibility. If you are producing a continuous, standardized product with homogeneous (the same) throughput for a mass market maybe it looks, for those who design work organization, like an extremely efficient way of organizing. Where there is no such mass market and a heterogeneous (diverse) rapidly changing and unpredictable throughput (due to customer demand or product innovation) then what may be required is a more flexible, committed, itinerant, and skilled workforce capable of exercising discretion to cope with uncertainties and fluctuations in demand and technology. The mechanistic conception of people needs to be replaced with an alternative approach to human beings.

The Human Relations Movement

The roots of human relations are to be found in the nineteenth century in, for example, Émile Durkheim's (1858–1917) analysis of anomie (a pathology, a form of social breakdown; see Durkheim 1984) and his concern about social solidarity and integration. The human relations movement began to emerge during the First World War and was concerned with the selection, testing, and classification of army recruits which required psychological testing. These developments ought to increase employees' productivity and personal satisfaction by easing difficulties rather than using sanctions (Lupton 1971). The starting point was a series of experiments at the Western Electric Company's Hawthorne plant in Chicago in 1924. First the relationship was investigated between lighting, temperature, humidity, frequency of rest breaks, and employees' productivity (Roethlisberger and Dickson 1939). Two groups of employees were selected and isolated in another part of the plant. One group experienced changes in their working conditions while the other did not. The productivity of each group was monitored and it was found that output of the experimental group increased regardless of how illumination was manipulated. Even when lighting was reduced to the equivalent of a candle, output continued to increase. Output of the control group also steadily increased.

The second set of experiments took place in the relay assembly test room in 1927 and looked in more detail at the effect of working conditions (also reported by Homans 1959). Here six women were watched as they assembled telephone relays. They put together parts and fixed them with screws, expected to complete five relays in six minutes. For the experiment they were assured that the object was to determine the effect of certain changes in working conditions such as rest periods, lunches, and shorter working hours. They were told to work at a comfortable pace. Again, no matter what the researchers did, even lengthening the working day and reducing rest periods, productivity increased. The researchers explained this by saying that the employees had been made to feel special; they had been the centre of attention. They had been given a 'test room observer', they had frequent interviews with the superintendent ('a high officer in the company'), and their views about the experiment were sought. The operators knew that they were taking part in what was considered an important and interesting experiment. Their work was expected to produce results 'which would lead to the improvement of the working conditions of their fellow employees' (Homans 1959: 586). This had increased their morale, which led to the increase in productivity. Further when they went for physical examinations to monitor their health they were given ice cream and cake. Relationships within the group also improved during the period of the experiment so that when one of them had a birthday, each of the others would bring her a present and she would respond by offering the group a box of chocolates. If one of them was tired, the others would 'carry' her, agree to work especially fast to make up for the low output expected from her. They became friends and socialized together out of work. The group developed a self-appointed leader who was ambitious and saw the experiment as a chance for personal distinction and advancement; there was then the development of an organized social group which led to improved output.

This behaviour is contrasted with that of their old department, which was discussed in conversations with each other and the observers. They had not enjoyed the constraints of supervision in their old department but felt 'relief from some form of constraint, particularly the constraint of supervision' (Homans 1959: 587) in the test room; they were disparaging about the supervisors in the department. It is curious (as Homans 1959: 595 notes) that the women felt they were free from pressure of supervision in the test room yet they were far more thoroughly supervised than they ever had been in their regular department.

Further interviews revealed that workers were banding together informally to protect themselves against practices which 'they interpreted as a menace to their welfare' (Homans 1959: 588). In response to the 'menace' they adopted a standard of what they felt to be a proper day's work and none of them exceeded it by very much. They resented the wage incentive system, usually some form of group piece-work (where the group would be paid for the number of pieces they produced), implied it was not working satisfactorily, used informal practices to punish and bring into line those who exceeded the accepted standard, and developed informal leadership to keep the group working together and enforcing its rules. They felt that seeking promotion was futile. Interviews with another group in 1931 revealed that while the management thought the adjustments the group made to small parts in the telephone equipment were complex, it was actually quite simple. The operators had however 'put a fence around the job' and took pride in telling how the apparatus, which no one could make work properly, was adjusted by them. Telephone engineers would seek their expertise. The operators would 'fool around' doing all sorts of wrong adjustments and taking two hours and in this way prevented people 'on the outside' from finding out what they really did. They delighted in telling the interviewer how they were pulling the wool over everybody's eyes. An informal organization had developed a leader who dealt with any outsiders—engineers, inspectors, or supervisors. This informal leader answered any questions. For keeping new operators from exceeding group norms of output, another leader was developed. While the supervisors were largely aware of this situation of informal leadership, they felt powerless to do anything about it.

Later research in the early 1930s involved the detailed observation of a group of fourteen men in a seven-month period who worked in the bank-wiring observation room. This time the men stayed in their normal work setting and a financial incentive scheme was introduced to reward group output. The men appeared to control their output, limiting it to what they thought was a 'fair day's work' for the pay they received. The group determined the maximum and minimum output norm. Any deviants were punished. If one of the employees did something that was not considered quite proper, one of his fellow workers had the right to 'bing' him. Binging consisted of hitting him with a stiff blow on the upper arm. The person who was struck usually took the blow without protest and did not strike back. If he turned out too much work he was called names like 'Speed King' or 'The Slave' (Homans 1959: 592).

The studies are now famous for identifying the importance of social needs in the workplace and the way work groups can satisfy these needs by restricting output and engaging in all kinds of unplanned activities. In identifying the informal organization based on friendship and groups and unplanned interactions existing alongside the formal organization designed by management, the research dealt an important blow to classical management theory. The informal organization included the emotional, non-rational, and sentimental aspects of human behaviour in organizations, the ties and loyalties that affected workers, the social relations that could not be encompassed by the organization chart but shaped behaviour regardless. Other theorists who influenced the development of this perspective included Mary Parker Follett (Kanter 1977).

The answer to problems of output restriction and resistance, according to Mayo (1949) writing on the Hawthorne research, was to develop managerial social skills so that the workers felt more disposed to work better with management. Morale and motivation could be improved if managers were better able to elicit cooperation through being more sensitive to workers' social needs. Management was encouraged to intervene in the informal organization and build a new moral order which would 'create and sustain consent' (Thompson and McHugh 2002: 49).

It is interesting that researchers have noted that Mayo was deeply distrustful of collective sentiment. He wanted to reduce the likelihood of workplace unrest (Sewell et al. 1999). Mayo believed in industrial harmony (Rose 1988: 115). In some respects his views were not too dissimilar from those of Frederick Taylor. He is also found to have allowed management to remove trouble makers from an experiment (Brewis and Linstead 1999). The Hawthorne experiments have come under close scrutiny by researchers and been found to be inadequate. Carey (1967) made it clear that these studies are replete with erroneous interpretations and do not demonstrate much of what everyone thought they did. For example the conclusion that relaxed and friendly supervision causes higher productivity is refuted by Carey, who argues the opposite—because of higher productivity the managers became more relaxed. Further, the increase in productivity was caused by a simple change of people in the work group. Two recalcitrant male workers were dismissed halfway through the study and were replaced with two women who needed jobs to help with their financial problems. It was their efforts and prodding that led to the increase in group output, and it was only after this output increase that management relaxed their coercive style of supervision (Weick 1969).

Similarly Brown (1976) and more recently Acker and Van Houton (1992) have noted how the Hawthorne studies produced questionable or incomplete interpretations of their results since they failed to consider adequately the gender dimensions of organizational processes. The men were observed under normal working conditions while the female group was in an experimental situation. Despite the fact that output was increased by the women and restricted by the men, the overall findings were presented as an explanation of the behaviour of employees per se.

It is also interesting to note, as Kanter (1977) has done, that while the first thrust in management theory—planning and decision making—put the 'rational man' into management, the second thrust concerning motivation and morale (acknowledging the human order behind the machine) did not significantly change this aspect of the management image. The traits of the masculine ethic seen as necessary for effective management did not change. Human relations theories may have made inroads adding a 'feminized' element to the old masculine ethic, influencing new forms of organization using teams and project management systems, yet the masculine ethic of rationality has dominated the spirit of managerialism and has given the manager role its defining image. It told men how to be successful as men in the new organizational world. Such an image also provided a rationale for where women belong in management. If they belonged it was in people-handling staff functions like personnel, at the 'emotional' end of management, excluded from the centres of power (Kanter 1977).

Rationality? Fitting Workers to Jobs?

Frederick Taylor argued that jobs and individuals should be matched. As employees are not universally similar, in the interests of efficiency, jobs and workers should be matched in terms of necessary skills and intelligence required. It has always been in employers' interests to fit workers to jobs but the First World War brought the issue into sharp relief. The provision of munitions and people for the war forced the government of the time to intervene in the management of factories to accelerate efficiency. When the United States entered the First World War in 1917 the scale of activities changed and the army's Committee for Psychology was established to place recruits, from the subnormal to officer material, using psychological tests; they claim to have tested almost 2 million men. The Industrial Fatigue Board in Britain in 1918 was set up to investigate and promote mechanisms of efficiency; it looked at rest, working hours, ventilation, and lighting systems. Psychological tests were also developed at this time so individuals could be tested and placed. C. S. Myers, founder and director of the National Institute of Industrial Psychology, began work in Britain in 1921. Industrial psychology has been dominated by the need to use psychometric testing to fit workers to jobs since this time. Wartime produced the technology for mass psychometric selection. While in the USA this generally tested ability, in Britain the tests were based on specific job needs to help select, for example, air pilots (see Hollway 1991; Rose 1988). 'Applied psychology thus achieved much favourable publicity, massive development funds and full respectability' (Rose 1988: 92). After the First World War, selection tests were used more widely and spread to the spheres of education and business. Unfortunately the tests were used for far more sophisticated purposes than those for which they were intended and, as a consequence, failed to meet expectation, resulting in a backlash of feeling against the use of psychological tests. The Second World War revived interest in ability testing again. Progress in testing had been made and a number of tests were developed to measure separate dimensions of ability. It became possible to assess those aspects of individual's competence which were of specific relevance to the individual's situation and the purpose of the assessment.

Social Darwinism, the application of Darwinist biology to society, provided the framework for a new psychology of individual differences. The relation of psychology of individual differences to psychometrics was 'symbiotic' (Hollway 1991: 57); one fed off the other. Where psychometrics provided the method, the theory was individual differences. Darwinism had enabled theory in terms of populations rather than individuals. Social

---

AN EXAMPLE OF EUGENICS: A CUSTOM-MADE BABY

A French scientist claims to be able to guarantee the sex of your baby if you use his method. The method is called 'Rightbaby' and is sold for £199 (*The Scotsman*, 3 November 1997, p. 12). It offers what every consumer wants, choice. But can any engineered gender selection be natural or is this eugenics? Is it ethically acceptable? A value judgement is being made on the basis of gender. It has been calculated that there are a hundred million 'missing women' who have been aborted or died as infants because of gender preferences (Boseley 2002). What do you think?

More recently the story of the Masterton family has been brought to the fore in the media (e.g Boseley 2002) with their wish to ensure their next child was female, having lost their only female child in a bonfire accident. A sperm-sorting machine called Microsort has led to the birth of some 300 babies whose gender was selected by their parents. Organizations sell the use of this technology while other organizations like the Human Fertilization and Embryology Authority (HFEA) try to regulate its use.

Darwinism, at the turn of the century, was concerned with improving the fitness of the race, genetic inheritance, and national efficiency. Eugenics gave a new political salience to the question of individual differences.

Eugenics

Eugenics was the science of improving stock which takes cognizance of all influences that tend to give the more suitable races or strains of blood a better chance of prevailing speedily over the less suitable than they otherwise would have had (Hollway 1991). Eugenics sees individual differences as largely determined by genetic inheritance. If an individual's performance is genetically determined, no attempt will be made to change it. You just need to group, place, and regulate individuals.

Eugenics has become a topical subject again since Scandinavian governments have been found to have executed a plan to purify the Nordic race through enforced sterilization. Those branded low class or mentally slow were sterilized. More than 60,000 women in Sweden were sterilized between 1935 and 1996 (*Guardian*, 30 August 1997, p. 14). It has been acknowledged that 60,000 Americans underwent forced sterilization in the name of science and improvement of the human breeding stock (Engel 2002); this process was only stopped in 1979. In the early twentieth century a British scientist called Sir Francis Galton proposed that the British population be divided into 'desirables', 'undesirables', and 'passables'. The first group would be encouraged to have children, the second discouraged, and the third left alone. Bertrand Russell, who suggested the state issue colour-coded procreation tickets, also expressed the need for eugenics in Britain. Those who reproduced without the ticket would be fined. H. G. Wells hailed eugenics as the first step towards the removal of detrimental types and the fostering of desirable ones. Eugenics appears to be a topic raised for discussion on a regular basis. Both eugenics and the psychology of individual differences are derived from statistical theory of population distribution based on the normal curve. In Britain Cyril Burt was the most prominent representative of the psychology of individual differences, in particular the genetic determination of intelligence testing.

Intelligence Testing: Testing People

Burt compared the IQ (Intelligence Quotient) scores of identical twins with less closely related siblings. He gathered a large set of data on identical twins that were raised separately. After Burt's death his work was closely scrutinized by Leon Kamin (1974, 1981). Carelessness and fraud was suggested, first by the *Sunday Times* (Gillie 1976) and later by Burt's official biographer (Hearnshaw 1979). Burt had failed to indicate which tests of intelligence he was using and published his papers with co-authors who could not be located; the co-authors were unknown to the institutions listed as their place of employment and were unknown to members of the scientific community at that time (Cernovsky 1997). His findings showed identical correlation coefficients for twin samples (see also Butler and Petrulis 1999); since IQ tests are not a precise tool it is unlikely that an identical IQ would be obtained even when testing the same person over time. These and other facts led to the uncomfortable conclusion that Burt had manufactured the data to support his belief that intelligence is largely inherited. Yet before being discredited, Burt influenced British social policies, for example, in schooling and the workplace.

While Burt was primarily an educational psychologist, he also worked with industrial psychologists to turn his attention to vocational guidance. In vocational guidance the measurement of general intelligence in children and the interests of employers come together to fit the person to the job. Burt claimed that the mental level of each child should be measured then the education most appropriate to that level should be given so that the child is guided into a career 'for which his measure of intelligence has marked him out' (Burt 1924: 71).

Burt testified to British government committees that children's intelligence levels were largely fixed by the age of 11 or so and were accurately measurable by standard tests given at that age. He helped produce the 'eleven plus' examination which streamed the top scoring minority into grammar schools or top streams at comprehensive schools and the rest into less challenging classes. It was virtually impossible for a child in a non-grammar secondary school to move and grammar school education was required for acceptance into university (Fancher 1985).

Despite the assumption that IQ is static, Flynn (1987) is able to show data from fourteen countries indicating IQ gains ranging from five to twenty-five points in one generation. This increase suggests powerful environmental influences that affect performance in IQ tests. Howe (1998) shows how intervention can produce lasting change. Yet many write as if this was not the case (e.g. Murray 1996). Other environmental factors likely to influence IQ differences are related to infant malnutrition or whether or not you have skipped breakfast (Spring et al. 1992)!

The public assumes that intelligence testing is infallible and this has very negative consequences for those groups seen as 'genetically inferior' as 'proven' by 'science'. Intelligence tests have a very narrow focus on skills and tasks acquired in schooling; they do not test creativity or social intelligence (like the ability to know yourself or perceive the emotional states or social behaviour of others). Many treat intelligence as if it is inherited through genes and as unchangeable during life (see Fox and Prilleltensky 1997: ch. 8 by Zack Cernovsky for a full discussion). Despite classical textbooks warning that it is unlikely that any test can be fair to more than one cultural group, numerous psychologists still misinterpret IQ scores from other cultures as indicating genetic inferiority of these groups. In the late 1960s a scientific discussion erupted on whether black peoples were genetically less intelligent than whites. The issue became less popular in the 1970s when some researchers demonstrated, using the same logic and tests, that Asians in the USA on average scored more in intelligence than whites. It is difficult, if not impossible, to finds tests that are culture free (Hofstede 1997).

Intelligence testing is so unreliable that even those who have been described as geniuses have been awarded low IQ scores. Cultural differences, for example, count for the ten-point gap in the IQ scores between white and black Americans. Yet in spite of this, there are still those like Christopher Brand, a psychologist at the University of Edinburgh, who continue to claim than it is a 'scientific fact' that white Americans and Asians are more intelligent than blacks. In the USA Hernstein and Murray (1994) in *The Bell Curve* documented the alleged intellectual inferiority of African Americans. Not only did the result harm the research participants who had been given Standford-Binet or other tests, but it weakened the available social support for those from black and minority groups by stigmatizing them as genetically inferior, thus strengthening the larger culture's racist attitudes (Brown 1997).

There is no inherent quality of intelligence which can indicate high potential (Howe 1997). Education and family background are better predictors of future success. Had George Stephenson, the nineteenth-century railway engineer, been given an intelligence test, he would probably have received a low score as he did not go to school, could not write his name, or do more than simple arithmetic by the age of 18. What intelligence tests have done is to set a threshold for entry into occupations that makes access to high-status jobs difficult for people with low scores. Large-scale research on army recruits from the Second World War found the median IQ scores increased and the range of scores decreased with occupational status. The median score for accountants was 128 with a range from 94 to 154 while the median scores for labourers was 88 with range of scores from 46 to 145 (Harrell and Harrell 1945). If you accept that this is an accurate reflection of ability, it shows that some labourers have the intelligence to be accountants and vice versa!

We all seem to know that a high IQ is about being clever, being good at thinking, good at solving abstract problems. According to Beloff (1992) we also assume that such power lies in the domain of men. Three separate studies show how, compared with male self-perceptions, females invariably underestimate their IQ. Further, females project higher IQs on to their fathers than on to their mothers (Beloff 1992; Higgins 1987; Hogan 1973). Young women students will, then, see themselves as intellectually inferior to young men. Women see themselves as inferior to their fathers and men as superior to their mothers. Issues of power, self-perception, gender, and IQ are clearly linked.

Vocational Guidance: Testing then Fitting People to Jobs

Cyril Burt claimed that the results of the measurement of intelligence corresponded with existing forms of classification of the school population and could also justify the sorts of jobs which less intelligent adults should choose. The idea is that making a fit between individuals and jobs can create a world of industrial harmony and productivity. Misfits were those who, by virtue of being in the wrong job, did not match up to the new methods and speeds introduced into production (Hollway 1991: 64). Vocational guidance for school leavers was of interest to industrial psychologists because if natural abilities and aptitudes could be measured, there would be no waste generated by those who found themselves in jobs which they did not 'fit'. As the vocational tests were applied almost entirely to mechanized jobs, all that was being tested would be aptitudes like finger dexterity and hand–eye coordination. These ideas were adopted by producers like the chocolate manufacturer, J. S. Rowntree, who believed that vocational selection would enable his company to reduce the number of cases in which work was experienced as monotonous. Automatic machinery would suit the lowest grade of worker. Rational scientific management practices could enable the employer to select the right worker for the job. From this basic assumption psychometric testing (the measurement of mental ability) was developed. The 'science' produces a battery of methodologies and techniques for selecting the 'right person for the job'.

The Psychometric Testing Industry: Testing People for Jobs

It is estimated that 100,000 psychometric tests are taken each day in Western countries (Cole 1997). The tests are used to assist the recruitment process, for mid-career appraisal, and outplacement. The best-known tests are personality tests: Cattell's 16PF personality questionnaire, Eysenck Personality Inventory/Questionnaire, and the Myers Briggs Type Indicator. The 16PF consists of sixteen factors, like unassertive/dominant and objective/sensitive measured through 185 multiple-choice questions (in its fifth edition) completed in 45–60 minutes. An Institute for Personality and Ability Testing copyrights the questionnaires and those administering them ought to be trained. Most researchers outside the Cattell establishment, including Eysenck, have been unable to replicate the sixteen factors.

There is little agreement amongst psychologists about how the term personality is defined or which aspects of personality can be measured. Personality is tested through a definition and measurement of traits. Eysenck's personality test looks at a small number of different types or basic dimensions on which people differ—unstable/stable and introvert/extrovert. The dimensions are bipolar so you can be high on extroversion and low on introversion. The types or dimensions are made up of traits, so traits of the extrovert would be sociable, excitable, and impulsive.

No personality test will be totally accurate. Behaviour and personality will vary over time; a personality test has a 'shelf life' of just six months. Behaviour will change depending on the situation. People cannot be expected to behave consistently regardless of the situation (Mischel 1968). The tests are relying on self-report data that means respondents need to have some insight into their most characteristic behaviour; that level of insight will vary from person to person. Interestingly the 16PF contains a measure of the extent to which respondents attempt to present themselves in a favourable or unfavourable manner. It is assumed that personality tests can be distorted and that people may want to present themselves in the best possible light.

STOP

Social desirability, presenting yourself in the best possible light, is thought to be best measured by statements like 'I am always happy to help someone however inconvenient' or 'As I child I always did as I was told to do' or 'I have no undesirable habits or vices'. If you answer 'yes' to these, you may be identified as deliberately distorting the result, self-deceiving, or producing a highly positive, if not inaccurate self-image. Would this be fair? The personality test interpreter is expected to gather supportive evidence to assess whether or not genuine socially desirable behaviour is part of your disposition. How would they do this?

Recently there has been a growth of interest in emotional intelligence; the topic has enjoyed remarkable popularity in professional and popular literature in the United States (Fineman 2000). Emotional Intelligence is defined as 'the ability to perceive emotions, to access and generate emotions so as to assist thought, to understand emotions and emotional knowledge, and to reflectively regulate emotions so as to promote emotional and intellectual growth' (Mayer and Salovey 1997: 5). It is about effectively joining emotions and reasoning (for a fuller description see George 2000 or Landon 2002). It has four elements—how aware you are of your own emotions, ability to accurately express your emotions, the awareness of others' emotions, and the ability to accurately express others' emotions and express empathy. Emotional intelligence is thought to lead to enhanced functioning in a variety of aspects of life such as achievement and close relationships (Goleman 1995) but may play a particularly important role in leadership effectiveness (George 2000). For example, emotional intelligence is thought to contribute to constructive thinking or the ability to solve problems with a minimum of stress (Epstein 1990). Further, because leaders who are high on emotional intelligence are better able to understand and manage their own emotions, they may be more likely to engage in constructive thinking to build and maintain high levels of cooperation and trust. Several measures of emotional intelligence have been developed (Mayer et al. 1997; Salovey et al. 1995). These are 'diagnostic instruments' with self-report rating scales designed to profile emotional intelligence.

When promoting products like the emotional intelligence profile, it is rarely acknowledged that the individual probably understands only a tiny fraction of his or her motives, intentions, or feelings (Scheff 1997). Further, how would you, as a potential employer, be able to judge if the self-report instrument had been completed with compliance, self-interest, and an instrumental orientation in mind? You may only be selecting the person on the basis of his or her ability to display certain emotions—to perform 'emotional eugenics' (Briner 1999). It is also unlikely that it will be noted in promotional literature that engaging with employees' feelings is likely to be the most fragile of all managerial activities (Warhurst and Thompson 1998). Emotional intelligence is just one way in which alignment of the individual with a set of categories dictated by an organizational ideal may be achieved. Making emotions calculable makes them amenable to management and control. Emotions can be treated as a commodity and given a market value, just like other forms of capital (Landon 2002).

It should be noted that in a review of managerial psychology, Smith and George (1994) say that non-work-related personality tests used as selection tools are poor predictors of job success and should be treated with caution. Despite this poor validity, personality tests remain in popular use. They are being used by management consultants to dupe clients and to satisfy the demand for assessment of personality. There is a worldwide abuse of personality testing going on, Smith and George believe. Thompson and McHugh (2002: 234) note that personality testing and inventories effectively perform the same function for an organization as stereotypes do for an individual or group. They help to sort a bewildering variety of information about a person into categories which can be more easily comprehended and evaluated. They aim to point to characteristics useful or damaging to the organization.

The psychometric testing industry is particularly apt at making sweeping claims, providing evidence, for example, of women's inadequacies as employees. Glenn Wilson says that the reason 95 per cent of bank managers, company directors, judges, and university professors in Britain are men is because men are 'more competitive' and because 'dominance is a personality characteristic determined by male hormones' (1994: 62, 63). Women who do achieve promotion to top management positions 'may have brains that are masculinized' (1994: 65). Psychology is deeply implicated in the patriarchal control of women (Wilkinson 1997). Women's alleged limited achievements are seen as due to biological differences, therefore unchangeable, or as a problem of social skills where the solution is assertiveness training. This locates women as the problem and says nothing about the social context, organizational structures, policies, or procedures that discriminate against women. The underlying assumption behind personality testing is that managerial ability is related to personality factors. Those factors will not include the ability to hold down a job, run a household, and bring up children. It fulfils the expectations of existing managers—mainly white, male, middle class, and middle aged—about what makes a good manager (Hollway 1984). People unable or unwilling to make the correct responses automatically select themselves out, regardless of managerial potential. The utility of psychometric testing is its cost-saving ability to predict who is capable or willing to be trained. The pragmatic psychology of Taylorism is at work here. If the person can do the job, as long as they have the 'right' personality, they will be a 'fit' employee.

■ SUGGESTIONS FOR FURTHER READING

1. Fincham, R., and Rhodes, P. (1999), *Principles of Organizational Behaviour* (3rd edn.), Oxford: Oxford University Press. This book has sections dealing with issues like personality and intelligence testing.

2. Thompson, P., and McHugh, D. (2002), *Work Organizations* (3rd edn.), Houndmills: Palgrave. Chapter 3 in particular asks you to think about the ideology underlying Taylorism. Chapter 15 is useful on personality testing.

3. Rose, M. (1988), *Industrial Behaviour* (2nd edn.), Harmondsworth: Penguin. This book is particularly good for describing, in greater depth, the thinking and rationale behind Taylorism and Human Relations.

4. Cernovsky, Z. Z. (1997), 'A Critical Look at Intelligence Research', chapter 8 in D. Fox and I. Prilleltensky, *Critical Psychology: An Introduction*. London: Sage. This chapter demands you take a really critical view of intelligence research.

5. Noon, M., and Blyton, P. (2002), *The Realities of Work* (2nd edn.), Houndmills: Palgrave Macmillan. Chapter 6 on 'Work Routines and Skill Change' is particularly strong on Taylorism, Fordism, and the deskilling debate (whether it is right to assume that there is a trend where managers use technology to deskill jobs).

6. Landon, M. (2002), 'Emotion Management: Dabbling in Mystery—White Witchcraft or Black Art?', *Human Resource Development International*, 5/4: 507–21. This article is very strong on making some interesting cases for being wary of psychometric testing, particularly emotional intelligence.

7. Hollway, W. (1991), *Work Psychology and Organizational Behaviour*, London: Sage, Chapter 4 is on fitting workers to jobs. Other chapters will be useful for helping understand the history of work psychology.

■ WEB LINKS

www.accel-team.com/scientific/scientific_02.html This web page gives you more information about Taylorism, briefly describes Taylor's predecessors in job design, and has links to other early management theorists.

www.socsci.mcmaster.ca/~econ/ugcm/3ll3/taylor/sciman takes you to Taylor's original work of 1911.

■ QUESTIONS

1. What are the advantages of scientific management according to Taylor? What disadvantages in employing scientific principles have been shown to exist?

2. You have seen here the 'logic' of job design. Clegg (1984) shows how the processes of work simplification can be reversed. If you were a manager would you try to humanize work? Why or why not?

3. Read Smith and George (1994) and decide, from their review, what selection methods you might employ if you wanted to hire a manager.

4. What implications are there for managers to draw from the science of eugenics?

5. Carol Vorderman, the TV presenter, known for being 'a brain with beauty', has an IQ of 157. In an interview she said: 'while I'm not stupid, I didn't get a particularly good degree—a third' (Radio Times 1997). Is IQ a good predictor of degree result? What other factors contribute?

■ **GROUP EXERCISE**

Organizations make attempts to shape the way individuals experience, understand, judge, and conduct themselves (Foucault in Rose 1996). Individuals are expected to regulate themselves by being educated and solicited into an alliance between their own personal objectives and ambitions and those of the organization. There is a 'eugenics of the human soul' (Rose 1990) going on. How do you think this is done? What are your own personal experiences of this?

■ **REFERENCES**

Acker, J., and Van Houton, D. R. (1992), 'Differential Recruitment and Control: The Sex Structuring of Organisations', ch. 1 in A. J. Mills and P. Tancred (eds.), *Gendering Organizational Analysis*, London: Sage.

Ackroyd, S., and Crowdy, P. A. (1990), 'Can Culture be Managed?', *Personnel Review*, 19/5: 3–13.

Argyris, C. (1964), *Integrating the Individual and the Organization*, New York: Wiley.

Babbage, C. (1989), *The Economy of Machinery and Manufactures* (4th edn.; first published in 1832), London: William Pickering.

Beloff, H. (1992), 'Mother, Father and Me: Our IQ', *Psychologist* (July), 309–11.

Blacker, F. H., and Brown, C. A. (1978), *Job Redesign and Management Control*, London: Saxon House.

Blauner, R. (1964), *Alienation and Freedom*, Chicago: University of Chicago Press.

Boseley, S. (2002), 'Gender Machine Put to the Test', *Guardian*, 23 Oct., found at www.guardian.co.uk/uk_news/story/0,3604,817172,00.html

Braverman, H. (1974), *Labor and Monopoly Capital: The Degradation of Work in the Twentieth Century*, New York: Monthly Review Press.

Brewis, J., and Linstead, S. (1999), 'Gender and Management', ch. 2 in L. Fulop and S. Linstead (eds.), *Management: A Critical Text*, Houndmills: Macmillan.

Briner, R. (1999), 'The Neglect and Importance of Emotion at Work', *European Journal of Work and Organizational Psychology*, 8/3: 323–46.

Broadbent, J., Dietrich, M., and Roberts, J. (1997), 'The End of the Professions?', ch. 1 in J. Broadbent, M. Dietrich, and J. Roberts (eds.), *The End of the Professions? The Restructuring of Professional Work*, London: Routledge.

Brown, L. (1997), 'Ethics in Psychology: Cui Bono?', ch. 4 in D. Fox and I. Prilleltensky (eds.), *Critical Psychology: An Introduction*, London: Sage.

Brown, R. (1976), 'Women as Employees: Some Comments on Research in Industrial Sociology', ch. 2 in D. L. Barker and S. Allen (eds.), *Dependence and Exploitation in Work and Marriage*, Harlow: Longman.

Buchanan, D. A. (1985), 'Canned Cycles and Dancing Tools: Who's Really in Control of Computer Aided Machinery?', Paper presented to the 3rd Annual Labour Process Conference, Manchester.

Burrell, G. (1997), *Pandemonium: Towards a Retro-Organizational Theory*, London: Sage.

Burt, C. (1924), 'The Mental Differences between Individuals', *Journal of the National Institute of Industrial Psychology*, 11/2: 67–74.

Butler, B. E., and Petrulis, J. (1999), 'Some Further Observations Concerning Sir Cyril Burt', *British Journal of Psychology*, 90: 155–60.

Carey, A. (1967), 'The Hawthorne Studies: A Radical Criticism', *American Sociological Review*, 32: 403–16.

Cernovsky, Z. Z. (1997), 'A Critical Look at Intelligence Research', ch. 8 in D. Fox and I. Prilleltensky, *Critical Psychology: An Introduction*, London: Sage.

Child, J. (1972), 'Organizational Structure, Environment and Performance: The Role of Strategic Choice', *Sociology*, 6: 1–22.

Clegg, C. W. (1984), 'The Derivations of Job Designs', *Journal of Occupational Behaviour*, 5: 131–46.

Cole, N. (1997), 'Personality put to the test', *The Scotsman*, 24 Oct., p. 1.

Corbett, M. (1994), *Critical Cases in Organizational Behaviour*, Houndmills: Macmillan.

Davis, L. E., Canter, R. R., and Hoffman, J. (1955), 'Current Job Design Criteria', *Journal of Industrial Engineering*, 6: 5–11.

Dore, R. P. (1973), *British Factory—Japanese Factory*, London: Allen & Unwin.

Drucker, P. F. (1989), *The Practice of Management*, Oxford: Heinemann Professional Publishing.

Durkheim, E. (1984), *The Division of Labour in Society*, trans. W. D. Halls, London: Macmillan.

Edwards, R. C. (1978), 'The Social Relations at the Point of Production', *Insurgent Sociologist*, 8/2–3: 109–25.

Engel, M. (2002), 'State Says Sorry for Forced Sterilizations', *Guardian*, 23 May; found at www.guardian.co.uk/international/story/0,3604,709818,00.html.

Epstein, S. (1990), 'Cognitive-Experimental Self-Theory', in L. Pervin (ed.), *Handbook of Personality Theory and Research*, New York: Guilford Press, pp. 165–91.

Fancher, R. E. (1985), *The Intelligence Men: Makers of the IQ Controversy*, London: Norton.

Fineman, S. (1996), 'Emotion and Organizing', ch. 3.3 in S. R. Clegg, C. Hardy, and W. R. Nord (eds.), *Handbook of Organization Studies*, London: Sage Publications.

——(2000) (ed.), *Emotion in Organizations*, London: Sage.

Flynn, J. R. (1987), 'Massive IQ Gains in 14 Nations: What IQ Tests Really Measure', *Psychological Bulletin*, 101: 171–91.

Ford, H. (1923), *My Life and Work*, London: William Heinemann.

Fox, D., and Prilleltensky, I. (1997) (eds.), *Critical Psychology: An Introduction*, London: Sage.

Friedman, A. (1977), 'Responsible Autonomy versus Direct Control over the Labour Process', *Capital and Class*, 1 (Spring), 43–57.

George, J. M. (2000), 'Emotions and Leadership: The Role of Emotional Intelligence', *Human Relations*, 8: 1027–55.

Gillie, O. (1976), 'Crucial Data Faked by Eminent Psychologist', *Sunday Times*, 24 Oct.

Goleman, D. (1995), *Emotional Intelligence*, New York: Bantam Books.

Grint, K. (1991), *The Sociology of Work: An Introduction*, Cambridge: Polity.

Hackman, J. R., and Lawler, E. E. (1971), 'Employee Reactions to Job Characteristics', *Journal of Applied Psychology Monograph*, 55/3: 259–86.

Harrell, T. W., and Harrell, M. S. (1945), 'Army Classification Test Scores of Civilian Occupations', *Educational and Psychological Measurement*, 5: 229–39.

Hearnshaw, L. S. (1979), *Cyril Burt: Psychologist*, London: Hodder & Stoughton.

Hernstein, R. C., and Murray, C. (1994), *The Bell Curve: Intelligence and Class Structure in American Life*, New York: Free Press.

Herzberg, F., Mausner, B., and Snyderman, B. (1959), *The Motivation to Work*, New York: Wiley.

Higgins, L. (1987), 'The Knowing of Intelligence', *Guardian*, 10 Feb.

Hofstede, G. (1997), *Cultures and Organizations: Software of the Mind*, New York: McGraw Hill.

Hogan, H. W. (1973), 'IQ: Self Estimates of Males and Females', *Journal of Social Psychology*, 106: 137–8.

Hollway, W. (1984), 'Fitting Work: Psychological Assessment in Organizations', in J. Henriques et al., *Changing the Subject: Psychology, Social Regulation and Subjectivity*, London: Methuen.

——(1991), *Work Psychology and Organizational Behaviour: Managing the Individual at Work*, London: Sage.

Homans, G. C. (1959), Group Factors in Worker Productivity, in E. Maccoby, T. M. Newcomb, and E. L. Hartley (eds.), *Readings in Social Psychology* (3rd edn.), London: Methuen, pp. 583–95.

Howe, M. (1997), *IQ in Question*, London: Sage.

——(1998), 'Can IQ Change?', *Psychologist* (Feb.), 69–72.

Johnson, P., and Gill, J. (1993), *Management Control and Organizational Behaviour*, London: Paul Chapman.

Kamin, L. (1974), *The Science and Politics of I.Q.*, Potomac, Md.: Erlbaum.

——(1981), Chapters 12 to 20 and 22 in H. J. Eysenck and L. Kamin (eds.), *Intelligence: The Battle for the Mind: H. J. Eysenck versus Leon Kamin*, London: Macmillan.

Kanter, R. (1977), *Men and Women of the Corporation*, New York: Basic Books.

Landon, M. (2002), 'Emotion Management: Dabbling in Mystery—White Witchcraft or Black Art?', *Human Resource Development International*, 5/4: 507–21.

Leidner, R. (1993), *Fast Food, Fast Talk: Service Work and the Routinization of Everyday Life*, Berkeley, Calif.: University of California Press.

Littler, C. R. (1985), 'Taylorism, Fordism and Job Design', ch. 2 in D. Knights, H. Wilmott, and D. Collinson (eds.), *Job Redesign: Critical Perspectives on the Labour Process*. Aldershot: Gower.

Lupton, T. (1971), *Management and the Social Sciences*, Harmondsworth: Penguin.

McGregor, D. (1960), *The Human Side of Enterprise*, New York: McGraw Hill.

Mayer, J. D., and Salovey, P. (1997), 'What is Emotional Intelligence: Implications for Educators', in P. Salovey and D. Sluyter (eds.), *Emotional Development, Emotional Literacy and Emotional Intelligence*, New York: Basic Books, pp. 3–31.

————and Caruso, D. (1997), 'Multifactor Emotional Intelligence Scale', New Caanan, Conn.: unpublished manuscript.

Mayo, G. E. (1949), *The Social Problems of Industrial Civilization*, London: Routledge & Kegan Paul.

Mischel, W. (1968), *Personality and Assessment*, New York: Wiley.

Monanari, J. R. (1979), 'Strategic Choice: A Theoretical Analysis', *Journal of Management Studies*, 16: 202–21.

Murray, C. (1996), Murray's précis, *Current Anthropology*, 37 suppl. (Feb.): S143–51.

Noble, D. F. (1974), *America by Design*, New York: Oxford University Press.

——(1979), 'Social Choice in Machine Design: The Case of Automatically Controlled Machine Tools', in A. Zimbalist (ed.), *Case Studies in the Labor Process*, New York: Monthly Review Press, pp. 1–50.

Noon, M., and Blyton, P. (2002), *The Realities of Work* (2nd edn.), Houndmills: Palgrave.

Radio Times (1997), 'Why am I on TV so much? Probably because I'm cheap' (4–10 Oct.), 15–16.

Roethlisberger, F. J., and Dickson, W. J. (1939), *Management and the Worker*, Cambridge, Mass.: Harvard University Press.

Rose, M. (1988), *Industrial Behaviour* (2nd edn.), Harmondsworth: Penguin.

Rose, N. (1990), *Governing the Soul: The Shaping of the Private Self*, London: Routledge.

——(1996), 'Identity, Genealogy and History', in S. Hall and P. du Gay (eds.), *Questions of Cultural Identity*, London: Sage.

Salovey, P., Mayer. J. D., Goldman, S. L., Turvey, C., and Palfai, T. P. (1995), 'Emotional Attention, Clarity, and Repair: Exploring Emotional Intelligence Using the Trait Meta-Mood Scale', in J. W. Pennebaker (ed.), *Emotion, Disclosure and Health*, Washington DC: American Psychological Association, pp. 125–54.

Scheff, T. J. (1997), *Emotions, the Social Bond and Human Reality*, Cambridge: Cambridge University Press.

Sewell, G., Fulop, L., Linstead, S., and Rifkin, W. D. (1999), 'Managing Teams', ch. 6 in L. Fulop and S. Linstead (eds.), *Management: A Critical Text*, Houndmills: Macmillan.

Sims, D., Fineman, S., and Gabriel, Y. (1993), *Organizing and Organizations*, London: Sage.

Smith, M., and George, D. (1994), 'Selection Methods', in C. L. Cooper and I. T. Robertson (eds.), *Key Reviews in Managerial Psychology: Concepts and Research in Practice*, Chichester: Wiley.

Spring, B., Pingitore, R., Bourgeois, M., Kessler, K. H., and Bruckner, E. (1992), 'The Effects and Non-Effects of Skipping Breakfast: Results of Three Studies', paper presented at the 100th Annual Meeting of the American Psychological Association, Washington, DC, August.

Stearns, P. N. (1989), 'Suppressing Unpleasant Emotions: The Development of a Twentieth-Century American', in A. E. Barnes and P. N. Stearns (eds.), *Social History and Issues of Human Consciousness*, New York: NY University Press.

Taska, L. (1995), 'The Cultural Diffusion of Scientific Management', *Journal of Industrial Relations*, 37/3: 427–61.

Taylor, F. W. (1911), *Principles of Scientific Management*, New York: Norton & Co.

Taylor, J. C. (1979), 'Job Design Criteria Twenty Years Later', in L. E. Davis and J. C. Taylor (eds.), *Design of Jobs* (2nd edn.), Santa Monica, Calif.: Goodyear.

Thompson, P., and McHugh, D. (2002), *Work Organizations: A Critical Introduction* (3rd edn.), Houndmills: Palgrave.

Ure, A. (1835), *The Philosophy of Manufactures*, London: Charles Knight.

Walker, C. R., and Guest, R. H. (1952), *The Man on the Assembly Line*, Cambridge, Mass.: Harvard University Press.

Warhurst, C., and Thompson, P. (1998), 'Hands, Hearts and Minds: Changing Work and Workers at the End of the Century', in P. Thompson and C. Warhurst (eds.), *Workplaces of the Future*, Basingstoke: Macmillan.

Watanabe, T. (1990), 'New Office Technology and the Labour Process in Contemporary Japanese Banking', *New Technology, Work and Employment*, 5/1: 56–67.

Weick, K. (1969), *The Social Psychology of Organizing*, Reading, Mass.: Addison-Wesley Publishing Company.

Wilkinson, S. (1997), 'Feminist Psychology', ch. 16 in D. Fox and I. Prilleltensky (eds.), *Critical Psychology: An Introduction*, London: Sage.

Wilson, F. M. (1987), 'Computer Numerical Control and Constraint', in D. Knights and H. Wilmott (eds.), *New Technology and the Labour Process*, London: Macmillan.

Wilson, G. (1994), 'Biology, Sex Roles and Work', in C. Quest (ed.), *Liberating Women . . . from Modern Feminism*. London: Institute of Economic Affairs, Health and Welfare Unit, pp. 59–71.

Zeitlin, J. (1983), 'The Labour Strategies of British Engineering Employers 1890–1922', in H. Gospel and C. Littler, *Managerial Strategies and Industrial Relations*, London: Heinemann.

3 Rationality and Bureaucracy

The logic and rationale of Taylorism, human relations, and job design were described in the last chapter. In this chapter we will be looking at bureaucracy as it represents a continuous drive towards rationalization and efficiency in organizations. We start with the work of Max Weber.

While Taylor had been a theorist-practitioner, Max Weber (1864–1920) was a writer on sociology and politics. He described the process of rationalization underlying Western history, a trend where the traditional or magical criteria of action were replaced by technical, calculative, or scientific criteria. Weber's (1930) study of the rise of capitalism argued that the 'spirit of capitalism' owed a lot to the practices and thoughts of the Calvinist Church which, in turn, was enmeshed in logical, calculative thought, rationality that had spread from science, through politics and into the new Protestant Church. Rationalization is a process whereby the means chosen to pursue ends can be determined by logical and rational calculation. The continuous drive towards greater rationalization and efficiency, according to Weber, is clear in every sphere of social, economic, and political life. With this process relations between people increasingly come to take the form of calculations about the exchange and use of the capabilities and resources. One key place where this happens is in bureaucracies.

All organizations make provision for their continuance to ensure they meet given aims. Bureaucracy helps them do this. Bureaucracies are enterprises or political parties or other organizations (like the Church) where people discharge functions specified in advance according to rules. Authority is wielded as tasks are allocated, coordinated, and supervised. Tasks are regulated through the organization's structure. The bureaucratic structure has become dominant in modern society, in the public and private sector.

Weber's starting point is authority. The claims to legitimacy of authority come from three different sources:

1. Rational grounds where there is a belief in the rules and rights of those in authority to issue commands. This is legal authority.

2. Traditional grounds where there is sanctity or sacredness of tradition and legitimacy of status (traditional authority).

3. Charismatic grounds where there is devotion to sanctity, heroism, or character of an individual (charismatic authority).

With legal authority obedience is owed to the office whoever is in it; they have a right to issue commands. Legal authority is to be found in bureaucracy. In contrast a monarch or a feudal lord would have traditional authority and dynamic, influential characters would have charismatic authority. With legal authority and bureaucracy there is a levelling of status.

In Weber's view, what are the characteristics of bureaucracy? Modern officialdom functions in the following manner (adapted from Gerth and Wright Mills 1948):

1. There is the principle of fixed and official areas of administration, which are usually ordered by rules or regulations. Activities are distributed as official duties. The authority to give commands about these duties is distributed in a stable way and strictly delimited by rules concerning the coercive means which officials have. Only suitably qualified individuals are employed.

2. The hierarchy means that there is a firmly ordered system where those in lower office are under the command of those in higher office.

3. The management of the office is based upon written documents, which are preserved in their original form. The officials, the office materials, and the files make up the bureau or office.

4. Specialized office management presupposes thorough and expert training.

5. When the office is fully developed, official activity demands the full working capacity of the official.

6. The management of the office follows general rules that can be learnt.

The official is in a vocation which requires work over a long period and for which the official needs to be qualified. Holding office is not to be exploited for, for example, rents or the exchange of services, as has been the case in the past. The official manages faithfully in return for security of employment. The job, at least in public authorities when Weber wrote, was held for life. Loyalty should be impersonal and functional, not personal, like that of the vassal, slave, or disciple; the official is not the personal servant of a ruler. The official enjoys social esteem. A superior authority appoints them. The official receives a fixed salary for the job and is set on a career within the hierarchical order.

STOP When you were reading about the slave, the vassal, the official, what gender did you envisage them being? Bologh (1990: xiv) argues that Weber opens up a world of men who struggle for power, men who strive to dominate their world and give meaning to, and find meaning in, that world. Is she right?

Weber was keen to stress the technical advantages of bureaucratic organization. The decisive reason for the advance of bureaucratic organization has been its purely technical superiority over every other form of organization. There is precision, speed, lack of ambiguity, knowledge of the files, continuity, discretion, unity and uniformity, strict subordination, reduction of friction and of material and personal costs. All these are raised to the optimum in a strictly bureaucratic organization. There are calculable rules so there is a 'calculability' of consequences. Scientific management has a role to play in this process as it provides the ideal vehicle for the imposition of military discipline in the factory. Techniques such as Taylor's 'shop cards' specifying the daily routines of employees are ideal for this process of bureaucratization.

Business is discharged 'without regard for persons' (Weber 1978: 226); the division of labour in administration is put into practice according to purely objective criteria. All love, hatred, and purely personal irrational and emotional sentiments are excluded. In contrast the lord of older societies was capable of being moved by personal sympathy, kindness, favour, or gratitude. With rationalization comes the use of calculative devices and techniques, formally rational means, the division of labour, sets of rules, accounting methods, money, technology, and other means for increasing that rationality. There will, however, always be unintended consequences; bureaucracy could also manifest features that were 'materially irrational'. For example bureaucracy can threaten individual freedom. Weber recognized that bureaucracy might become an 'iron cage' (1930: 181) and speculated that the domination of the official in modern society could become more powerful than the slave owner of eras past. Weber wrote on many topics, including the history of the piano and Freudianism (see Runciman 1978), but is probably best known in management for his work on bureaucracy.

Since Weber wrote about the ideal bureaucracy, a good deal of work has focused on the dysfunctions of the bureaucratic form, the menace of bureaucracy, for example by Merton (1936), Gouldner (1954), and Selznick (1949). These writers, as well as questioning the perfection of the 'ideal type', discussed whether the opposition between organizational efficiency and the freedom of the individual was possible. The routine and oppressive aspects of bureaucracy were highlighted to show it as a 'vicious circle' that develops from the resistance of the human factor to the mechanistic rationalist theory of behaviour which is being imposed on it. The very resistance tends to reinforce the use of the bureaucracy. For example in Gouldner's view, impersonal bureaucratic rules evolve because they alleviate the tensions created by subordination and control, but at the same time they perpetuate the very tensions that bring them into being. They particularly reinforce the low motivation of the workforce that makes close supervision necessary.

As we have seen the ideal type of bureaucracy is governed by a formal set of rules and procedures which ensures that operations and activities are carried out in a predictable, uniform, and impersonal manner. Personal relationships are excluded from organizational life. Zygmunt Bauman (1989) shows the importance of bureaucratic organization to the death camps in Nazi Germany.

AN EXAMPLE OF BUREAUCRACY IN PREGNANCY?

Pregnant women in the UK may see up to forty health care professionals on a 'production line' basis and may never see the same midwife twice. They are unlikely to know the names of those helping deliver the baby. If anything goes wrong with the delivery, the patient is likely to be even more distanced (Burrell 1997: 145).

Both women and the medical profession organize and manage productive lives, seeking to control, routinize, and make predictable the process of pregnancy and birth (Brewis and Warren 2001). An example of this is the 'birth plan' that Western women are usually encouraged to plan for their labour. Another example is the screening done to prevent genetic 'disorders'.

What other elements of bureaucracy are likely to be witnessed during pregnancy and birth?

Can bureaucracy be devoid of emotion? We think of bureaucracy, organizational order, and efficiency as matters of rational, non-emotional activity. Cool clear strategic thinking should not be sullied by messy feelings. Good organizations are places where feelings are managed, designed out, or tamed. We have known for four decades, since C. Wright Mills (1951) wrote about white-collar workers, that they need to control their feelings and that facial expressions (e.g. a smile) became a matter of professionalism. 'She [sic] must smile when it is time to smile' (Mills 1963: 272). It is thought that emotions interfere with rationality (Fineman 1996). That rationality and effective leadership would be damaged by, for example, a sign that you cannot cope (Sachs and Blackmore 1998). It is however just the expression of some emotions that are frowned upon. Anger and competitiveness are generally condoned in bureaucratic organizations while others like sadness, fear, and some forms of sexual attraction and vulnerability are taboo (Martin et al. 1998: 434). Emotion management operates through the exclusion of negative emotions, emotions that neither contribute to productivity nor are easy to deal with. But can organizations, and in particular bureaucracy, be free of all unwanted emotion? Can you, for example, imagine a political party free of all public embarrassment?

Recently writers (e.g. Acker 1990; Brewis and Grey 1994; Martin 1990; Witz et al. 1996) have suggested that while the rational-legal model presents itself as gender neutral, it actually constitutes a new kind of patriarchal structure. Ferguson (1984) also argues that bureaucracy is an organization of oppressive male power. Bureaucracy is both mystified and constructed through an abstract discourse of rationality, rules, and procedures. ('Discourse', as defined in the work of Foucault, refers to what is regarded as acceptable, both in terms of what is permitted to be said and thought, who can and cannot speak and with what authority; also who is regarded as normal or abnormal.) The reality of organizational life is constituted through discourses which have a 'normalizing' effect on individuals, defining what and who is normal, standard, and acceptable (Thomas 1996). Bureaucracy is a construction of male domination. In response bureaucrats, workers, and clients are 'feminized' as they develop ways of managing their powerlessness that at the same time perpetuate their dependence.

Pringle (1989), using the case of secretaries, shows how the relationship between the boss and the secretary is the most visible aspect of a pattern of domination based on desire and sexuality to be found in modern bureaucratic structures. Secretaries seem to contradict the criteria of the ideal bureaucracy. For example they are far from being specialized as they can be called upon to do just about anything. There may be considerable overlap between their work and that of their boss. In bringing to bear the emotional, personal, and sexual, they represent the opposite of rationality, as discursively constituted. She argues that the concept of rationality excludes the personal, the sexual, and the feminine. The personal, sexual, and feminine are perceived as associated with chaos and disorder and in opposition to rationality; the concept of rationality is thus seen to have a masculine base.

> **STOP**
>
> **Secretaries, Sex, and Work**
>
> While no one seriously believes that secretaries spend much time on their bosses' knee, sexual possibilities colour the way in which the boss–secretary relationship is seen. Outside the sex industry, it is said to be the most sexualized of all workplace relationships (Pringle 1989). Is Pringle right?

Pringle and others (e.g. Burrell 1984, 1987; Hacker and Hacker 1987) have questioned whether bureaucratic forms have banished sexuality from organizational life. While the complete eradication of sexuality from bureaucratic structures has been a goal that many top decision makers have pursued, many managements content themselves with the incorporation and close containment of sexual relations in the non-work field. Human features, like love, comfort, and sexuality, have been gradually expelled from bureaucratic structures and relocated in the family. Faced with this curtailment, significant numbers of men and women have resisted, so acts of intimacy have taken place in the past and will continue to take place in the future. This view stresses how male sexuality is routinely privileged within organizational practices as sexuality and power are intertwined in everyday social interactions.

Men, then, are more likely to match the requirements of bureaucratic organizations than women are. It is the male body, its sexuality, minimal responsibility in procreation, and the conventional control of emotions that pervades work and work organizations (Acker 1990). Bureaucrats need to be highly controlled or regimented, lacking in desire, isolated in performance, and disassociated from self; this is 'the' male body being privileged (Witz et al. 1996).

Rationalization and the Service Sector

More recently jobs in the service sector have expanded, challenging employers to rationalize workers' self-presentation and feelings as well as their behaviour (as we also see in the chapter on culture and others). Employers may try to specify how workers, such as a flight attendants, look, how their hair should be styled and, in the case of women, how their make-up should look. Employers may try to specify what employees say, their demeanour, their gestures, and even their thoughts. To do this they use scripts, uniforms, dress codes, rules, and guidelines for dealing with customers and co-workers, instructions about how best to think of the work and customers.

This routinization of human interaction is disconcerting but explicit rules have become a significant feature of employment contracts in many mass service industries. For example, the guidelines in personal appearance issued to Walt Disney World employees include 'Fingernails should not extend more than one-fourth of an inch beyond the fingertips' (Leidner 1993: 9). These explicit rules include feeling rules (Fineman 1995): 'First we practice a friendly smile at all times with our guests and among ourselves. Second, we use friendly courteous phrases. "May I help you" . . . "Thank you" . . . "Have a nice day" . . . "Enjoy the rest of your stay" and many others are all part of our working vocabulary' (Walt Disney Productions 1982: 6). The 'Magic Kingdom', also known as 'the smile factory' expects each member of staff, known as 'the cast', to show a constant smile even to those who are difficult, offensive, or threatening. They also have a system of staff surveillance but the cast seek out blind spots (a large rock, a concrete pillar) to have a rest, conversation, or smoke. The staff then resist these feeling rules by taking an illegitimate break (Van Maanen 1991). They are also known to slap visitors hard across their chests with the seat belt of ride vehicles if they misbehave.

Values and attitudes can be constructed and influenced through training programmes and corporate culture. Hochschild (1983) shows how recurrent training for flight attendants is aimed at reinforcing the 'inside-out' smile. She documents how flight attendants were trained to repeat 'I know just how you feel' to calm passengers furious over a missed connection or other failures of service. She also showed, in the case of flight attendants, that the result of regulating what she called 'emotion work' (the work of creating a

---

AN EXAMPLE OF THE RULES: A CLEAN-SHAVEN EMPLOYEE IN A TIE IS BEST?

Safeway has a preference for employing clean-shaven men. Perhaps they would like to consider the following story (*Scotland on Sunday*, 9 November 1997, p. 21). An upper-class woman employed a decidedly scruffy gardener who allowed a shadow of stubbly growth to appear on his chin. His employer did not like it but did not want to offend him by asking him to shave. She asked him one day how long he thought a person should go before shaving if they wanted to avoid looking scruffy. He looked at her thoughtfully and then replied 'I would say with a light growth like yours, every two days should be fine.'

Two men have recently questioned the issue of men's dress code in the office. The first, working in a JobCentre in Stockport, objected to the dress code for men which included wearing a collar and tie; he was disciplined for not wearing them. He argued at a tribunal that it was unfair that men had to wear a collar and tie when women could turn up to work wearing what they liked, including t-shirts and football shirts. This he said amounted to unlawful sex discrimination; males were being treated less favourably than their female colleagues. The tribunal agreed with him (Bradley 2003; Manners and McMyn 2003). A second male JobCentre employee, in Birmingham, was banned from wearing jeans to work. In response, he turned up to work in a kilt, lumberjack shirt, and loud multicoloured tie. He said that his employers 'seemed happy for me to go to work like this, even though I looked like a pillock' (Manners and McMyn 2003).

particular emotional state in others, often by manipulating your own feelings) was that the attendants were alienated from their feelings, their faces, and their moods. Some showed signs of resistance, for example, by spilling a Bloody Mary over an offensive passenger's lap. Here is another story: 'A young businessman said to a flight attendant, "Why aren't you smiling?" She put her tray back on the food cart and said, "I'll tell you what. You smile first, then I'll smile". The businessman smiled at her. "Good," she replied. "Now freeze and hold that for fifteen hours."' (Hochschild 1983: 127.)

Smiling is not always interpreted as intended by 'rational' organizations. The 'smile' is not always 'read' correctly by customers. One woman attacked a check-out operator for 'flirting' with her husband. There have been numerous examples of obscene phone calls to operators (Keenoy 1990, reported in Burrell 1992).

The effect of increased rationalization on the workforce is, however, not always negative. Some will accept the tight scripting because it saves them having to make the effort of thinking of appropriate words to say or ways to act. The standards of good work have been clarified for them, the routines can act as shields against the insults and indignities a worker might have to accept from the public (Leidner 1993: 5). Others will refuse to smile (Hochschild 1983) or will insist on their right to their own style (Benson 1986).

Most of us know how to behave with service workers in order to fit the organizational routines. We have been fitted into the routine of 'involuntary unpaid labor' (Glazer 1984) when we serve ourselves petrol at the petrol station, gather up, bring, and unload groceries from our baskets in the supermarket, and clear away our rubbish in fast food restaurants. We know not to order items in fast food restaurants that are not on the menu and we know to line up for service. The garish colours and plastic seats are designed to make sure we do not linger too long.

The Case of McDonald's

The routinization to be found at McDonald's shows a close link with the logic of Taylorism, maximizing managerial control of work and breaking work down into its constituent tasks which can be preplanned. The key to McDonald's success is its uniformity and predictability. Customers know exactly what to expect. McDonald's promises that every meal will be served quickly, courteously, and with a smile. It promises fast service, hot food, and clean restaurants. To do this it needs to use the principles of scientific management coupled with centralized planning, central designed training programmes, approved and supervised suppliers, automated machinery, meticulous specifications, and systematic inspections. As a result, 'a quarter-pounder is cooked in exactly 107 seconds. Our fries are never more than 7 minutes old when served.' Each restaurant aims to serve any order within sixty seconds (Beynon 1992: 180). Customers are channelled through the restaurant by its layout and design and through the service routines and relatively restricted menu on offer.

About three-quarters of the outlets are owned by franchisees rather than the corporation, so owners retain control over pay scales, for example, but the company requires that

---

AN EXAMPLE: HOW TO COOK A HAMBURGER

Here is an example of the original McDonald's procedure for cooking hamburgers. Those grilling the burgers were instructed to put hamburgers down on the grill moving from left to right, creating six rows of six burgers. As the first two rows are furthest away from the heating element, they were instructed to flip the third row first, then the fourth, fifth, and sixth before flipping the first two (Love 1986: 141–2). How would you feel if instructions as detailed as this were to be found in recipe books? Would you follow the instructions (*a*) in your own home, (*b*) for an employer?

---

every outlet's production methods and products meet McDonald's precise specifications. The regimentation covers food preparation, bookkeeping, purchasing, dealing with workers and customers, and virtually every aspect of the business. The food production is the most visible aspect for the customer. A 'bible', an operations and training manual, demonstrates the proper placement and amount of ketchup, mustard, and pickle slices on each type of hamburger available. Lights and buzzers tell the crew when to take French fries out of the fat, the French fry scoops specify the size of portion and allow the worker to fill a bag and set it down in one continuous motion, and specially designed ketchup dispensers squirt the correct portion of ketchup. Crew are also told in what sequence the products customers order are to be gathered, what arm motion is to be used in salting the batch of fries, and to double-fold each bag before presenting it to the customer. Only minor variations in the execution of its routines are allowed. Customers are referred to as 'guests' so that all customers are potentially treated with respect and courtesy.

There are rules about safety, hygiene, and uniform. All workers have to wear a clean uniform complete with hat and nametag. Brightly coloured nail polish, wearing more than two rings, and dangling jewelry are forbidden. Leidner (1993) shows how extensively these dress code rules stretched. For example one window worker always wore a piece of adhesive tape on his ear to hide a gold earring. While the tape was probably more offensive than the earring, management considered it less offensive.

Performance is rated and each worker is awarded stars (worn on a badge) which are linked to pay and promotion prospects. The performance rating is made on the basis of an assessment which lists criteria such as: 'Greeting the customer: 1. There is a smile 2. Greeting is pleasant, audible, sincere 3. Looks customer in the eyes' (from McDonald's 'Counter Observation Check List' quoted in Fineman 1995). McDonald's training centre near Chicago is called Hamburger University. The 'university' is on a 'campus', the director is called 'the dean', and the trainers are 'professors'. The trainers work from scripts prepared for them. They try to produce managers 'with ketchup in their veins'. Crew, managers, and franchisees learn that there is a McDonald's way of doing business and that any diversion from this would be wrong. The full training programme requires between 600 and 1,000 hours of work and is required of all those who wish to own a McDonald's outlet.

While the routinization and extreme standardization is clear, McDonald's does favour some experimentation. When an employee produces a new idea, it can be adopted (the

Egg McMuffin and the Big Mac are examples of employee ideas) but the corporation will experiment, test, and refine the idea before it is implemented in a uniform way. You will find that some products too differ depending on national or local context, despite the uniformity of approach. For example, in Norway McDonald's sells grilled salmon sandwiches with dill sauce on a whole grain bread (Ritzer 1998: 85).

Ritzer (1998, 2000) argues that fast food restaurants like McDonald's are the new model of rationalization which have replaced the bureaucratic structure. He talks of McDonaldization, defining it as a process by which the principles of the fast food restaurant are coming to dominate more and more sectors of American society as well as the rest of the world. He believes that McDonaldization affects education, work, travel, the family, and every other sector of society. The McDonald's model has proved to be irresistible. Four basic dimensions lie at the heart of McDonald's success:

1. Efficiency: it offers us the optimum method of getting from a state of being hungry to a state of being full.

2. It offers food and service that can be easily quantified and calculated. We feel that we are getting a lot of food for a modest amount of money. People think that it will take less time to go to McDonald's, eat the food, and return home than to prepare the food at home.

3. It offers predictability. We know that the burger we eat in one town will be the same as in another and that the one we order next week will be identical to the one we eat today.

4. Control is exerted over human beings, especially through the substitution of non-human technology for human. The humans do a limited number of tasks precisely as they are told to do them. Limited menus, few options, and uncomfortable seats lead diners to do what management wants them to do—eat quickly and leave. Technology replaces human labour where the soft drink dispenser shuts off when the carton is full; the programmed cash register eliminates the need for cashiers to calculate prices.

The experience of working in a fast food restaurant is included in Gabriel's (1988) book on working lives in catering (see also 'The View from Below' chapter, below). He interviewed in three London outlets of one fast food company. Virtually all the staff were in their teens or early twenties and management were only slightly older. About one-third of the workers worked part-time and several were students; most lived with their parents and for many it was their first job. Few expected to stay for more than a year.

The jobs offered little intrinsic satisfaction and very few people found their jobs enjoyable. Most respondents spent most of their time in just one job like cleaning, sweeping, serving at the counter, or in the kitchen. To get through the day they had to fantasize. Nineteen of the twenty-six workers said they kept their minds on other things while they worked; only working on the till required concentration. Many had developed a contempt for the work they did ('crap jobs'). Some played games, like catching a girl's eye as she entered the restaurant and seeing if she joined your queue (if they were a heterosexual male). Some added personal touches to the burgers they put together and wrapped, or bent the rules of how many burgers to make in any one batch, to see if they could get away with it. Breaking the rules, adding personal touches, and playing games broke the drudgery of work. As Burawoy (1981, 1985) notes, these games give some degree of control to workers and are tolerated by management because they enhance the efficiency of work. We are left wondering then, does increasing routinization really lead to efficiency or is a human relations view more appropriate?

There is a downside to the fast food industry, says Ritzer. For example, the fast food restaurant can be a dehumanizing setting in which to eat or work. It can feel like dining or working on an assembly line. It minimizes contact among human beings. It serves food which is high in calories, fat, sugar, and salt content. It has run foul of environmentalists as well as nutritionists. It contributes to a homogenization around the world; diversity of food choice is being reduced or eliminated.

McDonald's did not, as Ritzer notes, develop in a historical vacuum; it had important precursors providing the principles of the assembly line, scientific management, and bureaucracy. Although the fast food restaurant adopts elements of these precursors, it takes a quantum leap in the process of rationalization. The basic dimensions of McDonaldization—efficiency, calculability, predictability, increased control through technology—are manifest not only in fast food restaurants but in a wide and increasing array of social settings throughout the world like shopping malls, home shopping, preprepared meals. They are also evident in factory farming. Burrell (1997: 138) takes this point one stage further when he says that McDonald's is an organization dependent on the profitable death of cattle and chickens in profusion. Without automated death, the cost of the Big Mac would be higher. The Nazi concentration camps, he notes, relied upon the relative automation of death too (see also Bauman 1989).

Ritzer (1998) has gone on to document the continuation, if not acceleration, of the rationalization process in a book called *The McDonaldization Thesis* and in another about credit cards (Ritzer 1995). He argues that we have a 'new means of consumption' (1998: 1) in fast food restaurants, credit cards, tourism, shopping malls, superstores, home shopping television networks, and many more. Using Mannheim's thinking on rationalization, Ritzer believes that McDonaldized systems, through their rules, regulations, scripts, and so on, encroach upon and ultimately threaten the ability of people working with these systems to think intelligently. Central planning and considerable control exerted over franchisees, employees, and customers bring us back to a Weberian image of an iron

---

AN EXAMPLE OF MCDONALD'S AND EXPLOITATION?

Seventeen-year-old women are forced to work 9–10 hours a day, seven days a week in a factory in Vietnam which manufactures the toys for McDonald's Happy Meals. Wages are well below subsistence levels. Wages do not even cover 20 per cent of the daily food and travel costs of workers, let alone their families. Overcome by fatigue and poor ventilation, 200 women fell ill. Appeals from human and labour rights groups failed to influence the management of the factory (Alfino et al. 1998: xiii–xiv)

cage of rationalization. Ritzer says that this iron cage is currently being constructed, piece by piece, by the various organizations and institutions that follow the McDonald's model. It may be more escape-proof than Weber ever imagined.

Credit cards and fast food restaurants share some interesting similarities. Both represent radical change in society yet neither was highly innovative. Both rely heavily on advertising; both have been forced to engage in price competition and have tried to target teenage populations. While McDonald's rationalized the delivery of prepared food, the credit card rationalized the consumer loans business. Prior to credit cards, the process of obtaining a loan was slow, cumbersome, and non-rationalized. It now requires little more than the filling out of a short questionnaire. Credit bureaus and computerization mean that credit records can be checked and applications approved or rejected rapidly. The unpredictability of whether a loan will be approved has been greatly reduced. Credit card loans, like fast food hamburgers, are being served up in a highly rationalized assembly line.

There are also degrees of McDonaldization to be found in surprising areas of life. Academia might be one domain immune to it. But Ritzer believes that McDonald's has influenced academia and even medicine and law. For example, in the case of universities, parents and students are increasingly approaching the university as consumers in the same way that they approach other consumption items. They are looking for low price, convenience, efficiency, and absence of hassle. Universities have responded by opening satellite campuses in suburban areas or smaller towns not well served by a central university. They provide plenty of parking space and advanced technology. Television, video, or video-conferencing can now transmit courses. We confront a future of accelerating McDonaldization. McDonald's will remain powerful until the nature of society changes so dramatically that McDonald's is no longer able to adapt. Like scientific management, the assembly line, and bureaucracy, it leads to an ever more rational world.

Ritzer is not without his critics. Ritzer is accused of offering a reductive analysis and expressing cultural elitism that is insensitive to the variety and diversity of consumer practices and local variations. It is argued, for example by Parker (1998, 2002) that Ritzer is making the judgement that the food and service are not as good as they used to be in traditional restaurants; he is condemning contemporary practices and is nostalgic for an older, quieter, slower world. He is accused of neglecting gender analysis and the meanings that McDonald's has for women or for people of different classes, races and regions. He is also accused of being too pessimistic (Alfino et al. 1998).

A Thought

It could be argued that the last two chapters are misleading. Currently the book leads you to understand that there has been a linear development of management thinking from early theorists like Taylor and Babbage to the present day. Tsoukas and Cummings (1997) present an alternative view. They argue that we should abandon the idea that there is a development of thinking about organization and management that is underpinned by progression, that we are part of a continuous progress. Rather than seeing the history of management as a 'stairway to heaven' upwards and onwards, it should be viewed as a kaleidoscope, containing a number of discrete fragments, revealing a pattern, as Foucault (1966) did. The sequence of patterns from the kaleidoscope obeys no inner logic and conforms to no universal norm of reason. Fragments from the past will reappear now and again. What support do you find for this thought? Would you agree with Tsoukas and Cummings? What would be the rationale for presenting a non-linear view of management thinking?

■ SUGGESTIONS FOR FURTHER READING

1. Thompson, P., and McHugh, D. (2002), *Work Organizations*, Houndmills: Palgrave. Chapter 3 discusses Weber, bureaucratic control, and its contradictions.
2. Alfino, M., Caputo, J. S., and Wynyard, R. (1998) (eds.), *McDonaldization Revisited: Critical Essays on Consumer Culture*, London: Praeger. This book offers a number of criticisms of the McDonald's thesis from different perspectives and is useful for helping us think through the weaknesses of Ritzer's otherwise compelling arguments.
3. Schlosser, E. (2001), *Fast Food Nation: What the All-American Meal is Doing to the World*, London: Penguin. Schlosser is a journalist who offers all sorts of interesting facts about fast food, like that Americans now spend more money on fast food than on higher education, personal computers, or new cars. On any given day, about a quarter of the adult population in the USA visits a fast food restaurant.
4. Noon, M., and Blyton, P. (2002), The Realities of Work (2nd edn.), Basingstoke: Palgrave Macmillan. Chapter 7 on emotional work. This chapter defines emotional labour and demonstrates why it is important. It also looks at employee's reactions to emotional labour.
5. Putnam, L. L., and Mumby, D. K. (1993), 'Organizations, Emotion and the Myth of Rationality', ch. 2 in S. Fineman (ed.), *Emotion in Organizations*, London: Sage. This chapter shows how emotion is rooted in a 'myth of rationality'. It positions emotion as central to the process of organizing.
6. Watson, T. (2002), *Organizing and Managing Work*, Harlow: Pearson. Chapter 7 on the structure, culture, and the struggle of management control contains a good section on the ubiquity and inevitability of bureaucracy as well as its failings and contradictions.
7. Barry, J., Chandler, J., Clark, H., Johnston, J., and Needle, D. (2000) (eds.), *Organization and Management: A Critical Text*, London: Business Press. Chapter 1 by John Chandler—'Organizational Behaviour and the Individual: A Critique of a Consensus'—discusses emotion and bureaucracy as well as morality.

■ WEB LINKS

Ritzer, G. (McDonaldization: George Ritzer Interview), found at **http://tienxs.virtualave.net/george.html**. In *Fast Food, Fast Talk*, attending Hamburger University, Robin Leidner observes how McDonald's trains the managers of its fast food restaurants to standardize every aspect of service, found at **www.ucpress.edu/books/pages/6158.html**

Bureaucracy can affect some lives very dramatically. The story 'Rabbit Proof Fence' by Doris Pilkington Garimara shows the impact of government policy and bureaucracy on the lives of three Aborigine girls taken away from their family in 1931. Official government policy decreed that all 'half caste' children (born of Aboriginal mother and 'white' father) be taken away from kin and land in order to be 'made white'. The architect of the removal policy was the Chief Protector of Aborigines, a man driven by the vision of a society cleansed of 'half castes'. See **www.rabbitprooffence.com.au/news/Prejudice.html**

■ QUESTIONS

1. Why should management, thinking about rationalization, be seen as a kaleidoscope and not in a linear fashion?

2. Gabriel (1988) found that workers in the fast food industry said the main point of their job was to earn their own money. Why was this the case? If you have worked in the fast food industry, what was the main point for you?

3. George Ritzer argues that McDonaldization constrains or eliminates people's creativity. Discuss.

4. Burger King have had a slogan—'You want it? You got it!'—implying that the customer's wish was their command. What do you think would happen if you asked for your burger to be medium rare?

5. Pringle (1989) says that her study of secretaries vividly illustrates the working of modern bureaucracy. How does she do this? Which of her arguments might you wish to disagree with?

6. Filby (1992) described the everyday life in a betting shop. The management tried, and partly succeeded, in using women's bodies and personalities to promote the product but the female employees 'turned the tables' (Thompson and McHugh 2002: 144). How did they do this?

7. In 1997 a TV investigation videotaped local restaurant workers sneezing into their hands while preparing food, licking salad dressing off their fingers, picking their noses, and flicking cigarette ash into food about to be served. In May 2000 three employees at Burger King were arrested for putting spit, urine, and cleaning products into the food. They had allegedly tampered with the Burger King food for eight months (Schlosser 2001: 222). What other stories does Schlosser (2001) tell about behaviour at work that might make you think twice about eating fast food again?

■ GROUP EXERCISE

Leidner (1993) found that McDonald's workers do not say that they are dissatisfied with their jobs. Ritzer (1998) says that this is a disturbing finding. If most of your life is spent in McDonaldized systems there is little or no basis for rebellion against your McDonaldized job because you lack a standard against which to compare and to judge such a job. More generally there is no basis for rebellion against the system or for seeking out an alternative. McDonaldization is an iron cage from which there is no escape and not even any interest in escape. Do you agree? Divide the class in two. One half should find arguments to support Ritzer and the other half to argue against.

■ REFERENCES

Acker, J. (1990), 'Hierarchies, Jobs, Bodies: A Theory of Gendered Organizations', *Gender and Society*, 4/2: 139–58.

Alfino, M., Caputo, J. S., and Wynyard, R. (1998) (eds.), *McDonaldization Revisited: Critical Essays on Consumer Culture*, London: Praeger.

Bauman, Z. (1989), *Modernity and the Holocaust*, Cambridge: Polity.

Benson, S. P. (1986), *Counter Culture: Saleswomen, Manager and Customers in American Department Stores 1890–1940*. Urbana, Ill.: University of Illinois Press.

Beynon, H. (1992), 'The End of the Industrial Worker?', in N. Abercrombie and A. Warde (eds.), *Social Change in Contemporary Britain*, Cambridge: Polity.

Bologh, R. W. (1990), *Love or Greatness: Max Weber and Masculine Thinking—a Feminist Inquiry*, London: Unwin Hyman.

Bradley, R. (2003), 'Employers Get a Dressing Down', *The Scotsman*, 28 Mar., p. 6.

Brewis, J., and Grey, C. (1994), 'Re-eroticizing the Organization: An Exegesis and Critique', *Gender, Work and Organization*, 1/2: 67–82.

——and Warren, S. (2001), 'Pregnancy as Project: Organizing Reproduction', *Administrative Theory and Praxis*, 23/3: 383–406.

Burawoy, M. (1981), 'Terrains of Contest: Factory and State under Capitalism and Socialism', *Socialist Review*, 11/4: 58, 83–124.

——(1985), *The Politics of Production*, London: Verso.

Burrell, G. (1984), 'Sex and Organizational Analysis', *Organization Studies*, 5/2: 97–110.

——(1987), 'No Accounting for Sexuality', *Accounting, Organization and Society*, 12: 89–101.

——(1992), 'The Organization of Pleasure', ch. 4 in M. Alvesson and H. Wilmott (eds.), *Critical Management Studies*, London: Sage.

——(1997), *Pandemonium: Towards a Retro-Organizational Theory*, London: Sage.

Ferguson, K. E. (1984), *The Feminist Case against Bureaucracy*, Philadelphia: Temple University Press.

Filby, M. (1992), 'The Figures, the Personality and the Bums: Service Work and Sexuality', *Work, Employment and Society*, 6/1: 23–42.

Fineman, S. (1995), 'Stress, Emotion and Intervention', ch. 6 in T. Newton (with J. Handy and S. Fineman), *Managing Stress: Emotions and Power at Work*, London: Sage.

——(1996), 'Emotion and Organizing', ch. 3.3 in S. R. Clegg, C. Hardy, and W. R. Nord (eds.), *Handbook of Organization Studies*, London: Sage.

Foucault, M. (1966), *The Order of Things: An Archaeology of the Humanities*, London: Tavistock & Routledge.

Gabriel, Y. (1988), *Working Lives in Catering*, London: Routledge & Kegan Paul.

Gerth, H. H., and Wright Mills, C. (1948), from *Max Weber: Essays in Sociology*, trans. H. H. Gerth and C. Wright Mills, London: Routledge & Kegan Paul.

Glazer, N. Y. (1984), 'Servants to Capital: Unpaid Domestic Labor and Paid Work', review in *Radical Political Economics*, 16: 61–87.

Gouldner, A. (1954), *Patterns of Industrial Bureaucracy*, Glencoe, Ill.: The Free Press.

Hacker, B. C., and Hacker, S. (1987), 'Military Institutions and the Labor Process: Non-Economic Sources of Technological Change, Women's Subordination and the Organization of Work', *Technology and Culture*, 28: 743–75.

Hochschild, A. R. (1983), *The Managed Heart: Commercialization of Human Feeling*, Berkeley, Calif.: University of California Press.

Keenoy, T. (1990), Personal communication reporting research at Cardiff Business School, reported in Burrell (1992).

Leidner, R. (1993), *Fast Food, Fast Talk: Service Work and the Routinization of Everyday Life*, Berkeley, Calif.: University of California Press.

Love, J. (1986), *McDonalds: Behind the Arches*, Toronto: Bantam.

Manners, W., and McMyn, J. (2003), 'Tie Case Throws Dress Codes into Confusion', *The Times*, Law, p. 3.

Martin, J. (1990), 'Re-reading Weber: Searching for Feminist Alternatives to Bureaucracy', paper presented to the Academy of Management in San Francisco.

——Knopoff, K., and Beckman, C. (1998), 'An Alternative to Bureaucratic Impersonality and Emotional Labor: Bounded Emotionality at The Body Shop', *Administrative Science Quarterly*, 43: 429–69.

Merton, R. K. (1936), 'The Unanticipated Consequences of Purposive Social Action', *American Sociological Review*, 1: 894–904.

Parker, M. (1998), 'Nostalgia and Mass Culture: McDonaldization and Cultural Elitism', ch. 1 in M. Alfino et al. (eds.), *McDonaldization Revisited: Critical Essays on Consumer Culture*, London: Praeger.

——(2002), *Against Management*, Cambridge: Polity Press.

Pringle, R. (1989), 'Bureaucracy, Rationality and Sexuality: The Case of Secretaries', in J. Hearn, D. L. Sheppard, P. Tancred-Sheriff, and G. Burrell (eds.), *The Sexuality of Organizations*, London: Sage.

Ritzer, G. (2000), *The McDonaldization of Society* (new century edition), Newbury Park, Calif.: Sage.

——(1995), *Expressing America: A Critique of the Global Credit Card Society*, Thousand Oaks, Calif.: Pine Forge Press.

—— (1998), *The McDonaldization Thesis: Explorations and Extensions*, London: Sage.

Runciman, W. G. (1978), *Max Weber: Selections in Translation*, Cambridge: Cambridge University Press.

Sachs, J., and Blackmore, J. (1998), 'You Never Show You Can't Cope: Women in School Leadership Roles Managing their Emotions', *Gender and Education*, 10/3: 265–79.

Schlosser, E. (2001), *Fast Food Nation: What the All-American Meal is Doing to the World*, London: Penguin.

Selznick, P. (1949), *TVA and the Grass Roots*, Berkeley, Calif.: University of California Press.

Thomas, R. (1996), 'Gendered Cultures and Performance Appraisal: The Experience of Women Academics', *Gender, Work and Organization*, 3/3 (July), 143–55.

Thompson, P., and McHugh, D. (2002), *Work Organizations* (3rd edn.), Houndmills: Palgrave.

Tsoukas, H., and Cummings, S. (1997), 'Marginalization and Recovery: The Emergence of Aristotelian Themes in Organization Studies', *Organization Studies*, 18/4: 655–83.

Van Maanan, J. (1991), 'The Smile Factory', in P. Frost, L. F. Moore, M. R. Louis, C. C. Lundberg, and J. Martin (eds.), *Reframing Organizational Culture*, Newbury Park, Calif.: Sage.

Walt Disney Productions (1982), *Your Role in the Walt Disney World Show*, Orlando, Fla.: Walt Disney Productions.

Weber, M. (1930), *The Protestant Ethic and the Spirit of Capitalism*. London: Allen & Unwin.

——(1978), *Economy and Society: An Outline of Interpretive Sociology*, ed. G. Roth and C. Wittich, Berkeley, Calif.: University of California Press.

Witz, A., Halford, S., and Savage, M. (1996), 'Organized Bodies: Gender, Sexuality and Embodiment in Contemporary Organizations', ch. 8 in L. Adkins and V. Merchant (eds.), *Sexualising the Social*, London: Macmillan.

Wright Mills, Charles (1951), *White Collars: The American Middle Class*, Oxford: Oxford University Press.

——(1963), *Power, Politics and People: The Collected Essays of C. Wright Mills*, Oxford: Oxford University Press.

4 What Work Means

So far we have looked at how the rationale behind jobs has influenced job design. But what do jobs mean to those who do them? What does work mean, why do people work, and what do they hope to get out of it?

Intuitively we know one of the prime reasons individuals give for working is to earn money. Yet we are usually aware that there are other reasons too—to use our skills, for a feeling of worth, a sense of dignity. This chapter looks at what research tells us about what work means to those who do it. Looking at what unemployment means gives us more clues about what work means, but this will be tackled in a later chapter.

Most people will say that earning money is the prime reason they go to work. In a British survey (Rose 1994) 68 per cent of respondents said they worked for the money to provide money for basic essentials or to buy extras and enjoy some economic independence from the primary earner in a household. Economic need may be contingent on family composition. It may be that the earnings of minority ethnic women are more important to their households than for many white households (Phizacklea and Wolkowitz 1993; Westwood 1988).

> **STOP**
>
> **Ask yourself the 'lottery question' (Corbett 1994). Imagine you have won a lottery or inherited a large sum of money and could live comfortably for the rest of your life without working; what would you do about work? Would you continue working in the same or a different job or could you imagine stopping work altogether?**

In the British survey 26 per cent (Rose 1994) said they did not work for money but for 'expressive' reasons (intrinsic rewards like a sense of enjoyment, satisfaction, and a sense of achievement) so economic reasons are not a sufficient explanation for economic activity. Pakistani and Bangladeshi women record the lowest levels of economic activity despite living in the most disadvantaged households (Blackburn et al. 1997).

Work is, then, more than a means towards the end of earning a living; people work for more than money. If work were purely a means to an economic end there would be no way of explaining the dislocation and deprivation individuals feel when they retire. Intrinsic reward is clearly important too, perhaps more so than money. More qualitative research, for example through individual interviews (as opposed to more quantitative survey research), shows similar findings. Respondents show that they are less concerned about earning than somebody wanting them 'for what I can do' (Sharpe 1984: 78; see also Sayers 1988).

Measuring what constitutes meaningful work is a complex task (Hodson 2002). Job satisfaction is one measure but there are other indicators. The experience of creativity can contribute significantly to meaning and dignity at work. The ability to take pride in work is a core foundation for meaningful work. For example a worker is able to boast that a year's work of production has been delivered by them without any rejects (Seider 1984). Conflict, either with managers or with co-workers can undermine satisfaction. Work groups that are diverse, less integrated and cohesive report greater dissatisfaction (Maznevski 1994). Research shows that groups that are diverse have lower levels of member satisfaction and higher rates of labour turnover than more homogeneous groups (Milliken and Martins 1996). Respect for workers' rights as organizational stakeholders is another contributor to satisfaction, for example managers refraining from abusive practices (Adler and Borys 1996), providing job security, and avoiding lay-offs. Management leadership manifested through the maintenance of a viable and well-functioning organization and a respect for workers is of crucial importance for satisfaction and meaning of work (Hodson 2002).

Maintaining dignity at work is something workers from all walks of life struggle to achieve (Hodson 2001). Dignity can be achieved through taking pride in productive accomplishments even if those accomplishments may be modest by someone else's standards. Dignity is also realized through resistance against abusive bosses or bad management. In defending dignity workers establish themselves as active agents with some control over their work lives. Without dignity, work becomes unbearable. Employees can find themselves confronting abusive conditions and a chaotic mismanaged workplace (Juravich 1985) or chronic overwork and exhaustion (Cavendish 1982) or defending their competence and autonomy (Bosk 1979) or avoiding downsizing and lay-offs (Smith 1990). Each of these conditions present challenges to working with dignity and shows how dignity is attained and defended (Hodson 2001).

What about people who do not have to work? People who win the pools or the lottery continue to work even if they hold jobs that could be described as dull, routine, and repetitive (Brown 1954). If individuals are asked if they would continue working if they had enough money to live comfortably for the rest of their life, a majority will say they would continue to work (Gallie and White 1993; Morse and Weiss 1955). Men in middle-class occupations will point to the loss of interest and accomplishment they found in their jobs; those in working-class jobs typically mention the lack of activity they would experience (Morse and Weiss 1955). Where the status of work is low, money will be stressed as the principal reward (Friedmann and Havighurst 1954). At higher occupational levels intrinsic job components like opportunity for self-expression, interest value of work, were more valued. At lower occupational levels, extrinsic job components like pay and security were more valued (Centers and Bugental 1966). One explanation might be that those in higher-level jobs, with intrinsic job components, design jobs for those in lower levels and have no interest in designing them with the same intrinsic components.

Research from the USA shows that jobs in the new economy are very mixed in what they offer in terms of meaning. Reich (1991) calculated that just 20 per cent of the jobs in the new economy were intrinsically satisfying and economically rewarding. These jobs belong to the journalists, designers, architects, and lecturers whose work has creativity at its core as they communicate complex ideas. These are the 'fortunate fifth'. These jobs can be contrasted with the 25 per cent who regularly perform routine tasks and the 30 per cent who deliver a variety of mundane services. The recent growth in call centre jobs in Britain leaves you wondering how intrinsically satisfying they are.

Vecchio (1980) revisited Morse and Weiss's findings. While he also found that the majority of workers would desire to continue working, he also discovered a 39 per cent increase in the number of male workers who would stop working if given the opportunity. One explanation for this is that there has been a real decline in the perceived value and meaning of work. Alternatively it may be that a leisure ethic is replacing the traditional work ethic.

Classic studies of male workers demonstrate that the meaning of work is not confined to the workplace. Dennis et al. (1969) showed how the dangerous difficult conditions in mining created a male culture of mutual dependence which continued outside in leisure and other activities. The men defined themselves almost exclusively in terms of their work.

Dubin (1956) concerned himself with looking at the 'central life interests' of workers. Work was seen as a central life interest of adults in most societies and the capitalist system was seen to rest upon the moral and religious justification that the Reformation gave to work, as Weber (1930) pointed out. Dubin, however, found that for almost three out of four industrial workers, work and the workplace were not central life interests. People's life histories had their centres outside work; this was where they looked for human relationships, feelings of enjoyment, happiness, and worth. Yet, as Dubin notes, much management activity is directed at restoring work to the status of central life interest through human relations; management's efforts seem then to be at odds with reality.

In spite of Dubin's findings, managements and researchers have sought to discover more about what work means to people and what can be done to increase productivity. Researchers moved on to dedicate themselves to trying to understand what motivated employees or what satisfied them (for example, Herzberg 1966, 1968). Some researchers saw both employee productivity and alienation as a problem (Hackman and Oldham 1975). (Alienation is discussed in the next chapter.) It was thought that redesigning jobs to reduce problems of alienation and boredom would increase productivity. Job enrichment and job redesign were seen then as solutions. In order to measure and understand what happened to jobs when they were changed, in America Turner and Lawrence (1965) measured employee perceptions of task attributes. Based on that work, Hackman and Oldham (1975) developed the Job Diagnostic Survey (JDS). The theory underlying the tool was that experienced meaningfulness of work is enhanced by skill variety (using different skills and talents), task identity (doing a job from beginning to end with a visible outcome), and task significance (the degree to which the job has a substantial impact on the work or lives of other people). Hackman et al. (1975: 61) claimed that the JDS gauged the 'objective characteristics of the jobs themselves'. Similarly Sims et al. (1976) developed the Job Characteristics Inventory (JCI) while in Britain a Job Components Inventory was developed (Banks et al. 1983). The JDS and JCI would diagnose existing jobs as an input to planned job redesign.

Job redesign meant any attempt to alter jobs with the intent of increasing the quality of work experience and productivity such as job rotation, job enrichment, and sociotechnical systems design. Typically changes involved providing employees with additional responsibilities for planning, setting up, checking their own work, and for making decisions about methods and procedures, for establishing their own work pace (within limits), and sometimes for relating directly with the client who sees the results of their work (Hackman 1977). For example a basic job involved the assembly of a small pump used in a washing machine. The assembly line worker assembled a particular part of the job with five others on an assembly line. The job was redesigned so that each worker assembled a whole pump, inspected it, and placed his own identifying mark on it; workers were given more freedom to control their pace of work. As a result total assembly time decreased, quality improved, and cost savings were realized (Hackman 1977: 99). As job design became a quaint relic of the 1970s new initiatives emerged under new brand names like 'high performance work design' (Buchanan 1987).

There were some serious problems with the measures of job characteristics (Aldag et al. 1981; Salancik and Pfeffer 1977; Stone and Gueutal 1985). The job characteristics that were measured had been derived from a search of the literature, reflective thinking, and by trial and error. The dimensions then may or may not have coincided with the dimensions along which individuals generally perceive jobs to vary; they may just represent the idiosyncratic way in which Turner and Lawrence viewed jobs.

The questions for us now are, could job redesign have been 'sold' to employers if it did not bring with it the promise of increased efficiency and productivity? Were employers really interested in what jobs meant to individuals with a view to increasing what they might mean and offer in terms of intrinsic rewards? Did employers have altruistic motives and were they interested in their employee's quality of work life? Many are now disillusioned with the ideals of job design. For many teachers of organizational behaviour, job redesign is seen as a dated 1970s fad. Examples are to be found in the literature of new work designs which failed due to, for example, cost (Klein 1982, cited in Clegg 1984), because the role of supervisors was threatened (Cummings 1978; Lawler et al. 1973) or because changes were resented and opposed by other groups (Clegg 1982). Complex job design may be exceptionally difficult to implement for a mixture of historical, economic, and psychological reasons (Clegg 1984) so it is little wonder that few major initiatives of this kind have been attempted and survived.

AN EXAMPLE ABOUT ANONYMITY

Hackman and Oldham (1975) recommend that employees take the Job Diagnostic Survey under conditions of anonymity. I discovered, from personal experience of consultancy work, how necessary this was when the managing director of the company where I had used a similar diagnostic instrument, to look at motivation and morale, asked me to identify the most disaffected employees so he could sack them. I did not comply with his request.

Some social scientists had much to say about how jobs should be redesigned and an international Quality of Working Life movement began in 1972 with a conference (Davis and Cherns 1975). However other social scientists, particularly sociologists and political scientists, were more critical of the job redesign movement (Blacker and Brown 1978) and what it sought to achieve. One of these criticisms was that attempts to improve quality of working life amounted to little more than 'human relations' management (showing concern for employee's social needs, their personal problems, making them feel important) and a cosmetic activity to help managers increase collective endeavour (Blacker and Brown 1980). Job redesign may just serve to control behaviour. Changes are only peripheral (Blacker and Brown 1980). A possible effect of job redesign is 'to divert attention away from a recognition of more fundamental sources of inequality' (Child 1973: 243).

Alan Fox (1973: 219) spoke of how job redesign did not address the principle of hierarchical rewards or the possibility of increases in intrinsic reward at the cost of efficiency. Job design could be described as a management control device. Instead of bringing fundamental change, job redesign only addressed marginal issues while the legitimacy of prevailing power structures and current business frameworks remained. Impartial science was claimed but poor research designs were used. The criteria used in evaluation studies were usually managerially rather than psychologically oriented as their emphasis was on organizational efficiency rather than an individual's psychological growth (Blacker and Brown 1978). While management had a definite interest in seeing workers as thinking social beings with the potential to work together more productively, they also had an interest in limiting these potentials. Fineman (1996) says that the people presented are 'emotionally anorexic'. They may have dissatisfaction and satisfaction, be alienated or stressed, will have preferences, attitudes, and interests but these are noted as variables for managerial control. Managers had no wish to forfeit control and there were limits to what they could 'sensibly', in their view, do (Nichols 1976: 22; see also Thompson and McHugh 2002). This issue of managerial control is explored in a later chapter but we will turn our attention in the next chapter to look more at what work means for those in lower levels of the hierarchy and how they feel about their jobs, particularly those who work on assembly lines.

■ SUGGESTIONS FOR FURTHER READING

1. Noon, M., and Blyton, P. (2002), 'The Meaning of Work', ch. 3 in *The Realities of Work* (2nd edn.), Basingstoke: Macmillan. This chapter provides an answer to the question of why work. It also looks at the influence of culture and religion on answers to this question. The issue of work ethic is also discussed.

2. Watson, T. (1997), 'Work: Meaning, Opportunity and Experience', ch. 4 in *Sociology, Work and Industry* (3rd edn.), London: Routledge.

3. Morse, N. C., and Weiss, R. S. (1955), 'The Function and Meaning of Work and the Job', *American Sociological Review*, 20. This is classic, but flawed work on the topic.

4. Vecchio, R. P. (1980), 'The Function and Meaning of Work and the Job: Morse and Weiss (1955) Revisited', *Academy of Management Journal*, 23/2: 361–7.

5. Corbett, J. M. (1994), *Critical Cases in Organizational Behaviour*, Houndmills: Macmillan, ch. 2 on the meaning of work, motivation, and commitment.

6. Grint, K. (1998), *The Sociology of Work* (2nd edn.), Cambridge: Polity Press. Chapter 1 on what is work includes a section on orientations to work as well as describing historical rhetorics of work.

■ WEB LINKS

www.v-p-c.com/jobs/practice/redesign.htm discusses job redesign and its principles in relation to veterinary practices.

www.managementlearning.com/revb/vroomm/ takes you to a web site (a motivation book review) that includes a critique of Morse and Weiss.

■ QUESTIONS

1. By looking at unemployment, we can understand more about what employment might mean to people. What can be learnt about what work means by looking at research on unemployment?

2. Some researchers, like Hakim (1991) and Coward (1992) have argued that women are less committed to their careers than men. Others (like Bradley 1997; Spencer and Taylor 1994; Demos in Walter 1996) have shown strong attachment to the labour force among women. Read their findings and draw your own conclusion.

3. Would money be cited as a principal reward for nurses (for example see Orzak 1959)?

4. Mismanagement is a central obstacle to working with dignity. Discuss (see Hodson 2001).

■ GROUP EXERCISE

Work 'is quintessentially a social phenomenon, a world of symbolic representation, meanings and interpretations rather than a world of self-evident objective facts' (Grint 1998: 46). Discuss.

■ REFERENCES

Adler, P. S., and Borys, B. (1996), 'Two Types of Bureaucracy: Enabling and Coercive', *Administrative Science Quarterly*, 41/1: 61–89.

Aldag, R. J., Barr, S. H., and Brief, A. P. (1981), 'Measurement of Perceived Task Characteristics', *Psychological Bulletin*, 90/3: 415–31.

Banks, M. H., Jackson, P. R., Stafford, E. M., and Warr, P. B. (1983), 'The Job Components Inventory and the Analysis of Jobs Requiring Limited Skill', *Personnel Psychology*, 36/1: 57–66.

Blackburn, R., Dale, A., and Jarman, J. (1997), 'Ethnic Differences in Attainment in Education, Occupation and Lifestyle', in V. Karn (ed.), *Employment, Education and Housing among Ethnic Minorities in Britain*, London: HMSO.

Blacker, F. H., and Brown, C. A. (1978), *Job Redesign and Management Control*. London: Saxon House.

————(1980), 'Job Redesign and Social Change: Case Studies at Volvo', ch. 8 in K. D. Duncan, M. M. Gruneberg, and D. Wallis (eds.), *Changes in Working Life*, Chichester: Wiley.

Bosk, C. L. (1979), *Forgive and Remember*, Chicago: University of Chicago Press.

Bradley, H. (1997), 'Gender and Change in Employment', ch. 5 in R. Brown (ed.), *The Changing Shape of Work*, Basingstoke: Macmillan.

Brown, J. C. (1954), *The Social Psychology of Industry*, Baltimore, Md.: Penguin.

Buchanan, D. (1987), 'Job Enrichment is Dead: Long Live High-Performance Work Design', *Personnel Management* (May), 40–3.

Cavendish, R. (1982), *Women on the Lone*, Boston: Routledge & Kegan Paul.

Centers, R., and Bugental, D. E. (1966), 'Intrinsic and Extrinsic Job Motivations among Different Segments of the Working Population', *Journal of Applied Psychology*, 50/3: 193–7.

Child, J. (1973) (ed.), 'Organization: A Choice for Man', in *Man and the Organization*, London: Allen & Unwin.

Clegg, C. W. (1982), 'Modelling the Practice of Job Design', in J. E. Kelly and C. W. Clegg (eds.), *Autonomy and Control at the Workplace: Contexts for Job Redesign*, London: Croom Helm.

——(1984), 'The Derivations of Job Designs', *Journal of Occupational Behaviour*, 5: 131–46.

Corbett, M. (1994), *Critical Cases in Organizational Behaviour*, Houndmills: Macmillan.

Coward, R. (1992), *Our Treacherous Hearts*, London: Fontana.

Cummings, T. G. (1978), 'Self-Regulating Work Groups: A Socio-Technical Synthesis', *Academy of Management Review*, 3: 625–34.

Davis, L. E., and Cherns, A. B. (1975), *The Quality of Working Life*, i and ii, New York: Free Press.

Dennis, N., Henriques, F., and Slaughter, C. (1969), *Coal is our Life*, London: Tavistock.

Dubin, R. (1956), 'Industrial Workers' Worlds: A Study of the "Central Life Interests" of Industrial Workers', *Social Problems*, 5: 138–42.

Fineman, S. (1996), 'Emotion and Organizing', ch. 3.3 in S. R. Clegg, C. Hardy, and W. R. Nord (eds.), *Handbook of Organization Studies*, London: Sage.

Fox, A. (1973), 'Industrial Relations: A Social Critique of Pluralist Ideology', in J. Child (ed.), *Man and Organisation*, London: Allen & Unwin.

Friedmann, E. L., and Havighurst, R. J. (1954), *The Meaning of Work and Retirement*. Chicago: University of Chicago Press.

Gallie, D., and White, M. (1993), *Employee Commitment and the Skills Revolution*, London: Policy Studies Institute.

Grint, K. (1998), *The Sociology of Work* (2nd edn.), Cambridge: Polity.

Hackman, J. R. (1977), 'Work Design', ch. 3 in J. R. Hackman and J. L. Suttle (eds.), *Improving Life at Work*, Santa Monica, Calif.: Goodyear.

——and Oldham, G. R. (1975), 'Development of the Job Diagnostic Survey', *Journal of Applied Psychology*, 60/2: 159–70.

————Janson, R., and Purdy, K. (1975), 'A New Strategy for Job Enrichment', *California Management Review*, 17: 57–71.

Hakim, C. (1991), 'Grateful Slaves and Self-Made Women: Fact and Fantasy in Women's Work Orientations', *European Sociological Review*, 7/2: 101–21.

Herzberg, F. (1966), *Work and the Nature of Man*, New York: Staples Press.

——(1968), 'One More Time: How Do You Motivate Employees?' *Harvard Business Review* (Jan.–Feb.), 46/1: 53–62.

Hodson, R. (2001), *Dignity at Work*, Cambridge: Cambridge University Press.

——(2002), 'Demography or Respect? Work Group Demography versus Organizational

Dynamics as Determinants of Meaning and Satisfaction at Work', *British Journal of Sociology*, 53/2: 291–317.

Juravich, T. (1985), *Chaos on the Shop Floor*, Philadelphia: Temple University Press.

Klein, L. (1982), 'Design Strategies in Theory and Practice', paper presented at the 20th International Congress of Applied Psychology, University of Edinburgh.

Lawler, E. E., Hackman, J. R., and Kaufman, S. (1973), 'Effects of Job Redesign: A Field Experiment', *Journal of Applied Social Psychology*, 3: 49–62.

Maznevski, M. L. (1994), 'Understanding our Differences: Performance in Decision-Making Groups with Diverse Members', *Human Relations*, 47/5: 531–52.

Milliken, F. J., and Martins, L. L. (1996), 'Searching for Common Threads: Understanding the Multiple Effects of Diversity in Organizational Groups', *Academy of Management Review*, 21/2: 402–33.

Morse, N. C., and Weiss, R. S. (1955), 'The Function and Meaning of Work and the Job', *American Sociological Review*, 20.

Nichols, T. (1976), 'Management, Ideology and Practice', in *People at Work*, Block 5, Unit 15, Milton Keynes: The Open University Press.

Orzak, L. (1959), 'Work as a Central Life Interest of Professionals', *Social Problems*, 7: 125–32.

Phizacklea, A., and Wolkowitz, C. (1993), *Homeworking Women: Gender, Racism and Class at Work*, London: Sage.

Reich, R. (1991), *The Work of Nations*, New York: Knopf.

Rose, M. (1994), 'Skill and Samuel Smiles: Changing the British Work Ethic', in R. Penn, M. Rose, and J. Rubery (eds.), *Skill and Occupational Change*, Oxford: Oxford University Press.

Salancik, G. R., and Pfeffer, J. (1977), 'An Examination of the Need-Satisfaction Models of Job Attributes', *Administrative Science Quarterly*, 22: 427–57.

Sayers, S. (1988), 'The Need to Work: A Perspective from Philosophy', in R. E. Pahl (ed.), *On Work: Historical, Comparative and Theoretical Approaches*, Oxford: Basil Blackwell.

Seider, M. (1984), *A Year in the Life of a Factory*, San Pedro, Calif.: Singlejack.

Sharpe, S. (1984), *Double Identity: The Lives of Working Mothers*, Harmondsworth: Penguin.

Sims, H. P., Szilagyi, A. D., and Keller, R. T. (1976), 'The Measurement of Job Characteristics', *Academy of Management Journal* (June), 195–212.

Smith, V. (1990), *Managing the Corporate Interest: Control and Resistance in an American Bank*, Berkeley: University of California Press.

Spencer, L., and Taylor, S. (1994), *Participation and Progress in the Labour Market: Key Issues for Women*, Dept. of Employment Research Series, no. 35. Sheffield: Dept. of Employment.

Stone, E. F., and Gueutal, H. G. (1985), 'An Empirical Derivation of the Dimensions along which Characteristics of Jobs are Perceived', *Academy of Management Journal*, 28/2: 376–96.

Thompson, P., and McHugh, D. (2002), *Work Organisations* (3rd edn.), Houndmills: Palgrave.

Turner, A. N., and Lawrence, P. R. (1965), *Industrial Jobs and the Worker*, Cambridge, Mass.: Harvard University Press.

Vecchio, R. P. (1980), 'The Function and Meaning of Work and the Job: Morse and Weiss (1955) Revisited', *Academy of Management Journal*, 23/2: 361–7.

Walter, N. (1996), 'Bringing out the Women in New Labour', *Guardian* (29 Feb.).

Weber, M. (1930), *The Protestant Ethic and the Spirit of Capitalism*, London: Allen & Unwin.

Westwood, S. (1988), 'Workers and Wives: Continuities and Discontinuities in the Lives of Gujarati Women', in S. Westwood and P. Bhachu (eds.), *Enterprising Women: Ethnicity, Economy and Gender Relations*, London: Routledge, pp. 103–31.

5 | The View from Below

We have explored briefly what work might mean to people, and we have looked at the rationality behind how work is organized and jobs allocated, but what do employees feel about work? How do they view their jobs?

The concept of alienation forms, for many, a useful starting point for understanding how people feel about work. Marx, in the *Economic and Political Manuscripts*, shows that there are various aspects to the experience. The work, according to Marx, is external to the worker

> that is not part of his nature, that consequently he does not fulfil himself in his work but denies himself, has a feeling of misery, not of well being, does not develop freely a physical and mental energy, but is physically exhausted and mentally debased. A worker therefore only feels at home in his leisure, whereas at work he feels homeless. His work is not voluntary but imposed, forced labour. (Bottomore and Rubel 1963: 177–8)

Weber too argued that alienation is a state or a feeling in which the job is external to the individual (Weber 1926/1947); it results primarily from lack of autonomy at work. There are links to learning here as over time, work alienation is institutionalized in the minds of employees in a continuing sequence of conditioning (Argyris 1985, 1990). Employees learn not to ask questions, answer back, or question management authority. This then results in increased organizational rigidity and inefficiency as organizational members experience job dissatisfaction and low levels of organizational commitment (Efraty et al. 1991). There are also links to leadership as research (Sarros et al. 2002) has shown that transformational leadership (considerate leadership based on more personal relationships between managers and followers) is associated with lower work alienation. Leadership style can have a significant impact on feelings of work alienation.

Marx (1963) and Braverman (1974) would identify structural conditions and technologies as generating alienation in the workplace. It would be possible to look, for example, at the impact of centralization and work technology on job autonomy, participation, and well-being (Zeffane and MacDonald 1993). It would be possible to look at individual's perceptions, feeling, and consciousness of alienation within specified work conditions and relationships, as some researchers have done (Ashforth 1989; Kakabadse 1986; Kanungo 1982). Work alienation occurs when employees perceive that the work environment is personally detrimental to their needs, values, and sense of well-being (Kanungo 1982).

However the meaning and measurement of work alienation is problematic and fraught with ambiguity (Geyer and Schweitzer 1981). A number of different interpretations of the concept have emerged. It is usually thought of as consisting of three main components:

1. Powerlessness—lack of control over the work activities, lack of autonomy and participation.

2. Meaninglessness—the inability to comprehend the relationship of your work contribution to a larger purpose, when workers feel they contribute little to the overall production process and so do not see the significance of their role in it. According to the Job Characteristics Model, employees experience meaninglessness at work when their jobs are narrow in scope. If job tasks are dull, boring, unchallenging, and separate from other work activities, then employees might feel their work contribution is meaningless.

3. Self-estrangement—when the work process is perceived as alien to the individual and independent of their contributions, for example where external rewards serve to limit the creative contributions of employees. It occurs where jobs are narrow in scope and depth and are unable to provide employees with intrinsic job satisfaction and fulfilment. Researchers have attempted to tap into the extent of self-estrangement by asking individuals if work is a central life interest (Dubin 1956) and whether the employees prized self-image is fulfilled at work (Wilensky 1964).

How is the experience of alienation and degrading work documented in research?

The Experience of the Assembly Line

An early account of concrete experiences of factory work can be found in the work of Simone Weil (see Grey 1996), who worked in an electrical plant and a metalworking factory in Paris in 1934–5. The highly mechanized work was degrading, humiliating, and shaming for the individual. For example, she describes how she worked on a stamping press where the pieces were difficult to position, producing 600 pieces in less than three hours before having a half-hour to reset the machine. She had to adapt to the 'slavery'. She felt disgust at being forced to strain and exhaust herself, 'with the certainty of being bawled out either for being slow or for botching' (Weil 1987: 159). Workers are oppressed, they are treated as means rather than as ends in themselves. The clearest manifestation of oppression is to be found, not in class, but in the organization of production, she says. Taylorism, bureaucratization, and management are all implicated in the development of forms of oppression.

A more recent experience of the assembly line is described by Michael Moore. 'This insane system known as the assembly line is designed to deny individuality and eliminate self worth', says Moore in the foreword to Ben Hamper's (1992) book *Rivethead*. This book is written by a journalist and tells his story of finding a job and working at General Motors' Truck and Bus Plant in Michigan. Initially he worked on an assembly line installing clips and screws inside rear wheel wells. Then he learnt how to spot weld so he could do his neighbour's job on the line too and they could 'double-up'—do two jobs for an hour or two and then have one or two hours' break. He complains about the monotony of the job (being faced with the same job every few minutes) in spite of being able to take these long breaks where he could read two newspapers, a magazine, and a good chunk of a novel each evening. In this world, 'workers suffer and cope through drink or madness'.

Some further realities of working on assembly lines in Britain and France are captured in accounts from researchers Ruth Cavendish and Robert Linhart. Ruth Cavendish's (1989) account of her seven-month experience of working in a motor components factory was so contentious that she had to go to considerable lengths to disguise the identity of the company. Ruth was an assembler and she learnt the job by sitting by a woman at a bench. The benches were at each side of a conveyor belt; each line had fifteen operators including two operators who sat at the end and mended incorrectly assembled or faulty products. The line produced 500 or 1,000 'sets' of assembled components each one or two days which meant each operator performed the same operation over and over 500 or 1,000 times. Sometimes Ruth would do up to five different jobs a day and was completely exhausted. She says that she had terrible pains in her neck and back and found it hard to keep up with the work on the line, but because the work kept coming, she had to keep on. Most days she worked so hard that she did not have time to look up or had to work extra fast so that she could have enough time between tasks to unwrap a piece of chewing gum or take a sip of tea. You could not blow your nose or flick hair out your eyes without losing valuable seconds. It was very hot and the ventilation was poor. The repetition of the work and being controlled by the speed of the line was hard to take.

The work and the speed of the line was set by management and was not negotiable. To keep the components moving at a steady pace, all the jobs on the line ought to have taken the same length of time, but some were harder to complete than others so there would be pile-ups of work. It took several weeks to become proficient in any one job. The best way to learn it was to have an experienced operator show you how to do it, how to hold the components, how to move your fingers, and which order to do the different operations so you could cut out unnecessary movements. If you could not keep up with the speed required, you were out. From that bench you could see all 200 staff on main assembly; you could see who was talking to whom, who went to the coffee machine or toilet, and how many times a day they went, who was late. The women were 'doing time'. Much of the language found in these accounts is similar to that used in prisons.

Linhart (1989) worked on the Citroën car assembly line. This time the line appeared to be slow moving and the operators were working at a resigned monotonous pace. The crash of a new car body arriving every three or four minutes marked out the rhythm of the work. Since the work moved, the workers also had to move in order to stay with the car. Each man had a well-defined area for the operations he had to perform, although the boundaries were invisible. If the man worked fast he had a few seconds to spare. He could then either take a very short break or intensify the effort to 'go up the line' to gain a little more time, working further ahead, outside his normal area, together with the worker at the previous position on the line. Gaining one or two minutes meant that he could smoke a cigarette. If, on the other hand, you worked too slowly, your work slipped back. By the end of the first day Linhart says his limbs were painful and he felt exhausted and anxious due to the repetition of the same movement over and over again. It was not unusual for a new recruit to give up after the first day 'driven mad by the noise, the sparks, the inhuman pressure of speed, the harshness of endlessly repetitive work, the authoritarianism of the bosses and the severity of the orders, the dreary prison-like atmosphere'. After five months in the plant, the management announced that the work shift would be extended by forty-five minutes to ten hours. This provoked a strike where Linhart was one of the organizers. After the strike there was a 'systematic persecution'; the management knew how to make each of the 'hardliners' give in their notice, and succeeded in doing so.

These writers vividly describe the endless pressure and the continual fear of slipping behind with work. They want to do a good job; the control system hooks the worker into a manic concern for throughput (Littler 1989). Few aspects of work provide intrinsic satisfaction but individuals become resigned to the daily drudge; these workers would not be in a strong position in a labour market.

AN EXAMPLE OF BEING A MACHINE OPERATOR AND MAKING WORK MANAGEABLE

Between 1944 and 1945 Donald Roy worked as a radial drill operator in a factory. He was a secret participant observer particularly interested in restriction of output, why workers did not work harder. Roy (1960) outlines how workers who are subject to monotonous tasks make their experiences bearable by adding meaning to their day. Work at the factory was tedious (simple machine operation) and for a twelve-hour day, six days a week. The group in which Roy worked had established a series of events for structuring the day. There was a peach time instigated by Sammy when two peaches would be shared. Then there was 'banana time' (where Sammy provided a banana but Ike ate it, as he had stolen it from Sammy's lunch box; Sammy made futile protests). Window time, pick-up time (when a man came to cart away boxes), fish time, and coke time followed in quick succession. Various pranks and food consumption were linked with the times. Ditton too (1979) describes the social construction of time and how the workers in a bakery broke the day up into 'digestible fragments to make it psychologically manageable' (1979: 160).

Donald Roy (1960) also describes horseplay, boisterous play, in this work setting. One worker, Ike, would regularly switch off the power to Sammy's machine whenever Sammy went to the toilet or water fountain. Sammy invariably fell victim to the plot by attempting to operate his machine on his return. This blind stumbling into the trap was always followed by indignation and reproach from Sammy, smirking satisfaction from Ike, and a mild scolding from a third worker. When would Ike weary of the prank or when would Sammy learn to check his power switch? There was, Roy observed, a pattern to the interaction. A system of roles had formed, a sort of pecking order or hierarchy. It was a controlling frame of status, a matter of who can do what to whom and get away with it. Roy concludes that one source of job satisfaction lay in the interaction between members of the group. Horseplay, conversation, sharing of food and drink reduced the monotony of simple, repetitive operations to the point that the long workdays became manageable. (See excerpts from *Banana Time* in Salaman and Thompson 1973).

Some writers, following Marx, would argue that workers such as these are being exploited and alienated. There is a fundamental tension between the needs of capital and the needs of labour within capitalist economies. The worker is robbed of part of the value of the labour. 'In reality they [workers] are paid only the equivalent in monetary terms of the value they produce in part of the working day, say five out of eight hours' (Burawoy 1979: 23). As well as being exploited economically, they are alienated from the products of their labour. Since they do not own or control the products of their labour, their needs and capacities are subordinated to the requirements of capital accumulation. The psychological consequence is that the worker feels a stranger to his or her work (Thompson and McHugh 1990).

Burawoy (1979) worked as a machine operator at the engine division of Allied Corporation producing, among other things, agricultural equipment. This was the same plant Donald Roy had worked and researched in thirty years before. The central question for Burawoy was 'Why do workers work as hard as they do?' Why did he find himself actively participating in the intensification of his own exploitation and even losing his temper when he couldn't? He describes a series of games the operators played in order to achieve levels of production that earned incentive pay. The rules of the game were experienced as a set of externally imposed relationships, like informal alliances. The art of 'making out' (maximizing bonus pay in a piece-rate system) was to manipulate those relationships with for example, the foreman, superintendent, scheduling man, other operators, or truck drivers to your best advantage.

Truck drivers were responsible for bringing the stock from the aisles, where it was kept, to the machine. Truck drivers could hold you up considerably if you hadn't befriended them, particularly at the beginning of the shift when they were in great demand. The foreman acted as a referee and expediter in the game of making out. The foreman could point out more efficient set-ups, help make special tools, persuade inspectors to pass work and so on, so the job could be done faster and you could earn more.

The shop-floor culture revolved around making out. Each worker was sucked into a distinctive set of activities and language which went with those activities. The pressure to make out could also lead to conflict between workers. The games workers play are not usually created in opposition to management but emerge out of struggle and bargaining. Management participates in the game by organizing it and enforcing the rules. The game is entered into for its 'relative satisfactions'. The satisfaction of that need reproduces consent and material wealth.

Burawoy (as Jermier et al. 1994: 7 note) did not draw out the implications for understanding shop-floor resistance from this analysis. The game was, though, a way of testing self-esteem in which these factory workers became locked into practices that led to their own exploitation and subordination. Burawoy's account has been critiqued in some detail (Collinson 1992; Knights 1990; Thompson 1990; Willmott 1990). He is criticized for not investigating workplace subjectivity enough, for example, neglecting gender and sexual identity.

AN EXAMPLE OF THE GAME

Burawoy has described the games that workers play as a way of making out and creating space outside managerial surveillance (see also Pahl 1988). Stewart Clegg (1987) produces an interesting example of 'making out' in the 'inclemency rule'. Clegg worked on a building site. On construction sites in the UK joiners have an agreement that they do not have to work in 'inclement' weather. There is, though, no operational definition of how bad the weather has to be before it is called inclement. One day the worker unit leader decided it was inclement so the workmen downed tools, went to their hut, and brewed tea. After about ten minutes the site foreman came down and asked them to go back to work. It was drizzling lightly with rain. The first time this happened Clegg thought 'OK I know the joiners don't like getting wet and we don't work when it is raining.' But when it happened again a few days later, and the men downed tools, it was hardly raining at all. This went on several times over a period of two or three weeks. Clegg's explanation was that the joiners were using the inclemency rule to put pressure on incompetent managers to organize the job more effectively so that the materials and supplies the joiners needed to do the job were there on time and the joiners could increase their bonus. Since supplies were not arriving, the joiners were taking up slack time for 'inclemency'. They were putting pressure on management to increase control and thus more effectively exploit them.

Class and Gender

Focusing on issues of class and gender at work, Anna Pollert (1981) has described the differing situations and identities of men and women in a cigarette factory in Bristol. She talks about how the women were subject to a double burden of male oppression and capitalist exploitation. Women were pushed down, discriminated against, and unfree, much like black and minority ethnic groups, immigrants, and other oppressed groups. She describes, in some detail, the lived experience of factory life and work in the home. The domestic background was a distinctive part of the women workers' consciousness. Women workers are workers in a man's world yet they also create their own. Women remain separate, they import their own world, and maintain a dual existence.

> **STOP** Anna Pollert (1981) asks, 'Does it make any difference being a woman worker? Is work seen or felt differently from a man?' How would you answer these questions and how does she answer them?

Similarly Westwood (1984) describes how home and work are part of the one world for women working in a company she calls Stitchco. Westwood is an anthropologist and was a participant observer for over a year working with the women on a wide variety of machines producing socks, tights, sweaters, and cardigans. Using a Marxist framework she begins with the point that these women, formally free labourers, sell their labour power to employers for wages and so enter the world of social production and relations of exploitation in the workplace which give them a class position. But these women were also workers in the home, exploited through the gift of unpaid labour to men who were husbands and fathers. She and Cynthia Cockburn (1983) would argue that the sex-gender system and class structure are two interlocking systems from which women's subordination is generated and reproduced.

Westwood's book examines both the way in which women enter waged employment and become classed subjects and how working makes them a worker and a woman. Shop-floor culture offers, to women at work, a version of woman and they take upon themselves elements of this in ways that tie them more firmly to a 'feminine' destiny and the culture of femininity. Women in the labour market are affected by their domestic lives; being a woman counts. Women of colour are faced with an additional ideological hurdle of racism.

The factory employed over 2,000 workers; women made up nearly two-thirds of these workers. Nearly half the workers were Afro-Caribbean and Asian. The gendered division of labour was clear. While the men were knitters, mechanics, dyers, and top managers, the women worked in the finishing process, in personnel, and white-collar jobs. The finishing jobs women did were low paid, repetitive, and based upon dexterity, which is conceived of as a natural attribute, not a skill; they joined fabric together, bar-tacked hems, and operated button-sewing machines. A woman might sew side seams all day, every day, for weeks at a time. Unlike the assembly line that controlled the flow of work, the machinist was dependent on the supervisor to bring work to her. This could be an endless source of frustration and aggravation. The individual worker had no control over what she would do but tried to boost her speed on each operation in order to secure the highest rate for the job. The women disliked being moved between jobs but management looked for flexibility in the use of their labour power.

The work was physically tiring, noisy, and monotonous. Illness was a common response to the job. The women were expected to meet targets of production each day and had to work under tremendous pressure to earn a bonus. Monotony was eased through conversation, jokes, fierce quarrels, and passing sweets around. The women's work was domesticated by them. For example they used the phrases 'my machine' and 'my chair', and adorned their machines with family photos or a picture of the current heart-throb. A common practice was to wear slippers at work. They made aprons from company fabrics to protect their clothing. The aprons were embroidered and edged. These collusive practices reinforced a definition of woman that was securely tied to domestic work in the home. Engagements and weddings were major events to be celebrated by all. Like the women in Anna Pollert's study, these women brought the world of home to work.

> **STOP**
>
> We have just seen how women personalize objects at work—'my machine, 'my chair'. Do you think men do the same? Could this be to do with ownership and power—'my secretary, my office—or the need for personal space?

The Experience of Catering Work

Researchers argue that little has been written on the class relations at the point of production. Helping redress the balance, like the other researchers in this chapter, Gabriel
(1988) (whom we also meet in Chapter 3) documents working lives in catering. He says
that catering workers frequently complain that they are taken for granted and academic
researchers who talk about the 'service sector' rarely trouble themselves to find out what
catering work is like. Even the public with whom the catering workers come into daily
contact seldom seems to register their existence. Work in hotels and catering differs little
in kind and quality from similar work in manufacturing, argues Wood (1992: 16).

Jobs in catering are low paid, have poor job security and union representation, and are
mainly done by part-time employees and women workers. Catering jobs have a sense of
subservience which is not associated with other jobs. For many of the ancillary workers
Gabriel interviewed in a hospital kitchen, the job had become a prison; they felt trapped
in their job because they lacked training, because their command of English was limited,
or because of age, nationality, and background. In contrast the cooks in the hospital
kitchen did not feel trapped and expressed pride and achievement in their jobs. But cooks
in a cook-freeze kitchen were far less happy. The kitchen was a faithful adoption of Taylorist principles in mass catering—splitting cooking from planning, making tasks simple
and tightly controlled, and reducing the skill, initiative, and thinking required of cooks
to a bare minimum. There were pockets of resistance; for example, one of the supervisors
started cooking curried and vegetarian meals and used her initiative, ability, and skill.
Like the workers in Anna Pollert's study, domestic responsibilities dominated the
women's thinking about work; the main asset of the job was that the hours of work and
holidays fitted with the schools.

The literature does not just document a single researcher's findings though. Wood
(1992) draws on a range of studies in the hotel and catering industry to construct a
sociological account of employment there. He argues that the hospitality industry has
attracted little research attention compared to manufacturing. Wood aims to relate what
is known about hotel and catering work to wider issues in industrial sociology-led trends
towards deskilling and flexible working and trends in industrial conflict. He shows how
hotel and catering work is largely exploitative, degrading, poorly paid, unpleasant,
insecure, and taken as a last resort or because it can be tolerated in the light of family
commitments and other constraints. Some will value and enjoy their work in the industry but they are in the minority. How then do people cope?

An in-depth study, using participant observation, by Paules (1991) of women who
waited at tables in a family-style restaurant in New Jersey demonstrates how the dictates
of management can be resisted. She describes how these women protected and enhanced
their position at work while absorbing the abuse of a hurried and often abusive public.
The waitress's subordination to her customers is proclaimed; she is directed to wear a uniform that recalls a housemaid's dress and is prohibited from eating, drinking, and resting
in public view. She is to address each customer as sir or ma'am while the customers call
her by her first name. The greater part of her income comes from tips, conferred as gifts
by strangers, as her wages are below the national minimum wage. Despite this she is not

passive and powerless. She can boost tip income by increasing the number of customers she serves. This is accomplished by securing the largest and busiest sets of tables, 'turning' the tables quickly (taking the order, delivering the food, clearing, and resetting the table as fast as possible), and by controlling the flow of customers through the restaurant. In order to compete effectively with other waitresses, she does not take formal breaks. Waitresses had been known to refuse to serve customers who had not tipped them on an earlier occasion. She can resist the demands of management and customer either silently or with open confrontation.

Working-Class Kids, Working-Class Jobs: The Case of Care Assistants

Why do working-class individuals continue to enter working-class, gender-stereotyped jobs? Why do working-class boys look for heavy manual work (Willis 1977) and trades like plumber, electrician, and forestry? Why do working-class girls still swarm towards traditional female occupations like nursing and rarely, for example, seek training as electricians, joiners, technicians, and computer operators? We might expect that new production patterns, new systems of education and training, coupled with the promise of lifting barriers to opportunity might have dislocated the processes of class and gender reproduction of careers. Yet little has happened to counteract the influence of class, race, and gender on career choice (Cockburn 1987; Jones and Wallace 1990; Mirza 1992).

Bates (1993) explores the experiences of a group of young women who chose jobs in the field of institutional care. Careworkers, like many other female workers, find they are using a wide range of domestic skills. The work can be physically and emotionally demanding, involving a range of tasks from bed making, food serving, bathing, lifting the elderly, sitting with the dying, and laying out the dead. It is low paid and involves long and often socially inconvenient hours of work. Some of the tasks they have to do are stressful and traumatic, like dealing with violence, incontinence, and death. In order to cope they have been found to 'switch off' from their job (Bates 1993). Swearing and being sworn at, getting a 'belt', and occasionally delivering one, were seen as given parts of a day's round. There was a perpetual tension between caring for and processing people. The limits to the caring came not from the women themselves but from the occupational culture and levels of resourcing. The girls expressed a pride in what they did, how they coped with death and their growing 'toughness' in becoming unflinching in the face of harsh facts of life. The paradox was that, despite the gruelling nature of the work, the girls came to accept it and even became enthusiastic. These jobs were not their initial choices at school (they would have preferred jobs like nursery nurse, beauty therapist, typist) but they failed to gain entry into the relevant courses or jobs so found themselves on a YTS 'Caring' course. The girls changed their definitions of themselves and their approach to the job in order to accommodate it in the light of labour market realities—high unemployment and job scarcity. They were able to challenge feelings of disgust, inferiority, and shame and convert them into feelings of pride and a job 'right for' them. Their family lives had exposed them to experiences such as care of the young or elderly, crowded conditions, demanding physical work, verbal and physical aggression, so they appeared to be the ideal candidates for care jobs.

Why Work at Home? The Experience of Homeworking

What is the reality of homeworking for individuals? Allen and Wolkowitz (1987) showed how it involved long hours, was punctuated by strict deadlines from employers, demanding family members, and was relied upon for a regular household income. A key factor in producing homeworking labour was women's responsibility for unpaid work, looking after young children and elderly relatives, coupled with the ideological constraints affecting women, such as a woman's rightful place is in the home. Racism in the labour market and discrimination against the disabled were other factors producing homeworking.

'Teleworking' has received a good deal of attention in the media. This media preoccupation is directed at largely professional jobs and the more boring data-entry clerk or women preparing your bills do not usually feature in these stories. Teleworking, Huws et al. (1990) showed, is only adopted by managers who see it as solving an immediate, concrete problem, such as the retention of valued staff or of cutting costs. The teleworkers do the work for equally practical reasons, such as having no alternative or for childcare reasons. The need to combine work and childcare was a primary motive for Huws et al.'s predominately European female group. Similarly Christensen (1989), in a US sample of 7,000 women, found that values related to family, work, and money drove the initial decision to work at home. In contrast, Olson's (1989) largely US male sample gave work-related reasons. Over 50 per cent said the reason they first decided to work at home was to increase productivity; only 8 per cent said that it was to take care of their family.

Christensen (1989) directly challenges media images of homeworking involving computer-based work as offering freedom and independence. For example, she found that computers are not the central factor in the proliferation of homework; only one in four clerical workers and one in three professional workers were using them. A large number of clerical homeworkers had the legal status of independent contractor but worked for only one employer and had little control over the amount and timing of their work. In some cases the women had worked in offices for the same company and the shift to home-based work meant the loss of employees' status, rights, and benefits. She also showed that homework did not reconcile the tension between the need to earn money and the need or desire to care for children. The majority of women in the survey did not manage to work when their children were around or awake. Homeworking was stressful and isolating.

Phizacklea and Wolkowitz (1995) provide evidence of the realities of homeworking for a sample of thirty white English-speaking and nineteen Asian homeworkers in Coventry. The nine (all white) clerical workers were paid between £2.90 and £3.25 an hour but none of these workers received holiday leave and only one paid National Insurance so was eligible for the state sickness pay scheme. Despite the absence of employment rights, clerical homeworkers' levels of job satisfaction were comparatively high. They had relatively high earnings for homework, relatively low hours, and little variation in the flow of work.

The forty manual homeworkers in the survey were sewing or knitting machinists, dress-makers, doing other forms of assembly and packing, or childminders. Manual homework was found to be sharply divided along ethnic lines. All the clothing assembly was done by Asian women. Fifteen of the nineteen Asian women either assembled whole garments or stitched pieces such as collars and cuffs; hourly earnings varied between 75p and £3.50. The white manual homeworkers were spread over a larger range of occupations, worked shorter hours than the Asian women, and had slightly higher average hourly earnings. The cultural stereotype is of Asian women homeworkers who work at home because their husbands want them to, so it was interesting that only 10 per cent of the Asian women said they preferred to work at home.

Further research showed how female homeworkers were segregated into female occupational ghettos; few women would be able to use homework as a way out. These workers did not have much access to the assistance offered to the self-employed. Perceptions of the disadvantages of homeworking were widely shared; there were more responses to the question about disadvantages of homeworking than advantages. The disadvantages included the low or unpredictable earnings, work-related health problems, and the inconvenience of working at home.

What then can we conclude about the view from below? The first point is that it is worth researching and understanding in order to gain insight into how employees feel and think about work. How they feel and react will be shaped by the context and content of what is being resisted so the nature of resistance will vary across space and time. The second is that most employees are not class-conscious revolutionaries about to overthrow managerial ownership or control. Nor are they passive docile automatons. In the next chapters we look at sexuality and the sex typing of jobs, then misbehaviour and how it may be construed.

Case Study: A Tale of Two Friends and of Jobs Worth Having

(Adapted from a piece by Wythe Holt and found on Alabama Public Radio's web site (see **www.wual.ua.edu**). Wythe Holt is a lawyer, historian, and writer who lives in Alabama, USA. He is University Research Professor of Law at the University of Alabama.)

I have a friend who took a job at the Mercedes plant in Tuscaloosa County. A high school graduate, my friend had worked steadily for several years as a pipefitter in a much smaller local plant. He was glad when Mercedes called him, thinking it was a dream job. The pay is better than $17 an hour and he began to accrue sick leave and vacation leave from the moment he signed the contract.

However, he has already turned down lots of voluntary overtime. He says the job, on an assembly line, is both astoundingly boring and very hard on him physically. He does the same thing over and over and over all day long, although as a pipefitter he did many different tasks. The Mercedes job also requires a type of physical activity in a cramped space that leaves him hurting and exhausted at work's end every day. The dream job is more like a nightmare—though, for that money, this sturdy and healthy young man with family cannot afford to quit. He is trapped.

Assembly line jobs—such as those at Mercedes, or at McDonald's—have always been like this. Listen to writer and auto factory worker Harvey Swados, describing assembly line work in 1957: '[Workers] hate work that is mindless, endless, stupefying, sweaty, filthy, noisy, exhausting, insecure in its prospects, and practically without any hope of advancement. The plain truth is that factory work is degrading . . . to any man who ever dreams of doing something worthwhile with his life.' As President Teddy Roosevelt said a century ago, 'Far and away the best prize that life offers is the chance to work hard at work worth doing.' All of us dream of doing something worthwhile with our lives, and all of us are and want to be good workers. But boring work, degrading work, miserable work, dehumanizing work is not work worth doing.

I have another friend who may beg to differ with me about this. He is a very effective, hard-working, pleasant, brilliant, and—best of all—militantly progressive State Senator. African American himself, he represents thousands of African Americans, and his primary political goal is to help his community and his constituents achieve the basics of human dignity and respect. The vast bulk are poor and otherwise beset with all of the racist and degrading legacies of slavery which black folk in Alabama's Black Belt must still endure every single day. Eliminating poverty seems of prime importance in the scheme of achieving dignity and respect. Many of my friend's constituents have no work and little chance to work, especially for $17 an hour.

The State Senator works hard to bring all sorts of economic development to the Black Belt. Most pertinently, he has worked tirelessly to get another new automobile plant established near Montgomery, so that high-paying jobs will be available to his needy constituents and community members. He is very supportive of 'jobs'.

My position is different. I say that, with all respect, my friend the State Senator is being short-sighted and unmindful of history in his solution for poverty and lack of respect in the Black Belt. I say he is failing to take into account the experience that workers in the first world have always had with economic development—experiences like those of my friend at Mercedes. I say that the work provided to workers by existing capitalist producers of 'jobs' will not actually pay them well, will sap their self-respect because it will treat them with utter indignity, will only strengthen racist attitudes, and will thus augment rather than cure poverty, racism, and discontent.

I say these things because auto assembly line jobs, indeed all existing jobs and economic development, occur within a system of capitalism. History amply demonstrates that work, in capitalism, inevitably brings workers neither real wealth, nor an end of racist treatment, nor dignity and respect. It does the opposite.

It is no accident that assembly line jobs are boring and require almost no skill. That is how they were designed. Skilled workers—craftspersons—know enough about the manufacturing process to control it themselves. They don't need bosses. They don't like being herded into factories, the historical reason for which is so that bosses can control production, keep workers captive, and sap the individuality and courage of the workers. Skilled workers protest the control that bosses implement. They form unions and they strike, in order to regain control and reassert their dignity.

So bosses deskill workers. They divide up the tasks of production into minute and boring repetitive segments, requiring no skill. They demand absolute obedience, and deny workers any opportunity for ingenuity or innovation. They steal the knowledge of the manufacturing process out from under the workers' hats. Andrew Carnegie did this to skilled steelworkers in 1894. Henry Ford did it to skilled auto machinists 20 years later.

The great guru of this deskilling process, an engineer named Frederick W. Taylor, said that 'under our system, the workman is told just what he is to do and how he is to do it. Any improvement he makes upon the orders given him is fatal to success.' Taylor expected assembly lines to be worked on 'by men who are of smaller caliber, and therefore cheaper,' than the skilled workers they replaced.

To capitalists, then, the good worker is stupid and cheap. Workers are not primarily people to capitalists, they are costs. And they are treated accordingly, without any say in plant location or relocation, without job security, under conditions frequently unhealthy or dangerous, usually without benefits or vacation. Unless, that is, a union is somewhere in the picture.

In a universe of unskilled workers, there is no such thing as a high-paying job. We can thank unions, or the pressures applied by organized workers, for any job which pays well. Mercedes pays $17 an hour, and those instant benefits, only to keep the United Auto Workers from organizing its plant. All of these auto manufacturers are flooding into Alabama primarily because it is not a heavily unionized state.

We also can thank unions and militant workers for the 40-hour week, vacations, weekends off, pensions, Social Security, the minimum wage, and whatever safety standards may exist. If unions go, so will these worker benefits, especially including high-wage jobs. We have seen a huge drop in worker purchasing power and in benefits such as pensions, health insurance, and overtime pay in the thirty years that organized labour has been on a decline in the US.

Moreover, no matter how high industrial unions pushed hourly wages, the pay for workers never has been as high as what is earned by those in management. The highest-paid worker gets less than the starting salaries offered to inexperienced college graduates without dependants.

Finally, racism is the boss's tool. Bosses need to divide workers off from each other, to keep them from organizing into unions. Among the most important methods used to accomplish this has been the fostering of racism. Historians Peter Linebaugh and Marcus Rediker demonstrate that the huge numbers of unskilled workers produced by the beginnings of the industrial revolution in the 17th and 18th centuries around the Atlantic Ocean—sailors, slaves, the unskilled, and their allies—did not exhibit racism toward each other. Racism grew among skilled and unskilled workers in the US in the 17th, 18th, and 19th centuries, as historians Edmund Morgan and Marlon Riggs show, because it was fostered by business elites, slave owners, and other property owners.

So, we have a paradox. Poverty-stricken, job-challenged workers in the Black Belt need jobs, especially high-paying industrial jobs, but modern industry treats workers like dirt, will only increase racism, and will pay well only under the pressure of unions. Can I justly counter my friend the State Senator by urging folks NOT to take the $17 jobs which come to them through 'development?' No. But I can say that, in capitalism, jobs without unions are fatal in the long run. I can say that anyone urging my fellow humans to take such jobs MUST also explain what unions have meant for workers, how workers are inevitably hurt without strong union organization, and how they can and must take union organization with them into the jobs.

Jobs worth having, jobs which foster dignity and respect, will come NOT from development, not from capitalism, but solely from worker awareness and worker organization.

Is the writer right in what he says? What points can you agree with? What points would you take issue with? How would you do that? What evidence would you use to support your argument?

■ SUGGESTIONS FOR FURTHER READING

1. Burawoy, M. (1979), *Manufacturing Consent: Changes in the Labour Process under Monopoly Capitalism*, Chicago: University of Chicago Press. This book is a classic of its time and is an example of how participant observation is done. Pahl, R. E. (1988), *On Work, Thirty Years of Making Out*, Oxford: Basil Blackwell, ch. 8 by M. Burawoy provides more on Burawoy's work.

2. Noon, M., and Blyton, P. (2002), *The Realities of Work* (2nd edn.), Houndmills Palgrave Macmillan, ch. 9 on survival strategies at work and for a critique of Burawoy.

3. Ackroyd, S., and Thompson, P. (1999), *Organizational Misbehaviour*, London: Sage, ch. 5, 'Only Joking?' This chapter discusses the use of humour and makes links to counter-culture.

4. Roy, D. (1960), 'Banana Time: Job Satisfaction and Informal Interaction,' *Human Organization*, 18: 156–68. This lively description of behaviour and the interpretation of it makes great reading.

5. Thompson, P., and McHugh, D. (2002), *Work Organizations* (3rd edn.). Houndmills: Palgrave, ch. 19 on motivation: the drive for satisfaction. This chapter discusses Roy's work in the context of motivation.

6. Gabriel, Y., Fineman, S., and Sims, D. (2000), *Organizing and Organizations* (2nd edn.), ch. 14 on serious joking has some interesting examples of how humour is used in organizations.

7. Watson, T. (2002), *Organizing and Managing Work*, Harlow: Pearson. Chapter 10 has a section on workplace mischief which is fun to read.

■ WEB LINKS

See **www.wual.ua.edu** for a fuller description of the case study in this chapter.

www.sociology.berkeley.edu/faculty/burawoy/ takes you to Michael Burawoy's web page and tells you more about his work.

■ QUESTIONS

1. Burawoy says that the 'game' metaphor is more than an explanation; it is also a tool of critique (1979: 92). Discuss. Or according to Burawoy, how does the capitalist labour process 'manufacture consent'?

2. Marx sees it as 'man's nature' to be 'his' own creator. Discuss (see Du Gay 1996: 11–15).

3. Hakim (1991) argues that women, particularly homeworkers, who willingly marry and accept the authority of husbands who have traditional views of women, should take the blame for

their poor situation in the labour market. Some women gratefully accept slave status. Phizacklea and Wolkowitz (1995) argue against this view. How do both sides present the argument and with whom would you agree?

4. Phizacklea and Wolkowitz (1995) say that researching homeworking is hard to do. Why?

5. How widespread is the 'electronic cottage' and does it offer increased autonomy or greater control over work? (See Huws et al. 1990; Phizacklea and Wolkowitz 1995; and other sources.)

6. Hassard (1996) shows how important time is in the studies by Roy, Ditton, and Cavendish. Why is time so important?

7. How would you explain how working-class kids continue to get working-class jobs (see Bates 1991; Mirza 1992; Willis 1977)? Why is it so inevitable? Can you find any research that demonstrates that this process is not inevitable?

■ GROUP EXERCISE

Divide the class up into small groups. Ask each individual to describe a job they have done using headings such as: features of the job I liked, features I disliked, the effect that the job had, what I learned from doing that job.

■ REFERENCES

Allen, S., and Wolkowitz, C. (1987), *Homeworking: Myths and Realities*, London: Macmillan.

Argyris, C. (1985), *Strategy, Change and Defensive Routines*, Pitman: Boston.

—— (1990), *Overcoming Organizational Defenses: Facilitating Organizational Learning*, Boston: Allyn & Bacon.

Ashforth, B. E. (1989), 'The Experience of Powerlessness in Organizations,' *Organizational Behavior and Human Decision Processes*, 43/2: 207–42.

Bates, I. (1991), 'Closely Observed Training: An Exploration of Links between Social Structures, Training and Identity', *International Studies of Sociology of Education*, 1: 225–43.

——(1993), 'A Job which is "Right for Me"? Social Class, Gender and Individualization', ch. 1 in I. Bates and G. Riseborough (eds.), *Youth and Inequality*. Buckingham: Open University Press.

Bottomore, T., and Rubel, M. (1963), Karl Marx: *Selected Writings in Sociology and Social Philosophy*, Harmondsworth: Penguin.

Braverman, H. (1974), *Labor and Monopoly Capital*, New York: Monthly Review Press.

Burawoy, M. (1979), *Manufacturing Consent: Changes in the Labour Process under Monopoly Capitalism*. Chicago: University of Chicago Press.

Cavendish, R. (1989), 'Women on the Line', ch. 8 in C. Littler (ed.), *The Experience of Work*, Milton Keynes: Open University Press.

Christensen, K. (1989), 'Home Based Clerical Work: No Simple Truth, No Simple Reality', in E. Boris and C. Daniels (eds.), *Homework: Historical and Contemporary Perspectives on Paid Labour at Home*, Chicago: University of Illinois Press.

Clegg, S. (1987), 'The Language of Power and the Power of Language', *Organization Studies*, 8/1: 61–70.

Cockburn, C. (1983), *Brothers: Male Dominance and Technological Change*, London: Pluto Press.

Cockburn, C. (1987), *Two-Track Training: Sex Inequalities and the YTS*, London: Macmillan.

Collinson, D. L. (1992), *Managing the Shopfloor: Subjectivity, Masculinity and Workplace Culture*, Berlin: De Gruyter.

Ditton, J. (1979), 'Baking Time', *Sociological Review*, 27: 157–67.

Dubin, R. (1956), 'Industrial Workers' Worlds', *Social Problems*, 3, 131–42.

Du Gay, P. (1996), *Consumption and Identity at Work*, London: Sage.

Efraty, D., Sirgy, J. M., and Claiborne, C. B. (1991), 'The Effects of Personal Alienation of Organizational Identification: A Quality-of-Work-Life Model,' *Journal of Business and Psychology*, 6/1: 57–78.

Gabriel, Y. (1988), *Working Lives in Catering*. London: Routledge & Kegan Paul.

Geyer, R. F., and Schweitzer, D. (1981) (eds.), *Alienation: Problems of Meaning, Theory and Method*, London: Routledge & Kegan Paul.

Grey, C. (1996), 'Towards a Critique of Managerialism: The Contribution of Simone Weil', *Journal of Management Studies*, 33/5: 591–611.

Hakim, C. (1991), 'Grateful Slaves and Self-Made Women: Fact and Fantasy in Women's Work Orientations', *European Sociological Review*, 7/2 (Sept.), 101–21.

Hamper, B. (1992), *Rivethead: Tales from the Assembly Line*, London: Fourth Estate.

Hassard, J. (1996), 'Images of Time in Work and Organization', in S. Clegg, C. Hardy, and W. R. Nord (eds.), *Handbook of Organization Studies*, London: Sage, ch. 3.5, or ch. 1 in K. Grint (ed.) (2000), *Work and Society: A Reader*, pp. 14–40.

Huws, U., Korte, V., and Robinson, S. (1990), *Telework: Towards the Elusive Office*, Chichester: Wiley.

Jermier, J. M., Knights, D., and Nord, W. R. (1994), 'Resistance and Power in Organizations: Agency, Subjectivity and the Labour Process', in J. Jermier, D. Knights, and W. R. Nord (eds.), *Introduction to Resistance and Power in Organizations*, London: Routledge, pp. 1–24.

Jones, G., and Wallace, C. (1990), 'Beyond Individualization: What Sort of Social Change?', in L. Chisholm et al. (eds.), *Childhood, Youth and Social Change*, Lewes: Falmer Press.

Kakabadse, A. (1986), 'Organizational Alienation and job climate: A Comparative Study of Structural Conditions and Psychological Adjustment,' *Small Group Behavior*, 17/4: 458–71.

Kanungo, R. N. (1982), *Work Alienation: An Integrative Approach,*' Praeger, New York.

Knights, D. (1990), 'Subjectivity, Power and the Labour Process', ch. 10 in D. Knights and H. Wilmott (eds.), *Labour Process Theory*, London: Macmillan.

Linhart, R. (1989), 'The Assembly Line', in C. Littler (ed.), *The Experience of Work*, Milton Keynes: Open University Press.

Littler, C. (1989), 'Introduction: The Texture of Work', in C. Littler (ed.), *The Experience of Work*. Milton Keynes: Open University Press.

Marx, K. (1963), *Early Writings*, ed. and trans. T. B. Bottomore, London: C. A. Watts.

Mirza, H. (1992), *Young, Female and Black*, London: Routledge.

Olson, M. (1989), 'Organizational Barriers to Professional Telework', in E. Boris and C. Daniels (eds.), *Homework: Historical and Contemporary Perspectives on Paid Labour at Home*, Chicago: University of Illinois Press.

Paules, G. F. (1991), *Dishing it out: Power and Resistance among Waitresses in a New Jersey Restaurant*, Philadelphia: Temple University Press.

Pahl, R. E. (1988), *On Work, Thirty Years of Making out*, Oxford: Basil Blackwell, ch. 8 by M. Burawoy.

Phizacklea, A., and Wolkowitz, C. (1995), *Homeworking Women: Gender, Racism and Class at Work*, London: Sage.

Pollert, A. (1981), *Girls, Wives and Factory Lives*, London: Macmillan.

Roy, D. (1960), 'Banana Time: Job Satisfaction and Informal Interaction', *Human Organization*, 18: 156–68; repr. in J. Hassard (ed.), *The Sociology of Time*, London: Macmillan, ch. 9.

Sarros, J. C., Tanewski, G. A, Winter, R. P., Santora, J. C., and Densten, I. L. (2002), 'Work Alienation and Organizational Leadership', *British Journal of Management*, 13: 285–304.

Salaman, G., and Thompson, K. (1973) (eds.), *People and Organisations*, Harlow: Longman for the Open University Press

Thompson, P. (1990), 'Crawling from the Wreckage: The Labour Process and the Politics of Production', in D. Knights and H. Wilmott (eds.), *Labour Process Theory*, London: Macmillan.

——and McHugh, D. (1990), *Work Organizations*, Basingstoke: Macmillan.

Weber, M. (1926/1947), *The Theory of Social and Economic Organization*, ed. Talcott Parsons, New York: Free Press.

Weil, S. (1987), *Formative Writings 1929–1941*, London: Routledge.

Westwood, S. (1984), *All Day Every Day: Factory and Family in the Making of Women's Lives*, London: Pluto Press.

Wilensky, H. L. (1964), Varieties of work experiences in H. Borrow (ed.), *Man in a World of Work*, Boston: Houghton Mifflin.

Willis, P. (1977), *Learning to Labour*. Farnborough: Saxon House.

Willmott, H. (1990), 'Subjectivity and the Dialectics of Praxis: Opening the Core of Labour Process Analysis', in D. Knights and H. Wilmott (eds.), *Labour Process Theory*, London: Macmillan.

Wood, R. C. (1992), *Working in Hotels and Catering*, London: Routledge.

Zeffane, R., and Macdonald, D. (1993), 'Uncertainty, Participation and Alienation: Lessons from Workplace Restructuring', *International Journal of Sociology and Social Policy*, 13/5–6: 22–52.

6 | Sexuality, Sex Typing, Managing Emotions, and Feeling in Control

In the last chapter we looked at the view from below, at the perspective of some employees. In Chapter 8 we will look at the view from above, the manager's reality. But what insights can be gained by taking a more external view, if we take a step outside the organization and look back in? In this chapter we look back into organizations and also concentrate on issues which are normally treated as if they are external to organizations—sexuality, emotions, 'deviancy', and feelings.

Sexuality in Organizations

What about bureaucracy and sexuality—do they mix? We saw earlier, in the chapter on rationality and bureaucracy, how in bureaucracies women are strangers in a male-defined world. There is evidence of women managers being perceived as threats to male self-image (Cockburn 1991; Sargent 1983). Women may play down their sexuality in order to 'blend in' (Sheppard 1989). In this chapter we look further into the issue of sexuality and how it is pertinent to understanding organizational behaviour. Issues of emotionality, sexuality, and intimacy are currently missing from descriptions of organizational life (Brewis and Grey 1994); they are seen as belonging to a private sphere. Women and sex are not welcome in the public sphere. Women, characterized as inherently passionate, sexual beings, are thought not to function as well as men in the rational public sphere as they are overly prey to their basic emotions. Popular myth says that women are too neurotic to be able to cope with public positions of responsibility and are more suited to 'instinctive' roles like caring for the young or infirm, or in supportive, helping, administrative roles. Sexuality here refers to sex roles, sexual preference, sexual attractiveness, and notions of masculinity and femininity in organizations. It is sexuality that marks men and women out as different and also marks out differences between groups, for example, gay men and lesbian women. It is interesting to note that most writing on sexuality in organizations assumes heterosexuality as given. 'Heterosexual' (like 'white', 'male', and 'able bodied') is almost always a silent term (Kitzinger et al. 1992). Only recently have there been studies looking at lesbians and gay men in work—the public sector (Skelton 1999; Humphrey 2000), the police (Burke 1993), and the military (Hall 1995).

Sex Typing of Jobs

Some jobs and professions have been sex typed as male. The legal profession is one good example of where this has happened. Male lawyers (with a few exceptions) and the professional bodies in England fiercely resisted the entry of women into the profession for three reasons (Podmore and Spencer 1982). First, they are a very conservative profession who oppose change. Secondly, and most importantly for our purposes here, the men felt that professional standards would be dangerously compromised by the entry of women into the profession. Maleness was one of the attributes of professionalism; maleness was part of the profession's character so that the admission of women was seen as threatening the very identity of the institutions. Men lawyers referred to stereotypes that portrayed women as emotional, illogical, and irrational. Women were seen as successful only if they suppressed the feminine side of their characters. This would mean 'unsexing' women, which would be deplored by the male legal establishment. So women should be excluded. The third reason was that they wished to exclude the competition women would present. Women in the profession feel that their careers have been shaped and fashioned by their gender; for example they find themselves channelled into particular types of work seen as fit for females, desk-bound work like conveyancing and divorce work. Women tend to be excluded from higher status and more remunerative work (particularly company and commercial law) as they are thought, by men, to be less effective in these areas (Podmore and Spencer 1982).

Social norms are often personified in sexual stereotypes. For instance a commonly held belief is that female bar staff should be attractive, warm-hearted, easy-going women, providing a shoulder for men to cry on, capable of taking and giving a joke. Such consensual objectivity has a reality independent of fact. The barmaid who is not attractive, is embarrassed by risqué humour, or unsympathetic to the cries for sympathy fails to comply with criteria for membership of the group 'barmaid' and is unlikely to be ignorant of that failure (Breakwell 1979).

Rosemary Pringle in her book *Secretaries Talk* (1989) shows how femininity and secretarial work are closely tied. Though most secretaries were men until the late nineteenth century and they retained a presence in secretarial work until the Second World War, secretarial work is currently seen as quintessentially feminine. Moreover, all women are assumed to be capable of secretarial work: 'typing is seen as something every woman can do—like washing up!' (Secretary in Pringle 1989: 3.) Men may perceive any woman in an office as the secretary and expect her to perform secretarial service in the absence of a secretary. Secretaries are also represented almost exclusively in familial or sexual terms as wives (e.g. office wife), mothers, spinster aunts, mistresses, and femmes fatales. The image is often of the 'sexy secretary' and the 'mindless dolly bird'. It is virtually impossible to talk about secretaries without making a set of sexual associations. In fact secretary/boss relations are seen by Pringle as the most sexualized of all employment relationships 'out side the sex industry itself' (1989: 158). Images of secretaries sitting around filing their nails or doing their knitting reinforce the idea that they do little work.

It is also men's labour that is sexualized. McDowell's (1997) research in the City of London shows how men 'do' masculinity. Organizations are structured by the social relations of sexuality (1997: 27). Men construct everyday work through heterosexual masculine discourse in different types of merchant banking. The stock exchange is a commercial market place, a space in which 'rampant male libido' (1997: 169) is celebrated. Work itself was described in terms of explicit sexual metaphors such as 'lift your skirt' (reveal your position), 'hard on' (rising market), 'rape the cards' (exaggerate expenses), and the 'consummation' of deals (1997: 148). Women and gay men are 'others' in this heterosexual culture. The men used terms like 'skirts', 'slags', 'brasses', and 'tarts' to describe women and emphasize how they were illegitimate outsiders. Similarly Knorr-Cetina and Bruegger (2000) are struck by the sexual vocabulary of the training rooms: 'I got shafted, I got bent over. I got blown up. I got raped. I got stuffed . . .'

> **STOP**
>
> **Loutish behaviour in the finance industry can cost companies a lot of money. American Express (the travel and finance company) agreed to pay $US31 million in a lawsuit for sex and age discrimination filed on behalf of more than 4,000 women. Two investment banks settled two sex discrimination cases in New York and London. In the London case an employment tribunal awarded the claimant almost £1.5 m, a record amount for a sex discrimination case in Britain (*The Economist* 2002).**

While it might be argued that merchant banking jobs are not inherently masculine, some jobs are seen as very much the masculine domain. One example is butchery. Women make up less than 1 per cent of butchers (Pringle and Collings 1993). Butchers continue to stress the inappropriateness of butchery for women. The 'woman butcher' is almost unthinkable as a cultural category. Women's place within the popularly mythologized butcher's shop is as the butcher's wife, as cashiers, or as shop assistants. There has been a reluctance to allow them to cut the carcasses up. A physical strength discourse helps keep women out of butchery; strength is needed to break up carcasses. It is also assumed that women will be afraid of knives and squeamish at the sight of blood (Pringle and Collings 1993).

Sex Stereotype and Emotions

Sexuality and emotions are clearly brought into work. Women are often required to display the sex stereotype in order to be effective in their work. Arlie Russell Hochschild (1983) was among the first scholars to show how extensively individuals, particularly employed women, are expected to manage their emotions; she uses the metaphor of a 'managed heart' to underscore the emotional control the women were required to exhibit. With this research we have a new angle on the experience of work and the view from below.

We saw earlier how Hochschild has described emotion work. Hochschild's (1983) study of US airline flight attendants shows how the attendants were trained to display an emotional commitment to the welfare and comfort of airline passengers; they were required to show a caring, courteous, friendly, and efficient front even when passengers were rude or arrogant. There were rules for grooming and personal attitudes. Customers had to be met with warmth and smiles; the smiles were to be 'inside-out' ones, felt and meant. Cabin crew at Delta Airlines were socialized during their training to believe, not only that they had to make customers feel cosseted and valued, but they had to genuinely experience positive regard for them and suppress both negative behaviour and negative emotions. This is 'emotional labour' for the flight attendants, particularly when it involves the semi-institutionalized expectation of flirting expected between (mainly) female air stewardesses and male airline passengers. This is reflected in advertising like 'We really move our tails for you to make your every wish come true' (Continental Airlines) or 'Fly me, you'll like it' (National Airlines) (see Hochschild 1983: 93). The company, then, manufactured the response to the client. 'Professionalism' requires this behaviour.

There are two main ways in which emotional labour is engaged, in surface and deep acting. The former involves pretending to feel 'what we do not'. We may be deceiving others about how we feel but not ourselves. Deep acting means deceiving yourself as well as others. There is a cost attached to this labour; the labour 'affects the degree to which we listen to feeling and sometimes our very capacity to feel' (Hochschild 1983: 21–2). Hochschild goes on to imply that many, perhaps most, women have had the kinds of training she observed among Delta flight attendants who were taught 'that an obnoxious person could be reconceived in an honest and useful way'. Such lessons were part of their 'anger desensitization' (1983: 25).

This emotional labour cannot be regarded as 'gender neutral'. Jobs requiring significant amounts of emotional labour are dominated by women (Taylor and Tyler 2000). The 'natural' skills and personality required to deliver quality service among telephone sales agents at 'Flightpath' appeared to be female ones. 'We are looking for people who can chat to people, interact, build rapport. What we find is that women can do this more, they're definitely more natural when they do it anyway . . . women are naturally good at that sort of thing' (Taylor and Tyler 2000: 84). The women were expected to put up with sexualized encounters from men on the phone. Similarly female flight attendants were thought to be best suited to the role because they were seen as more patient and caring of other's needs than men. The quality service delivered by flight attendants, the 'personal servic- ing' of passengers, increases relative to the cost of the service itself. Flight attendants working with first-class travellers are trained to introduce themselves, use passenger names, memorize their drink and meal requirements, and to provide a more 'personal' service. They were instructed to walk softly though the cabin, make eye contact with each passenger, and always smile at him or her.

   Tyler and Abbott (1998) have documented how women flight attendants are also asked to manage themselves as 'ornamental objects' (West and Zimmerman 1987: 141). Flight attendants are required to deploy skills and abilities that they are deemed to possess sim- ply by virtue of their sexual difference from men. The flight attendant is 'part mother, part servant and part tart' (Tyler and Abbott 1998: 440): essentialized, gendered, and sex- ualized. The skills are not remunerated or trained, but they are managed. These women are required to manage and monitor their bodies, be 'body conscious' and watch weight. An efficient and effective airline is signified by a 'slender' flight attendant. Applicants can be rejected if their weight is not considered to be in proportion to their height. They also need to look after their bodies in other ways, as rejection is associated with looking too old, having blemished skin, having hair too short, too messy, or too severe. They could also be rejected if their nails were too short or bitten, their posture was poor or legs too chubby. Others were rejected for having prominent teeth or having a weakness for choco- late. Poise and grooming are important for the image. All attendants are required to con- form to company-specific formal uniform and grooming regulations which stipulate clothing, shoes, hair, and make-up and height–weight restrictions. Only female flight attendants were weighed periodically during grooming checks. While men have to look clean and socially attractive, the women have to look 'polished' and sexually attractive. This they are expected to do at their own expense as no allowance is given for make-up, hairdressers, or fitness centres.

Masculinity and Managing Feelings

Research has shown that it is not just women who are required to manage their emotions at work. Management prescribes combinations of positive and negative feelings to help police officers and debt collectors adjust social interaction to organizational aims (Rafaeli and Sutton 1991). Training sessions show debt collectors how to adapt their display rules to the emotional reactions of debtors. Debt collectors are taught to express warmth with anxious debtors, neutrality or calmness with angry respondents, and urgency and disap- proval with reluctant customers. Rises, promotions, cash prizes, criticism, warnings, demotions, and firings are used to sanction those who deviate from the appropriate emotional displays.

Research has also shown how men are often reluctant to admit to vulnerability or fear at work. Prison officers, for example, view requests for help from colleagues as a show of professional weakness. Asking for help was tantamount to admitting you were not 'man enough' for the job. Asking for help, showing fear or emotion was not occupationally acceptable (Carter 1996). Can you think of other occupations where this might be the case?

One such occupation may be found in 'security' work at nightclubs and pubs—being a 'bouncer' or 'door supervisor' (see Monaghan 2002). In this setting fear can be hidden and managed through group solidarity. Research with over sixty door supervisors (only five were female) showed the importance of demonstrating solidarity with the 'comrades'. Solidarity was demonstrated between door staff in a masculinist way. Greeting and departure rituals such as the obligatory firm handshake represented a mundane manifestation of in-group ties while violence towards 'problematic' customers who physically assault door staff provide a more shocking indication of this commitment. Danger is an extremely important unifying factor and is implicated in dominating styles of body use. While the door staff face personal bodily injury, police arrest, and instant dismissal from the manager, this renders in-group cohesion salient at practical, cognitive, and emotional levels. Not only do they support staff at their own place of work. Workers at different venues can be in radio contact with others in adjoining pubs and clubs. If a violent incident erupted at one site, door teams could 'double up' with the intention of quickly resolving the conflict and reducing the risk of occupational injury. Door staff 'keep warm together' in an insecure world.

As other research has shown, the strong male coded emotions such as anger, hatred, and aggression sometimes actually prompted 'bloody revenge' (Mellor and Shilling 1997: 201). If 'you hit a doorman and, if the team is worth its salt, you'll pay in blood. That's the unwritten law' (Thompson 2000: 151; Monaghan 2002: 512).

Masculinity is very precarious and may be usurped in a public and humiliating manner. For example one doorman (Terry) 'took the piss' out of another (Paul) by refusing him access to a nightclub. Paul's reaction was tearful. Paul 'lost face', as he was, in this case, unable to tolerate the public exchange of insult and humour, and the overt conflict.

Managing Emotions and the Image of Professionalism: The Case of Prostitutes

Professionalism is also important for sex workers, prostitutes. Prostitution has been described as the mutually voluntary exchange of sexual services for money or other consideration (COYOTE 1988: 290). Others might argue that prostitution is always by force, is always a violation against women and an outrage to their dignity (e.g. Barry 1991, quoted in Van der Gaag 1994). Some argue that a firm distinction must be made between 'free choice' prostitution and all forms of forced and child prostitution (e.g. Delacoste and Alexander 1988). Organizations like Barnardos and The Children's Society have campaigned to bring about change in how those under 16 who work as prostitutes are seen, arguing they should be treated as victims of abuse. However free choice prostitution can be regarded as sex work and a form of work like any other. Many definitions rely on analogies of work or industry calling prostitutes saleswomen, women sex workers, or women who perform erotic labour (Boynton 1998), though women and girls involved in prostitution may not always perceive what they do as work or prostitution.

Sex workers generate future business by adopting an equivalent professionalism to that found in other jobs. For example, both flight attendants and sex workers have been found to separate the realms of experience into private and public domains (McKeganey and Barnard 1996). Publicly they are required to act in order to present a certain 'face'; privately they can let this go. Publicly flight attendants' faces and feelings help to make money, although not directly for themselves. Prostitutes' faces and bodies are a resource to make money for them.

Maintaining the public image requires individuals to distance themselves from the clients in some way. The most visible strategy prostitutes use to distance themselves from clients is explicitness. From the outset they make clear that they are sexually available but at a price. Negotiation and contract are central concerns for prostitution. Prostitution is governed by unwritten 'rules' but as the 'rules of the game' are not fixed for clients there are three considerations: what the prostitute is prepared to do, the nature of the client's request, and the amount of money on offer. All these have to be negotiated and agreed. Throughout the process of initial negotiation the women adopt an assertive business-like stance in the hope of securing client compliance so they can dictate the terms and conditions of the sale. A large part of the rationale for this resides in an acute awareness of the potential dangers of providing sex to men who for most part are total strangers. Once the deal has been negotiated, additional income is dependent on the skill of the prostitute and level of naivety of the client; extra charges are incurred by the client for 'extras' like touching (McKeganey and Barnard 1996).

While the prostitutes describe themselves as being in charge of the encounter with the client, the client will similarly feel they are in charge. As the client has the money, they have the power. The business relationship is 'managed' so that both parties feel they have control (McKeganey and Barnard 1996). The 'rules of the game', the unwritten code of conduct adopted by one group of prostitutes, are described by Sharpe (1998). These women claimed never to accept business without insisting their clients used condoms. Information about whether the vice squad were patrolling, information about punters (particularly 'funny punters'), attacks, violent incidents, or strangers 'on the patch' (new prostitutes, new police in the vice squad, media people, and researchers) was exchanged but the women never mixed socially beyond the boundaries of the patch. Most of the prostitutes developed a territorial affiliation and the 'poaching' of someone else's patch or customers was not appreciated or tolerated. The newcomer had to stand her ground and the war of attrition was played out until she was accepted or tolerated. The patch had a well-established internal market that controlled and regulated prices. If an individual moved her prices to attract more business she laid herself open to retribution from the others, at least verbal abuse and at worst a severe beating (Sharpe 1998).

Karen Sharpe (1998) noted that negotiations with the clients also followed 'rules'. Once it was ascertained what service the client required, he was informed of the prices and where the business would take place. Then the prostitute made the decision whether to accept or decline the business. Prices were invariably non-negotiable and the women always took the money first. The women always provided condoms; if a hotel room was used, the client would meet the cost. Again being in control was a major issue for the women—being in control of the situation, the client, the location, and what their children understood, were all-important for these women.

Feeling in Control: The Stripper

Strippers too express the feeling of being in control. The women describe themselves as powerful 'It's your show, you're higher than everyone else on that stage and you feel in control,' says Ninon. Melissa (a student at Oxford who works in the same show) says 'It's the only sexual relationship I've had where I feel completely in control' (*Scotland on Sunday*, 3 August 1997, p. 4).

'When I am on stage I am a sex goddess, I'm revered by every man in the room. I'm all powerful, they all want me but they can't have me' (Melissa Butler, quoted in the *Sun*: *Guardian*, 28 August 1997). A male stripper (Clarke 2003) was advised by a female stripper about the behaviour he should exhibit. Women expect to 'get interactive'. 'They want to laugh, scream and howl. The male stripper has to get among them, dance, flirt and expect to get a bit mauled.' He had not anticipated that a woman would bite him on his buttock; he was bitten so badly that he needed four stitches. This time he had lost control.

It is not only relationships with clients that sex workers manage. Relationships between prostitutes and police, for example, have to be managed too. For example to reduce the chances of being arrested by the police they use 'the courtesy of the road' which means, if the police come along, the prostitutes will move, walk off, or even just look in the opposite direction (McKeganey and Barnard 1996). Sharpe (1998) found that an unwritten rule with the police was that the women would not start working on the patch until six o'clock in the evening. If they came out before this they were immediately arrested and charged.

STOP

An Example of the Unwritten Rules

All jobs have unwritten rules attached to them. For example, when I worked as a hospital cleaner as a temporary worker, I found that temporary cleaners were given all the worst jobs to do, like cleaning up sewage from a broken ceiling pipe. Temporary cleaners could only use the cleaning equipment (floor polishers, etc.) when not needed by those with permanent cleaning jobs. The full-time cleaners had control. What jobs have you done and what unwritten rules applied? (We will look more at rules in Chapter 13.)

Images of stereotypical femininity in contemporary culture are associated with the good wife and mother, the good girl, reliable, passive, nurturing, often fragile, gentle, and emotional. Some prostitutes claim to challenge these stereotypes for all women by resisting the pressure to conform to the stereotype of being the good girl and by bringing into the public sphere and to many men the services women would usually perform in private for one man. They insist that prostitution is work and a service that anyone can offer or seek and that they should have the same rights and liberties as other workers (O'Neill 1997).

O'Connell Davidson (1995) describes some of the many similarities between sex workers and other self-employed individuals. One of the most difficult aspects of the prostitute's business is the flow of custom and therefore cash. About 90 per cent of the men break their appointments so it is difficult to control or reliably predict demand. One way to do this is to build up a regular clientele who more generally do keep the appointments they make. Some control can also be achieved over the nature and volume of demand through pricing systems, skills, and specialisms. The prostitute called Desiree in O'Connell Davidson's study catered for men who were better off, came to her premises, and had diverse and demanding requirements in terms of skill, equipment, and props. The clients were prepared to pay higher prices for these services than they would pay to a street prostitute. She plans and controls all aspects of her business: where and when to advertise, who to employ and tasks they are assigned, the pricing system, the services on offer, the hours and days of business. She also exercises a great deal of control over the details of transactions with clients and has a clearly defined split between her private and public self.

Issues concerning 'being in charge' or in control in both the public and private world seem to be important in managing sexuality in organizations. An interesting example of who is in charge can be found in some research by Martin (1990). Taking the example of a TV interview with a chief executive of a very large multinational organization she shows how organizational practices can break down the separation between the individual's public and private life. In this interview the chief executive talks of how a young woman is important to the launch of a new product the next day. In order for her to be prepared for the launch she had arranged to have a Caesarian section for the birth of her child. The company had 'insisted' she stay at home and her involvement with the product launch was going to be maintained and televised on closed circuit television.

Feelings

We have seen how traditional organizational theory has stressed the functional and how managers try to shape worker behaviour to organizational objectives using an armoury of rules, regulation, and inducements. The view is of a 'passionless organization' (Fineman 1994). Organizational theory needs to account for the process and interaction of emotions, felt and displayed, emotions as diverse as pride, jealousy, love, hate, happiness, despair, anger, grief, joy, fear, and excitement. Feelings connect us with our realities and provide internal feedback on how we are doing, what we want, and what we might do next. We work over our feelings, have feelings about feelings, and are guided by previous

Hochschild, A. R. (1983), *The Managed Heart: Commercialisation of Human Feeling*, Berkeley, Calif.: University of California.

Humphrey, J. (2000), 'Organizing Sexualities, Organization Inequalities: Lesbians and Gay Men in Public Service Occupations', *Gender, Work and Organization*, 6/3: 134–51.

Kitzinger, C., Wilkinson, S., and Perkins, R. (1992), 'Theorizing Heterosexuality', *Feminism and Psychology*, 2/3: 293–324.

Knorr-Cetina, K., and Bruegger, U. (2000), 'The Market as an Object of Attachment: Exploring Postsocial Relations in Financial Markets', *Canadian Journal of Sociology*, 25/2: 141–68.

McDowell, L. (1997), *Capital Culture: Gender at Work in the City*, Oxford: Blackwell.

McKeganey, N., and Barnard, M. (1996), *Sex Work on the Streets: Prostitutes and their Clients*, Buckingham: Open University Press.

Martin, J. (1990), 'Deconstructing Organizational Taboos: The Suppression of Gender Conflict in Organizations', *Organization Science*, 1/4: 339–59.

Mellor, P., and Shilling, C. (1997), *Re-forming the Body: Religion, Community and Modernity*, London: Sage.

Monaghan, L. F. (2002), 'Embodying Gender, Work and Organization: Solidarity, Cool Loyalties and Contested Hierarchy in a Masculinist Occupation, *Gender, Work and Organization*, 9/5: 504–36.

Mumby, D. K., and Putnam, L. L. (1992), The Politics of Emotion: A Feminist Reading of Bounded Rationality', *Academy of Management Review*, 17: 466–85.

O'Connell Davidson, J. (1995), 'The Anatomy of 'Free Choice' Prostitution', *Gender, Work and Organization*, 2/1: 1–10.

O'Neill, M. (1997), 'Prostitute Women Now', ch. 1 in G. Scambler and A. Scambler (eds.), *Rethinking Prostitution: Purchasing Sex in the 1990s*, London: Routledge.

Podmore, D., and Spencer, A. (1982), 'Women Lawyers in England: The Experience of Inequality', *Work and Occupations*, 9/3: 337–61.

Pringle, R. (1989), *Secretaries Talk: Sexuality, Power and Work*, London: Verso.

——Collings, S. (1993), 'Women and Butchery: Some Cultural Taboos', *Australian Feminist Studies*, 17: 29–40.

Rafaeli, A., and Sutton, R. I. (1991), 'Emotional Contrast Strategies as Means of Social Influence: Lessons from Criminal Interrogators and Bill Collectors', *Academy of Management Journal*, 34: 749–75.

Sargent, A. G. (1983), *The Androgynous Manager*. New York: AMOCOM.

Scambler, G., and Scambler, A. (1997) (eds.), *Rethinking Prostitution: Purchasing Sex in the 1990s*, London: Routledge.

Sennett, R. (1998), *The Corrosion of Character: The Personal Consequences of Work in the New Capitalism*, New York: W.W. Norton.

Sharpe, K. (1998), *Red Light, Blue Light: Prostitutes, Punters and the Police*. Aldershot: Ashgate Publishing.

Sheppard, D. (1989), 'Organizations, Power and Sexuality: The Image and Self Image of Women Managers', in J. Hearn, D. L. Sheppard, P. Tancred Sheriff, and G. Burrell (eds.), *The Sexuality of Organization*, London: Sage.

Skelton, A. (1999), 'The Inclusive University? A Case of the Experiences of Gay and Bisexual Higher Education in the UK, in P. Fogelberg, J. Hearn, L. Husu, and T. Mankkinen (eds.), *Hard Work in the Academy*, Helsinki: Helsinki University Press, Helsinki, pp. 190–209.

Taylor, S., and Tyler, M. (2000), 'Emotional Labour and Sexual Difference in the Airline Industry', *Work, Employment and Society*, 14/1: 77–95.

Tyler, M., and Abbott, P. (1998), 'Chocs Away: Weight Watching in the Contemporary Airline Industry', *Sociology*, 32/3: 433–50.

Thompson, G. (2000), *Watch my Back*, Sussex: Summersdale.

Van der Gaag, N. (1994), 'Prostitution: Soliciting for Change', *New Internationalist*, 252 (Feb.), 4–7.

West, C., and Zimmerman, D. H. (1987), 'Doing Gender', *Gender and Society*, 1: 125–51.

7 | When Organizational Behaviour is not so 'Good'

Organizational misbehaviour, resistance, and crime has been relatively neglected in textbooks of management and business. It is seldom thought of as 'organizational behaviour'. Yet resistance has been acknowledged since Karl Marx as taking many forms and derived from revolutionary class consciousness. For Marx, though, class-conscious radicalism was not very likely to occur as within capitalism there was the illusion of freedom and alienation was obscured; capitalism appears normal and inevitable, like the laws of nature. 'Real resistance' was broken down (Jermier et al. 1994). Acts such as sabotage, theft, or the intentional withholding of output can often be explained as reactions to frustrations (Spector 1997).

Theft

We all know people who cheat and probably cheat ourselves. Middle managers, often long servers, are among the chief culprits as they have the best understanding of how to cheat their company and cover their tracks (Ashworth 1999). We know how to cheat and thieve, even if we don't do it. In universities plagiarism is one form of cheating much despised; theft is equally despised by most. Every now and again newspapers report a story of theft that is bound to catch the eye. Punch (1996) cites the newspaper story of nuns who had fraudulently diverted money (about $5 million) from a hospital to build an indoor swimming pool and so they could have TV sets in all the cells in their luxurious convent. He also details three highly dramatic cases of business deviance, including the

---

SOME EXAMPLES OF BAD BEHAVIOUR

Bad behaviour in organizations takes all sorts of different forms. Here are just two examples:

A director of a charity would sleep through meetings with senior staff but afterwards request and receive reassurance from them that his input would be helpful.

Youth workers allowed youth clubs they were responsible for to fall into disuse, but falsified attendance figures to make it look as if they were still serving young people (Myers 2002). What examples have you witnessed?

case of Robert Maxwell. In one case £300 million went missing from pension funds; BCCI are estimated to have swindled $20 billion from depositors around the world (and run a 'black bank' within the bank), and then there was the Savings and Loan scandal where funds were siphoned off for personal gains. These cases, he says, blow apart the rationale and respectable myth of management. Top managers have manipulated their companies, regulators, and their environments for devious ends. To understand business crime and deviance we have to look at the nature of business, the realities of organizational life, and the dilemmas facing management.

It is estimated that three-quarters of all employees steal from their employers at least once (McGurn 1988; Ashworth 1999) and that many of these repeat such actions on a regular basis (Delaney 1993). Petty theft may include personal telephone calls, taking office stationery, and fiddling expenses. Employee theft has been blamed for 30–50 per cent of all business failures (Greenberg 1997). Companies sacrifice about 1 per cent of annual sales to petty pilfering which, for a major company, could cost as much as £70 million a year (Ashworth 1999). In Ditton's (1977) classic study of British bakery workers, so extreme was the theft in one bakery, and so widely accepted the practice, that supervisors had to plan for extra loaves to be baked each day to avoid running short.

Gerald Mars, a social anthropologist, looked at ways in which ordinary people cheat at work, how they steal from their organizations (Mars 1982). Cheating is endemic and integral to the rewards of work, he says. Fiddling is woven into the fabric of people's everyday lives. He sorts the cultures he sees in organizations into four groups: hawks, donkeys, wolves, and vultures. Each group has a distinct ideology, a set of attitudes, a set of rules, and a view of the world. Each plans to rob, cheat, fiddle, or short change subordinates, customers, employers, or the state.

Let us look at how he describes these groups he identifies. Hawks, he says, are individualists, who bend the rules to suit themselves. They are entrepreneurs, innovative professionals (including academics and journalists), and those who run small businesses. Hawkish entrepreneurs are also to be found among waiters, fairground buskers, and owner taxi drivers. The individuals' freedom to transact on their own terms is highly valued. Their aim is to 'make it'. An example would be a journalist claiming good expenses for a good story or claiming first-class travel but going second class, or a lawyer charging cheap time (by using trainee, unqualified, apprentice labour) but charging it at dear prices, charging full professional rates.

Donkeys are highly constrained by rules and isolated from each other. Unlike hawks who have a reasonably full choice in how they spend their time, donkeys have no such freedom. Some transport workers are donkeys, as their jobs isolate them and they feel dominated by rules (for example, those governing safety). Supermarket cashiers and machine minders are also highly constrained and isolated. These people will respond particularly where the constraints are strongest, by breaking or sabotaging the rules that constrain them; alternatively they will fiddle. These individuals can be either powerful or powerless depending on their actions. If they passively accept the constraints they are powerless; if they are disruptive and reject the rules, they can be extremely powerful. The example given is of a supermarket cashier who was able consistently to extract five times her daily wage in fiddled cash. She might do this by ringing up less than the total charge on the till then pocket the difference or by allowing her friends and family to take goods through the checkout that had not been paid for. She hated being treated like a programmed robot and fiddled to make her job more interesting. Fiddling gave her new targets, a sense of challenge, and hurt her boss.

Wolves work and steal in packs; they have a hierarchy, order, and internal controls that ensure that when they steal they do so with agreed rules and a well-defined division of labour. They have a leader and penalize their own deviants. Examples are a dock-work gang, refuse collectors, airplane crews, or miners. Refuse collectors will break the rules, riding on the back of the cart or leaving it unattended. They break the 'no gratuities rule' too and will sell dustbins to those who ask. They can also sell what they collect, for example, sofas, brass, and copper. An attack on one, an exertion of management control over the fiddle, will be seen as an attack on all.

Vultures need the support of the group for the fiddle but act on their own when 'at the feast'. They depend on support and information from colleagues but are also competitive and act in isolation for much of the time. As they rely on both cooperation and competition, their groups can be unstable and turbulent. Examples from this group include travelling sales people, driver-deliverers, and waiters. Waiters can overcharge for drinks from the bar; photocopy sales staff can sell paper they are supposed to give away; the delivery person can sell black economy clothing from the van. All rely on the actions of others to keep their 'scam' going.

Elsewhere Mars describes in greater depth the pilferage that takes place in a hotel in Blackpool where he worked (1989). Wages paid to waiting staff are comparatively low and labour turnover is high. Using this as justification, the waiting staff pilfers and indulges in 'the fiddle'. 'Knock-off' refers to a subtype of fiddle, the illicit acquisition of food, cutlery, and linen. Fiddles are regarded as entitlement, as part of the wages. This could be done by, for example, fiddling on tea and coffee. A waiter would receive an order for two coffees. He goes into the kitchen and orders one coffee on an order slip. He obtains a standard coffeepot, milk jug, and one cup and saucer from the staff in the kitchen. He needs an extra cup and saucer for his customers that he will have hidden in a strategic area near the lounge. A 'bent helper' in the kitchen can make sure there is enough coffee in the pot to serve two. The waiter charges the customer for two coffees but only puts the price of one, with the order slip, into the till. Bent helpers can be paid in beer rather than cash.

Some employers in manufacturing industry have tried to combat theft by locking their workers into factories. As a result of this measure, there have been some tragic accidents: 146 workers died in a fire in a locked New York garment industry sweatshop; 84 died in a fire in a toy-producing company in China, and 25 in a poultry plant in North Carolina (Nichols 1997: 108).

Research (e.g. Greenberg and Scott 1996) suggests that many individuals steal from their companies because they believe it is justified. They believe that the company is not providing them with a fair deal so to even up the score they appropriate company property. Supporting this view is the fact that such theft is often accompanied by a total absence of guilt.

Resistance at Disneyland

We touched on the limits to organizational culture's absorption in the chapter on culture but much more could be said. Van Maanen (1991) shows the limits to which overt company propaganda in the Disney organization can be effective. Satirical banter, mischievous winking, and playful exaggeration are to be found in the classroom with the new recruits. As one notes, 'It is difficult to take seriously an organization that provides its retirees with "Golden Ears" instead of gold watches after 20 or more years of service' (1991: 67). All the newcomers are aware that the label 'Disneyland' has both an unserious and artificial connotation. A full embrace of the Disneyland role would be as deviant as its full rejection.

Sometimes customers will overstep their role, insult an operator, challenge their authority, or disrupt the routines of the job. If a customer slights a ride operator, routine practices have been developed by the operators to deal with this. Common remedies include the 'seat-belt squeeze' where the deviant customer's seat-belt is adjusted to the extent that he or she is doubled over at the point of departure and left gasping. The 'break-toss' is where operators jump on the outside of a norm violator's car, unhitch the safety belt, then slam on the brakes, bringing the car to an almost instant stop while the driver flies over the bonnet. In the 'seat-belt snap' an offending customer receives a sharp quick snap of the hard plastic belt across the face or other part of the body while entering or exiting a seat-belted ride. The 'break up the party' gambit is a queuing device put into officious use to separate troublesome pairs into different units, thus forcing on them the pain of strange companions for the duration of a ride. Offensive guests can be drenched with water in the submarine ride. All these procedures, and more, are learnt on the job and enliven conversation time at breaks or after work. Naturally, though, operators are aware of the limits and if caught they know that restoration of corporate pride will be swift. Is this behaviour a sign of resistance to managerial control, demonstrating how ride operators are in control of their job and how it is managed? Should it be regarded as misbehaviour? Does it represent ways in which the operator copes with difficult demands of the job, especially difficult customers?

Resistance and Control among Nursing Auxiliaries and Care Assistants

Women are often portrayed as a compliant workforce but this is not necessarily the case. A study of work in a nursing home for older people (Lee-Treweek 1997) shows how female nursing auxiliary workers use resistance to get through each working day. The work is physically heavy, dirty (involving tasks such as washing soiled bodies), and low paid (wages can be as low as £1 per hour). It is assumed that this is women's work, easy and natural for women who are equipped to deal with bodily substances, are sympathetic, and that they might enjoy this type of work as 'caring people'. However, the main motivation for work was instrumental, earning a wage. Their carework had little to do with caring. Conveying this view to those outside the job was problematic for the auxiliaries.

The home's brochure advertised 'family type care' but the pressure to create the clean and orderly individual was far stronger. The main work for the nursing auxiliary was to create a sanitized 'lounge standard' patient. The product of the work was a clean, orderly, quiet patient; the work was about process and order, much the same as factory work.

Knowing the people was not about knowing patients as individuals, but about knowing the type of work and how to handle the patients. This knowledge was a source of both pride and resistance to the sheer drudgery and lack of control over the nature of the work. The nurses' knowledge and role was seen by the auxiliaries as inferior—it was clean work which was neither real nor necessary. The needs of the patient were often not met as 'needy' or 'sick' patients were reconstructed into attention-seeking, pretence, or wilful childishness; they were ignored even when they were talked about in their own presence. Incidents such as being hit by a patient were referred to as 'fun', so that personal toughness was elevated to a position of importance.

Similar disturbing descriptions of the realities of life for psychiatric nurses can be found (see Handy 1990). The issue of control over patients seems to be central in studies of nursing and care and of being tough, 'not being a bleeding, whining Minnie' (Bates 1990). Bates (1993) also shows how 16- to 18-year-old care assistants cope with violence, incontinence, and death in their daily work. To cope they 'switched off' and kept 'busy'. A significant proportion of the work the girls regarded as 'shit shovelling' (1993: 17). The social taboo of talking about incontinence was dealt with in part through a humorous language strategy: the reversal of shit to produce 'tish'. The trainee care assistants rejected and scorned the college tutor's stress of the need for sensitivity and genuine caring in their work. What they contested was the quality of care which they were expected to offer.

Lying

In 1968 Albert Carr argued that business is a game and, like other games, is played by its own set of rules. In particular he argued that bluffing (i.e. lying) is a convention that the rules of business both support and encourage. As business bluffing is conventional, it is not and should not be subject to norms applicable outside the business realm. Concern for morals appears to have disappeared from view.

Deception and lies have received little attention in the management literature yet we all know that they happen. People have ample opportunity either to lie or to tell the truth in the course of their work. Workers constantly report their behaviour or give information to others. The truck driver reports the number of hours on the road, the nurse charts vital signs, the public accountant audits, and the forester reports a tree census. Organizations generally rely on the reports to be accurate and honest but each of these individuals may have reasons to lie. We lie to avoid embarrassment or conflict, to impress others, cope with difficult situations, and to achieve personal gain. It has been estimated that between a half and a third of résumés, curricula vitae, contain lies (Cole-Golomski 1999; Edwards 1998; Prater and Kiser 2002). Lying jeopardizes information quality and therefore the integrity of organizations. It can have detrimental effects on how organizations function (Grover 1997).

Grover (1993a) has looked at the conditions under which employees tell lies. They will lie to protect their 'turf' or when faced with conflicting demands (role conflict). For example, the truck driver may lie about speeding because there is a conflict between organizational policy (which says speed limits must be followed) and external role demands (for example, they must pick the children up by six). The nurse's time may conflict with time demands of the job assignment, leading the nurse to report vital signs not actually measured. People may also lie out of self-interest, for example to get promoted, prevent themselves from being admonished, or to make more money. Grover (1993b) looks at the conditions under which professionals lie about their work behaviour. Again role conflict causes lying—when, for example, the physician has a professional ethic to cure patients by diagnosing and treating them as accurately as possible but may find that the costs of the procedure are prohibitive (prescribing Viagra, the impotency drug, is the example which springs to mind here).

Role conflict and self-interest will not explain all lying. Some people may have pathological tendencies toward lying, or may lie when instructed to do so by a superior, or as revenge in response to anger. Managers employ deceptive strategies to lie to workers about the opportunities of advancement, or deceive overworked individuals about possible relief, or create fear and anxiety by selective public reprimands. They will also display indiscriminate bursts of staged anger (Jackall 1980). Jackall (1980) also discusses how corporations lie. This was so, he says, in the case of thalidomide where, in order to continue high sales of the drug as a non-toxic tranquilizer, the managerial response to reports of children born with deformities was to 'Lie, suppress, bribe and distort' (The Insight Team 1979).

STOP

Would you Lie for your Boss?

A personal assistant told a court that lying was 'standard practice' in the City of London (Renshaw 1999). She created documents to help protect her boss. The former secretary to Colonel Oliver North said she was protecting her boss when she shredded nationally important documents in the Iran-Contra scandal in the USA. A personal assistant lied to her boss's wife about his whereabouts to cover up the boss's fling with a colleague. Another personal assistant says she often has to release information containing heavily inflated figures about attendances at seminars on behalf of her sales manager (Renshaw 1999). Would you lie? Under what circumstances would you lie?

ANOTHER EXAMPLE OF MISBEHAVIOUR? FEAR AND LOATHING

This can be a feature of organizational life too. It is documented in subject areas, like Organization Studies (Van Maanen 1995) when controversy breaks out between academics, in an 'academic blood sport called debate' (1995: 687). It happens in departments, sometimes to such an extent that a department is closed (Hayes 1998: 24). Here is how a story is told: 'Several of the key professors had come to hate each other for reasons known only to themselves and their mutual animosity grew so severe that they began putting obstacles in each other's paths and in the paths of the students of their rival professors. The bitterness became so intense that not a single student escaped having to undergo a great deal of pain and inconvenience. There were no victors, but every single person, whether student or professor, became a victim of this uncontrolled childish hatred.' One suspects that fear and loathing break out in all kinds of organizations.

Denial

Organizations can take on collective false images. For example an elite university department may be ridden with strife but maintain a positive, if false, public image. Its members may admit privately to the strife but in public they talk about how inspiring or stimulating it is to work there.

Recently Stanley Cohen (2001) has received acclaim for his study of denial—how we black out, turn a blind eye, shut off, and see only what we want to see. There are many occasions on which individuals and organizations are perfectly justified in claiming that an event did not happen, or not as it was alleged to have happened, or that it might have happened but without their knowledge. Denials and simple statement of fact are made in good faith. Evidence to counter evidence can be produced, claims checked, lies exposed, and proof presented. Games of truth are highly volatile.

There may be a conscious attempt to deceive, to lie. Cohen notes how no cognitive psychology textbook lists terms like denial in its index, yet denial may be perception without awareness, perceptual defence, a use of selective attention or simply perceptual error.

There are many horrific examples to be found in his work, drawing on the Holocaust and political murders. Concentration camps and prisons are organizations too. Businesses are involved in their creation and maintenance. In the case of the Holocaust the Post Office delivered notification of expropriation and deportation, the Finance Ministry confiscated wealth, businesses fired Jewish workers. Pharmaceutical companies tested drugs on concentration camp inmates. Travel agents booked one-way passages to camps; the same forms and procedures to book tourists going on holiday were used to send people to Auschwitz (Berenbaum 1993: 115). Companies bid for the contract to supply gas ovens. Others received the shaved hair from women's heads to process into felt while others melted down gold (10–12 kilograms a week by 1944) from jewelry and dental fillings. Each transaction was meticulously recorded by clerks (Cohen 2001). There are personal and collective denials of this history. Denial—in the sense of shutting out others' suffering—is the normal state of affairs.

Bullying

Research on bullying, sometimes referred to as 'mobbing' (particularly if it has involved singling a person out for victimization), has recently been undertaken in Europe, Scandinavia, the USA, and Australia. Organizations are places where bullying can take place. Bullying can take the form of persistent insults or offensive remarks, teasing, ridicule, persistent criticism, personal or even physical abuse, and usually involves a person with power in a hierarchy bullying a subordinate (Hoel et al. 2001). The victims of bullying can suffer from severe psychological stress symptoms such as anxiety, depression, irritability, and self-hate (Zapf et al. 1996). The prevalence of bullying, if defined as exposure to two acts per week for at least six months, reveals figures ranging from 2.7 per cent to 8 per cent of employees. If defined as at least one negative act in a week for six months, between 8 and 25 per cent of respondents can be classified as victims of bullying

(Mikkelson and Einarsen 2001). A study of Finnish business school graduates showed 8.8 per cent reported exposure to bullying at least occasionally during the previous twelve months (Salin 2001). A study of male workers in a Norwegian shipyard revealed the prevalence of bullying to be as high as 17 per cent (Einarsen and Skogstad 1996). Some have shown that women are significantly over-represented among those classifying themselves as bullied (Hoel et al. 2001) but others have found approximately equal victimization rates for men and women (Einarsen and Skogstad 1996; Leymann 1992).

Greater pressure on managers for increased competitiveness can create an environment ripe for bullying (Lewis 1999). Organizational restructuring is one time when workplace bullying may be facilitated because restructuring can lead to job insecurity as people worry about possible redundancies and the extra demands it can put on remaining employees (Kearns et al. 1997). One study found that 60 per cent of managers had experienced large-scale restructuring in the previous twelve months—such processes feed perceptions of job insecurity that make employees feel vulnerable (Worral and Cooper 1999). However poor work design, deficient leadership, a socially exposed victim, unresolved escalated conflict (Zapf 1999) or a low moral standard in a department can also lead to bullying (Einarsen 1999).

Some would argue that the very act of managing, then, can be seen as bullying. 'Institutionalized tyranny' divests employees of their former identities and drives home the overriding importance of compliance. Some researchers believe that organizations simply facilitate petty tyranny rather than actively promoting it (e.g. Ashforth 1994). However others take a less generous view and argue that management requires the exercise of power and by its very nature promotes tyranny of varying degrees of subtlety (Alvesson and Deetz 1996; Mumby and Stohl 1996).

Most research in this area has looked at percentages of employees being bullied by using a survey, questionnaire method. Respondents are given a list of items like the incidence of verbal abuse or practical jokes and asked how often they have been subjected to that negative act in the last six months. The person may not however see these incidents as bullying. Research on bullying has shown that many victims are either unaware of the fact that they are being bullied or will not admit this is the case (Mikkelsen and Einarsen 2001). When the Finnish professionals with a university degree in business studies were provided with a definition of bullying, 8.8 per cent of respondents (as we have seen) reported they had at least occasionally been bullied during the past twelve months. However when presented with a list of 32 predefined negative and potentially harassing acts, as many as 24 per cent reported they had been subjected to at least one of the negative acts on a weekly basis (Salin 2001).

Recently researchers have looked at how the term bullying was used by employees in a call centre, just using interviewing rather than a questionnaire (Liefooghe and Mackenzie Davey 2001). They found that the rules regarding call-handling time, threat of dismissal, discipline, sickness policies, and being forced to change jobs to fit in with the needs of the organization were all seen as bullying. The organization itself rather than individuals within it were seen as responsible for the bullying practices.

Sabotage

Few academic studies exist on sabotage. It is often a rational and calculative act. Sabotage is deliberate action or inaction that is intended to damage, destroy, or disrupt some aspect of the workplace environment (the property, product, process, or reputation). Examples include destruction of machinery or goods, work slowdowns, passing on defective work, flattening tyres, scratching cars, intentionally misplacing important paperwork, offering a chemical company's new formula to a competitor, erasing financial records, or introducing a computer virus. Taylor and Walton (1971: 219) define sabotage as 'the conscious act of mutilation or destruction' that reduces tension and frustration. They quote the case of a frustrated salesman in a Knightsbridge store who demobilized a machine which shuttled change around the store by ramming a cream bun down its gullet and the time a half-mile of Blackpool rock had to be throw away as it carried the terse words 'F . . . Off'. Industrial sabotage may be an attempt to reduce tension and frustration, an attempt to ease the work process (by creating a break time), a way of having fun, or an attempt to assert control. It also may be an important index of underlying industrial conflict.

An early study of sabotage can be found in Dubois (1979). While sabotage may be done by workers, it can also be done by management, he says. Non-productive time is sabotage—when machines are out of order, there is poor planning, shortage of raw materials, inadequate consideration of siting of machinery—all of these can be seen as management sabotage. Lock-outs and strikes bring production to a halt. Sabotage by management is far more serious than sabotage from workers. Sabotage, LaNuez and Jermier (1994) argue, is a result of low levels of control. Both managers and workers can experience low levels of control due to mergers and restructuring, increased use of monitoring and other control techniques, technological changes that replace skilled labour with less skilled labour, and displacement. Sabotage can be seen as a strategic weapon that can be used by any person to revise power imbalances or seek to re-establish control of their work or workplace. Similarly they may choose to 'whistleblow', to disclose illegal, unethical, or harmful practices in the workplace to parties who might take action (see Miceli and Near 1997; Rothschild and Miethe 1994).

Struggles over Time

The control over working time is always a source of struggle between workers and managers. In spite of employer opposition, 'Saint Monday' was kept as a rest day in Birmingham throughout the nineteenth century. Workplace studies have shown that time is struggled over and negotiated. The accounts show that the action with respect to time might be in an effort to relieve the monotony of work, as in Roy's (1960) study of machine operators, or as a way of creating time away from work, as in Ditton's (1979) study of a factory bakery.

Recently Heyes (1997) has shown how workers in a chemical plant created opportunities for overtime and enhanced earnings through what management termed 'illegitimate' absenteeism and the workers called 'knocking'. Knocking took two forms. In one a pair of workers from separate shifts would collaborate; a worker might deliberately go sick for a shift while his workmate would voluntarily provide cover at an overtime premium. The following week the roles would be reversed and the gains from knocking were thus shared. The second form was known as the '8 plus 4' system. A worker on an eight-hour day shift would volunteer to work the extra four hours of someone who had been unable to fulfil (had knocked off) a twelve-hour shift. Again there was an explicit, reciprocal agreement in order to enhance joint incomes. Workers also regarded occasional absences (3.5 per cent of contractual hours on average) as a necessary means of gaining relief from the pressures of a hard, physically intensive, and dangerous job.

Organizational Misdemeanour: Does Organizational Romance Fit?

Organizational romances are commonplace and have increased in number (Collins 1983; Mainiero 1993; Roy 1974). Organizations are natural breeding grounds for romantic involvements. There is abundant evidence that individuals tend to prefer others with similar attitudes (Smith et al. 1983) and similar attitudes are often found amongst people working together. The Alfred Marks Bureau (1991, 1995) found that 58 per cent of respondents in their surveys had experienced at least one relationship at work and over half the romantic relationships that start off in the office end in marriage.

STOP

Consensual Relationships between Staff and Students at University

University teachers are advised not to develop intimate relationships with students. If they do develop a consensual relationship, the university teacher is asked to declare that a relationship has developed and ask that another member of staff assess the student's work. Is this what you witness as good practice?

Romantic relationships can, however, produce a serious practical problem because they can distort the smooth functioning of organizations (Quinn 1977). There have been some high-level cases of romantic entanglements that have had devastating effects on careers. The Cecil Parkinson (senior politician)—Sara Keays (his secretary) affair in Britain and the Mary Cunningham (Bendix corporation)—Willam Agee case in the USA demonstrate the career risks (Harrison and Lee 1986). Initially couples usually try to keep their relationship a secret because some organizations have explicit rules against romantic relationships and fear of gossip and disapproval fosters secrecy. Where one or both participants is married, the predominant fear is that family members find out. There can be negative impacts if favouritism or special treatment is shown to the new partner in the relationship; this causes jealousy and resentment (Lobel et al. 1994). Sometimes hostility can be generated by the romance in a work group and output and productivity lowered (Mainiero 1986). Couples can experience role conflict, conflict between personal and professional roles. For example, if the lovers attend a presentation ceremony dinner along with the company's top executives. During dinner someone at the table suggests to the male executive that it is inappropriate to bring his lover along as her corporate status is not the same as the other executive guests (Collins 1983). A more disruptive impact can come about when the affair ends (Warfield 1987). In office romances that cross the lines of authority in an organization there is the potential for exploitation of the relations. For example, sexual favours to the boss could be returned for promotion. Conversely a boss may manipulate a subordinate by threatening to withdraw from the relationship unless a work deadline is met (Mainiero 1993). In the most extreme cases the affair can lead to a harassment claim. There have been a number of high-level harassment cases recently, for example Bill Clinton/Paula Jones (American Lawyer 1997; Macleans 1998; Taylor 1997) and Anita Hill/Clarence Thomas (Trix and Sankar 1998).

It would be wrong to leave the impression that the impact of romantic relationships is only negative. Mainiero (1989) describes several cases in which couples reported that their personal and professional lives were enhanced by an office romantic involvement. For example, one couple found that when a deadline had to be met, they worked together at home to meet that deadline. In another case the couple reported they had benefited from each other's critical comment on management style and work behaviour. The sexual harassment research literature tends to show, however, that for every happy outcome, there are many more unhappy ones.

Sexual Harassment

Harassment too is, of course, misbehaviour (Wilson 2000, 2003; Wilson and Thompson 2001). Sexual harassment can take many forms from leering, whistling, and suggestive gestures through to sexual blackmail. Much of the teasing, flirting, and joking that goes on at work between the sexes is not sexual harassment because it is mutual. Most sexual behaviour at work is seen as benign or positive (Witz et al. 1994). Sexual behaviour becomes harassment when it is unwanted and intrusive, when it offends and threatens. In the workplace harassers are usually male supervisors or managers.

Women are more likely to define more experiences as harassing than men. Sexual harassment is a pervasive problem; it is estimated that just over half of British working women have been harassed (Industrial Society 1993). Women are most likely to be harassed where they are in jobs dominated by men. For example a study of policewomen (Gregory and Lees 1999) found that nearly all had experienced some form of sexual harassment. Sexual harassment has recently become widespread over the telephone, particularly in call centres (Sczensky and Stahlberg 2000). Most of those harassed do nothing about it; they hope the offender will stop. The victims often fear not being taken seriously if they complain, do not want to challenge the position of the harasser, or fear reprisals. Sexual harassment remains, then, common organizational behaviour.

Gossip

Gossip too is intrinsic to organizational life (Noon and Delbridge 1993). It is idle chat or conversation which can be positive or negative (Fine and Rosnow 1978), malicious or harmless (Guendouzi 1996), praise or blame (Elias and Scotson 1965), cooperative or competitive (Guendouzi 2001). Gossip is associated almost exclusively with women; studies of oral culture confirm this (e.g. Jones 1980) but men too participate in it and can be the subject of study (see Johnson 1994).

Gossip flourishes in close-knit communities and facilitates social bonds between people (Harrington and Bielby 1995). In organizational behaviour, gossip is informal communication of value-laden information about members of a social setting (Noon and Delbridge 1993). It is about exchange of information between at least two people about a non-present third party (Blum-Kulka 2000). Gossip serves many functions. It can provide the gossiper with a means of indirect attack, having lower risk than a direct attack. It can be used to impart information, influence others, or as entertainment. It may secure personal gain or status for the gossipers, if they have information considered important. It can be motivated by self-interest amongst rivals. The power dynamics of gossip are that the balance is tilted in favour of the producer and not the consumer (Harrington and Bielby 1995).

The most interesting gossip is information that deals with violations of moral codes (Shibutani 1966). The more scandalous the information and the more it concerns people within the group, the more gossip-worthy the information. But this could be dangerous information to spread so the potential gossiper has to consider who to tell and the impact the information might have. For women in particular where the social conventions of femininity carry with them obligations of 'behaving nicely' (Coates 2000) the risk for malicious gossip instigators is being labelled 'a bitch' (Guendouzi 2001).

STOP

An Example of Deceit or Impression Management?

The gossip in one company was that the managing director, who was rumoured to be in personal debt, was said to 'dress down' when she met tax inspectors in an attempt to conceal her spending and engender their sympathy (Myers 2002).

Gossip and power are linked (Kurland 2000). One effect of negative gossip is that it may enhance coercive power (see the chapter on power). When the gossiper relates negative news about a third party, recipients may infer that the gossiper could also spread negative information about them. Positive gossip in contrast is likely to affect reward power as the recipient may infer that the gossiper could spread positive information about them. It is apt to influence expert power if it facilitates the exchange of data and helps build a knowledge base. It may detract referent power of the gossiper if gossip is seen as a small or petty activity but positive gossip can enhance the reputation of people.

The business literature deals with gossip as bad and something that should be eradicated by managers; employees who are gossiping are not working hard enough. However gossip plays a vital role in group formation, regulation, and perpetuation so the removal of gossip is not possible unless there is a complete ban on all communication. Other commentators suggest that managers should accept the existence of gossip as a natural part of organizational life and attempt to manipulate it for their own benefit (Davis 1973; Hirschhorn 1983). However gossip can help the functioning of an organization, it can communicate rules, values, and morals. It facilitates the diffusion of organizational tradition and history and maintains the exclusivity of the group. It may provide an explanation of matters that otherwise would not have been clear so can relieve feelings of insecurity and anxiety; it can smooth interpersonal and intergroup strains. It may be a vehicle for social change (Noon and Delbridge 1993). Gossip may also be fun.

Fun

Fun has been touched upon in other chapters, particularly where we have looked at how individuals resist organizational culture's constraints. The presence of horseplay and humour is also found in research on hospitals (Goffman 1968), coalmines (Pitt 1979), building sites (Riemer 1979), schools (Willis 1977), and shop floors (Burawoy 1979; Pollert 1981; Roy 1960). Humour serves many purposes. Roy described how the machinists avoided 'going nuts' by teasing and using mock aggression. Racial hostility was found to be diluted by humour in Burawoy's study. Linstead (1985) found that joking was closely related to resistance and sabotage. Joking helped establish an informal world outside the constraints of management control. Showing the collective elements of joking and exploring the contradictions and divisions that characterize shop-floor relations, Collinson (1988) focuses on gender identity and working-class resistance in a lorry-producing factory. He shows that humour served as resistance both to the tightly controlled repetitious work tasks and to the organization of production. The men wanted to make the best of the situation and enjoy the company of others. They were concerned to show that they could laugh at themselves. The use of nicknames like 'Fat Rat', 'Bastard Jack', 'Big Lemon', and 'The Snake' created a mythical and imaginary world. 'Electric Lips' was unable to keep a secret. 'Pot Harry' had broken all the drinking pots, mugs, by dropping them. They also wanted to differentiate themselves from white-collar staff and managers. They did this by, for example, expressing how manual work was the very essence of masculinity. The joking culture was a symbol of freedom and autonomy. The uncompromising banter of the shop floor, permeated with swearing, ridicule, displays of sexuality, and pranks, was contrasted, exaggerated, and elevated above the middle-class politeness, cleanliness, and more restrained demeanour of office staff.

Humour could also mean conformity. There were demands of group conformity, specific rules that led to social survival. Individuals had to be able to take a joke, laugh at themselves, and expected others to do the same. They needed to be aggressive, critical, and disrespectful. Apprentices had to learn to accept degrading initiation ceremonies. Humour also meant control, being used as pressure to conform to routine shop-floor values and practices, mutual control, and discipline. For example, there was a steady stream of cutting remarks to control 'deviants', lazy workers.

There are choices in how managers view the issues discussed here. They can clamp down on the activities and exercise greater control; this is likely to lead to further resistance. Or they can learn to live with these realities, as authors like Mars suggest. Fox (1973) offers us a framework to help consider potential conflict. He says there are two frames of reference, the unitary and pluralist perspective. If managers adopt a unitarist perspective they believe that within their organization there is the potential for unity, partnership, and harmony, if it does not already exist. In this organization there will be one source of authority and one focus of loyalty; the organization could, and maybe does, function much like a healthy functioning sports team. Management and workers should be striving jointly to meet company goals. Individuals should accept the authority of those who manage and managers are best qualified to manage. Managers motivate and promote an *esprit de corps*. Your organization is like a team, striving to achieve common goals. Any conflict is either negligible, caused by poor communication, stupidity, or the work of agitators. This view, Fox would argue, would wish to deny that theft, strikes, conflict, and sabotage exist. This view is only maintained because it suits the needs of management. Denial of conflict may be one way in which managers cope with conflict; denial of reality is one way psychologists have found individuals cope (Edwards 1990).

A pluralist perspective would represent a more accurate description of what really happens; it would accept the existence of several different but related interest groups, each with its own leaders, loyalties, and objectives. Management and workers are two different groups who have conflicting interests. Here conflict, sabotage, and so on are seen as inevitable and a natural component of work. A certain amount of overt conflict is welcomed as a sign that aspirations are neither being drowned by hopelessness nor suppressed by power (see Armstrong and Dawson 1989, for a fuller description of the frames of reference).

A third and radical approach would say that a pluralist ideology does not address the full extent of conflict. It does not fully appreciate the differences in power between managers and workers. This approach would focus on the power differences between various groupings and would show that management's power is greater than it appears. Employees are totally dependent on the organization and have little power or influence. Sabotage, theft, fun, and so on are some of the few ways employees have of undermining managerial power and control. What perspective would be useful in considering the next case of a game involving making tips and cheating?

A Case: The 'Game of Making Tips' and Cheating in Casinos

Worker solidarity in the casino industry in the United States is induced by the industry's shared tip structure in which individual dealer's tips are pooled together and split evenly among all workers (Sallaz 2002). Tipping constitutes 75 to 85 per cent of a dealer's income. As the most experienced dealer's income was dependent on the tip-making ability of the least experienced and newest of dealers, new workers were 'taken under the wing' of veteran dealers and taught the group's tip-making tactics.

The standard method of tipping is to offer a 'toke bet'. The player places a smaller side bet 'for the dealer' next to their bet before the game begins. If the player wins the dealer earns a tip which is deposited in a 'toke box' and evenly distributed among all the dealers at the end of the shift. The dealer is only tipped when the player wins, otherwise both bets to the house. The maximum tips will be made if dealing is fast. Non-tippers are treated rudely and forced off the table. Novice players (who are likely not to know about toke bets and tipping) find that attention will be drawn to the tipping structure by, for example, the dealer thanking a tipper in an exaggerated tone. Having made players aware of the toke system, dealers must make clear that tips are not gratuities or gifts but rather a fee for service rendered. Dealers might whisper advice to a player, improving the 'service'. Veteran roulette dealers can, with varying degrees of accuracy and consistency, 'set the ball down' in particular numbers by coordinating their spinning of the ball with that of the wheel (Sallaz 2002).

Dealers have regularly cheated. They might slyly pocket money when supervisors were out of sight or use special shuffling techniques to 'set the deck' for a confederate playing at the table (Nelson 1978). In the past despotic control managers and owners of casinos have used severe tactics to stop cheating. Owners would walk the floor and monitor workers. If dealers were caught cheating, they were fired on the spot (Binion 1973; Nelson 1978). If the cheating was serious, two others would hold the dealer down. A third 'goon' would wield a baseball bat and bring it down on the dealer's hands, smashing them beyond repair. 'The dealer was then dragged through the casino, with the blood dripping from his crushed fingers' (Reid and Demaris 1963: 52).

Actions designed to stop cheating, with less serious consequences, involved instructing workers never to display emotions while dealing. The advice was to 'dummy up and deal' (Solkey 1980). Talking to players was seen as risky behaviour and seldom necessary. Shuffling machines and multi-deck shoes served to maximize the speed and security of dealing by eliminating dealer skill and discretion. Electronic surveillance technology is used to monitor workers closely. A black ceiling globe houses a video camera above each table and relays to a central control room staffed by surveillance specialists. The dealer's uniforms are designed to maximize security. Tight cuffs on long sleeved shirts ensure they do not slide chips up their sleeves; aprons prevent them from accessing their pockets while at the tables.

■ SUGGESTIONS FOR FURTHER READING

1. Giacalone, R. A., and Greenberg, J. (1997), *Antisocial Behaviour in Organizations*, London: Sage.
2. Mars, G. (1984), *Cheats at Work: An Anthropology of Workplace Crime*, London: Unwin Paperbacks.
3. Noon, M., and Blyton, P. (2002), *The Realities of Work* (2nd edn.), Basingstoke: Palgrave Macmillan. See 'Time and Work' in chapter 4 and chapter 9 on survival strategies that discusses how and why employees 'fiddle'. These chapters help challenge the view that all rule bending is problematic.
4. Punch, M. (1996), *Dirty Business: Exploring Corporate Misconduct. Analysis and Cases*, London: Sage.

5. Brewis, J. (2000), 'Sex, Work and Sex at Work: Using Foucault to Understand Organizational Relations', ch. 5 in J. Barry et al. (eds.), *Organization and Management: A Critical Text*, London: Thompson Learning. You will find links here with the chapters on power and control and rationality and bureaucracy.

6. Ackroyd, S., and Thompson, P. (1999), *Organizational Misbehaviour*, London: Sage. This book documents all kinds of misbehaviour. You will see lots of connections between this book and many of the chapters here.

7. Gabriel, Y., Fineman, S., and Sims, D. (2000), *Organizing and Organizations* (2nd edn.), London: Sage. Chapter 13 is on sex in organizations.

■ WEB LINKS

For more on Stanley Cohen see **www.lse.ac.uk/people/s.cohen@lse.ac.uk/**

Or **www.mngt.waikato.ac.nz/depts/sml/journal/vol3_2/croci.htm** for more on the work of Maurice Punch, a former professor at The Netherlands School of Business.

■ QUESTIONS

1. Compare and contrast two of Punch's (1996) cases of organizational misdemeanour.

2. What, according to the research, are the negative impacts of romantic relationships at work? What are the positive aspects? How have organizations responded?

3. Academics have criticized the film *Disclosure* for the way in which it portrays sexual harassment in an organization. What is wrong with the film (see Brewis 1998)?

4. Even when people are trained, paid, and told to be nice, it is hard for them to do so all of the time. Why? (See, for example, Van Maanen 1991.)

5. Handy (1990) describes how psychiatric nurses have both to control and to care for the mentally ill, which creates some highly distressing consequences. What is the problem, as described by Handy (see Handy 1990 and 1995)?

6. 'Sabotage is bound up with the private ownership of the means of production and will disappear only when that does' (Dubois 1979: 213). Discuss.

7. There is a danger that in the case of careworkers, the researcher (Lee-Treweek) is 'throwing stones at angels'. Read the article yourself and see how Lee-Treweek would handle this criticism. If you had done this research and found nothing positive to say about the careworkers, how would you have handled this?

■ GROUP EXERCISES

1. Put groups of students into the roles of hawks, vultures, donkeys, wolves, and managers. Ask them to research their potential role and be prepared the next week to play out their roles with the managers. The managers wish to stop the thieving practices. The hawks, vultures, donkeys, and wolves want to maintain the status quo.

2. Describe some of your own experiences of theft, sabotage, or fun at work to the class or use video extracts to illustrate. Divide the class into groups and ask students to share their experiences. Ask that a spokesperson from each group comes to the front and presents the stories from their group they liked best to the rest of the class.

■ REFERENCES

Alfred Marks Bureau (1991), *Meeting Your Partner at Work: A Quantitative Report on the Frequency and Effects of Relationships at Work* (Dec.), Borehamwood, Herts: Alfred Marks Bureau.

——(1995), *Does Cupid Work in Your Office?* (Feb.), Borehamwood, Herts: Alfred Marks Bureau.

American Lawyer (1997), 'Principles, Politics and Paula Jones', *American Lawyer*, 19/1: 49.

Alvesson, M., and Deetz, S. (1996), 'Critical Theory and Post Modernism: Approaches to Organizational Studies', in S. R. Clegg and C. Hardy (eds.), *Studying Organization: Theory and Method*, London: Sage.

Armstrong, P., and Dawson, C. (1989), *People in Organizations* (4th edn.), Cambridge: ELM Publications.

Ashforth, B. (1994), 'Petty Tyranny in Organizations', *Human Relations*, 47/7: 755–78.

Ashworth, J. (1999), 'Blowing the Whistle on the Office Fraudsters', *The Times*, 26 Jan., p. 17.

Bates, I. (1990), 'No Bleeding, Whining Minnies: The Role of YTS in Class and Gender Reproduction', *British Journal of Education and Work*, 3: 91–110.

——(1993), 'A Job which is "Right for Me"? Social Class, Gender and Individualization', ch. 1 in I. Bates and G. Riseborough (eds.), *Youth and Inequality*, Buckingham: Open University Press.

Berenbaum, M. (1993), *The World Must Know: The History of the Holocaust as Told in the United States Holocaust Museum*, Boston: Little, Brown & Co.

Binion, L. B. (1973), 'Some Recollections of a Texas and Las Vegas Gaming Operator', Reno: University of Nevada Oral History Program cited in Sallaz 2002.

Blum-Kulka, S. (2000), 'Gossipy Events at Family Dinners: Negotiating Sociability, Presence and the Moral Other', in J. Coupland (ed.), *Small Talk*, Harlow: Pearson.

Brewis, J. (1998), 'What is Wrong with this Picture? Sex and Gender Relations in Disclosure', ch. 4 in J. Hassard and R. Holliday (eds.), *Organization Representation: Work and Organizations in Popular Culture*, London: Sage.

Burawoy, M. (1979), *Manufacturing Consent*, Chicago: Chicago University Press.

Carr, A. Z. (1968), 'Is Business Bluffing Ethical?', *Harvard Business Review*, 46/1: 143–53.

Coates, J. (2000), 'Small Talk and Subversion: The Female Speakers Backstage', in J. Coupland (ed.), *Small Talk*, Harlow: Pearson.

Cohen, S. (2001), *States of Denial: Knowing about Atrocities and Suffering*, Cambridge: Polity Press.

Cole-Gomolski, B. (1999), 'Job Applicants Finding Fake Credentials on the Web', *Computerworld*, 7 Sept., 32/36: 6.

Collins, E. G. (1983), 'Managers and Lovers', *Harvard Business Review*, 16/5: 142–53.

Collinson, D. L. (1988), 'Engineering Humour: Masculinity, Joking and Conflict in Shop Floor Relations', *Organization Studies*, 9/2: 181–99.

Davis, K. (1973), 'The Care and Cultivation of the Corporate Grapevine', *Management Review*, 62: 53–5.

Delaney, J. (1993), 'Handcuffing Employee Theft', *Small Business Report*, 18: 29–38.

Ditton, J. (1977), *Part-Time Crime: An Ethnography of Fiddling and Pilferage*, London: Macmillan.

Ditton, J. (1979), 'Baking Time', *Sociological Review*, 27: 157–67.

Dubois, P. (1979), *Sabotage in Industry*, Harmondsworth: Penguin.

Edwards, A. (1998), 'True or False?', *Business Journal: Serving Jacksonville and Northeast Florida*, 7 Aug., 13/443: 33.

Edwards, J. R. (1990), 'The Determinants and Consequences of Coping with Stress', ch. 8 in C. Cooper and R. Payne (eds.), *Causes, Coping and Consequences of Stress at Work*. Chichester: John Wiley.

Einarsen, S. (1999), 'The Nature and Causes of Bullying at Work', *International Journal of Manpower*, 20/1–2: 16–27.

——and Skogstad, A. (1996), 'Bullying at Work: Epidemiological Findings in Public and Private Organizations', *European Journal of Work and Organizational Psychology*, 5: 185–201.

Elias, N., and Scotson, J. L. (1965), *The Established and the Outsiders*, London: Frank Cass.

Fine, G. A., and Rosnow, R. L. (1978), 'Gossip, Gossipers and Gossiping', *Personality and Social Psychology Bulletin*, 4/1: 161–8.

Fox, A. (1973), 'Industrial Relations: A Social Critique of Pluralist Ideology', in J. Child (ed.), *Man and Organization*, London: Allen & Unwin.

Giacalone, R. A., and Greenberg, J. (1997), *Antisocial Behaviour in Organizations*, London: Sage.

Goffman, E. (1968), *Asylums*, Harmondsworth: Penguin.

Greenberg, J. (1997), 'The Steal Motive: Managing the Social Determinants of Employee Theft', ch. 5 in R. A. Giacalone and J. Greenberg, *Antisocial Behaviour in Organizations*, London: Sage.

——and Scott, K. S. (1996), 'Why do Workers Bite the Hands that Feed Them? Employee Theft as a Social Exchange Process', in B. M. Staw and L. L. Cummings (eds.), *Research in Organizational Behavior*, 18, Greenwich, Conn.: JAI Press, pp. 111–56.

Gregory, J., and Lees, S. (1999), *Policing Sexual Assault*, London: Routledge.

Grover, S. L. (1993*a*), 'Lying, Deceit and Subterfuge: A Model of Dishonesty in the Workplace', *Organizational Science*, 4/3: 478–95.

——(1993*b*), 'Why Professionals Lie: The Impact of Professional Role Conflict on Reporting Accuracy', *Organizational Behavior and Human Decision Processes*, 55: 251–72.

——(1997), 'Lying in Organizations: Theory, Research and Future Directions', ch. 4 in R. A. Giacalone and J. Greenberg (eds.), *Antisocial Behaviour in Organizations*, London: Sage.

Guendouzi, J. (1996), 'Gossip: Some Problematics for Definitions and Gendered Talk', in *Papers in Linguistics for the University of Manchester*, i. 61–75, Manchester: University of Manchester Press.

——(2001), 'You'll think we're always bitching: The Functions of Cooperativity and Competition in Women's Gossip', *Discourse Studies*, 3/1: 29–51.

Handy, J. (1990), *Occupational Stress in a Caring Profession*, Aldershot: Avebury.

——(1995), 'Rethinking Stress: Seeing the Collective', ch. 4 in T. Newton (with J. Handy and S. Fineman), *Managing Stress: Emotion and Power at Work*. London: Sage.

Harrington, C. L., and Bielby, D. D. (1995), 'Where did you hear that? Technology and the Social Organization of Gossip', *Sociological Quarterly*, 36/3: 607–28.

Harrison, R., and Lee, R. (1986), 'Love at Work', *Personnel Management* (Jan.), 20–4.

Hayes, R. P. (1998), *Land of No Buddha: Reflections of a Sceptical Buddhist*, Birmingham: Windhorse Publications.

Heyes, J. (1997), 'Annualized Hours and the "Knock": The Organization of Working Time in a Chemicals Plant', *Work, Employment and Society*, 11/1: 65–81.

Hirschhorn, L. (1983), 'Managing Rumors during Retrenchment', *SAM Advanced Management Journal*, 48: 5–11.

Hoel, H., Cooper, C. L., and Faragher, B. (2001), 'The Experience of Bullying in Great Britain: The Impact of Organizational Status', *European Journal of Work and Organizational Psychology*, 10/4: 443–65.

Industrial Society (1993), *No Offence? Sexual Harassment, How it Happens and How to Beat it*, London: Industrial Society.

Insight Team of The Sunday Times of London (1979), *Suffer the Children: The Story of Thalidomide*, New York: Viking, esp. ch. 7.

Jackall, R. (1980), 'Structural Invitations to Deceit: Some Reflections on Bureaucracy and Morality', *Berkshire Review*, 15: 49–61.

Jermier, J. M., Knights, D., and Nord, W. R. (1994) (eds.), *Resistance and Power in Organizations*, London: Routledge.

Johnson, S. (1994), 'A Game of Two Halves: On Men, Football and Gossip', *Journal of Gender Studies*, 3/2: 145–54.

Jones, D. (1980), 'Gossip: Notes on Women's Oral Culture', *Women's Studies International Quarterly*, 3/193–8, repr. in D. Cameron (ed.), *The Feminist Critique of Language, A Reader*, London: Routledge, pp. 242–50.

Kearns, D., McCarthy, P., and Sheehan, M. (1997), *Organizational Restructuring: Considerations for Workplace Rehabilitation, Australian Journal of Rehabilitation Counselling*, 3/1: 21–9.

Kurland, N. B. (2000), 'Passing the Word: Toward a Model of Gossip and Power in the Workplace', *Academy of Management Review*, 25/2: 428–39.

LaNuez, D., and Jermier, J. M. (1994), 'Sabotage by Managers and Technocrats: Neglected Patterns of Resistance at Work', in J. M. Jermier, D. Knights, and W. R. Nord (eds.), *Resistance and Power in Organizations*, London: Routledge.

Lee-Treweek, G. (1997), 'Women, Resistance and Care: An Ethnographic Study of Nursing Auxiliary Work', *Work, Employment and Society*, 11/1 (Mar.), 47–63.

Lewis, D. (1999), 'UK Workplace Bullying: HRM Friend or Foe?', paper presented at the ninth European Congress on Work and Organizational Psychology, Helsinki, Finland, cited in Liefooghe and Mackenzie Davey (2001).

Leymann, H. (1992), *Adult Bullying at Swedish Workplaces: A Nation-wide Study Based on 2438 interviews*, Sweden: Swedish National Board of Occupational Safety and Health.

Liefooghe, A. P., and Mackenzie Davey, K. (2001), 'Accounts of Workplace Bullying: The Role of Organization', *European Journal of Work and Organizational Psychology*, 10/4: 375–92.

Linstead, S. (1985), 'Breaking the "Purity Rule": Industrial Sabotage and the Symbolic Process', *Personnel Review*, 14/3: 12–19.

Lobel, S. A., Quinn, R. E., St Clair, L., and Warfield, A. (1994), 'Love without Sex: The Impact of Psychological Intimacy between Men and Women at Work', *Organizational Dynamics*, 23: 5–16.

McGurn, T. (1988), 'Spotting the Thieves who Work among Us', *Wall Street Journal* (7 Mar.), 16A.

Macleans (1998), 'Is Clinton Home Free?' *Macleans*, 111: 15, 13.

Mainiero, L. A. (1986), 'A Review and Analysis of Power Dynamics in Organizational Romances', *Academy of Management Review*, 11/4: 750–62.

——(1989), *Office Romance: Love, Power and Sex in the Workplace*, New York: Macmillan.

——(1993), 'Dangerous Liaisons? A Review of Current Issues Concerning Male and Female Romantic Relationships in the Workplace', ch. 6 in E. A. Fagenson (ed.), *Women in Management: Trends, Issues and Challenges in Managerial Diversity*, London: Sage.

Mars, G. (1982), *Cheats at Work*. London: Allen & Unwin.

Mars, G. (1989), 'Hotel Pilferage: A Case of Occupational Threat', ch. 21 in C. Littler (ed.), *The Experience of Work*, Milton Keynes: Open University Press.

Miceli, M. P., and Near, J. P. (1997), 'Whistle-Blowing as Antisocial Behavior', ch. 7 in R. A. Giacalone and J. Greenberg (eds.), *Antisocial Behaviour in Organizations*, London: Sage.

Mikkelsen, E. G., and Einarsen, S. (2001), 'Bullying in Danish Work Life', *European Journal of Work and Organizational Psychology*, 10/4: 393–413.

Mumby, D. K., and Stohl, C. (1996), 'Disciplining Organizational Communication Studies', *Management Communication Quarterly*, 10/1: 50–72.

Myers, P. (2002), 'Customers, Boardrooms and Gossip: Theme Repetition and Metapatterns in the Texture of Organizing', *Human Relations*, 55/6: 669–90.

Nelson, W. (1978), *Gaming from the Old Days to Computers*, Reno: University of Nevada Oral History Program.

Nichols, T. (1997), *The Sociology of Industrial Injury*, London: Mansell.

Noon, M., and Delbridge, R. (1993), 'News from behind my Hand: Gossip in Organizations', *Organization Studies*, 14/1: 23–36.

Pitt, M. (1979), *The World on our Backs*, London: Lawrence & Wishart.

Pollert, A. (1981), *Girls, Wives, Factory Lives*, London: Macmillan.

Prater, T., and Kiser, S. B. (2002), 'Lies, Lies and More Lies', *SAM Advanced Management Journal*, 67/2: 9–14.

Punch, M. (1996), *Dirty Business: Exploring Corporate Misconduct. Analysis and Cases*, London: Sage.

Quinn, R. E. (1977), 'Coping With Cupid: The Formation, Impact and Management of Romantic Relationships in Organizations', *Administrative Science Quarterly*, 22: 30–45.

Reid, E., and Demaris, O. (1963), *The Green Felt Jungle*, New York: Trident Press.

Renshaw, R. (1999), 'Should you cover up for the boss? *The Times*, 24 Nov., Crème, p. 7.

Riemer, J. W. (1979), *Hard Hats*, London: Sage.

Rothschild, J., and Miethe, T. D. (1994), 'Whistleblowing as Resistance in Modern Work Organizations', ch. 8 in J. M. Jermier, D. Knights, and W. R. Nord (eds.), *Resistance and Power in Organizations*. London: Routledge.

Roy, D. F. (1960), 'Banana Time: Job Satisfaction and Informal Interaction', *Human Organization*, 18: 158–68.

——(1974), 'Sex in the Factory: Informal Heterosexual Relations between Supervisors and Work Groups', in C. Bryant (ed.), *Sexual Deviancy and Social Proscription*, New York: Human Sciences Press.

Salin, D. (2001), 'Bullying among Professionals: The Role of Work Overload and Organizational Politics', paper presented at the 10th European Congress on Work and Organizational Psychology, Prague, May, and cited in Mikkelsen and Einarsen (2001).

Sallaz, J. J. (2002), 'The House Rules: Autonomy and Interests among Service Workers in the Contemporary Casino Industry', *Work and Occupations*, 29/4: 394–427.

Sczensky, S., and Stahlberg, D. (2000), 'Sexual Harassment over the Telephone: Occupational Risk at Call Centres', *Work and Stress*, 14/2: 121–36.

Shibutani, T. (1966), *Improvised News: A Sociological Study of Rumor*, Indianapolis: Bobbs-Merrill.

Smith, E. R., Becker, M. A., Byrne, D., and Przybyla, D. P. (1993), 'Sexual Attitudes of Males and Females as Predictors of Interpersonal Attraction and Marital Compatibility', *Journal of Applied Social Psychology*, 23/13: 1011–34.

Solkey, L. (1980), *Dummy up and Deal*, Las Vegas: GBC Press.

Spector, P. E. (1997), 'The Role of Frustration in Antisocial Behaviour at Work', in R. A. Giacolone and J. Greenberg, *Antisocial Behaviour in Organizations*, London: Sage, ch. 1.

Taylor, L., and Walton, P. (1971), 'Industrial Sabotage: Motives and Meanings', in S. Cohen (ed.), *Images of Deviance*, Harmondsworth: Penguin, pp. 219–45.

Taylor, S. (1997), 'Her Case against Clinton', *American Lawyer*, 18/9: 56.

Trix, F., and Sankar, A. (1998), 'Women's Voices and Experiences of the Hill-Thomas Hearings', *American Anthropologist*, 100/1: 32.

Van Maanen, J. (1991), 'The Smile Factory: Work at Disneyland', ch. 4 in P. J. Frost, L. F. Moore, M. R. Louis, C. C. Lundberg, and J. Martin (eds.), *Reframing Organizational Culture*. London: Sage.

——(1995), 'Fear and Loathing in Organization Studies', *Organization Science*, 6/6: 687–92.

Warfield, A. (1987), 'Co-worker Romances: Impact on the Work Group and on Career Oriented Women', *Personnel*, 64/5 (May), 22–35.

Willis, P. (1977), *Learning to Labour*, London: Saxon House.

Wilson, F. M. (2000), 'The Subjective Experience of Sexual Harassment: Cases of Students', *Human Relations*, 53/8: 1081–97.

——(2003), *Organizational Behaviour and Gender*, London: McGraw Hill.

——and Thompson, P. (2001), Sexual Harassment as an Exercise of Power', *Gender, Work and Organization*, 8/1: 61–83.

Witz, A., Halford, S., and Savage, M. (1994), 'Organized Bodies: Gender, Sexuality, Bodies and Organizational Culture', paper presented to the BSA Conference: Sexualities in the Social Context, University of Central Lancashire, March.

Worral, L., and Cooper, C. L. (1999), *Quality of Working Life 1998 Survey of Manager's Changing Experiences*, London: Institute of Management.

Zapf, D. (1999), 'Organizational, Work Group Related and Personal Causes of Mobbing/Bullying at Work', *International Journal of Manpower*, 20/1–2: 70–85.

Zapf, D., Knorz, C., and Kulla, M. (1996), 'On the Relationship between Mobbing Factors, and Job Content, Social Work Environment and Health Outcomes, *European Journal of Work and Organizational Psychology*, 5/2: 215–37.

8 | The View from Above: What Managers Do

We have looked at the realities of work and work design mainly for workers. But what about managers? What do they do and what are their jobs like?

We all manage. In all societies people are involved in the complex and demanding work of organizing their lives, accomplishing ordinary tasks, and maintaining routines. We manage our resources, our time, and sometimes others, but we are not called managers. Those who are called managers will be experts who are trained and employed to shape, organize, and regulate. They will be managing large, medium-sized, and small production or service organizations—stores, hospitals, hotels, factories, voluntary organizations, cooperatives—so the job of manager will differ from organization to organization. Many people are managers without having the title of manager, for example nursing administrators, farmers, head teachers, prison governors, and bishops are all managers of people and resources. All are vested with formal authority within their organizations. Management is about having power and control over people while achieving a measure of voluntary compliance from them.

How then is management defined? Management can be defined as 'mental (thinking, intuiting, feeling) work performed by people in an Organizational context' (Kast and Rosenzweig 1985). Stewart defines management as a level, a position above foreman and above first-level supervision (Stewart 1994: 2). It is power and social context that differentiate managers from non-managers. As Grint (1995) notes, what managers do is little different from what anyone might do, but the context within which the act of management occurs differentiates the manager from the non-manager.

Henri Fayol, a French businessman, was one of the first managers (along with others like Gulick and Urwick 1937) to use his experience to theorize about the manager's job, to generalize about all managerial work (Fayol 1949). He did this by describing the functions that all managers perform. They plan, organize, motivate, control, and coordinate. This very clear-cut traditional account of what managers do can still be found in current management textbooks. This view gives us the theory but is the everyday reality of what managers do like this? Mintzberg (1970, 1973), Kotter (1982*a* and 1982*b*) and Stewart (1974, 1982*a*) all criticized Fayol's simplistic functional view of management. Mintzberg described the classical functions as 'folklore' (1975).

STOP

What Do Managers Do? A Joke

A big corporation hired several cannibals. 'You are all part of our team now,' said the HR rep during the welcoming briefing. You get all the usual benefits and you can go to the cafeteria for something to eat, but please don't eat any of the other employees.' The cannibals promised.

Four weeks later their boss remarked, 'You're all working very hard, and I'm satisfied with you. However, one of our secretaries has disappeared. Do any of you know what happened to her?' The cannibals all shook their heads no. After the boss had left, the leader of the cannibals said to the others, 'Which one of you idiots ate the secretary?'

A hand raised hesitantly. The leader of the cannibals continued, 'You fool! For four weeks we've been eating managers and no one noticed anything, but no, you had to go and eat the secretary!'

Research to discover what managers actually did began in earnest in the 1950s, with a study by Carlson in 1951 (Stewart 1994; Hales 1999). Carlson looked at the work of seven Swedish and two French executives over a four-week period. Managers are described as reactive socializers, not machine-like decision makers, who, in Grint's (1995: 48) words 'fought fires with words and networks of colleagues and subordinates'.

Henry Mintzberg (1973) theorized having observed five chief executives work for a week. In *Mintzberg on Management* (1989) he describes how he used a stopwatch (much as Frederick Taylor had done before him) to observe in the course of one intensive week the activities of five chief executives of a major consulting firm, a well-known teaching hospital, a school system, a high-technology firm, and a manufacturer of consumer goods. He says that if you ask managers what they do they will most likely tell you that they plan, organize, coordinate, and control, giving you a traditional account in Fayol's terms. But if you watch them, do not be surprised if you cannot relate what you see to those four words. Where would the activity of presenting a gold watch to a retiring employee fit into those four Fayol categories, for example?

There are four myths, Mintzberg says, about managers' jobs that do not bear up under scrutiny:

1. The manager is a reflective, systematic planner.
2. The effective manager has no regular duties to perform.
3. The senior manager needs aggregated information that a formal management information system best provides.
4. Management is becoming a science and a profession.

Evidence suggests that managers work at an unrelenting pace. The work is characterized by brevity. For example half the activities engaged in by the five chief executives Mintzberg studied lasted less than nine minutes and only 10 per cent exceeded one hour. It is also characterized by variety and discontinuity. Chief executives are strongly oriented to action and dislike reflective activities. There are a number of regular duties to perform including negotiating, ceremonies (like presiding at special dinners),

Are you lonely?

Hate having to make decisions?

Rather talk about it than do it?

Then why not

HOLD A MEETING

You can: Get to see other people

Sleep in peace

Offload decisions

Learn to write volumes of meaningless notes

Feel important

Impress (or bore) your colleagues

And all in work time!

'MEETINGS'
The Practical Alternative to Work

processing information that connects the organization with its environment. Managers favour telephone calls and meetings, not formal information systems. In two British studies, for example, managers spent an average of 66 and 80 per cent of their time in oral communication. This helps explain, at least in part, why managers are reluctant to delegate tasks—most of the important information they carry is in their heads and has not been recorded. Managers certainly do not, in Mintzberg's view, practise a science. They seek information by word of mouth, rely on what they call judgement and intuition and what Mintzberg would call ignorance. As a result the job of a manager is enormously difficult and complicated. They are overburdened yet cannot delegate. They are forced, then, to do tasks superficially. Scientific attempts to improve managerial work are impossible.

Mintzberg defines the manager as a person in charge of an organization or one of its subunits, which can include bishops, prime ministers, and vice-presidents. What all these people have in common is that they have all been vested with formal authority over the unit. From formal authority comes status that leads to various interpersonal relations. From these comes access to information. Information is used to make decisions and strategy. As a result of looking at managerial work and describing it, Mintzberg distinguishes between three main roles the manager plays: in interpersonal aspects, receiving and disseminating information (as a nerve centre for information), and as decision maker. These three roles were then divided into ten subdivisions.

Interpersonal roles	Informational roles	Decisional roles
Figurehead	Monitor	Entrepreneur
Leader	Disseminator	Disturbance Handler
Liaison	Spokesperson	Resource Allocator
		Negotiator

As figurehead there are duties of a ceremonial nature like meeting local dignitaries. As the persons in charge, managers are responsible for the work of the people in their unit, so are leaders. As a liaison they are making contact outside their vertical chain of command, spending as much time with peers and others outside their units (e.g. clients, suppliers, government officials) as with their own subordinates. Due to interpersonal contact with those below in the hierarchy and a network of contacts, managers are at the nerve centre of their unit. They will not know everything but will typically know more than their subordinates. This information needs to be processed. As a monitor they scan their environment for information (including gossip and speculation). They share and distribute this information in the disseminator role. In their role as spokesman (Mintzberg doesn't use inclusive language) managers send some of their information to people outside their units, for example to consumer groups.

Managers also play a major role in decision making. As entrepreneur they seek to improve the unit and adapt it to changes in the environment. They seek and initiate new ideas. Some of the chief executives Mintzberg studied have as many as fifty development projects running at any one time. In the role of disturbance handler they are responding to pressures, for example if a strike looms or if a major customer is declared bankrupt. They decide what resources go where, as resource allocator and as negotiator they find negotiations a way of life.

These roles are not easily separated and form an integrated whole. No role can be pulled out with the job left intact. Mintzberg believes that this description of managerial work should be more important to managers than any prescription that can be offered. Managers' effectiveness is significantly influenced by insight into their own work. Their performance is dependent on how well they understand and respond to the pressures and dilemmas of the job they do. Managers are challenged systematically to share their privileged information with subordinates, to step back to see the broader picture on offer, and to make use of analytical inputs. They need to control their time carefully.

A few studies have attempted to test Mintzberg's roles in actual operating situations (McCall and Segrist 1980; Lau et al. 1980; Kurke and Aldrich 1983; Snyder and Wheelan 1981). Minzberg's role theory is accused of failing to deliver something it promises. It promises to offer explanation of managerial behaviour; it does not answer the question why managerial behaviour is as it is. Instead it only categorizes that behaviour (Hales 1999). It is criticized for lacking specificity, and not pointing out the relationship between his role types and organizational effectiveness. It is developed on the basis of the questionable practice of not going beyond the observable work activities themselves. Managers could be thinking about job-related problems long after they leave work; we know for example that some managers may work many hours even before coming into the office (Carroll and Gillen 1987). Since managerial work is mental, it is not directly observable. Physical activities of managers do not indicate exactly what they do. It is impossible to measure managerial work without questioning managers about the purpose of their telephone calls, conversations, and so on. Although managers may make brief contacts, this does not mean that they are not planning, controlling, or investigating, all of which require information (Carroll and Gillen 1987).

Kotter (1982*a*) conducted a detailed analysis of what fifteen successful general managers did and how they spent their time. He compared his data with those of Mintzberg in the USA (1973) and Stewart (1979) in the UK. All three agree that managers' work is largely reactive rather than proactive and is varied, fragmented, and frequently interrupted. This research gives a different picture of the hectic day that contrasts with the theorist's view of a manager who plans, organizes, and controls. The research also shows how important interpersonal skills are for managers. Successful managers spend time establishing informal networks, creating or being involved in cooperative relationships with people. Most managers spend three-quarters or more of their time with others (Stewart 1997). The emphasis is on frenetic, disjointed activity, using informal methods of disseminating and collecting information, and a realization of the paramount importance of people skills. As Alimo-Metcalfe (1992) notes, these skills are difficult to measure and simulate in situations where you wish to judge if a manager has these skills. Equally difficult to measure are the necessary political skills. Studies of British and American managers have shown how they spend nearly all of their time with other people, trying to find out what is happening, trying to persuade others to cooperate, and less often trying to decide what ought to be done. They need to know how to trade, bargain, and compromise. The more senior they are, the more political will be the world in which they live (Stewart 1997).

Studies have repeatedly shown that managerial activity is high on oral communication (see also Kanter 1977). Gowler and Legge (1996) go beyond this assertion to say that such verbal activity involves the use of rhetoric, that is the use of a form of word delivery which is lavish in symbolism and involves several layers or textures of meaning. Managers use a rhetoric of bureaucratic control that is highly expressive, constructing and legitimizing managerial prerogative in terms of a rational, goal-directed image of organizational effectiveness. This rhetoric is political. Not only do managers spend most of their time talking, they generate a culture, in an anthropological sense, which is maintained and transmitted from one generation to another. Meaning may be generated through rituals, myths, magic, totemism, and taboo, in the same way as is documented in distant cultures by social anthropologists. This talk, especially the rhetoric, may be the way in which social control is maintained.

The issue of social control arises again when we look at the hours managers are required to work. Pahl (1995) notes the consistent patterns of long work hours and few holidays that characterize managerial work. Watson's (1994) participant observation study of managers shows how long work hours, especially in the evening, were seen as a measure of commitment to the organization. Male managers in particular deliberately stayed at work late in the evening, wasted time, artificially extended meetings, and criticized managers who left at 7.15 p.m. Similarly Coyle (1995) notes the long hours managers worked in the five UK organizations where she conducted research (see Collinson and Collinson 1997). Surveys have shown how managers are working increasingly long hours. Austin Knight UK (1995) found that 45 per cent of senior male managers said they were working more than fifty hours a week. An Institute of Management survey (1995) showed that 60 per cent of respondents stated that their workload had 'greatly increased' over the past two years. The Institute's 1996 survey showed that 80 per cent of respondents confirmed an increase in their workload over the past year. As a result most were experiencing signs of stress. Many managers now experience job insecurity and uncertainty. Fear of redundancy can create an imperative to appear visibly committed to the job to maximize limited promotion opportunities. Such presenteeism has been found to be highly gendered—it is more likely to be recognized by women but practised by men (Simpson 1998).

While many similarities can be found in managerial jobs, there can also be differences. Kotter (1982a) found the jobs of the general managers he studied differed. He also found that managers did their jobs differently, as also noted by Stewart (1982b). Stewart showed how every manager does the job in their own way, choosing, for example, to be outward focused, spending much time with people outside the organization building business, or inward looking, spending most of their time developing relations with and managing their own staff. Johnson and Gill (1993) believe that there is little consensus about what managers' everyday activities are. This is made worse because management is not an undifferentiated, homogeneous occupational group. But there must be some consensus to be found. Grint (1995) concludes that in Britain, at least, management seems to be mainly concerned with talk and manic attempts to stamp out numerous 'fires'. They dash from one emergency to the next, resolving short-term problems and crises whilst keeping production going. The typical manager's day involves 'keeping the show on the road, and managing to keep one's head above water when all around are losing theirs to stress' (1995: 66).

Drucker (1989) does not describe what the manager does but describes what a manager should do. He says, for example that managers should put economic performance first, as they can only justify their existence and authority by economic results. The ultimate test of management is business performance. Their second function is to make a productive enterprise out of human and material resources; the transmutation of resources requires management. The third and final function of management is to manage workers and work. In practice managers discharge these three functions in every action. His is a very practical approach to management, a guide for those working in management.

In a similar prescriptive vein, Kanter (1987) examined the conditions that support innovation and change, coupled with the experiences and activities of the innovators that bring this about. She looked at how people acquire and use power in empowering organizations and how this contributes to innovation and the mastery of change. She used ten core research companies and found that to manage effectively, corporate entrepreneurs need to work through participative teams to produce small changes that will add up later to big ones. They need 'power skills' to persuade others to invest information, support, and resources in new initiatives driven by an entrepreneur. They need the ability to manage the problems associated with the greater use of teams and participation as well as an understanding of how change is designed and constructed in an organization.

A power approach to manager and management would say that the distinguishing feature of the professions is their ability to gain societal recognition as professions. This approach emerges from the Chicago School of symbolic interactionists who argue that professions are essentially the same as other occupations. There is no precise and unique definition of professions; it is just a title claimed by certain occupations at certain points in time. Professional rewards are sufficient for people to want and to strive for professional status.

Has there been a revolution in management and what interests do managers serve? Some, like Burnham (1945), have argued that a managerial revolution has come about. Specialist knowledge and skills of managerial experts have become crucial to the successful running of increasingly large and complex businesses and bureaucracies. The dominance of owners of wealth is undermined and a new class of professional salaried managers exercises control. The counter-argument is that the criteria of performance under which managers operate are oriented to ownership interest. The more successful managers tend to be those who internalize profit-oriented values and priorities. Corporate profits are prerequisites for high managerial income and status (Zeitlin 1989). The ownership of wealth and control of work are closely related; both managers and owners play their parts in the same 'constellations of interest' (Scott 1979; see also Watson 1997).

We saw earlier how Mintzberg questions the view that management is becoming a profession. Is it a profession now? What would the characteristics of a profession be? The taxonomic or classification approach would say that a profession possesses specialized skills, the necessity of intellectual and practical training, and the perceived collective responsibility for maintaining the integrity of the profession as a whole via a professional body (see Dietrich and Roberts 1997: 23). This is done through, for example, barriers to entry and occupational closure.

Is management a profession? During the 1980s British management education and training became a matter for public concern, debate, and action. A number of reports (Constable and McCormick 1987; Handy 1987; Mangham and Silver 1986) showed that the range and quality of provision of education and training fell well below that of

America, Europe, and Japan (Reed and Anthony 1992). British management was, in some areas, a 'spurious elite' (Handy et al. 1988: 168). British managers were embedded in a centuries-old technique and culture of rule that emphasized stability at the expense of innovation and compromise at the expense of confrontation (Fox 1983: 33). They seemed to lack the entrepreneurial zeal and basic technical competence of managerial elites in other countries. British management relied on a model of status rather than occupational professionalism. They lacked developmental, educational, and training opportunities. While other professionals, in law, medicine, accountancy, and architecture, for example, spent up to seven years in apprenticeship and further study, British managers did nothing to apply the procedures of professionalism to management. As the practice of management is so diversified and bereft of occupational organization and control, they cannot generate effective professional authority and closure.

Management and Men

It is interesting to note (as Collinson and Hearn 1996 have done) how Mintzberg uses 'manager' and 'he' interchangeably; he remains silent about the inherently gendered assumptions he makes about management. Drucker does the same. His book *The Practice of Management* (1989) is aimed 'at being a guide for men in major management positions . . . For younger men in management—and for men who plan to make management their career' (1989: preface). What does this tell us about who should be successful in management?

Most managers are men and men are associated with organizational power, yet male domination of management is a subject that has received little scrutiny (Collinson and Hearn 1996). Management has been portrayed as a masculine concept, about controlling, taking charge, and directing. Journalistic profiles of male executives and 'captains of industry' present heroic macho images emphasizing struggle, battle, a willingness to be ruthless, brutal, a rebellious nature, and an aggressive, rugged individualism (Neale 1995). Managers were frequently depicted as masculine, abrasive, and highly autocratic 'hard men' who insisted on the 'divine right of managers to manage' (Purcell 1982).

Kanter (1977) has studied men and women in management. She notes how the 'masculine ethic' can be identified as part of the early image of managers in the writings of Taylor, Weber, and Chester Barnard. This masculine ethic elevates the traits assumed to belong to some men to necessities for effective management: a tough-minded approach to problems, analytic abilities to abstract and plan, a capacity to set aside personal, emotional considerations in the interests of task accomplishment, and a cognitive superiority in problem solving and decision making. These characteristics supposedly belonged to men, but then, practically, all managers were men. However, when women tried to enter management jobs, the masculine ethic was invoked as an exclusionary principle.

Middle Management

There are some gloomy views of middle management. There are a number of reasons why middle managers may be frustrated, disillusioned individuals, according to Dopson and Stewart (1990).

1. They are in the middle of a long hierarchy and may have been bypassed by top management's efforts to increase employee involvement.

2. They have to cope with conflicting expectations of those above and below them in the hierarchy. They are squeezed between the demands of the strategies they cannot influence and the ambitions of independent-minded employees (Kanter 1986). They can get caught in crossfire between departments and customers or suppliers.

3. They have lost technical expertise to administrative tasks.

4. There is career disillusionment among middle managers. They can no longer expect lifetime careers, they express frustration, dissatisfaction, and powerlessness. Some commentators have talked about the 'end of the career' in management (Handy 1989; Osterman 1996).

As if this is not bad enough, middle managers have been under attack as organizational downsizing and re-engineering have reduced their numbers in the 1980s and 1990s (Scarborough and Burrell 1996). While opinions vary as to the extent of the reduction (Dopson and Stewart 1990) middle managers have been a target as they are seen to add costs, slow down decisions, and obstruct flow of information (Dopson and Neumann 1998; Thomas and Dunkerley 1999). The downsized, re-engineered, flatter organization has less need for people whose primary role is to transmit senior manager's orders down the organizations, particularly when they fail to perform the role effectively. They have also been considered to have a negative impact on change, being obstructive and resistant to change.

This gloomy view is counteracted by a number of writers who show that information technology has led to a reshaping of middle managers' role rather than to its decline. For example, Dopson and Stewart (1990) found that a smaller number of middle managers had a greater responsibility for a wider range of duties for which they were clearly accountable. They were described as more important than in the past because they are in slimmer, flatter organizations, have more responsibility, and are seen by top management as having a major role in implementing change. Most managers were positive about the changes and how their jobs had changed. Middle managers found themselves closer to top management and strategic decisions. They had their own clear area of responsibility with more control over resources and could more legitimately take decisions within their own areas. The traditional career model for managers has to be revised (McGovern et al. 1998).

Success in Management

Careers in organizations have undergone a transformation as organizations have reformed and reshaped, culling layers of the management hierarchy, rethinking employment contracts, and revising what they are prepared to offer in terms of careers (Arnold 1997). The meaning of career success needs to be revisited by organizations in the light of change. Career success has frequently been presented as something that can be objectively quantified through external criteria such as hierarchical position and salary level (Melamed 1995; O'Reilly and Chatman 1994). Managers' own conceptions of success have generally been excluded from research into careers (Herriot et al. 1994). When own conceptions of success are researched, a minority of individuals includes reaching the most senior levels of management as criteria for success. The majority though use a range of internal and intangible criteria such as achievement, accomplishment, personal recognition, and influence to define career success in their own terms (Sturges 1999).

Women managers have been found to view career success as a process of personal development which involves interesting and challenging work coupled with balance with the rest of their life (Marshall 1984; Powell and Mainiero 1992). In contrast salary and rank have been shown to correlate with career satisfaction for men (Russo et al. 1991). Women managers' different ideas about career success are likely to be influenced by their socialization as women. Also the constraints they perceive are likely to affect their careers in organizations, where they remain in a minority and where hierarchical success is seen to be very difficult to achieve (Davidson and Cooper 1992; Poole et al. 1993). Sturges (1999) found that women managers and older managers appear less inclined to define career success in terms of hierarchical and financial progression.

Some researchers believe that success at work and success at home are linked. Draughn (1984) questioned if men who perceive themselves as successful in work will perceive themselves as successful in the role of husband! She found that indeed the middle-aged man's perception of success in work is related to his perception of success in the husband role. It was also found that men's perceptions of job competence increased as the level of income increased.

The Reality for the Woman Manager

Women managers experience unique sources of stress related to their minority status and gender; these pressures result in higher levels of overall occupational stress compared to their male counterparts (Davidson 1996; Davidson and Cooper 1992). Women managers experience strain coping with discrimination, prejudice, and sex stereotyping; there is a lack of role models, they feel isolated, they have to cope with being the 'token woman' and with higher work/home conflicts.

Since the 1980s there has been talk of a glass ceiling preventing women managers progressing. Lack of family-friendly employment policies, poor access to training, the pattern of career development, and informal barriers contribute to this glass ceiling. Gregg and

Machin (1993) note that only 8 per cent of top UK executives are female and the number of females drops dramatically as you move to the top of the hierarchy. A survey of British management salaries (Institute of Management 1994) recorded a fall in the number of women managers from 10.2 per cent in 1993 to 9.8 per cent in 1994. This downward trend has also been noted in the USA, other countries in Europe, and in Australia (Fagenson 1993). Women managers earn less than men in the same jobs, with the largest pay gaps found at the extreme top of the hierarchies.

Wajcman (1996) studied the attitudes and experiences of men and women managers and showed how women who made it into senior positions were in most respects indistinguishable from men in equivalent positions. They had similar backgrounds, attitudes, and worked the same long hours. However, this was not enough to guarantee success as their career progression was still blocked. The most commonly cited barrier was the senior management 'club', the prejudice of colleagues, lack of career guidance, and family commitments. She concludes that it is men who have the power to define what constitutes occupational success and men who dominate it.

Double Jeopardy: The Reality for the Black and Ethnic Minority Woman Manager

The American literature on women managers has been accused of making African-American women managers invisible (Nkomo 1988). The double jeopardy faced by African-American women managers helps secure their position at the very bottom of the managerial hierarchy. In the USA white women hold 38 per cent of the executive administrative and managerial positions while women 'of color' represent only 5 per cent (Hite 1996).

If you are young, female, and black in Britain the chances are slim that you will find a job to reflect your academic ability or potential (Mirza 1992). Ethnic minority women are under-represented in the professional field compared to white women (Bhavnani 1994). Yet little research has been devoted to the plight of the black and ethnic manager woman in Britain (Davidson 1997). Davidson, in her study of thirty black and ethnic minority managers, shows how these women face the double negative effects of sexism and racism. These women had fewer, if any, role models and were more likely to feel isolated. They had to contend with stereotypical images based on gender and ethnic origin and were more likely to experience performance pressure. As one noted, 'I feel under enormous pressure to perform well. White people always seem to be looking to me to fail. If I fail, though, I let down all black women' (1997: 46). They have greater home/social/work conflicts, particularly with regards to the family and black community. As a result, 80 per cent reported negative psycho-social and health outcomes which were related to sexism and racism at work. Bhavanani (1994) notes how there is some evidence from local government which suggests that the segregated patterns of black women's professional areas actually block access into senior management positions. For example, black women in education were given opportunities to use their background as relevant experience but when they attempted to move out of these areas their work experience became a barrier to parity of status. There is also evidence that black staff employed at managerial level in local government are primarily recruited for directing services towards black users. There may then be new forms of resegregation emerging.

Similarly, racism is likely to be experienced by black male managers, yet there is little research evidence on this. There have been attacks on the army and prison service recently for discriminating on grounds of race. There are, for example, only nine black prison officers in the grade of principal officer in Britain's jails yet one in five inmates are from ethnic minorities. Of more than 28,000 officers only 2.5 per cent are from ethnic minorities and only six are at junior governor level (*Observer*, 10 August 1997).

Hotel Management

Hotel management: is it the same as or different from other management? Research into the occupation of hotel management is fairly recent, most taking place in the 1980s. Hotel management has been found to be notoriously insular (Wood 1992: 80). Those training in hotel and catering management are generally separated off from those studying management or business. Hotel and catering trainees are usually required to do periods of industrial placement as a form of pre-entry socialization. Two-thirds of hotel managers have been found to have had no work experience outside the hotel industry (Baum 1989; Guerrier 1987). Formal qualifications do not seem to affect the position on entry, promotion prospects, or career patterns, for example most managers find themselves in very junior positions at first in spite of qualifications. Most managers will have to move jobs in order to gain experience of specific functions and different types of hotels.

Hotel managers engaged in a larger number of activities than their counterparts in other industries, saw less of their peers, and were rarely involved in group situations. They spent less time alone because of time spent directly supervising staff and due to customer contact. Generally they dislike sitting behind a desk and see the important job as being out and about in the hotel. Like other managers they work long hours. In Mintzberg's terms, hotel managers place emphasis on leadership and entrepreneurial roles (Wood 1992).

Managers in luxury international hotels are required to deliver a highly standardized service, controlled and maintained with the help of volumes of operating manuals. Coupled with this they need to provide an 'authentic' (non-routinized and individualized) service in a variety of cultural contexts to gain competitive advantage (Jones et al. 1997). How do they ensure that rules are followed, standards maintained, staff act consistently, yet provide a non-routinized and individualized service? Various methods are used which include customer feedback and careful selection and training of employees who have internalized 'appropriate' corporately determined values. Well-trained, socialized, and informed employees can be empowered to make good decisions. Jones et al. (1997) give us the case of 'Americo', a multinational hospitality company. Here empowered employees are asked to 'do whatever it takes' to ensure that every guest leaves satisfied. The company advertises this aim by showing a waiter on night duty driving round town to find a favourite night-time drink and a porter retracing a guest's journey on a tram to retrieve a lost wallet. But creating these empowered employees was not a simple task for managers if employees had already been socialized to accept a more directive management style or where employees felt they were being asked to take on duties that managers were paid to have. Empowerment also meant less need for as many layers of management so some lost their jobs.

Managers are always faced with dilemmas, for example like the ones posed here by the need to standardize and customize, control and empower. For managers then there is no best way to manage, 'only partial routes to failure' (Hyman 1987: 30). Managers face complexities in their social and organizational worlds. With management we have a highly structured order permeated by relational networks that, in Reed's (1989: 93) words, 'simultaneously sustain and undermine the viability of the former'. Whether managers are able or willing to overcome the obstacles that stand in the way of constructing a more meaningful and satisfactory work environment remains to be seen.

■ SUGGESTIONS FOR FURTHER READING

1. Thomas, A. B. (2003), *Controversies in Management* (2nd edn.), London: Routledge. Chapter 2, 'What is Management? A Term in Search of a Meaning', provides a useful discussion.

2. Noon, M., and Blyton, P. (2002), *The Realities of Work*, Houndmills: Palgrave. Pages 210–11 would help answer the question of whether management is a profession.

3. Thompson, P., and McHugh, D. (2002), *Work Organizations*, Houndmills: Palgrave. Chapter 7 on management also discusses whether management can be a profession.

4. Watson, T. (2002), *Organising and Managing Work*, Harlow: Pearson. Pages 84–92 discuss making sense of what managers do.

5. Gowler, D., and Legge, K. (1996), 'The Meaning of Management and the Management of Meaning', in S. Linstead, R. Grafton Small, and P. Jeffcutt (eds.), *Understanding Management*, London: Sage. Chapter 2 discusses the rhetoric of management and the moral necessity of hierarchy, accountability, and achievement.

6. Grint, K. (1995), *Management: A Sociological Introduction*, Cambridge: Polity, for a discussion on how rational managers' work is.

7. Watson, T., and Harris, P. (1999), *The Emergent Manager*, London: Sage. This book looks at the process of becoming a manager and considers how people connect the ways they manage in life to their development as managers.

■ WEB LINKS

This web site talks about a book that tells you what great managers do differently: **www.humanresources.about.com/library/weekly/aa070900a.htm**—you might want to critique it in the light of what you now know.

www.1668homeguide.com/office_business_work_26.htm is similar.

See **http://sol.brunel.ac.uk/~jarvis/bola/mintzberg/** for a description of Henry Mintzberg's views on managerial work.

■ QUESTIONS

1. How rational is management (see Grint 1995)? Are managers 'firefighters' because they are 'mimetic pyrophobes', i.e. they are addicted to fear of fire or because they are responsible for the 'chronically inflammable' (Hales 1999)?

2. What are the differences in the findings from Stewart, Kotter, and Mintzberg on what managers do? How far do they help us understand why managers do what they do? (See Hales 1999.)

3. How would you decide on the attributes of a successful manager in any job?

4. What is it about management behaviour that makes it masculine? What are the parallels to be found in shop-floor behaviour (see Collinson 1992)? Does management need to be dominated by men? (See Collinson and Hearn (1996) and Wensley (1996).)

5. How do men master themselves (see Hollway 1996)?

6. 'Representing management as a predominantly technical activity creates an illusion of neutrality' (Alvesson and Wilmott 1996: 12). Discuss.

7. How often have you opened a book on management and seen any reference to race? Why do you think this is the case?

■ GROUP EXERCISES

1. Can management be considered a profession? One-half of the class should argue the case that it is while the other should argue that it is not. What prospect is there for change?

2. Middle management work is a moving, complex picture. There appear to be both pessimistic and optimistic pictures of what is happening to middle management. Research the topic for yourselves and debate, in class, the optimistic versus the pessimistic view (see also Balogun 2003).

■ REFERENCES

Alimo-Metcalfe, B. (1992), 'Different Gender—Different Rules', ch. 11 in P. Barrar and C. L. Cooper (eds.), *Managing Organizations*. London: Routledge.

Alvesson, M., and Wilmott, H. (1996), *Making Sense of Management: A Critical Introduction*, London: Sage.

Arnold, J. (1997), *Managing Careers in the 21st Century*, London: Paul Chapman.

Austin Knight UK (1995), *The Family Friendly Workplace*, London: Austin Knight.

Balogun, J. (2003), 'From Blaming the Middle Manager to Harnessing its Potential: Creating Change Intermediaries', *British Journal of Management*, 14/1: 69–84.

Baum, T. (1989), 'Managing Hotels in Ireland: Research and Development for Change', *International Journal of Hospitality Management*, 8/2: 131–44.

Bhavnani, R. (1994), *Black Women in the Labour Market: A Research Review*, Manchester: Equal Opportunities Commission.

Burnham, J. (1945), *The Managerial Revolution*, Harmondsworth: Penguin.

Carlson, S. (1951), *Executive Behaviour: A Study of the Workload and Working Methods of Managing Directors*, Stockholm: Strombergs.

Carroll, S. J., and Gillen, D. J. (1987), 'Are the Classical Management Functions Useful in Describing Managerial Work?', *Academy of Management Review*, 12/1: 36–51.

Collinson, D. L. (1992), *Managing the Shopfloor: Subjectivity, Masculinity and Workplace Culture*, Berlin: De Gruyter.

——and Collinson, M. (1997), 'Delayering Managers: Time-Space Surveillance and its Gendered Effects', *Organization*, 4/3: 375–407.

——and Hearn, J. (1996) (eds.), *Men as Managers, Managers as Men*, London: Sage.

Constable, J., and McCormick, R. (1987), *The Making of British Managers*, London: British Institute of Management.

Coyle, A. (1995), 'Women and Organizational Change', Research Discussion Series, 14, Manchester: Equal Opportunities Commission.

Davidson, M. J. (1996), 'Women in Employment', in P. Warr (ed.), *Psychology at Work*, London: Penguin.

——(1997), *The Black and Ethnic Minority Woman Manager: Cracking the Concrete Ceiling*, London: Paul Chapman.

——and Cooper, C. L. (1992), *Shattering the Glass Ceiling: The Woman Manager*, London: Paul Chapman.

Dietrich, M., and Roberts, J. (1997), 'Beyond the Economics of Professionalism', ch. 2 in J. Broadbent, M. Dietrich, and J. Roberts (eds.), *The End of the Professions? The Restructuring of Professional Work*, London: Routledge.

Dopson, S., and Neumann, J. E. (1998), 'Uncertainty, Contrariness and the Double-Bind: Middle Manager's Reactions of Changing Contracts', *British Journal of Management*, 9: 53–70.

——and Stewart, R. (1990), 'What is Happening to Middle Management?', *British Journal of Management*, 1: 3–16.

Draughn, P. S. (1984), 'Perceptions of Competence in Work and Marriage of Middle Age Men', *Journal of Marriage and the Family*, 46/2: 403–9.

Drucker, P. F. (1989), *The Practice of Management*, Oxford: Heinemann Professional Publishing.

Fagenson, E. (1993) (ed.), *Women in Management*, Newbury Park, Calif.: Sage.

Fayol, H. (1949), *General and Industrial Management*, London: Pitman.

Fox, A. (1983), 'British Management and Industrial Relations: The Social Origins of a System', in M. Earl (ed.), *Perspectives on Management*, Oxford: Oxford University Press.

Gowler, D., and Legge, K. (1996), 'The Meaning of Management and the Management of Meaning', ch. 2 in S. Linstead, R. Grafton Small, and P. Jeffcutt (eds.), *Understanding Management*, London: Sage.

Gregg, P., and Machin, S. (1993), 'Is the Glass Ceiling Cracking? Gender Compensation Differentials and Access to Promotion among UK Executives', National Institute of Economic and Social Research, Discussion Paper 50, London: NIESR.

Grint, K. (1995), *Management: A Sociological Introduction*, Cambridge: Polity.

Guerrier, Y. (1987), 'Hotel Managers' Careers and their Impact on Hotels in Britain', *International Journal of Hospitality Management*, 6/3: 121–30.

Gulick, L., and Urwick, L. (1937), *Papers on the Science of Administration*, New York: Columbia University Press.

Hales, C. (1999), 'Why Do Managers Do What They Do? Reconciling Evidence and Theory in Accounts of Managerial Work', *British Journal of Management*, 10/4: 335–50.

Handy, C. (1987), *The Making of Managers*, London: London Manpower Services Commission, National Economic Development Council, and British Institute of Management.

——(1989), *The Age of Unreason*, London: Business Books.

——Gordon, C., Gow, I., and Randlesome, C. (1988), *Making Managers*, Oxford: Pitman.

Herriot, P., Gibbons, P., Pemberton, C., and Jackson, P. R. (1994), 'An Empirical Model of Managerial Careers in Organizations', *British Journal of Management*, 5: 113–21.

Hite, L. M. (1996), 'Black Women Managers and Administrators: Experience and Implications', *Women in Management Review*, 11/6: 11–17.

Hollway, W. (1996), 'Masters and Men in the Transition from Factory Hands to Sentimental Workers', ch. 2 in D. L. Collinson and J. Hearn (eds.), *Men as Managers, Managers as Men*, London: Sage.

Hyman, R. (1987), 'Strategy or Structure? Capital, Labour and Control', *Work, Employment and Society*, 1/1: 25–55.

Institute of Management (1994), *The 1994 National Management Salary Survey*, London: Institute of Management.

——(1995), *Survival of the Fittest: A Survey of Managers' Experience of and Attitudes to Work in the Post Recession Economy*, London: Institute of Management.

Johnson, P., and Gill, J. (1993), *Management Control and Organizational Behaviour*, London: Paul Chapman.

Jones, C., Taylor, G., and Nickson, D. (1997), 'Whatever it Takes? Managing "Empowered" Employees and the Service Encounter in an International Hotel Chain', *Work, Employment and Society*, 11/3: 541–54.

Kanter, R. (1977), *Men and Women of the Corporation*, New York: Basic Books.

——(1986), 'The Reshaping of Middle Management', *Management Review*, 19–20.

——(1987), *The Change Masters: Corporate Entrepreneurs at Work*, London: Unwin Books.

Kast, F. E., and Rosenzweig, J. E. (1985), *Organization and Management: A Systems and Contingency Approach* (4th edn.), New York: McGraw Hill.

Kotter, J. P. (1982a), *The General Managers*, London: Free Press.

——(1982b), 'What Effective General Managers Really Do', *Harvard Business Review*, 60/6: 156–67.

Kurke, L. B., and Aldrich, H. E. (1983), 'Mintzberg Was Right! A Replication and Extension of the Nature of Managerial Work', *Management Science*, 29: 975–84.

Lau, A. W., Newman, A. R., and Broedling, L. A. (1980), 'The Nature of Managerial Work in the Public Sector', *Public Management Forum*, 19: 513–21.

McCall, M. W., and Segrist, C. A. (1980), *In Pursuit of the Manager's Job: Building on Mintzberg*, Greensboro, NC: Center for Creative Leadership.

McGovern, P., Hope-Hailey, V., and Stiles, P. (1998), 'The Managerial Career after Downsizing: Case Studies from the "Leading Edge"', *Work, Employment and Society*, 12/3: 457–77.

Mangham, I., and Silver, M. (1986), *Management Training: Context and Practice*, London: Economic and Social Research Council.

Marshall, J. (1984), *Women Managers: Travelling in a Male World*, Chichester: John Wiley.

Melamed, T. (1995), 'Careers Success: The Moderating Effect of Gender', *Journal of Vocational Behviour*, 47: 35–60.

Mintzberg, H. (1970), 'Structured Observation as a Method of Studying Managerial Work', *Journal of Management Studies*, 7: 87–104.

——(1973), *The Nature of Managerial Work*, New York: Harper & Row.

——(1975), 'The Manager's Job: Folklore and Fact', *Harvard Business Review*, 53/4: 49–61.

——(1989), *Mintzberg on Management*, New York: Free Press.

Mirza, H. S. (1992), *Young, Female and Black*, London: Routledge.

Neale, A. (1995), 'The Manager as Hero', paper presented at the Labour Process Conference, Blackpool, Apr.

Nkomo, S. M. (1988), 'Race and Sex: The Forgotten Case of the Black Female Manager', in S. Rose and L. Larwood (eds.), *Women's Careers: Pathways and Pitfalls*, London: Praeger.

O'Reilly, C. A., and Chatman, J. A. (1994), 'Working Longer and Harder: A Longitudinal Study of Managerial Success', *Administrative Science Quarterly*, 39/12: 603–27.

Osterman, P. (1996) (ed.), *Broken Ladders: Managerial Careers in the New Economy*, Oxford: Oxford University Press.

Pahl, R. (1995), *After Success: Fin-de-siecle Anxiety and Identity*, Cambridge: Polity.

Poole, M. E., Langan-Fox, J., and Omedei, M. (1993), 'Contrasting Subjective and Objective Criteria as Determinants of Perceived Career Success: A Longitudinal Study', *Journal of Occupational and Organizational Psychology*, 66: 39–54.

Powell, G. N., and Mainiero, L. A. (1992), 'Cross-currents in the River of Time: Conceptualizing the Complexities of Women's Careers', *Journal of Management*, 18/2: 215–37.

Purcell, J. (1982), 'The Rediscovery of the Management Prerogative: The Management of Labour Relations in the 1980s', *Oxford Review of Economic Policy*, 7/1: 33–43.

Reed, M. (1989), *The Sociology of Management*, London: Harvester Wheatsheaf.

——and Anthony, P. (1992), 'Professionalizing Management and Managing Professionalizing: British Management in the 1980s', *Journal of Management Studies*, 29/5: 591–613.

Russo, N., Kelly, R. M., and Deacon, M. (1991), 'Gender and Success-Related Attribution: Beyond Individualistic Conceptions of Achievement', *Sex Roles*, 25/5 6: 331–50.

Scarborough, H., and Burrell, G. (1996), 'The Axeman Cometh: The Changing Role and Knowledge of Middle Managers', in S. Clegg and G. Palmer (eds.), *The Politics of Management Knowledge*, Thousand Oaks, Calif.: Sage.

Scott, J. (1979), *Corporations, Classes and Capitalism*, London: Hutchinson.

Simpson, R. (1998), 'Presenteeism, Power and Organizational Change: Long Hours as a Career Barrier and the Impact on the Working Lives of Women Managers', *British Journal of Management*, Conference Issue, 9 (special issue), 37–50.

Snyder, H. H., and Wheelan, T. L. (1981), 'Managerial Roles: Mintzberg and the Management Process Theorists', *Proceedings Academy of Management*, 249–53.

Stewart, R. (1974), 'The Manager's Job: Discretion versus Demand', *Organizational Dynamics*, 2/3: 67–80.

——(1979), *Managers and their Jobs*, London: Macmillan.

——(1982*a*), 'A Model for Understanding Managerial Jobs and Behavior', *Academy of Management Review*, 7: 7–14.

——(1982*b*), *Choices for the Manager*, Maidenhead: McGraw-Hill.

——(1994), 'Managerial Behaviour', Templeton College Management Research Paper. Oxford: Templeton College.

——(1997), *The Reality of Management* (3rd edn.), Oxford: Butterworth Heinemann.

Sturges, J. (1999), 'What it Means to Succeed: Personal Conceptions of Career Success Held by Male and Female Managers at Different Ages', *British Journal of Management*, 10/3: 239–52.

Thomas, R., and Dunkerley, D. (1999), 'Careering Downwards? Middle Managers' Experiences in the Downsized Organization', *British Journal of Management*, 10: 157–69.

Wajcman, J. (1996), 'Women and Men Managers: Careers and Equal Opportunities', ch. 12 in R. Crompton, D. Gallie, and K. Purcell (eds.), *Changing Forms of Employment: Organizations, Skills and Gender*, London: Routledge.

Watson, T. (1994), *In Search of Management*, London: Routledge.

——(1997), *Sociology, Work and Industry* (3rd edn.), London: Routledge.

Wensley, R. (1996), 'Isabella Beaton: Management as "Everything in its Place"', *London Business School Strategy Review*, 7/1: 37–46.

Wood, R. C. (1992), *Working in Hotels and Catering*, London: Routledge.

Zeitlin, M. (1989), *The Large Corporation and Contemporary Classes*, Cambridge: Polity.

9 | Motivation

Having looked at the rationale behind job design and described what work means and how it might be experienced, this chapter turns to theories of motivation to see what attempts have, and can, be made to improve the quality of working life for employees. Motivation theory tends to be dominated by psychology, but sociology also has an interesting contribution to make to our understanding of how motivation may be viewed as a social construction. It is useful to us when meaning is lost from jobs. Seivers (1986) for example has argued that motivation only became an issue for management as organizational theorists when meaning was either lost or disappeared from work; motivation theories have become surrogates for the search for meaning (Thompson and McHugh 2002: 306).

When chief executives say that people are their biggest asset or their only source of competitive advantage, it suggests that they value their human resource. Advocates of humane work practices have long needed some proof that treating people well was good for business as well as good ethical behaviour. The 'right' motivation theory could potentially offer that proof. The right theory might explain a range of behaviour found in organizations and may even provide the key to increased productivity.

No fewer than 140 definitions of motivation have been found in the literature (Kleinginna and Kleinginna 1981). While Vroom (1964) defines it as 'a process governing choices made by persons or lower organisms among alternative forms of voluntary activity', Dewsbury (1978) says that the concept of motivation tends to be used as a garbage pail for a variety of factors whose nature is not well understood. Motivational models are commonly divided between those which focus on an individual's internal attributes, needs, drives, goals (content theories) and those that focus on the individual's interactions with the environment, cognitive judgements about rewards, costs, and preferences (process theories). Discussions of motivation theory usually start with the need theories, content theories, principally Maslow's need hierarchy and Herzberg's two-factor theory, both usually considered content theories.

Maslow's Theory

Maslow's hierarchy of needs tends to be treated as classical within the field of organizational behaviour, being referred to as a 'classic among classics' (Matteson and Ivancevich 1989: 369). It remains a conceptual starting point for motivation theory. In Maslow's (1943) theory of motivation there are thought to be five sets of needs which people possess and as you satisfy most of the needs at one level you move up to seek satisfaction at the next. These needs are innate and so are universal and unchanging. Physiological needs, the lowest needs for food and drink, are followed by safety needs, love needs, esteem needs, then finally the need for self-actualization, the desire to realize your ultimate potential. Self-actualization is defined as the 'desire to become more and more what one is, to become everything that one is capable of becoming' (1954: 92), a need that can be expressed in a range of ways both in and outside work.

Implicit in the idea that a person is motivated to satisfy needs is that needs serve as inevitable determinants of action. Maslow (1943) speaks of self-actualizing behaviour as a compulsive thing, as musicians who must make music and artists who must paint. This formulation provides an explanation of behaviour—I had to do it—and can aid in the maintenance of behaviour in the face of negative reactions about their worth or acceptability. But what about people who find themselves in jobs that will not help them satisfy higher-order needs? Individuals in lower-level occupations are more likely to be motivated by lower-order needs, physiological and safety needs, because these are not sufficiently gratified to allow needs at a higher order (self-esteem and self-actualization) to become prepotent, more powerful.

The strength of the theory lies in the fact that it supports management practices that encourage employee autonomy and personal growth as these will enable employees to satisfy esteem and self-actualization needs. Proper management of the ways in which people work and earn their living can improve them and improve the world and in this sense be a utopian revolutionary technique (Maslow 1965: 1). There are however limits to what can be achieved. It is appropriate only when employees are already developed (Maslow 1965: 15–33).

STOP | Linstead (2002) argues that Maslow's theory is kitsch (defined as worthless pretentiousness). Is he right?

A Critique of Maslow

Maslow's theory lacks empirical support (Wahba and Bridwell 1976) as Maslow himself admitted when in 1962 he wrote 'My motivation theory was published 20 years ago and in all that time nobody repeated it, or tested it, or really analyzed it or criticised it. They just used it, swallowed it whole with only the minor modifications' (Lowry 1982: 63).

In 1972 Alderfer suggested a revision of Maslow's need hierarchy. In Maslow's model if the individual is frustrated at a particular need level, he or she stays at that level until the need is satisfied. Once it is satisfied, the individual progresses to the next level of the hierarchy. Unfortunately empirical research has failed consistently to confirm this (e.g. Lawler and Suttle 1972; Rauschenberger et al. 1980; Hall and Nougaim 1968). For example Hall and Nougaim found that as managers advanced, safety needs became less important while higher-order needs were more important but this could be explained by a process of career change and advancement. Alderfer proposed that when an individual becomes frustrated at a particular need level he or she might regress to a lower level. He also suggested that instead of the five-level model, a more appropriate hierarchy would be based on three need levels (for existence, relatedness, and growth). This theory, though, has not received much more empirical support than Maslow's.

Cullen (1994) goes one step further than Alderfer and says Maslow's methodology is suspect. It has also been accused of being occupationally biased (Friedlander 1965), culturally biased (Nevis 1983), male biased (Cullen 1994; Cullen and Gotell 2002), better understood as a mythical quest for the meaning of life, and elitist (Shaw and Colimore 1988). The needs hierarchy serves to legitimate and perpetuate exploitative relations (Knights and Wilmott 1974/5: 219; Buss 1979). At the same time it allows for finding imagination, ingenuity, and creativity in the average person (McGregor 1960) and supports the move away from the more negative assumptions of human nature underlying the practices of scientific management. It could be said then to contain contradictory premisses. There is a 'democratic' one that emphasizes authenticity, self-fulfilment, and respect for the choices, preferences, and values of each individual. At the same time there is an 'aristocratic' premiss which emphasizes vocational competence, self-criticism, and deference to the choices, preferences, and values of the self-actualizing elite (Aron 1977; Cullen 1997). For Maslow the 'good' society is one in which the 'biological elite' are given the opportunity to develop their superiority, but are protected from the 'almost inevitable malice of the biologically non-gifted' (Hoffman 1996: 71) who cannot accept the reality that their inferiority is a matter of biological chance. The theory has intuitive appeal and influence because it is concerned with individual superiority and social dominance (Cullen 1997).

Do people in reality only tend to seek out the company of others once they have had enough to eat (Watson 1996)? It is not difficult to think about problems with Maslow's hierarchy of needs. It is possible that they have structurally different hierarchies or that they differ in their concept formation so no two of us use identical categories or categorization rules. It is also possible that these needs are not hard-wired biological and/or psychological mechanisms but cognitive processes. Uncertainty in the workplace might lead to an emphasis on affiliation motives—the more uncertain the environment, the more likely individuals are to exert more effort to develop and maintain relationships (Veroff et al. 1984).

STOP

Watson (2002) argues that students just 'surface learn' so that motivation is linked with Maslow. This approach is typified in the phrase 'Motivation, that's Maslow isn't it?' Is he right? Look at Watson's (2002 and 1996) argument and evaluate for yourself how useful Maslow's theory is to a practising manager.

Frederick Herzberg's Theory

Herzberg (1968) says there is a manager in every audience who thinks the simplest, surest, and most direct way of motivating someone is to kick them in the 'ass'—give them the KITA, as he abbreviated it. There are various forms of it. The literal one is inelegant, contradicts the precious image of benevolence that most organizations cherish, and often results in the employee just kicking you in return. Positive KITA rewards the desired behaviour (like autonomous working—Thompson and McHugh 2002) but is not motivation. Herzberg's theory of motivation starts with the premise that the factors involved in producing job satisfaction and motivation are separate and distinct from the factors that lead to job dissatisfaction. These two feelings are not opposites of each other. The opposite of job satisfaction is no job satisfaction while the opposite of job dissatisfaction is no job dissatisfaction.

Herzberg believes that the growth or motivator factors that are intrinsic to work are achievement, recognition for achievement, the work itself, responsibility, and growth or advancement. These factors are to do with the job content. Motivators are the primary cause of job satisfaction. Motivators cause positive job attitudes because they satisfy the worker's need for self-actualization (Maslow 1954), the individual's ultimate goal.

Hygiene factors stand in contrast to motivators. Hygiene factors are the primary cause of unhappiness in work. The hygiene factors that are to do with the context of the job are extrinsic to the job and include company policy, administration, supervision, interpersonal relationships, working conditions, salary, status, and security.

Twelve different investigations informed the theory, research which included a diverse range of employees: lower-level supervisors, professional women, agricultural administrators, men about to retire from management positions, hospital maintenance personnel, nurses, food handlers, military officers, engineers, teachers, housekeepers, accountants, foremen, and engineers. Interviewees were asked open-ended questions about their jobs, when they felt bad or good about their jobs (Herzberg et al. 1959). They were asked what job events had occurred in their work that had led to extreme satisfaction or extreme dissatisfaction.

In an attempt to enrich jobs, management, Herzberg argues, has horizontally loaded jobs. For example they might challenge the employee by increasing the amount of production expected of them. Instead of tightening 10,000 bolts a day, see if they can tighten 20,000 bolts. This merely enlarges the meaninglessness of the job. Instead Herzberg recommends enriching work by vertical loading. This can be done by removing some controls while retaining accountability, by increasing the accountability of individuals for their own work, giving a complete natural unit of work (e.g. giving an employee a whole job rather than a small part). The supervisor or manager could grant additional authority to an employee, make periodic reports directly available to the worker rather than the supervisor, introduce new and more difficult tasks, or assign individual specialized tasks enabling them to become experts. Not all jobs can be enriched though, nor do all jobs need to be enriched.

Herzberg's theory suggested that a job should enhance employee motivation to the extent that it provides opportunities for achievement, recognition, responsibility, advancement, and growth in competence. These principles gave rise to a series of generally successful job enlargement experiments in the American Telephone and Telegraph Company, summarized by Ford (1969). A number of researchers though were unable to provide empirical support for some of the major tenets of the theory (e.g. Dunnette et al. 1967; Hinton 1968; King 1970).

Critique of Herzberg

Many critics find it a little strange and a little more than coincidence that Herzberg's two sets of factors fit so neatly into two boxes—intrinsic contributing to job satisfaction and extrinsic to dissatisfaction. Researchers have questioned whether these are separate and distinct factors giving different outcomes. It is conceivable for example that a new company policy (a hygiene factor) could have a significant effect on a worker's interest in the work itself or their success with it (Locke 1976; Tietjen and Myers 1998). In a study by Ewan (1963) it was found that hygiene factors, dissatisfiers, actually acted as satisfiers while satisfiers (motivators) sometimes acted in the predicted manner and sometimes caused both satisfaction and dissatisfaction.

Researchers have also questioned whether the differences in result reflect defensive processes at work within the individual. Individuals may be more likely to perceive the causes of satisfaction within the self and therefore describe experiences invoking their own achievement, recognition of advancement in their job. On the other hand dissatisfaction is attributed, not to personal inadequacies, but to factors in the work environment (Vroom and Maier 1961). Put simply, employees interviewed were taking credit for the satisfying events such as advancement or recognition, while blaming others such as supervisors, subordinates, and peers for dissatisfying situations (Locke 1976).

Locke (1976) also criticizes Herzberg's analysis for placing an emphasis on the number of times a particular factor was mentioned. Even though a dissatisfying factor is recorded numerously, this does not necessarily imply that this factor is a significant problem or even an irritation to the worker. Locke suggests that the measurement of intensity of satisfaction or dissatisfaction, rather than frequency, could have been used.

Centers and Bugental (1966) set out to look at the strength of intrinsic and extrinsic job factors in a sample of the entire working population. Respondents were asked 'Which of these things is the most important factor keeping you in your present job?' (1966: 194). Answers included extrinsic factors such as pay, good co-workers, and job security while the intrinsic included interesting work, skilled work, and job satisfaction. They found that intrinsic job components were more valued among white-collar groups than blue-collar groups. The extrinsic job components were more valued in blue-collar groups. No consistent sex differences appeared in the extent to which they valued intrinsic or extrinsic job satisfaction in general though men placed a slightly higher value than women on self-expression in their work. They conclude that job motivations of workers at higher level stem from the work itself, the skill required, and the interest value of the work. At lower levels job motivations are centred in facts external to the work itself. These findings are not surprising if one considers what else there is to value except extrinsic factors in low-level jobs. Further individuals in low-level occupations may not be sufficiently grati-fied to allow higher-order needs to become prepotent.

More recently the issue of trust in a supervisor, fundamental to good relationships with the supervisor, could be an important variable in predicting job satisfaction (and there-fore reported absence and desire to quit). Trust was found to be just as important as intrin-sic factors (Cunningham and MacGregor 2000.) Fostering or maintaining trusting relationships between individuals who have to work together could help enhance the benefits from improving the design of a job.

McClelland's Need for Achievement Theory

Motives are believed to function to energize and direct behaviour. David McClelland and his colleagues are specifically interested in how people are motivated to achieve, in need for achievement. The achievement motive is defined in McClelland's theory as a process of planning and striving for excellence (McClelland et al. 1953). People with a high need for achievement have a strong desire to assume personal responsibility for performing a task; they tend to set difficult goals and have a strong desire for feedback about their performance (McClelland et al. 1953). McClelland believes that there is a connection between the need for achievement and economic growth—the more individuals have a need for achievement, the greater economic growth. Innate and early-learned need for achievement is an essential characteristic of entrepreneurs.

David McClelland and his colleagues believe that there are two types of motives that can be identified using different research instruments. Implicit motives develop early in childhood, at a preverbal stage and tend to be poorly represented and difficult to articu-late. Self-attributed motives are thought to develop later in childhood and are more read-ily accessible to consciousness. Implicit motives are assessed indirectly with projective instruments, typically the Thematic Apperception Test (TAT). Participants might be given four minutes to create a story in response to one of 4–6 black and white pictures used to assess need for achievement (e.g. a picture of female scientists, an executive or architect at a desk). The supporting theory argues that people will project their own feelings, motives, and needs into the picture. Participants are asked to write a story in response to a question or questions about for example what is going on in this situation, what has led up to it, and what has happened in the past. The stories are then analysed by a coder who has to interpret what has been said in the story; they search for projected expressions of achievement. McClelland and his colleagues have devised a scoring system for need for achievement (McClelland et al. 1953).

The second technique for assessing need for achievement is through questionnaire. Self-attributed motives are assessed with self-report questionnaires containing for exam-ple true/false questions like 'I enjoy difficult work.' (For a recent application see Thrash and Elliot 2002.) The scale and questions that have been most commonly used to look at need for achievement are the achievement scale, from the Personality Research Form which assesses conscious motivation (Jackson 1974). However it has been noted that it does not include need for mastery (*sic*), need for work, and competitiveness, which are seen to overlap with or be components of need for achievement (Helmreich and Spence 1978). Goal commitment and perceived goal difficulty could also be components of need for achievement (Johnson and Perlow 1992). These scales are likely now to be added in research on need for achievement to give a multi-component view of need for achievement.

Critique of McClelland's Need for Achievement Theory

There have been some questions raised about this relationship between need for achievement and entrepreneurs (Frey 1984; Gilleard 1989). Other writers have argued that the influencing attributes of entrepreneurs are paramount (Furnham 1992); the successful entrepreneur is someone who can 'get things done through other people' (Timmons et al. 1985: 115). Entrepreneurs need managerial skills (Hisrich 1990). The argument that need for achievement is the dominant motive disposition for entrepreneurs may be in conflict then with other research (Langan-Fox and Roth 1995).

The projective test has been criticized for being complicated and time consuming both in administration and scoring (Gjesm and Nygard 1970). It is seen by some to be subjective. It is difficult to interpret the stories and the interpreter may need clinical psychology experience to be competent (see Hansemark 1997). It is criticized for having low predictive validity and reliability (Fineman 1977; Entwhistle 1972).

Early research using projective measurement techniques found that women have a lower need for achievement than men (McClelland et al. 1953; Veroff et al. 1953). This was explained in part by seeing the need to compete as a masculine attribute. However more recent research shows that women in general possess comparable need for achievement (Lips and Colwill 1978; Stein and Bailey 1975) or higher need for achievement than men (Veroff et al. 1975; Chusmir 1985).

The most obvious weakness with the questionnaire is that subjects make choices about what can be seen as socially acceptable. They can create an ideal picture of themselves. Links between questionnaires and projective tests are questionable. Fineman (1977) found no correlation between the results of questionnaires and TAT tests.

Equity Theory of Motivation

This is a cognitive or process theory of motivation put forward by Stacey Adams of the General Electric Company in 1963. It deals with two questions—what do people think is fair and equitable and how do they respond when they feel they are getting far more or far less than they deserve (Walster et al. 1978)? The theory suggests that people are capable and willing to perceive fairness in their immediate environment. People act in the light of what they regard as fair. They compare their input or 'investments' (Homans 1961) such as ability, skill, age, education, effort, and training to outcomes like monetary rewards, praise, status, and improved promotion opportunities. They also compare their reward to that of others with whom they make the comparison. For example if a skilled worker is currently earning a certain wage but finds that other similarly skilled workers in a different company are earning more, then that skilled worker can be expected to experience feelings of deprivation if there is no obvious reason for the underpayment. They then have to make a 'cognitive adjustment' in order to deal with the inequity. They could, for example, lower their inputs, their work contribution, or attempt to raise their outcomes like pay. They may decide to redefine their reference group, the individuals with whom they made the comparison, so in this case they might find another group of skilled workers in a different company with whom to make the comparison. They could change their perceptions of the skills involved in doing their job, saying, for example, the skills used in this job are not as many as those used in company X. Alternatively they could convince themselves that they are well compensated in other ways. Adams (1963) lists eight different courses of action that could be taken to reduce inequity.

In an example used to support the theory Adams (1963) discusses the case of check-out staff at supermarkets. Employed there are a cashier and a 'bundler', a person who takes the bought goods out of the trolley and puts them in bags ready for the customer to take away. Under normal conditions the cashier's job was of a higher status, better paid, permanent, and full-time whereas bundling was of lower status and lower pay, and was usually done by part-time employees who were often young. Psychologically bundlers were usually perceived as working for cashiers. As the employees in both groups varied in sex, age, and education, a bundler could be directed to work for a cashier whose status (as determined by sex, age, and education) was lower. For example a male university student of 21 years of age could be ordered to work for a secondary-school female cashier of 17. The response of the bundlers to this perceived inequity was to reduce their work speed. Consequently there was a cost to the store; those stores with greatest inequity between lower-status cashiers and higher-status bundlers experienced greater cost of operating the services. It cost approximately 27 per cent more to operate the stores in which the inequity was higher.

Evidence from other researchers has been found to support the theory. Some of the findings stress the negative ways in which workers can redress inequality. Underpayment leads to lowered job performance (Lord and Hohenfeld 1979; Prichard et al. 1972). Underpaid workers paid on a piece-rate basis have been found to produce more goods of lower quality (Prichard 1969). Another form of reaction to underpayment is disruptive, deviant behaviour such as vandalism and theft (Hollinger and Clark 1983). Acts of employee theft may be an effective means of increasing outcomes in order to reduce feelings of underpayment inequity. Pilferage can be seen as 'a morally justified addition to wages . . . an entitlement due from exploiting employers' (Mars 1974: 224). Greenberg (1990) found that in manufacturing plants, where a temporary 15 per cent pay cut was introduced, the workers felt highly underpaid and employee theft rates were as much as 250 per cent higher than under normal pay conditions. Higher rates of theft are found where limited information was given in an insensitive manner; lower rates are found if the basis for underpayment is thoroughly and sensitively explained to workers (Greenberg 1990).

However equity theory also shows that the cognitive adjustment can be more positive. Underpaid workers are motivated to perceive the tasks they perform as highly interesting so as to cognitively justify their performing them in exchange for low wages (Deci 1975;

AN EXAMPLE OF A PROBLEM OF INEQUITY AT THE BANK AND IN THE FORCES

Paris-born bank clerks worked side by side with other clerks who did identical work and earned identical wages but were born in the Provinces. The Parisians were dissatisfied with their wages for they considered that Parisian breeding was an input into the wage bargain which deserved monetary compensation. The bank management, while recognizing that place of birth distinguished the two groups, did not consider birthplace relevant in the exchange of services for pay (Crozier 1960).

This is an interesting finding in the light of a court case where former Gurkha soldiers from Nepal, who served in the British army, lost their battle for equal pay and pensions in the courts. Differential treatment was seen as lawful given the difference of living in Britain and Nepal (Tait 2003). Yet only the year before, Gurkha war veterans, subjected to brutal treatment in Japanese prisoner of war camps, won a case of unequal treatment and racial discrimination. They were awarded £10,000 each in compensation. They had been excluded for compensation payments awarded to British survivors of the camps in the 1950s (Norton-Taylor 2002). Is this inequity what you would have anticipated or expected?

Lepper and Greene 1978). Opportunities to work in large, private offices or to have large desks have been recognized as valued organizational rewards (Konar et al. 1982). Employees enhance the value of non-monetary aspects of their job in order to make up for being underpaid (Lepper and Greene 1978; Greenberg 1989). Currently however equity theory does not help us fully understand when the various reactions to inequality will occur and how they are interrelated (Cook and Parcel 1977; Greenberg 1993).

It is interesting that only some of the research on equity theory has examined if there are differences between women's sense of equity and men's (e.g. Greenberg 1989). There appears to be no reported difference yet it was a factor under consideration in the early studies (see Adams 1963). Researchers who have followed Adams appear to ignore sex referring to all subjects as 'he' (for example Prichard 1969) while others, for example Harder (1991), assume you realize that as the subjects are baseball players they will all be men.

Expectancy Theory of Motivation

Expectancy theory is another process of cognitive theory and can also be applied to pay and motivation. Expectancy theory admits the possibility that individuals may have different goals or needs and that individuals may perceive different connections between actions and their achievement of goals. In 1957 Georgopolous et al. sketched the mechanics of expectancy theory in their path goal theory. Seven years later Vroom (1964) published his expectancy theory of work motivation. Vroom's formulation postulates that the motivational force for an individual is a function of the expectancy that certain outcomes will result from their behaviour and the valence or desirability of these outcomes. It is suggested that individuals consider alternatives, weigh costs and benefits, and choose a course of action of maximum utility. The decision by an individual then to work on a particular task and expend a certain amount of effort is a function of their probability estimate that they can accomplish the task and the probability estimate that accomplishing the task will be followed by certain outcomes. This is dependent on the valence, the desirability of the outcomes. Different rewards can be accrued by the individual as a result of effort or performance. Extrinsic outcomes are rewards distributed by some external agent like the boss or the organization. Intrinsic rewards are mediated by the individual and are personal rewards like self-fulfilment and self-esteem.

Expectancy theory proposes that motivation and work-related behaviour can be predicted if we know about workers' strength of desire for various outcomes and the probability of achieving them. (For an application of the theory in an industrial setting, with a discussion of its weaknesses see Reinharth and Wahba 1976.) Here are some examples of how it works. First it assumes, as we have seen, that an individual perceives that effort is positively correlated with level of performance so experienced secretaries who believe they can increase the number of words they type per minute by exerting greater effort have a high effort–performance expectancy. Less experienced typists may realize that no matter how much effort they put in performance is fixed at a low level; they have low effort–performance expectancy. The theory predicts that the person with the high effort–performance expectancy will be more motivated to perform. Secondly it assumes that a person's expectations of reward will be tied to his or her level of performance. A sales person who is paid on commission is likely to have high performance–outcome expectancy. A person who works with no prospect of receiving a bonus has low performance–outcome expectancy. The former will be more motivated to perform than the latter. Thirdly, valence, the degree to which an individual values a particular reward means the more people value the reward they receive for their effort, the more motivated they will be to receive the reward. Rewards for which people generally have high valence include salaries, bonuses, promotion, and recognition. However individuals will differ. As an employer you can increase the effort employees expend by increasing the expectation that greater effort will lead to a higher level of performance, by strengthening the perceived link between results and rewards, and by ensuring that employees value the rewards given for high performance.

This then is the basic theory but it has been made more complex by the number of factors that are now recognized as affecting the basic components. Lawler (1970) first modified the basic theory by introducing two variables that affect the effort–performance expectancy. The first is ability, the individual's skill level. An employee must not only possess the skills but be able to apply them. The more confidently people believe they can apply their skills to solve new tasks, the higher the effort–performance expectancy. Past experience will affect a person's confidence in his or her problem-solving approach. The second is past experience as it also affects motivation. Satisfaction is a measure of how well the extrinsic and intrinsic rewards for performing a job satisfy the individual's needs and desires.

Wahba and House (1974) report that expectancy theory has a great deal of potential for understanding job behaviour and work motivation. The predictions of expectancy theory are generally supported by research. However the magnitude of the support varies from study to study. Most studies deal only with limited parts of the theory rather than the whole theory. Consequently the predictions of the whole theory are virtually unknown. Further there are unresolved methodological and logical issues, for example inadequate clarification of concepts like expectancy and valence.

Arvey and Mussio (1973) found little support for expectancy theory and job performance and satisfaction in their study of female clerical workers. A common criticism of expectancy theory is that it is unlikely that individuals actually carry out all of the complicated calculations implied by the model. Wanous et al. (1983) imply that expectancy mechanisms only come into play when there is a period for reflection on the possible outcomes. It may help us understand the important decisions an individual is making (Guest 1984).

Some Thoughts on Motivation

Herzberg relied on verbal accounts from individuals of their motivation. Should we, as social scientists, always take a person's word and not question it? If we cannot see motives, how do we know they are real? Do we know that motives are not produced to create a 'case' or a 'position'? These are the kinds of questions about motivation that Laurie Taylor (1972)—the sociologist turned radio journalist—has asked. People may lie, he argues, to continue their deviant behaviour or to explain the initial reason for their act. There are only a limited range of acceptable justifications for behaviour and these may be adopted as we are acting. Once articulated they become reasons for continuance. People typically cite motives that they consider will be regarded as satisfactory or acceptable. Put crudely we tell people what we think they want to hear (Taylor and Walton 1971). If we are no longer able to articulate such motives, then we may give up the behaviour. Motives are not inner biological mainsprings of action but linguistic constructs that organize acts. Motives are not mysterious internal states, but typical vocabularies with clear functions in particular social situations (Wright Mills 1940). Each audience may be offered a different account.

To illustrate how motives serve a particular purpose and can have a clear function, Taylor uses the case of sexual deviants. Taylor (1972) investigated sexual deviancy, looking at the range of justifications which are available to deviants, the role of others in determining which are acceptable, and the variables which restrict the acceptance or development of motives. He discovered that friends will be told a similar story to that which is provided for the magistrate or psychiatrist. The majority of the responses had in common a reference to factors beyond the individual's control. They refer to certain forces or circumstances outside the person which impinge upon him often in a sudden or unexpected manner. For example they may say they had a breakdown in mental functioning at the time of the offence, or that they were overcome by a desire which compelled them to act against their will. When magistrates were asked how likely they thought a statement to be true, it was found that the explanations offered by offenders were accorded significantly more credibility if the explanation was that the offender did not assert any conscious control over his behaviour. Magistrates reject statements made by offenders who claim that their action was intentional or meaningful (like 'I get sexual

---

A CASE FOR MOTIVATION?

A loan company called Purple Loans (part of the GE Capital group of finance brokers) invested in Special Air Service (SAS) military style training to improve the motivation of staff (see 'The Motivators', *Money Programme*, BBC, 2002). The company hoped in particular to improve teamworking and communication, that the training would result in people working more closely together, and therefore increase the number of sales. At the end of the training one of the staff members said that she felt as though if she set her mind to any task, she could do it. The training had made her feel more confident and motivated to achieve.

What could be the potential benefits of SAS training on sales staff?

How would you research the impact of this type of training on a sales team?

How would you know if they were more highly motivated?

---

satisfaction out of it') (see also Taylor and Walton 1971). Taylor (1972) finishes by asking us if we are prepared to go on accepting that a large section of our society is subject to sudden blackouts and irresistible urges over which they lack any control. We ought to question articulated motives.

Thinking about Job Satisfaction and Positive Outcomes for Organizations

The literature is in dispute as to the extent to which increased job satisfaction leads to improved performance. Brayfield and Crockett (1955) conclude there is no evidence of a relationship between job satisfaction and performance. However Iaffaldano and Muchinsky (1985) conclude that there is a weak relationship and Petty et al. (1984) demonstrate there is a strong relationship. Studies have revealed that satisfied employees are more likely to have low absenteeism and turnover (Tett and Meyer 1993; Barling et al. 1990; Pierce et al. 1991; Eby et al. 1999).

Job satisfaction and motivation are difficult subjects to study as there are so many views on offer, and so many of them offer contradictory positions. It is then a subject where arguments need to be weighed and balanced. There are few easy solutions to be found in this research. One way in which managers have tried to increase motivation and efficiency is through empowerment. This is the subject of the next chapter but first we will look at how much power management have and how much they appear to be willing to share.

■ SUGGESTIONS FOR FURTHER READING

1. Walster, E., Walster, G. W., and Berscheid, E. (1978), *Equity: Theory and Research*, Boston: Allyn & Bacon. This book discusses many of the experiments that have been done to show what happens at work when people feel they have been treated with inequity. It gives you some idea as to what you can expect to find.

2. Thompson, P., and McHugh, D. (2002), 'Motivation: The Drive for Satisfaction', ch. 19 in *Work Organizations* (3rd edn.), Houndmills: Palgrave. This chapter provides a critical introduction to motivation. It makes some controversial remarks to make you think, like 'managers often appear to be better at demotivating workers than at enthusing them with the spirit of the enterprise' (p. 314).

3. Fulop, L., and Linstead, S. (1999), 'Managing Motivation', ch. 7 in L. Fulop and S. Linstead, *Management: A Critical Text*, Houndmills: Macmillan. This chapter is useful in discussing motivation critically and linking motivation with concepts like commitment, emotion, and trust.

4. Brotherton, C. (1999), 'Individual Performance at Work: The Problem of Motivation', ch. 3 in *Social Psychology and Management: Issues for a Changing Society*, Open University Press, Buckingham. This chapter provides another critical appraisal of motivation so lacking in most mainstream texts.

5. Brooks, I. (2003), *Organizational Behaviour: Individuals, Groups and Organization* (2nd edn.), Harlow: Pearson. Chapter 3, 'Motivation to Work', includes a good critique of Maslow.

6. Cullen, D., and Gotell, L. (2002), 'From Orgasms to Organizations: Maslow, Women's Sexuality and the Gendered Foundations of the Needs Hierarchy', *Gender, Work and Organization*, 9/5: 537–55. Another critique of Maslow.

7. Watson, T. (2002), *Organizing and Managing Work*, Harlow: Pearson. Chapter 9 critically discusses motivation theories.

▓ WEB SITES

For a biography of Maslow and description of his theory on self-actualization see **www.ship.edu/~cgboeree/maslow.html**. Typing the word 'Maslow' into a search engine like Google leads to a whole host of web sites.

For a description of Herzberg and other motivation theorists see **www.accel-team.com/human_relations/ hrels_05_herzberg.html**

▓ QUESTIONS

1. In 1972 Martina Horner concluded that there was a high and perhaps increasing incidence of the motive to avoid success found in women. The predominant message was that highly competent women, when faced with conflict between their feminine image and expressing their competencies, adjust their behaviour to the sex stereotype. Do you think this finding would be replicated today?

2. 'The pathway to company profit is also the pathway to self actualisation' (Rose 1996). Discuss.

3. Critically assess McClelland's theory of need for achievement.

4. It might be possible for organizations to motivate their employees to act ethically or unethically. How? (See Fudge and Schlacter 1999.)

5. When individuals find themselves participating in inequitable relationships they become distressed. The more inequitable the relationship, the more distress individuals feel. Does this hold true if you are over-rewarded, or only if you are under-rewarded? (Answer to be found in Walster et al. 1978: 17). Has other research supported this finding? (See for example Jaques 1961; Prichard et al. 1972.)

■ GROUP EXERCISE

There are huge inequities in the salaries of male football players in Britain. Research what football players or male and female tennis players are paid. Could equity theory be applied here? What are the advantages and disadvantages of the inequitable payment for the motivation of players?

■ REFERENCES

Adams, S. (1963), 'Toward an Understanding of Inequity', *Journal of Abnormal and Social Psychology*, 67/5: 422–36.

Aron, A. (1977), 'Maslow's Other Child', *Journal of Humanistic Psychology*, 17/2: 9–24.

Arvey, R. D., and Mussio, S. J. (1973), 'A Test of Expectancy Theory in a Field Setting Using Female Clerical Employees', *Journal of Vocational Behaviour*, 3: 421–32.

Barling, J., Wade, B., and Fullagar, C. (1990), 'Predicting Employee Commitment to Company and Union: Divergent Models', *Journal of Occupational Psychology*, 63/1: 49–63.

Brayfield, A. H., and Crockett, W. H. (1955), 'Employee Attitudes and Employee Performance', *Psychological Bulletin*, 52: 396–424.

Buss, A. R. (1979), 'Humanistic Psychology as Liberal Ideology: The Socio-historical Roots of Maslow's Theory of Self Actualization', *Journal of Humanistic Psychology*, 19/3: 43–5.

Centers, R., and Bugental, D. E. (1966), 'Intrinsic and Extrinsic Job Motivations among Different Segments of the Working Population', *Journal of Applied Psychology*, 50/3: 193–7.

Chusmir, L. H. (1985), 'Motivation of Managers: Is Gender a Factor?' *Psychology of Women Quarterly*, 9: 153–9.

Cook, K. S., and Parcel, T. L. (1977), 'Equity Theory: Directions for Future Research', *Sociological Inquiry*, 47/2: 75–88.

Crozier, M. (1960), Personal communication, reported in S. Adams, 'Toward an Understanding of Inequity', *Journal of Abnormal and Social Psychology*, 67/5: 422–36.

Cullen, D. (1994), 'Feminism, Management and Self-Actualization', *Gender, Work and Organization*, 1/3: 127–37.

——(1997), 'Maslow, Monkeys and Motivation Theory', *Organization*, 4/3: 355–73.

——and Gotell, L. (2002), 'From Orgasms to Organizations: Maslow, Women's Sexuality and the Gendered Foundations of the Needs Hierarchy', *Gender, Work and Organization*, 9/5: 537–55.

Cunningham, J. Barton, and MacGregor, J. (2000), 'Trust and the Design of Work: Complementary Constructs in Satisfaction and Performance', *Human Relations*, 53/12: 1575–91.

Deci, E. L. (1975), *Intrinsic Motivation*, New York: Plenum.

Dewsbury, D. A. (1978), *Comparative Animal Behavior*, New York: McGraw Hill.

Dunnette, M. D., Campbell, J. P., and Hakel, M. D. (1967), 'Factors Contributing to Job Satisfaction and Job Dissatisfaction in Six Occupational Groups', *Organizational Behaviour and Human Performance*, 2: 143–74.

Eby, L., Feeman, D. M., Rush, M. C., and Lance, C. E. (1999), 'Motivational Bases of Affective Organizational Commitment: A Partial Test of an Integrative Theoretical Model', *Journal of Occupational and Organisational Psychology*, 72/4: 463–83.

Entwhistle, D. R. (1972), 'To Dispel Fantasies about Fantasy-Based Measures of Achievement Motivation', *Psychological Bulletin*, 77/6: 377–91.

Ewan, R. B. (1963), 'Determinants of Job Satisfaction', paper read at American Psychological Association, Philadelphia, September, cited in Wernimont (1966).

Fineman, S. (1977), 'The Achievement Motive Construct and its Measurement: Where are we now?', *British Journal of Psychology*, 68: 1–22.

Friedlander, F. (1965), 'Comparative Work Value Systems', *Personnel Psychology*, 18: 1–20.

Ford, R. N. (1969), *Motivation through the Work itself*, New York: American Management Association.

Frey, R. S. (1984), 'Need for Achievement, Entrepreneurship, and Economic Growth: A Critique of the McClelland Thesis', *Social Science Journal*, 21/2: 125–34.

Fudge, R. S., and Schlacter, J. L. (1999), 'Motivating Employees to Act Ethically: An Expectancy Theory Approach', *Journal of Business Ethics*, 18/3: 295–304.

Furnham, A. (1992), *Personality at Work*, London: Routledge.

Georgopolous, B. S., Mahoney, G. M., and Jones, N. W. (1957), 'A Path-Goal Approach to Productivity', *Journal of Applied Psychology*, 41: 345–53.

Gilleard, C. J. (1989), 'The Achieving Society Revisited: A Further Analysis of the Relation between National Growth and Need Achievement', *Journal of Economic Psychology*, 10/1: 21–34.

Gjesm, T., and Nygard, R. (1970), 'Achievement-Related Motives, Theoretical Considerations and Construction of the Measuring Instrument', Report no. 2, Sept., Fear of Failure project, University of Oslo.

Greenberg, J. (1989), 'Cognitive Re-evaluation of Outcomes in Response to Underpayment Inequity', *Academy of Management Journal*, 32/1: 174–84.

——(1990), 'Employee Theft as a Reaction to Underpayment Inequality: The Hidden Costs of Pay Cuts', *Journal of Applied Psychology*, 75: 561–8.

——(1993), 'Stealing in the Name of Justice: Informational and Interpersonal Moderators of Theft Reactions to Underpayment Inequality', *Organizational Behaviour and Human Decision Processes*, 54: 81–103.

Guest, D. (1984), 'What's New in Motivation', *Personnel Management*, May, 20–3.

Hall, D., and Nougaim, K. E. (1968), 'An Examination of Maslow's Need Hierarchy in an Organizational Setting', *Organizational Behaviour and Human Performance*, 3: 12–35.

Hansemark, O. C. (1997), 'Objective versus Projective Measurement of Need for Achievement: The Relation between TAT and CMPS', *Journal of Managerial Psychology*, 12/4: 280–9.

Harder, J. W. (1991), 'Equity Theory versus Expectancy Theory: The Case of Major League Baseball Free Agents', *Journal of Applied Psychology*, 76/3: 458–64.

Helmreich, R. L., and Spence, J. T. (1978), 'The Work and Family Orientation Questionnaire: An Objective Instrument to Assess Components of Achievement Motivation and Attitudes towards the Family and Career', *JSAS Catalog of Selected Documents in Psychology*, 8/35 (MS, No. 1677).

Herzberg, F. (1968), 'One More Time: How do you Motivate Employees?', *Harvard Business Review*, Jan.–Feb.

——Maunser, B., and Snyderman, B. (1959), *The Motivation to Work*, John Wiley & Sons, New York.

Hinton, B. L. (1968), 'An Empirical Investigation of the Herzberg Methodology and Two Factor Theory', *Organizational Behaviour and Human Performance*, 3: 286–309.

Hisrich, R. D. (1990), 'Entrepreneurship/Intrapreneurship', *American Psychologist*, 45: 209–22.

Hoffman, E. (ed.) (1996), *Future Visions: The Unpublished Papers of Abraham Maslow*, Thousand Oaks, Calif.: Sage.

Hollinger, R. D., and Clark, J. P. (1983), *Theft by Employees*, Lexington, Mass.: Lexington Books.

Homans, G. C. (1961), *Social Behavior: Its Elementary Forms*, London: Routledge & Kegan Paul.

Horner, M. (1972), 'Toward an Understanding of Achievement-Related Conflicts in Women', *Journal of Social Issues*, 28/2: 157–75.

Iaffaldano, M. T., and Muchinsky, P. M. (1985), 'Job Satisfaction and Job Performance: A Meta-analysis', *Psychological Bulletin*, 97/2: 251–73.

Jackson, D. N. (1974), *Personality Research Form Manual*, Port Huron, Mich.: Research Psychologist Press.

Jaques, E. (1961), *Equitable Payment*, New York: John Wiley & Sons.

Johnson, D. S., and Perlow, R. (1992), 'The Impact of Need for Achievement Components on Goal Commitment and Performance', *Journal of Applied Social Psychology*, 22/21: 1711–20.

King, N. (1970), 'A Clarification and Evaluation of the Two Factor Theory of Job Satisfaction', *Psychological Bulletin*, 74: 18–31.

Kleinginna, P. R., and Kleinginna, A. M. (1981), 'A Categorised List of Motivation Definitions with a Suggestion for a Consensual Definition', *Motivation and Emotion*, 5: 263–92.

Knights, D., and Wilmott, H. C. (1974/5), 'Humanistic Social Science and the Theory of Needs', *Interpersonal Development*, 5: 213–22.

Konar, E., Sundstrom, E., Brady, Mandel, D., and Rice, R. W. (1982), 'Status Demarcation in the Office, *Environment and Behavior*, 14: 561–80.

Langan-Fox, J., and Roth, S. (1995), 'Achievement Motivation and Female Entrepreneurs', *Journal of Occupational Psychology*, 68/3: 209–18.

Lawler, E. E. (1970), 'Job Attitudes and Employee Motivation: Theory, Research and Practice', *Personnel Psychology*, 23: 223–37.

——and Suttle, J. L. (1972), 'A Causal Correlation Test of the Need Hierarchy Concept', *Organizational Behavior and Human Performance*, 23: 251–67.

Lepper, M. R., and Greene, D. (eds.) (1978), *The Hidden Costs of Reward*, Hillsdale, NJ: Lawrence Erlbaum Associates.

Linstead, S. (2002), 'Organizational Kitsch', *Organization*, 9/4: 657–82.

Lips, H. M., and Colwill, N. J. (1978), *The Psychology of Sex Differences*, Englewood Cliffs, NJ: Prentice Hall.

Locke, E. A. (1976), 'The Nature and Causes of Job Satisfaction', in M. D. Dunnette (ed.), *Handbook of Industrial and Organizational Psychology*, Chicago: Rand McNally, pp. 1297–349.

Lord, R. G., and Hohenfeld, J. A. (1979), 'A Longitudinal Field Assessment of Equity Effects on the Performance of Major League Baseball Players', *Journal of Applied Psychology*, 64: 19–26.

Lowry, R. J. (1982) (ed.), *The Journals of Abraham Maslow*, Lexington, Mass.: Lewis.

McClelland, D. C., Atkinson, J. W., Clark, R. A., and Lowell, E. L. (1953), *The Achievement Motive*, New York: Appleton-Century-Crofts.

McGregor, D. (1960), *The Human Side of Enterprise*, New York: McGraw Hill.

Mars, G. (1974), 'Dock Pilferage: A Case Study in Occupational Theft', in P. Rock and M. McIntosh (eds.), *Deviance and Control*, London, Tavistock Institute, pp. 209–28.

Maslow, A. H. (1943), 'A Theory of Human Motivation', *Psychological Review*, 50: 370–96.

——(1954), *Motivation and Personality*, New York: Harper.

——(1965), *Eupsychian Management*, Homewood, Ill: Irwin.

Matteson, M. T., and Ivancevich, J. M. (eds.) (1989), *Management and Organizational Behavior Classics*, Homewood, Ill: BPI/Irwin.

Nevis, E. C. (1983), 'Using an American Perspective in Understanding another Culture: Toward a Hierarchy of Needs for the People's Republic of China', *Journal of Applied Behavioral Science*, 19: 249–64.

Norton-Taylor, R. (2002), 'Racist MoD ordered to compensate Gurkha PoWs: Landmark Ruling Finds Veterans were Irrationally Excluded from Payouts to British Survivors of Camps', *Guardian*, 28 Nov.

Petty, M. M., McGee, G. W., and Cavender, J. W. (1984), 'A Meta-analysis of the Relationships between Individual Performance', *Academy of Management Review*, 9/4: 712–21.

Pierce, J. L., Rubenfeld, S. A., and Morgan, S. (1991), 'Employee Ownership: A Conceptual Model of Process and Effect', *Academy of Management Review*, 16/1: 121–44.

Prichard, R. A. (1969), 'Equity Theory: A Review and Critique, *Organizational Behaviour and Human Performance*, 4: 75–94.

——Dunnette, M. D., and Jorgenson, D. O. (1972), 'Effects of Perceptions of Equity and Inequity on Worker Performance and Satisfaction', *Journal of Applied Psychology Monograph*, 56: 75–94.

Rauschenberger, J., Schmitt, N., and Hunter, T. E. (1980), 'A Test of the Need Hierarchy Concept', *Administrative Science Quarterly*, 25/4: 654–70.

Reinharth, L., and Wahba, M. A. (1976), 'A Test of Alternative Models of Expectancy Theory', *Human Relations*, 29/3: 257–72.

Rose, N. (1996), 'Identity, Genealogy and History', in S. Hall and P. Du Gay (eds.), *Questions of Cultural Identity*, London: Sage.

Seivers, B. (1986), 'Beyond the Surrogate of Motivation', *Organization Studies*, 7/4: 353–67.

Shaw, R., and Colimore, K. (1988), 'Humanistic Psychology as Ideology: An Analysis of Maslow's Contradictions', *Journal of Humanistic Psychology*, 28/3: 51–74.

Stein, A. H., and Bailey, M. M. (1975), 'The Socialization of Achievement Motivation in Females', in M. T. Mednick, S. S. Tangri, and L. W. Hoffman (eds.), *Women and Achievement*, Washington DC: Hemisphere, pp. 151–7.

Tait, N. (2003), 'Gurkhas Lose Case on Discrimination', *Financial Times*, 22 Feb., p. 2.

Taylor, L. (1972), 'The Significance of Interpretation of Replies to Motivational Questions: The Case of Sex Offenders', *Sociology*, 6/1: 23–40.

——and Walton, P. (1971), 'Industrial Sabotage: Motives and Meanings', in S. Cohen (ed.), *Images of Deviance*, Harmondsworth: Penguin, pp. 219–45.

Tett, R. P., and Meyer, J. P. (1993), 'Job Satisfaction, Organizational Commitment, Turnover Intention and Turnover: Path Analyses Based on Meta-analytic Findings', *Personnel Psychology*, 46/2: 259–93.

Thompson, P., and McHugh, D. (2002), *Work Organizations* (3rd edn.), Houndmills: Palgrave.

Thrash, T. M., and Elliot, A. J. (2002), 'Implicit and Self-Attributed Achievement Motives: Concordance and Predictive Validity', *Journal of Personality*, 70/5: 729–55.

Tietjen, M. A., and Myers, R. M. (1998), 'Motivation and Job Satisfaction', *Management Decision*, 36/4: 226–31.

Timmons, J., Smollen, L., and Dingee, A. (1985), *New Venture Creation* (2nd edn.), Homewood, Ill: Irwin.

Veroff, J., Wilcox, S., and Atkinson, J. W. (1953), 'The Achievement Motive in High School and College Age Women', *Journal of Abnormal and Social Psychology*, 48: 108–9.

——McClelland, L., and Ruhland, D. (1975), 'Varieties of Achievement Motivation', in M. T. Mednick, S. S. Tangri, and L. W. Hoffman (eds.), *Women and Achievement*, Washington, DC: Hemisphere, pp. 172–205.

Veroff, J., Reuman, D., and Feld, S. (1984), 'Motives in American Men and Women across the Adult Life Span', *Developmental Psychology*, 20, 1142–58.

Vroom, V. H. (1964), *Work and Motivation*, New York: Wiley.

——and Maier, N. R. (1961), 'Industrial School Psychology', *Annual Review of Psychology*, 12: 413–46.

Wahba, M. A., and Bridwell, L. G. (1976), 'Maslow Reconsidered: A Review of Research on the Need Hierarchy Theory', *Organizational Behavior and Human Performance*, 15: 212–40.

——and House, R. J. (1974), 'Expectancy Theory in Work and Motivation: Some Logical and Methodological Issues', *Human Relations*, 27/2: 121–47.

Walster, E., Walster, G. W., and Berscheid, E. (1978), *Equity: Theory and Research*, Boston: Allyn & Bacon.

Wanous, J. P., Keon, T. L., and Latack, J. C. (1983), 'Expectancy Theory and Occupational and Organizational Choices: A Review and Test', *Organizational Behavior and Human Performance*, 32: 66–85.

Watson, T. J. (1996), 'Motivation: That's Maslow, isn't it?', *Management Learning*, 27/4: 447–64.

——(2002), *Organizing and Managing Work: Organizational, Managerial and Strategic Behaviour in Theory and Practice*, Harlow: Pearson Education Ltd.

Wernimont, P. F. (1966), 'Intrinsic and Extrinsic Factors in Job Satisfaction', *Journal of Applied Psychology*, 50/1: 41–50.

Wright Mills, C. (1940), 'Situated Actions and Vocabularies of Motive', *American Sociological Review*, 15 (Dec.), 904–13.

10 Power, Control, and Resistance

Having looked at how managers have tried to motivate and control production through job design, and how managerial work is described, this chapter turns to look at the issue of how much power and control managers have. It begins by looking at how power is defined and where power comes from. It looks at the limits of managerial power and the issue of sharing power, empowerment.

Under the medieval guild structure, masters held the power over those who were employed. Power clearly derived from ownership and control of the means of production and was supported by the power of surveillance. Knowledge was important as power was derived from knowledge, from 'mastery' of the skills. The organization's status hierarchy and knowledge hierarchy coincided (Offe 1976). Increasing size and complexity of organizations brought about by the concentration of capital into larger units and the bringing together of different production processes meant that the unity of status and knowledge hierarchies became disrupted. Hardy and Clegg (1996) believe that modern organizations passed by the guild structures and as organizations grew larger, skills became increasingly fragmented and specialized and positions became more functionally differentiated. It was unlikely that any one person would have sufficient knowledge of all the processes to be able to control them in an adequate manner. Power was centralized. Modern organizations were designed to function as if they were a unitary organism. Power is structured into the organization design so that some will have more power than others. Obedience to those with power is central. But how is power defined and understood?

Management Power

Power has been defined by Weber (1978) as the ability to get others to do what you want them to do, even if this is against their will, or to get them to do something they otherwise would not (Dahl 1957). Weber, like Marx (1976) argued that power was derived from owning and controlling the means of production but went on to say that it was also derived from the knowledge of operations as much as ownership. Organizational members will use creativity, discretion, and agency as power, some more than others will. From the employer's viewpoint the employee represents the capacity to labour which must be realized as efficiently as possible. Standing in the way of this realization is the power of employees who may be more or less willing to work under managerial discretion and control. Managerial control can be increased or tightened through the hierarchy and discipline of the manager, and through rules and bureaucracy.

One of the simplest views on power can be found in French and Raven (1959), which was revised by Raven in 1965. They proposed six bases of power, resources that a person can use to change beliefs, attitudes, or behaviours of a 'target'. These six are reward, coercion, legitimacy, expertise, reference, and information. Coercive and rewards power can be seen in terms of tangible rewards and real threats—threats of being fired, promises of monetary rewards, bonuses or promotion. Personal approval from someone whom we like can result in quite powerful reward power; a threat of rejection or disapproval from someone we value highly can serve as a source for powerful coercive power. Legitimate power is based on a structural relationship between the influencing agent and the target. Implicitly or explicitly the agent says 'I have a right to ask you to do this and you have an obligation to comply'. Legitimate power is most obvious when it is based on some formal structure e.g. in a supervisor/subordinate relationship. Legitimate power can also be used in reciprocity—'I did that for you, so you should feel obliged to do this for me' (Gouldner 1960) or to gain equity—'I have worked hard and suffered, so it is only fair that you should do something which I ask of you' or in situations of responsibility or dependence—'I really depend on you to do this for me'. Sometimes a third party can be invoked. For example a supervisor could gain the assistance of a co-worker to persuade the recalcitrant worker. We each may have a number of power bases to choose from and combine.

How much power do workers have to resist managerial power and control? One of the early studies on this was by Crozier (1964) who looked at bureaucracy and power relations in a French state-owned tobacco company. The male maintenance worker's job was to fix machine breakdowns reported by the mainly female production workers. The production workers were paid on a piece-rate system and had been effectively deskilled. Their jobs and the workflow were tightly planned and controlled. The main uncertainty was machine stoppages. Machine stoppages were usually caused by the difficulties in conditioning the raw material and stoppages led to a decrease in the bonus the production workers could earn, so the production workers needed the machines to function and were dependent on the efficient working of the maintenance workers. The maintenance workers thus had a high degree of power over the production workers because they controlled the source of uncertainty. Comparable problems seemed to be handled better in other factories. The maintenance workers kept the maintenance and repair problems a secret and their skill as a rule-of-thumb skill, completely disregarding all blueprints and maintenance directions which they were able to make 'disappear from the plants' (1964: 153). The maintenance workers were able then to maintain relative autonomy, privilege, and power through their skills and knowledge. While the rationale of bureaucracy is the elimination of power relationships and personal dependencies, unintended results are yielded. Uncertainty, control, and power were linked as concepts. A theory of strategic contingency arose from the work of Hickson et al. (1971); central to this theory were four subunits connected by the major task element of the organization, coping with uncertainty. The balance of power between the subunits was dependent on how the units coped with uncertainty. The most powerful units were those least dependent on the other subunits and coping with the greatest systematic uncertainty. (For a critique see Clegg and Hardy 1996.) But this view assumes a unitary, cohesive organization, whereas the units are likely to be hierarchical with problems of consent and dissent.

How do managers and other elites bring about political quiescence (silence) and perpetuate the status quo? Bachrach and Baratz (1963) would say that they are in a position to use power to prevent decisions being taken over issues where there would be a conflict of interests, when they limit decision making to 'safe' issues. Power is exercised when they devote their energies to creating or reinforcing social and political values and institutional practices that limit the issues considered by, for example, agenda setting.

Lukes (1974) considers that Bachrach and Baratz do not go far enough so provides us with a radical view of power. Lukes asks us to look at latent unobservable conflict and the role of ideology in shaping perceptions and preferences contrary to the real interests of those who hold them. Lukes' radical concept is that 'A exercises power over B when A affects B in a manner contrary to B's interests' (Lukes 1974: 34). Power could be used to prevent conflict by shaping people's perceptions and preferences so that they accept their role in the existing order of things. Power helped sustain the dominance of elite groups and reduced the ability of subordinate interests to dissent.

More recently theorists have looked at disciplinary practices, the micro-techniques of power used in organizations, following in the steps of Foucault (1977). These are ways in which both individuals and groups become socially inscribed and 'normalized' through routine aspects of organizations. In studying managerial power this would mean that we would look at the 'rules of the game', which both constrain and enable action (Clegg 1975) and how the disciplinary gaze is put into action in organizations. An example of the disciplinary gaze might be an appraisal system. (Employee appraisal is a process where current performance in a job is observed and discussed in order to add to that performance.)

STOP

Is this an Example of the Disciplinary Gaze?

At the University of St Andrews staff are requested, if they make private calls, to prefix the number they dial with 77. They are subsequently issued with an itemized personal bill that they are required to pay. The bill lists the numbers dialed and the names of the people or organizations called and the cost of the call. If this is how private calls are logged, could this be the same for all other calls university staff make? What could telephone number information also be used for?

The rule systems that made up Weber's bureaucracy are reinterpreted under the auspices of disciplinary practices. Power is embedded in everyday life. Central to disciplinary practices is surveillance—personal, technical, bureaucratic, legal—seeking increasingly to control the behaviour and dispositions of the employee. Discipline is both a system of correction and a system of knowledge. Power then is much more than negation and repression of the actions of others. 'Rather than A getting B to do something B would not otherwise do, social relations of power typically involve both A and B doing what they ordinarily do' (Isaac 1987). From a manager's point of view, this means that managers have a right to manage.

Managerial Prerogative

Managers have a right to manage, they have the prerogative (Storey 1983). The boundaries of managerial prerogatives or rights give management its distinctiveness and are hotly defended. Justification for this comes from the fact that owners or managers have control over capital assets, they are supported by law, and managers should be left to manage as they see fit. Securing legitimation promotes willing compliance for their rules, policies, and decisions. Golding (1980) believes that the maintenance of prerogative depends on it not being overtly recognized or challenged; the belief in the rule of manager's right to control is 'blissful clarity' (1980: 772). It seems to go unchallenged because of employee socialization and the tendency to accept most aspects of the status quo. Managerial control may be impossible without a prerogative that in some way legitimates the right to control (Johnson and Gill 1993). But do they have an interest in empowering workers?

Managing to Empower?

Employee empowerment has become something of a managerial buzzword (Beirne 1999) and usually means 'the giving of power'. When it is defined in this way it concerns an individual's power and control relative to others as well as the sharing of power and control, and the transmitting of power from one individual to another with less. Terms such

---

AN EXAMPLE OF EMPOWERMENT AT 'FLIGHTPATH'

Good quality customer service was thought by managers at Flightpath to be produced by 'empowered' and 'autonomous' workers rather than through managerial prescription (Taylor and Tyler 2000). Empowered telephone sales agents would deliver quality customer service 'spontaneously' and 'naturally'. Yet the work of telephone sales agents was supervised and measured thoroughly. They were given individual monthly sales targets which they were expected to surpass. There were revenue targets relating to the value of airline services sold to customers. The number of calls per agent answered was measured, as was the amount of time spent in conversation with passengers per week and the amount of time spent between the termination of one call and the opening of a new one. Each individual had a target. Agents were further assessed on teamwork, commitment, and job skills. Appraisal of performance happened each week and performance-related pay was awarded. Does this sound like Taylorism or empowerment?

as employee involvement and participation have overlapping meanings. Kanter (1977, 1979, 1984) suggests that empowerment depends on developing the conditions in an organization for the circulation of power. Participative management with access to resources, information, and support can benefit the whole organization. The term can have a motivational meaning concerning people's feeling of behavioural and psychological investment in work (Koberg et al. 1999). Empowerment has been shown to affect managerial and organizational effectiveness (Spreitzer 1995). The word conjures up images of positive commitment and meaningful participation of workers in everyday management. Potentially empowerment can mean workers take more control over their jobs and working environment. They should be able to enhance the contributions they make as individuals and members of a team and also seize opportunities for personal growth and fulfilment. For Bowen and Lawler (1992) high involvement occurs when organizations give the lowest-level employees a sense of involvement in the total organization's performance. Information on performance is shared; people have the skills and power to act beyond their traditional roles and are rewarded for doing so. Examples of companies with high sustained involvement are hard to find but include W. L. Gore and the Body Shop (see Boddy 2002 for a discussion of both cases). To empower, managers are asked to create an atmosphere that supports and fosters mutual trust, to give people a sense of belonging and freedom to develop their interests in work, and to reorient the organizational culture to integrate empowerment. These are all vague, woolly prescriptions for managers to follow. However Bowen and Lawler (1992) list some of the benefits of empowerment—quicker on-line responses to customer needs, quicker responses to dissatisfied customers, employees feel better about their jobs and themselves, and empowered employees can be a great source of service ideas.

Research offers cautionary tales (Hales 2000; Wilkinson 1998). It tells us though that managers don't always want to empower and do not always see the benefits of empowerment. One of the most commonly cited barriers to the success of employee involvement is resistance from middle managers (Fenton-O'Creevy and Nicholson 1994). Ezzamel et al.'s research (1994) showed that middle managers were reluctant to give power to those below them as they wanted to retain control over the responsibilities and roles of others. Senior managers too may hold negative attitudes to empowerment (Fenton-O'Creevy 2001). While, for example, managers might go through the motions of empowerment, they may in fact be defending their own space and interests (Anthony 1990). Instances of greater worker 'voice' are exceptional (Peiperl 1996).

Empowerment can mean loading non-managerial jobs with managerial responsibilities without the commensurate means to discharge them (Geary 1994; Wilkinson 1998). Research tells us that selection and development costs of empowered employees can be high. You can get a slower or inconsistent service, fair play can be violated, and there are dangers if empowered employees make the wrong decisions (Bowen and Lawler 1992). Guidelines on making it happen are typically vague and over-generalized. Some employees might find that they are empowered due to decisions on other matters (e.g. in the National Health Service—see Beirne 1999). Sometimes a primary aim has been to cut costs and an unintended consequence of removing a layer of decision making has been an increase in duties for those below. Research confirms that the impetus towards empowerment frequently comes from technical and operational priorities often with little sensitivity being shown to the ethical and political issues. Employees can be ambivalent about taking power if they are going to be held personally accountable (Argyris 1998). Senior managers may believe that organizational change has led to the hierarchy being made flatter, more trust between management and managed, and better cooperation. But middle managers are more likely to believe that empowerment is a fiction (Doyle et al. 2000). Those at the bottom of the hierarchy are less likely to feel the positive effects of empowerment. The better educated and those with higher rank are more likely to experience feelings of empowerment (Koberg et al. 1999).

As we will see in Chapter 12, while teamwork may be about empowering workers, devolving responsibility, and reversing repressive workplace control structures, it can also mean intensifying attention. Instead of individuals exercising a degree of influence over their own work, they can now influence the work of others in their team through suggestion, demonstration, and exhortation. Life in teams can be stressful as individuals are subject to intense peer pressure to conform to group norms (see Barker 1993 for an example). Those who stand out as either good or bad workers will receive the scrutiny of their peers and then be subjected to sanction or reward or other forces determined by the team. Teamwork does not necessarily descend into tyranny though as McKinlay and Taylor's (1996) discussion of 'Pyramid' shows.

Teamwork can then contribute to managerial power surveillance. Managers have the right and the power to control and maintain surveillance.

THE CASE OF 'KAY ELECTRONICS': MANAGEMENT SURVEILLANCE AND CONTROL

At Kay Electronics (see Sewell and Wilkinson 1992) teams comprised twelve to forty members who were assembling printed circuit boards (PCBs). As the PCBs progressed they were subjected to electronic tests and the test results were relayed to a central inventory control database. At the start of each day the team members had yesterday's quality performance information displayed above their workstations in the form of 'traffic lights'. A red card signified that a team member had exceeded acceptable quality limits. A green card signified they had made no quality errors at all and an amber card signified that the operator had made some errors but they remained in an acceptable range. This display of management information unambiguously identifies for all those team members who are above average or good workers as well as those who are below average. As a result teams are likely to normalize their productive effort at the level of better performers. Persistent poor workers, identified by regular red cards, would be removed by management from the line, counselled, and retrained; repeated unsatisfactory performance would lead to dismissal. A persistent green card could mean that an individual was worthy of closer attention because they may have made some kind of innovation in the work process. While this may be a high-tech company, the 'traffic light' system copies ideas generated by Robert Owen at New Lanark textile mills in Scotland in the early 1800s (Randell 1994: 223). Letting employees know what was thought of their performance through the use of the 'silent monitors' is thought to encourage the good to improve.

Control and Surveillance

Wherever there is a need for efficiency, effectiveness, and coordination, structures of control will be found. Hierarchical control is often seen as tainted (Jermier 1998). As with power, we are uncomfortable discussing struggles for control. But processes of control are integral to the way organizations operate. We have been made aware of the excesses of control in the writings of novelists like George Orwell and Aldous Huxley. Their writings were designed to horrify, shock, and provoke thought and discussion.

Although all organizations use a mix of strategies of control, some scholars have argued that specific strategies have become popular in specific historical periods. For example, Edwards (1979) argued that managerial practices moved away from widespread use of coercive control in the late nineteenth century towards technological control (like the assembly line) and then on to bureaucratic control in the mid-twentieth century. Each shift was precipitated by changes in the nature of work and the climate of labour relations. More recently it has been argued that we make more use of post-bureaucratic control with advanced technology and of instilling emotions, values, and world-views congruent with the interests of more powerful parties (Wilkinson and Wilmott 1995).

Surveillance is one way in which this can be done. New information technologies increase the scope and reach of workplace surveillance and never before have employees been subjected to such intense scrutiny and monitoring (Sewell 1998). For example, new technology has allowed for the close monitoring of the activities of supermarket checkout operators, telesales staff, and long-distance truck drivers. Zuboff (1988) has talked about the 'information panopticon'. (The panopticon was originally a model of prison design devised in the eighteenth century where inmates were kept in single cells constructed in a ring surrounding a central watchtower. Inmates would be constantly visible from the observation tower.) Elite groups exercise control using computer-based production and information technology; armed with the new technology they consolidate better quality information (Robey 1981).

Technology

Technology is not just about machines—computers, washing machines, telephones, and so on—but also social relations. These technologies encourage some forms of interaction. There is little point in defining technology as devices and machines. As Kramarae (1988) noted, defining technology in this way would be like describing housework in terms of dust cloths and cleaning fluids without reference to the social systems which determine who it is who dusts and cleans. Technology can be described as 'the application of scientific and other knowledge to practical tasks by ordered systems that involve people and organizations, living things and machines' (Pacey 1983) or the transformation of science into a means of capital accumulation (Noble 1977; 1984). Technology is, then, a human, political, and social activity.

Technology is usually thought of as a masculine invention and activity. It is often assumed that women have not been very involved in the invention of technology. For example, there were no women among the qualified engineering professionals responsible for the food processor or the washing machine (Cockburn and Furst-Dilic 1994). However, many inventions have been made by women (see Trescott 1979; Warner 1979). Household technologies like refrigerators and washing machines were originally designed and manufactured for commercial laundries, hotels, and hospitals but have been scaled down for family use. These technologies, sold as 'labour-saving' devices, have not made the household easier to run or freed women for other activities (Cowan 1983). As the equipment has been introduced into the homes of families who could afford it, cleaning standards have been raised and it is still women who are doing the repetitive tasks. But what about factory technology?

Technology and power have been drawn together in research on the 'labour process', work initiated by Braverman (1974). Here power and technology were combined through the intermediary concept of control. Power was originally seen as exercised in a 'zero-sum' power game in which one party profits at the expense of another. The classical cases were documented by Marglin (1974) and Gorz (1972). Marglin cites the case of cotton and wool merchants who constructed a role for themselves using technology to control the activities of their workers rather than just to enhance productivity. A very different technology would be developed if maximum control had not been the main aim (Gorz 1972). Technology can have a major impact on work tasks, using judgement, discretion, decision making, and so reduce or eliminate the individual's opportunities for resistance (Beynon 1974; Nichols and Beynon 1977). More recent examples include Watanabe (1990), who describes how labour was deskilled and degraded in the banking sector (whose work was described in an earlier chapter), and Knights and Sturdy (1987), who argued that there had been a massive increase in routine work in the insurance industry and a polarization of skills.

However, it would be wrong to believe that technology always deskills jobs. Zeitlin (1983) shows how the introduction of new technology in the British engineering industry during the period 1890–1920 increased the margin of workers' control. Employers remained heavily dependent on skilled labour and vulnerable to craft militancy during boom periods. But the marginal gains by skilled employees were short-lived. Managerial intentions towards deskilling have been limited as Buchanan (1986), Wilson (1987), and others have shown. When Computer Numerically Controlled machines are introduced new demands are made on the workforce—programs need to be debugged and the production process monitored; workers' knowledge and skills prove to be essential. How long management is dependent on skills following the introduction of new technology is probably related to products, processes, and the configuration of power (Clegg and Wilson 1991). The locus of control cannot always be moved from workers to managers during technical change nor from managers to workers. Control ultimately does lie with management, though workers may resist it.

The Latest Technology 'Fad': Business Process Engineering (BPR)

BPR represents the latest in a series of managerial 'recipes' which advocate the use of technical/organizational changes. BPR has been described as 'the fundamental rethinking and radical design of business processes to achieve dramatic improvements in critical, contemporary measures of performance, such as cost, quality, service, and speed' and as 'a manifesto for revolution' (Hammer and Champy 1993: 32). It is the most recent in a long line of management innovations adopted by a wide spectrum of industry and commerce in Britain and the USA.

The distinctiveness, for Knights and McCabe (1998), of BPR is that it focuses upon radical change and is a process-based approach to the organization of work. The process is facilitated by the increased use of information technology. The implementation of new information technology is usually the main push for transforming the organization and is closely associated with BPR. BPR can include teamworking, empowerment, flatter hierarchies, and a customer orientation; the novelty rests in packaging these together to 'transform' organizations (Grint et al. 1996).

While BPR is widely discussed amongst management practitioners and proponents, they have widely different perceptions as to what BPR means. For some practitioners within the UK financial service industry, for example, it means short-term cost savings; for others it promises a radical future of change (McCabe et al. 1994). Examples of effective implementation are rare (Willcocks and Grint 1997). The claims and promises of BPR are also being challenged by academics (e.g. Grey and Mitev 1995). While practitioners may think that BPR presents the radically new, discontinuous future and recommend 'don't automate, obliterate', calling for organizational politics to be cast aside, Willcocks and Grint (1997) say that BPR is an inherently risky and political process.

Technology and Surveillance

Employers have always monitored the performance of their employees but in the last twenty years surveillance at work has increased with the introduction of information technology. This is to be found particularly in high-volume service operations like call centres such as those used in direct banking and insurance sales, where it is used to ensure work is being done. It has been described as 'the technological whip of the electronic age' (Fodness and Kinsella 1990). Calls are listened to by those who are monitoring levels of service quality and data collected on performance levels, like number of calls received or made. Those who are being monitored know their work is being seen but do not often know what information is being generated about them and their performance.

Kirsty Ball and David Wilson (1997; 2000) describe two case studies of the technology of surveillance, in a debt collection department in a building society and in a credit card division of a bank. In the debt collection department work varied according to the

---

AN EXAMPLE OF RESISTANCE TO CONTROL: STRIKE OVER 'SPY' SCHEME

Road maintenance workers went on strike in Dundee when 'spy' devices, satellite global positioning system devices, were planned to be installed in every maintenance vehicle. These devices can plot staff movements to within 10 metres. The location of the vehicles can be determined on a computer screen equipped with a street map at the company headquarters. The workers protested as they said the plan showed lack of trust from managers. The managing director said that no member of staff should have anything to fear but he conceded there was an element of management control: 'It will let us know that the workforce is where it is supposed to be and identify inappropriate or unauthorized use of vehicles' (*The Scotsman*, 12 October 1998).

---

complexity of the accounts in question and the length of time they had been in arrears. In the case of the credit card division the main activity was the inputting of credit card sales vouchers onto the computer system to charge the correct amounts to the customer. In both cases manager and supervisors could see what each operator and team had produced in a day. The performance statistics were a great source of stress to the operators as the calculation of them was secret. They would be given feedback on their performance and, in one company, if they persistently fell short of their targets, they were sacked.

Understanding organizations as political systems is a productive image that helps us understand more of the nature and functioning of organizations. Seeing organizations as political systems draws attention to the ways in which they can serves as sites where different values, forms of knowledge, and interests are articulated and embodied in decisions, structures, and practices. As political systems organizations use power and control; in so doing they provide meaning and personal identity as well as goods, services, and income. The issue of control is central to this book and is picked up again in the next chapter on organizational culture.

■ **SUGGESTIONS FOR FURTHER READING**

1. Collinson, D. (2000), 'Strategies of Resistance: Power, Knowledge and Subjectivity in the Workplace', ch. 8 in K. Grint (ed.), *Work and Society: A Reader*, Cambridge: Polity Press. This chapter discusses the options, knowledge, and agencies through which opposition to managerial power is initiated.
2. Hardy, C., and Clegg, S. R. (1996), 'Some Dare Call it Power', in S. R. Clegg, C. Hardy, and W. R. Nord (eds.), *Handbook of Organization Studies*, London: Sage, for more on power and organizations.
3. Noon, M., and Blyton, P. (2002), *The Realities of Work* (2nd edn.), Houndmills: Palgrave. Chapter 8 discusses knowledge, work, and power.
4. Thompson, P., and McHugh, D. (2002), *Work Organizations* (3rd edn.), Houndmills: Palgrave. Chapter 9 discusses issues of power, conflict, and resistance.

5. Hales, C. (2000), 'Management and Empowerment Programmes', *Work, Employment and Society*, 14/3: 501–19. This article compares and contrasts the rhetoric with the limited reality of empowerment. It takes evidence from a number of companies and settings to show how senior managers enthusiastically promote while junior managers reluctantly accept empowerment programmes.

6. Gabriel, Y., Fineman, S., and Sims, D. (2000), *Organizing and Organizations*, London: Sage, chapter 3 on rules are rules. This chapter discusses the rationality and rules in organizations. You will see some links to the chapter about bureaucracy and rationality.

7. Watson, T. (2002), *Organising and Managing Work*, Harlow: Pearson. Chapter 10 discusses power and politics in organizations.

■ WEB LINKS

See **www.gore.com/about/about_reading.html** for a reading list about W. L. Gore and how it operates as an organization.

See **www.thebodyshop.com/web/tbsgl/values.jsp** for more on the Body Shop and its espoused values

■ QUESTIONS

1. Sewell (1998) says that discipline can be maintained through teamwork and peer group scrutiny. Surveillance and teamwork are an unexpected combination. How are surveillance and teamwork combined?

2. Struggles for control are viewed with embarrassment or ignored, according to Jermier (1998). Why is this the case?

3. Search for research that would help you argue that the panopticon is as diverse in its use as the contexts in which it occurs (see Ball and Wilson 1997).

4. There is no system of managerial control that can completely eliminate the discretion of the employee. Discuss.

5. Many concepts used in organizational analysis, such as power, domination, control, and authority can be used as euphemisms for violence, most obviously in the police, military, and prisons (Hearn 1994). Discuss.

6. It could be argued that middle managers sabotage employee empowerment; alternatively they may be scapegoats for senior managers. Discuss. (See Fenton O'Creevy, 2001, see also Chapter 8 above.)

■ GROUP EXERCISE

Cautionary tales are offered about empowerment. What are the main messages? (See for example Beirne 1999; Wilkinson 1998.) Divide the class in two, one half to argue that the benefits of empowerment and the other half to discuss the failings.

■ REFERENCES

Anthony, P. (1990), 'The Paradox of the Management of Culture or "he who leads is lost"', *Personnel Review*, 19: 3–8.

Argyris, C. (1998), 'Empowerment: The Emperor's New Clothes', *Harvard Business Review*, 76: 98–105.

Bachrach, P., and Baratz, M. S. (1963), 'Decisions and Nondecisions', *American Political Science Review*, 57: 641–51.

Ball, K., and Wilson, D. (1997), 'Computer Based Monitoring and the Electronic Panopticon: A Review of the Debate and Some New Evidence from the UK', Working Paper. Birmingham: Aston Business School.

——(2000), 'Power, Control and Computer-Based Performance Monitoring: Repertoires, Resistance and Subjectivities', *Organization Studies*, 21/3: 539–65.

Barker, J. R. (1993), 'Tightening the Iron Cage: Coercive Control in Self Managing Teams', *Administrative Science Quarterly*, 38: 408–37.

Beirne, M. (1999), 'Managing to Empower? A Healthy Review of Resources and Constraints', *European Management Journal*, 17/2: 218–25.

Beynon, H. (1974), *Working for Ford*, Harmondsworth: Penguin.

Boddy, D. (2002), *Management: An Introduction* (2nd edn.), Harlow: Pearson.

Bowen, D. E., and Lawler, E. E. (1992), 'The Empowerment of Service Workers: What, Why, How and When', *Sloan Management Review* (Spring) 31–9.

Braverman, H. (1974), *Labor and Monopoly Capital: The Degradation of Work in the Twentieth Century*, New York: Monthly Review Press.

Buchanan, D. A. (1986), 'Canned Cycles and Dancing Tools: Who's Really in Control of Computer Aided Machining?', Working Paper Series, 1 (Mar.), Glasgow: University of Glasgow, Department of Management Studies.

Clegg, S. R. (1975), *Power, Rule and Domination*, London: Routledge.

——and Hardy, C. (1996), 'Organizations, Organization and Organizing', introd, to S. R. Clegg, C. Hardy, and W. R. Nord (eds.), *Handbook of Organization Studies*, London: Sage.

——and Wilson, F. (1991), 'Power, Technology and Flexibility in Organizations', in J. Law (ed.), *A Sociology of Monsters: Essays on Power, Technology and Domination*, London: Routledge.

Cockburn, C., and Furst-Dilic, R. F. (1994) (eds.), *Bringing Technology Home: Gender and Technology in a Changing Europe*, Buckingham: Open University Press.

Cowan, R. S. (1983), *More Work for Mother: The Ironies of Household Technology from the Open Hearth to the Microwave*, New York: Basic Books.

Crozier, M. (1964), *The Bureaucratic Phenomenon*, Chicago: University of Chicago Press.

Dahl, R. (1957), 'The Concept of Power', *Behavioral Science*, 20: 201–15.

Doyle, M., Claydon, T., and Buchanan, D. (2000), 'Mixed Results, Lousy Process: The Management Experience of Organizational Change', *British Journal of Management*, 11, Special issue, S59–S80.

Edwards, R. C. (1979), *Contested Terrain: The Transformation of the Workplace in the Twentieth Century*, New York: Basic Books.

Ezzamel, M., Lilley, S., and Wilmott, H. (1994), 'The "new organization" and the "new managerial work"' *European Management Journal*, 12/4: 454–61.

Fenton-O'Creevy, M. (2001), 'Employee Involvement and the Middle Manager: Saboteur or Scapegoat?', *Human Resource Management Journal*, 11/1: 24–40.

——and Nicholson, N. (1994), *Middle Managers: Their Contribution to Employee Involvement*, Employment Department Research Series, 28.

Fodness, K., and Kinsella, S. (1990), *Stories of Mistrust and Manipulation: The Electronic Monitoring of the American Workforce*, Cleveland, Oh.: National Association of Working Women.

Foucault, M. (1977), *Discipline and Punish: The Birth of the Prison*, Harmondsworth: Penguin.

French, J. R., and Raven, B. H. (1959), 'The Bases of Social Power', in D. Cartwright (ed.), *Studies in Social Power,* Institute for Social Research, Ann Arbor, MI, pp. 150–67.

Geary, J. (1994), 'Task Participation: Employees Participation, Enabled or Constrained', in K. Sisson (ed.), *Personnel Management* (2nd edn.), Oxford: Blackwell.

Golding, D. (1980), 'Establishing Blissful Clarity in Organizational Life: Managers', *Sociological Review*, 28/4: 763–83.

Gorz, A. (1972), 'Technical Intelligence and the Capitalist Division of Labour', *Telos*, 12: 27–41.

Grey, C., and Mitev, N. (1995), 'Reengineering Organizations: A Critical Appraisal', *Personnel Review*, 24/1: 6–18.

Gouldner, A. (1960), 'The Norm of Reciprocity: A Preliminary Statement', *American Journal of Sociology*, 81: 82–108.

Grint, K., Case, P., and Willcocks, L. (1996), 'BPR Reappraised: The Politics and Technology of Forgetting', in W. J. Orlikowski, G. I. Walsham, M. R. Jones, and J. I. Degross (eds.), *Information Technology and Changes in Organizational Work*, London: Chapman & Hull.

Hales, C. (2000), 'Management and Empowerment Programmes', *Work, Employment and Society*, 14/3: 501–19.

Hammer, M., and Champy, J. (1993), *Reengineering the Corporation: A Manifesto for Business Revolution*, London: Nicholas Brealy.

Hardy, C., and Clegg, S. R. (1996), 'Some Dare Call it Power', ch. 3.7 in S. R. Clegg, C. Hardy, and W. R. Nord (eds.), *Handbook of Organization Studies*, London: Sage.

Hearn, J. (1994), 'The Organization(s) of Violence: Men, Gender Relations, Organizations and Violences', *Human Relations*, 47/6: 731–54.

Hickson, D. J., Hinings, C. A., Lee, C. A., Schneck, R. E., and Pennings, J. M. (1971), 'A Strategic Contingencies Theory of Intraorganizational Power', *Administrative Science Quarterly*, 16/2: 216–29.

Isaac, J. C. (1987), *Power and Marxist Theory: A Realist View*, Ithaca, NY: Cornell University Press.

Jermier, J. M. (1998), 'Introduction: Critical Perspectives on Organizational Control', *Administrative Science Quarterly*, 43: 235–56.

Johnson, P., and Gill, J. (1993), *Management Control and Organizational Behaviour*, London: Paul Chapman.

Kanter, R. M. (1977), *Men and Women of the Corporation*, New York: Basic Books.

——(1979), 'Power Failure in Management Circuits', *Harvard Business Review*, 57.

——(1984), 'Innovation: The Only Hope for Times Ahead?', *Sloan Management Review*, 25: 51–5.

Koberg, C. S., Boss, R. W., Senjem, J. C., and Goodman, E. A. (1999), 'Antecedents and Outcomes of Empowerment', *Group and Organization Management*, 24/1: 71–91.

Knights, D., and McCabe, D. (1998), 'When "Life is but a Dream": Obliterating Politics through Business Process Reengineering?' *Human Relations*, 51/6: 761–98.

——and Sturdy, A. (1987), 'Women's Work in Insurance: Information Technology and the Reproduction of Gendered Segregation', in M. J. Davidson and C. L. Cooper (eds.), *Women and Information Technology*, Chichester: Wiley.

Kramarae, C. (1988), 'Gotta Go Myrtle, Technology's at the Door', in C. Kramarae (ed.), *Technology and Women's Voices: Keeping in Touch*. London: Routledge & Kegan Paul.

Lukes, S. (1974), *Power: A Radical View*, London: Macmillan.

McCabe, D., Knights, D., and Wilkinson, A. (1994), 'Quality Initiatives in Financial Services' (Research Report available from D. McCabe), Manchester: Financial Services Research Centre, Manchester School of Management, UMIST.

McKinlay, A., and Taylor, P. (1996), 'Power, Surveillance and Resistance', in P. Ackers, C. Smith, and P. Smith (eds.), *The New Workplace and Trade Unionism*, London: Routledge, pp. 279–300.

Marglin, S. A. (1974), 'What Do Bosses Do? The Origins and Functions of Hierarchy in Capitalist Production', *Review of Radical Political Economics*, 6: 60–112.

Marx, K. (1976), *Capital*, Harmondsworth: Penguin.

Nichols, T., and Beynon, H. (1977), *Living with Capitalism*. London: Routledge & Kegan Paul.

Noble, D. (1977), *America by Design: Science, Technology and the Rise of Corporate Capitalism*, New York: Alfred A. Knopf.

——(1984), *Forces of Production*. New York: Alfred A. Knopf.

Offe, C. (1976), *Industry and Inequality*. London: Edward Arnold.

Pacey, A. (1983), *The Culture of Technology*. Cambridge, Mass.: MIT Press.

Peiperl, M. (1996), 'Does Empowerment Deliver the Goods?', *Mastering Management*, Part 10: 2–4.

Randell, G. (1994), 'Employee Appraisal', ch. 7 in K. Sisson (ed.), *Personnel Management: A Comprehensive Guide to Theory and Practice in Britain* (2nd edn.), Oxford: Blackwell, pp. 221–52,

Raven, B. H. (1965), 'Social Influence and Power', in I. D. Steiner and M. Fishbein (eds.), *Current Studies in Social Psychology*, New York: Holt Rinehart & Winston, pp. 371–82.

Robey, D. (1981), 'Computer Information Systems and Organization Structure', *Communications of ACM*, 24: 679–87.

Sewell, G. (1998), 'The Discipline of Teams: The Control of Team-Based Industrial Work through Electronic and Peer Surveillance', *Administrative Science Quarterly*, 43: 397–428.

——and Wilkinson, B. (1992), 'Someone to Watch over Me: Surveillance, Discipline and the Just-in-Time Labour Process', *Sociology*, 26: 271–89.

Spreitzer, G. M. (1995), 'Psychological Empowerment in the Workplace: Dimensions, Measurement and Validation', *Academy of Management Journal*, 38/5: 1442–65.

Storey, J. (1983), *Managerial Prerogative and the Question of Control*, London: Routledge & Kegan Paul.

Taylor, S., and Tyler, M. (2000), 'Emotional Labour and Sexual Difference in the Airline Industry', *Work, Employment and Society*, 14/1: 77–95.

Trescott, M. M. (1979), *Dynamos and Virgins Revisited: Women and Technological Change in History*. Metuchen, NJ: Scarecrow Press.

Warner, D. (1979), 'Women Inventors at the Centennial', in M. M. Trescott (ed.), *Dynamos and Virgins Revisited*, Metuchen, NJ: Scarecrow Press.

Watanabe, T. (1990), 'New Office Technology and the Labour Process in Contemporary Japanese Banking', *New Technology, Work and Employment*, 5/1: 56–67.

Weber, M. (1978), *Economy and Society: An Outline of Interpretive Sociology*, ed. G. Roth and C. Wittich, Berkeley, Calif.: University of California Press.

Wilkinson, A. (1998), 'Empowerment: Theory and Practice', *Personnel Review*, 27: 40–56.

——and Willmott, H. (1995) (eds.), *Making Quality Critical: New Perspectives on Organizational Change*, London: Routledge.

Willcocks, L., and Grint, K. (1997), 'Re-inventing the Organization? Towards a Critique of Business Process Re-engineering', ch. 4 in I. McLoughlin and M. Harris (eds.), *Innovation, Organizational Change and Technology*, London: International Thomson Business Press.

Wilson, F. M. (1987), 'Computer Numerical Control and Constraint', in D. Knights and H. Wilmott (eds.), *New Technology and the Labour Process*, London: Macmillan.

Zeitlin, J. (1983), 'The Labour Strategies of British Engineering Employers, 1890–1922', in H. Gospel and C. Littler (eds.), *Managerial Strategies and Industrial Relations*, London: Heinemann.

Zuboff, S. (1988), *In the Age of the Smart Machine*, New York: Basic Books.

11 | Culture

Culture is a popular explanatory concept frequently used to describe a company, a rationale for people's behaviour, a guideline for action, a cause for condemnation or praise, or a quality that makes a company 'what it is' (Kunda 1992). The concept has been explicitly used only in the last few decades (Schein 1990). It is a fascinating but elusive topic for researchers. Organizational culture is defined simply by Deal and Kennedy (1982: 4) as 'The way we do things round here' but more fully by Hofstede (1991: 262) as 'the collective programming of the mind which distinguishes the members of one organization from another'. Schein (1985: 6) claims that the term 'should be reserved for the deeper level of basic assumptions and beliefs that are shared by members of an organization, that operate unconsciously, and that define in a basic "taken-for-granted" fashion an organization's view of itself and its environment'.

It would be reasonable to expect that organizations that are set up for similar purposes would have similar cultures. It would be reasonable to expect this to be especially so in those sectors where people move freely between organizations. But this has been found not to be the case. The National Health Service in Britain provides us with an example. Until recently each health authority was run according to the same tight guidelines set down by central government. Doctors were trained using a rotation scheme that required them to move between hospitals and specialties. The doctors found that each authority had its own distinctive features that made the experience of each novel (Dale 1994).

Culture is carefully defined by Schein (1990) as (a) a pattern of basic assumptions, (b) invented, discovered, or developed by a given group, (c) as it learns to cope with its problems of external adaptation and internal integration, (d) that has worked well enough to be considered valid and therefore (e) is to be taught to new members as the (f) correct way to perceive, think, and feel in relation to those problems (1990: 111). The culture of a particular group or organization can be distinguished at three fundamental levels at which the culture manifests itself: observable artefacts, value, and basic underlying assumptions (Schein 1990: 111).

Culture is commonly theorized as a pervasive, eclectic, layered, and socially constructed phenomenon which is generated through values, artefacts, structures, and behaviours (Detert et al. 2000; Silvester et al. 1999). Geertz (1973) sees organizational cultures as webs of meaning; culture itself is an ongoing creation of those who live within its influence. Meanings around which consensus has already evolved are incorporated as norms, beliefs, symbols, and values of organizational culture and become part and parcel of the way future interpretations are made. Values, beliefs, and shared meanings may be researched through interviews. Open-ended interviews can be very useful in getting at the level of how people feel and think about the culture. Questionnaires and survey instruments may prejudge the dimensions to be studied. There is no way of knowing whether the dimensions you are asking about are relevant or salient in that culture until you have examined the deeper levels. Assumptions are usually unconscious and may be observed through intensive observation, more focused questions, or self-analysis by members of a group.

Schein (1985) argues that we can gain some understanding at a superficial level of any culture by analysing artefacts produced and consumed by that culture. These are visible and can be deciphered or decoded by observation and analysis. To get a better feel for the ideas and orientations that have shaped the character and form of these artefacts, we need to understand the deeper value system. A value system is like a code of practice or behaviour; artefacts offer us clues to this deeper value system. Beneath the level of values there is a deeper level of 'taken-for-granted' unconscious assumptions. Unlike values and beliefs that exist at a conscious level and so may be challenged, the cultural forms and our ideas are not open to challenge. The unconscious shapes our norms like standards of behaviour, dress, personal interaction, our values and beliefs. Schein has been criticized by, for example, Collins (1998) for implying that cultural norms and values act as templates for thought and action and appear not to be open to change. However unconscious assumptions must be open to change and negotiation. They should be thought of as dynamic and social phenomena that will tend to evolve and change as people attempt to negotiate and bend the rules.

If this only gives us a superficial understanding, is this all we can expect to gain? Grint (1995: 162) must think so as he notes that 'Culture is rather like a black hole: the closer you get to it the less light is thrown upon the topic and the less chance you have of surviving the experience.' There is a lack of consensus about the nature of culture and its amenability to managerial manipulation (Wilmott 2000).

Since the late 1970s a vast body of literature has looked at the importance of organizational culture for organizational outcomes. Early writings on culture management were premissed on the assumption that culture management could lead to significant performance improvements (Deal and Kennedy 1982; Peters and Waterman 1982). A strong culture could be 'manufactured'. For example Deal and Kennedy (1982: 15) claimed 'The impact of a strong culture on productivity is amazing. In the extreme, we estimate that a company can gain as much as one or two hours of productive work per employee per day.' The emphasis was on improving efficiency, growth, and success. Ouchi (1981) for example proposed that this could be achieved through the creation of a strong, unifying organizational culture. 'Strong' cultures emphasized the values of 'being the best', of flexibility, initiative, innovation, of superior quality and service, being open participative companies where employees were seen as the most important asset (Peters and Waterman 1982: 285). Peters and Waterman (1982) were employed as consultants by McKinsay, a large, well-known management consultancy firm. In looking at excellence in organizational culture they say that there is a common culture to be found in excellent companies. This culture displays certain attributes like a bias for action so they make innovative decisions promptly, closeness to the customer so that they focus upon meeting and exceeding customer expectations, and values innovation. They place considerable emphasis on the importance of positive reinforcement, rewarding desirable behaviour. At IBM a senior manager adopted the practice of writing out a cheque as a reward for achievements he observed as he wandered about the organization. Well-known examples of companies who claim to have changed their culture are British Airways, who attempted to change the emphasis on flying routes to an emphasis on company service, and Nissan, who claimed they achieved an entirely new sentiment and identification from their labour force (Ackroyd and Crowdy 1990). Culture under this functionalist view is seen as a variable subject to management manipulation and control. Many culture interventions continue to focus on creating strongly unified values and are promoted as performance enhancing (Fey et al. 1999).

In *Change Masters* (1985) Rosabeth Moss Kanter tries to encourage North American companies to rekindle the spirit of innovation and enterprise. *Change Masters* studies ten major companies in depth. She concludes that if corporations are to flourish then the change masters must be allowed to redesign to tap the talents and skills of employees. Successful companies will create a climate that encourages change, will encourage antici-pation of external pressures, and will listen to new ideas. In similar terms to Peters and Waterman, she argues for the bias for action, companies that work through people, allow autonomy, and are value driven. In her later work, *When Giants Learn to Dance* (1989) she tells us that organizations must be fast, flexible, focused on their customers, and friendly, allowing staff to experiment and develop their skills.

Interest in culture was sparked too by Japanese business success, which was thought to arise from competitive advantage secured through national and corporate culture (Ouchi 1981; Pascale and Athos 1982). Through the 1970s Japanese industry managed to establish a solid reputation for quality, reliability, value, and service—attributes that others wished to emulate. A large and profitable literature capitalized on the idea that culture can be diag-nosed and changed to improve organizational effectiveness. It was thought that where US companies had adopted management practices that resembled those of the Japanese, as discussed by Peters and Waterman and Ouchi, they achieved financial success.

Functionalist management writers have prescribed how culture change may be achieved. Some have provided models for culture intervention, based on a typology or taxonomy of organizational culture, for example Harrison (1972) and Schneider (1994). Targeted change models espouse the adoption of focused means of culture change. For example Wilkinson et al. (1996) report a culture change effort dominated by training methods designed to change values. Gap or analytical frameworks champion culture change though analysing current culture, identifying the desired culture, and developing a programme of change to achieve the desired culture (e.g. Hawkins 1997).

Deal and Kennedy (1982: 15) claim that with a strong culture 'a company can gain as much as one or two hours of productive work per employee per day'. The prescriptive view shows how organizational culture can be designed and managed through the 'hearts and minds' of employees. The ideal employees are those who have internalized the organiza-tion's goals and values and no longer require rigid control. The trend has been towards a 'normative control' (Etzioni 1961), an attempt to direct the efforts of employees by con-trolling the underlying experiences, thoughts, and feelings that guide their actions (Kunda 1992: 11). Inherent conflict can be transformed into cooperation in the interests of both employee and employer. Through education, personal development, growth, and matu-rity employees become better, healthier people saved from alienation and conflict.

As Johnson and Gill (1993: 33) note, it is not clear whether the organizations Deal and Kennedy and Peters and Waterman observed developed in the way they have through chance and spontaneity (social control) or through conscious intent (administrative control). Some have argued that organizational culture management is designed more to improve control than directly to increase profitability. Wilmott (1993: 522) for example claims that cultural control is an intense and effective 'medium of domination'. The idea of equating the use of Japanese management practices with success in US companies was shaky to say the least (Legge 1994). Deal and Kennedy (1999) have themselves had to admit that the downsizing, outsourcing, and mergers that have characterized so much of management practice over the past twenty years have undermined relationships, trust, cohesion, and corporate culture. The design and empirical basis of Peters and Waterman's research is highly suspect. (For an excellent critique, see Guest 1992 and Collins 1998.)

The more critical researchers have then raised concerns regarding the conceptual feasibility of culture management (Ackroyd and Crowdy 1990; Legge 1994). Some reject the view that culture can be managed while others accept that culture may be malleable but change will be fraught with difficulties and ethical dilemmas. Some like Ogbonna and Harris (1998a) would argue that culture is not easily controlled but can be manipulated under certain but rare organizational conditions. They believe that organizational culture is not unitary; culture cannot be viewed in a unidimensional manner. There are likely to be different subcultures or types of culture in existence within organizations. Attempts to change culture may evolve in unpredictable ways (Ogbonna and Harris 1998b; Harris and Ogbonna 2002). Despite this scepticism, practitioners continue to attempt, often unsuccessfully, to bring about culture management initiatives. It may be that only adaptable cultural traits are linked to performance (Gordon and DiTomaso 1992) or that non-imitable, rare, and adaptable cultures may represent a source of competitive advantage (Barley 1991).

AN EXAMPLE OF GENDER, CULTURE, AND CONTROL

An example of a company that attempted to change its culture and control the behaviour of its employees is Emsite, a mining company in Australia. The management believed that employing large numbers of females helped improve the behaviour of male employees. Talking about the men, one of the managers said, 'I mean they're just your average peacock and it's amazing how they dress better, stay cleaner, behave more appropriately, when there are females around than when there are not' (Eveline and Booth 2002: 564). When women are part of the workforce, superintendents say better care is taken of equipment, there is less antagonism among men, and the overall safety record improves. Management then sees the women as 'minders' of the men. The male employees consented to this designation of women's housewifely position. With women around, male operators said the place was cleaner, women took orders more readily, there were fewer fights (between men), there was always someone different to talk to or to discuss family problems with (Eveline and Booth 2002: 566).

All was not positive though. A number of men refused to be trained by women to use equipment on which women excelled, particularly the huge computerized trucks and 824 dozer, which had been, designated 'women's machines'. The men called the women offensive names such as 'bush pigs' and 'dykes', and told sexually explicit stories and jokes. The 'belt shop' was designated 'male territory' and was lavishly adorned with lewd pin-ups. Men found they could keep women away or at least to a minimum with pornography.

Whatever your view, it has to be acknowledged that employees are not passive objects of control (Goffman 1961). They may accept, deny, react, reshape, rethink, acquiesce, rebel, or conform and create themselves within constraints imposed on them. Research, for example, on employee values and norms reflected in everyday practices (like restriction of output), shows direct conflict with the aims and objectives of management (Lupton 1963; Roy 1960). Hofstede (1998) believes that there are no shared values at the core of an organization's culture. While there is little doubt that practices are designed according to the values of the founder and significant top managers, this does not mean that all members of the organization share these values. Organizations can be composed of various subcultures that may be mutually antagonistic. These subcultures can compete overtly and covertly as different groups of organizational members seek to establish or impose their distinctive meaning systems and definitions of reality. There may be various sites of culture embedded in the various groups that make up the organization, creating subcultures or even counter-cultures (Smircich 1983*a*; see Smircich 1983*b*, for how networks of meaning can be researched). As Smircich (1983*a*) argues, organizations can only change those variables they 'have', like payment and information systems, mission statements, and corporate image. They cannot change what an organization 'is', the common values and beliefs which emerge from people's shared experiences. Individuals act out their work roles relying on customary definitions and understandings. These meanings are themselves embedded in class, regional, and national cultures. There will be distinctive patterns and connections that will be beyond the capacity of influence, never mind managerial control.

Hofstede's work looks at the relationship between national and organizational cultures. He claims to have successfully uncovered the secrets of entire national cultures (Hofstede 1980). He has studied differences in work-related values by analysing national cultures along five main dimensions—power distance, individualism/collectivism, masculinity/femininity, uncertainty/avoidance, Confucian dynamism (Hofstede 1991). Power distance refers to the extent to which the less powerful members of organizations, and institutions like families, expect and accept that power will be distributed evenly. Those societies with high power distance scores tend to exhibit more authoritarian management styles. In cultures high in individualism ties between individuals tend to be loose and there is an expectation that individuals are responsible for their own well-being. In collectivist societies there is a high degree of social solidarity; it would be less acceptable in this culture to dismiss workers for economic reasons. In masculine forms of society males are expected to be strong, tough, competitive, and assertive while women are expected to be meek, gentle, modest, caring, and nurturing. In more feminine societies both men and women are expected to demonstrate a degree of modesty and a concern for the quality of life. More feminine organizations would operate using intuition and negotiation while the masculine would use assertion and competition. Hofstede is, then, drawing on gender stereotypes here. Uncertainty avoidance is the extent to which members of a culture feel threatened by uncertainty and ambiguity. Those with high scores tend to have obvious routines and a need to be busy. Confucian dynamism is the extent to which societies adopt a short- or long-term approach to life. Those with a short-term approach demand quick results yet are respectful of traditions and social obligation. Those with a long-term approach also respect traditions but would argue that they have to be adapted to meet modern contexts.

Primary data was extracted for employee attitudes surveys within IBM subsidiaries in sixty-six countries between 1967 and 1973 (McSweeney 2002). For Hofstede culture is 'mental programming', 'software of the mind', subjective and territorially unique. The inhabitants of a particular nation individually carry a unique national culture. National culture is a common component of a wider culture that contains both global and subnational constituents.

Hofstede's work is criticized by a number of writers on culture (see Williamson 2002; Smith 2002; Hofstede 2002). There are richer conceptions of culture (e.g. Geertz 1973). It is possible to dismiss his project as an attempt to measure the unmeasurable (MacIntyre 1971; Smelser 1992). It is mainly his presuppositions and methodology that come under fire. Schein (1990) notes how culture in Hofstede's research is viewed as the property of groups that can be measured by questionnaires leading to Likert-type profiles. The problem with this approach is that it assumes knowledge of the relevant dimensions to be studied. Even if these are statistically derived from large samples of items, it is not clear whether the initial item set is broad enough or relevant enough to capture what may be the critical cultural themes for any given organization. It is not clear whether something as abstract as culture can be measured with survey instruments at all. Further the method is flawed as it is assumed that national samples can be taken from a single company, mainly marketing and sales staff (McSweeney 2002). It is then assumed that in IBM there is a single uniform monopolistic organizational culture, though he later acknowledged cultural heterogeneity.

Organizational cultures are not mirror images of the cultures of the wider society. There are other factors that shape the cultures of organization. The founders, for example, can act to shape the nature and conduct of a business. The nature of the business, the markets it serves, and the technology it uses all may influence the culture to some degree. Stakeholders too, like customers, can influence the nature and characteristics of the products or services.

Harris and Ogbonna (1998) found that initial objectives of management, to inculcate clearly defined cultural values in staff, resulted in a range of undesired responses. Some employees apparently genuinely, or instrumentally, complied with the newly espoused organizational culture traits but the majority of workers reacted to the culture change efforts in an ambivalent manner. They reinvented or reinterpreted the change in ways counter to the desires of management. Later research (Harris and Ogbonna 2002) shows how management efforts to impose time frames on culture change detrimentally ritualized the initiative which led to negative interpretations of the change like 'Every three months or so we get a pack—yeah, yeah—"this is how we're supposed to act this month". Yeah, yeah—this is now your philosophy for life!' In some cases the objectives were adulterated or hijacked by others for their own purposes. For example in one company the financial control department hijacked the aim of employee empowerment by reducing the management by 4,000 managers. Cultural traits could become eroded by high staff turnover as there was not enough time to train all new staff.

When and if we do find occupational cultures, shared values, and norms of behaviour, how can they best be described and researched? Stephen Barley (1991) argues that few organizational researchers have actually bothered to study the deep structure of a work setting; instead they have focused on symbols like stories, myths, logos, heroes, and so on, while failing to reveal the core of the system that lends a culture its coherence. He looks at the occupation of funeral directors' and analyses the meanings of funeral directors' activities, offering a seamlessly integrated interpretation of what may have otherwise appeared as disparate tasks. Closing the corpse's eyes, making the bed, opening the windows and curtains of the death room to allow fresh air to remove any odours, and embalming the body are all ways of making death seem lifelike. The strategic arrangement of the room is intended to reconstruct the room to how it would have looked before it became a death room. The corpse's features are posed to make it look as though it is having a restful sleep. Peaceful sleep will appear familiar and natural to the mourners so they are less likely to disrupt a smooth-flowing funeral. No emotionally disruptive hint of ambiguity or conflict is allowed to mar the funeral directors' choreographed presentation of a lifelike death. Barley (1991) provides us then with some insight and understanding of how the occupational culture created by the undertakers serves their purposes and makes their job easier.

For other researchers the focus has been on describing, but not prescribing, the relationship between culture and ideological and discriminatory practices (e.g. Collinson 1987, 1992; Mills 1988). One way of examining the culture of an organization is to look at its corporate image to see what and who is valued in the organization. A corporate image is the mental picture the clients, customers, employees, and others have of an organization. The impression is the combination of unconscious, unintended, conscious, and intended factors that arise. The source of this impression could be annual reports, advertisements, or in-house magazines. Clues to the culture of an organization can be found in its norms, its values, and its rituals. You can also look at the language of an organization, the metaphors, myths, and stories that are in common use or at the ceremonies, symbols, physical artefacts, taboos, and rites. For example Gherardi (1994) notes how the business environment echoes to the great male saga of conquest (of new markets) and of campaigns (to launch new products) while the services echo to the language of care and concern for needs, and relationality. The informal use of military, athletic, and sexual language in the workplace can produce a subtle separation between men and women and alienates those who do not participate in the use of sexual language (Bates 1988; Wilson 1992). Culture is a characteristic of the organization, not of individuals, but is manifested in and can be measured from the verbal and non-verbal behaviour of individuals. Traditionally, organizational culture has been studied through case-study description, often involving participant observation (Hofstede 1994). While these studies provide interesting insights, the problem is that different researchers might arrive at different conclusions.

Looking at occupational cultures can tell us more. Occupational cultures consist of ideologies (emotionally charged, taken-for-granted beliefs) and cultural forms (mechanisms for affirming and expressing those beliefs). Ideologies tell members what they ought to do (Trice 1993). Culture is a major carrier of social order. Cultures and subcultures bind people emotionally. Charismatic leaders are thought to be able to manage emotion. Corporate leaders for example have crafted their words and arranged the physical setting to create emotional images intended to capture the imagination of their audience and to 'move minds and hearts' (Fineman 1993). Companies such as IBM offer an elaborate social calendar and extensive training to impress the company spirit on new recruits so that employees report greater pride on seeing the IBM flag flying over corporate offices than when they see their national flag. Home sales organizations like Tupperware create a cozy, warm, and cheery party feeling for their domestic sales teams. Regular sales meetings and reward ceremonies have a distinctly evangelical tone to keep spirits high (Fineman 1993).

STOP

Thinking about the Language of Redundancy

In the early 1980s I interviewed a manager, in a declining industry, who talked of his fear that so many individuals would be made redundant that the organization would become 'anorexic' and too thin to function when an upturn in business came about. Some academics use metaphors of slimming to talk of delayering and redundancy. For example, Burrell (1992) talks of 'corporate liposuction' where senior managers have to 'slim down' the 'bulky' middle layers of the organization. What metaphors have you heard used recently to describe an organization and events?

Kunda (1992) provides us with a very detailed study of one organization and its culture, an example of successful culture management. He concentrated on how the culture was 'engineered', exploring, describing, and evaluating the reality behind the rhetoric of corporate culture. The company he looked at was called Tech Engineering, an intense and complex environment. The rhetoric was taken seriously by management and considerable time and energy was expended on embedding the rules, prescriptions, and admonitions of the culture into the fabric of everyday life. The company was portrayed as morally sound, organic, and undifferentiated. He describes how social reality was formed around key words and strong images. Relentless repetition was the rule and the ideological formulations were to be found in the ready-made words of wisdom, platitudes posing as insight and found in public places, in the mail, in workshops, and used in decoration—it became constant background noise. Metaphors characterizing Tech as a social entity were based on imagery of the family or analogies with moral institutions: religious or scientific. The ideal state was one of self-control and self-discipline. Many members managed to maintain a sense of freedom but they also experienced a pull that was not easy to resist, an escalating commitment to the corporation and its definitions of reality, coupled with a systematic and persistent attack on the boundaries of their privacy.

AN EXAMPLE OF HOW TO BREAK THE BOUNDARIES OF PERSONAL TIME AT WORK

An investment bank treats all its employees, from clerk to partner, to lunch. The employees each order up a very good lunch, from a menu, and it is delivered to their desks. What is the impact of this on the employee's behaviour? The effect on the employees is that they feel they have to sit at their desk at lunchtime, eat lunch, and carry on working. It is very hard for them to say, well, I think I'll take some time out now, having been given a gift of lunch.

While an organization may wish to engineer a culture, or a working atmosphere, it is not always totally successful in inducing harmonic relationships. Aktouf (1996) provides us with some excellent examples of how competence and promotability were displayed by charge-hands and workers in two breweries in Canada and Algeria where he worked as a participant observer. He looks at the signs and indicators that made middle- and lower-level employees look competent. They had to demonstrate that they had something extra or different from ordinary workers, for example, by being zealous and doing more work, by being ruthless, and by keeping their distance from other workers. There are some interesting omissions from the list of necessary attributes; for example, technical competence was not mentioned as an attribute necessary for being a foreman. Less surprisingly, the workers' idea of an 'ideal' foreman was found to be the exact opposite of that of management's. Career-minded employees had to learn to use the language of the power holder and adhere to their values, for example to talk about costs, productivity, rates, and so on, when dealing with superiors, particularly if senior managers were around. The required non-verbal symbolic activity included adopting behaviour that conformed to management prescriptions (like zeal in observing rules and quotas) and doing everything possible to help management, from 'seeing with the master's eye' to outright spying. Even more enlightening are the names given to promotion candidates, like 'blockheads', 'shit eaters', 'brown noses', and 'limp wrists' in Montreal, and to 'traitors', 'lickers', 'porters', and 'yes-men' in Algiers. However zealous management may be, then, in trying to promote a culture, they may be undermined by the workforce.

We have just seen how the language in the organization culture marks out managers' views of competence from the workers'. This differentiation can also be achieved through symbols. An earlier study of symbolism by Thompson (1983) reports on his work in a slaughterhouse. He documents the workers' interaction as they cope with the danger, strain, and monotony of their jobs, as well as the consumer-spending norms that trap them in their jobs. Non-verbal gestures were the primary form of communication in this work culture. Knives were used to beat against the tubs to communicate time. As managers had refused to install a clock in the work area the gesture symbolized the workers' efforts to regain the control that management had taken from them. These gestures cannot free them from their oppressive jobs or an oppressive work culture, though.

Ackroyd and Crowdy (1990) also look at the case of slaughterhouse men and raise questions about how much control management had over the work culture. Much of the culture could not be explained by (and was highly resistant to) management action. Management did not decide the precise nature of the division of labour. The work cycle and therefore the pace of the line varied with the kind of animal being processed. The men worked fast and hard, habitually aiming to finish available batches of animals in the minimum time. Toughness and strength were the heroic qualities of the culture. Typically they worked without a break until the work was done. Though management fixed meal breaks, the men, according to the batches they had to process, would vary them. High levels of sustained effort were needed to ensure large payouts from the piecework bonus system. This also removed the need for close managerial supervision. Each gang had a strong informal hierarchy dominated by the fastest and most accomplished workers. The gang decided how to distribute tasks and people and fixed the pace of the line. The lead, most senior man worked at the first work station where the animals were killed; he dictated the

---

AN EXAMPLE OF CREATING A CULTURE AT CONSULTANCYCO

The founding owner-manager of this company created a 'distinctive culture' (Grugulis et al. 2000). When it was first founded it consisted of a group of twelve friends who worked and socialized together. As the company grew these social events continued and were seen as an important part of the way the organization was managed. 'Work hard and play hard' appeared to be the way to describe the company culture. A 'culture manager' was appointed to manage the 'play'. The social events included weekends away, with families, nights out, competitions, and fund-raising. Employees were expected to want to actively participate. It was hoped that socializing together outside work would encourage employees to cooperate with one another in work and that subsidized social events would encourage loyalty. Families could join in on training days. The company's graduate open day was planned to coincide with Red Nose Day (a day of fun designed to raise money for charities).

   However the whole image is not all positive. The selection process sought to replicate the characteristics of the small group of friends who founded the company. Almost all were white, male, and aged between 20 and 40. Those who chose not to voluntarily participate in the social activities, those who criticized the company and who did not immerse themselves in the company culture were sacked. One is reminded of how home behaviour and regular church attendance were a condition of the $5 day for Henry Ford (Beynon 1984).

---

pace of work. The average pace of work led to a build-up at the work stations of the slower men; these men would be harassed (for example by flying entrails) into working harder and faster. Liquid excreta would be sprayed or practical jokes played on the lower-status members of the gang. Very few seemed to resent the harassment and degradation to which they were subjected, believing anyone was 'fair game'. Casual absenteeism was almost unknown and some of the men visited the plant while supposedly on vacation; they also brought their children to the plant and leisure activities were frequently communal. Would then management want to change the culture?

   Cultures are not self-consistent systems. Cultural ambiguity is found in this next case. At Hans Kardiner Design, a small European luxury gift retailer, candour was seen as a central value in the company culture. It appeared in a written list of company values and could be seen in practice to guide much behaviour. Staff meetings were held with frank exchanges of views. However when harsh decisions were made, almost tortured contortions were adopted that obscured what had been decided. For example the dismissal of staff was packaged in the guise of job opportunities, inviting staff to apply for posts they could not get or would not want or would not like. This disguise appeared to be unnoticed (P. Myers 2002).

Culture and Change

Studies of the impact of culture change have concentrated on the extent to which change objectives are achieved and the performance indicators of such change efforts (Denison 1990; Gordon and DiTomaso 1992). However there is a lack of attention to unintended impacts. Unintended consequences can impede or prevent the desired cultural change, as has been noted earlier (Ackroyd and Crowdy 1990; Legge 1994; Harris and Ogbonna 2002).

The culture of an organization is determined in part by its rules. (See also the chapters on stress and on routinization.) If change is to be brought about, some of those rules will have to change. One change that six major supermarkets in the UK brought about (see Ogbonna and Wilkinson 1990) was the development of 'surface acting skills'; staff were expected to tailor their responses carefully in order to please the customer. For example, cashiers were encouraged to smile all the time and note that the customer is always right. The customer is 'king' not 'punter'. The cashiers adopt these values for instrumental reasons (it disarms the customer) or under threat of sanction (I smile because I am told to). Random visits by bogus shoppers and head office management reinforce the threat of sanctions. Ogbonna and Wilkinson argue that these are not changes in values but changes in behaviour.

Other supermarkets have taken a different tack and decided to reward desired behaviour such as the friendly smile. If an employee is 'caught' being friendly to a mystery shopper, they are rewarded with a gift ranging from $25 to a new car (Rafaeli and Sutton 1987, 1989). In the UK McDonald's restaurants rate surface acting skills in their staff: whether there is a smile, the greeting is pleasant, audible, and sincere, the staff member looks the customer in the eyes, there is always a thank you, and some pleasant parting comment is used (Newton and Findlay 1996). Interactive style is thus stripped of its improvisation. Affective demeanour, precise words, and sometimes physical posture are scripted for production of the 'right' image.

Asda have tried to introduce a 'culture of service' (Du Gay 1996: 121), finding that in the Disney Corporation people were recruited and interviewed in threes to see how they related to others. One girl had been fired because she was too introverted and did not have enough eye contact to go with the 'Have a Nice Day' routine. Asda thus wanted to move attention to recruitment and training of employees and to their effective 'enculturation' into Asda's corporate norms and values.

Since consumers often resent the routinized interactions like the 'Have a Nice Day', seeing them as mechanical and phoney, organizations try to design routines that have some of the qualities of a more spontaneous interaction. For example, Marriot hotel porters were instructed to notice and comment on the home town of the guests whose bags they carried, to make the guests feel welcome. It becomes part of the service worker's job to hide the scripting through persuasive acting (Leidner 1993).

Hopfl (1995) recounts the story of being on a British Airways domestic flight between Manchester and London. Having made the pre-landing announcements, a female member of the cabin staff announced 'Ladies and gentlemen, I would just like to inform you that we have six cartons of milk left in the galley and if anyone is going home to an empty house or feels they can make use of them, please make yourself known to the cabin staff in leaving the aircraft.' The response to hearing of this, by a member of British Airways Cabin Crew Training, was shock. 'They're really not allowed to do that,' she countered with some consternation—despite emphasis in training on commitment to the customer. What was at issue was the extent to which improvisation around a specific role was possible or desirable and the extent to which this behaviour indicates a deviation from a faithful reading of a prepared script. When organizations bring about cultural change through scripting, rehearsing, and performing of roles, they cannot always guarantee the outcome they might like to see. While the acquisition of a 'service ethic' has led to a conscious performance orientation and a belief in the importance of well-rehearsed actors, appropriate staging, and setting, and, in effect, a compelling illusion, they cannot define the degree of discretion over improvisation around the role.

Delayering and redundancy can bring about change in culture and climate, producing an oppressive authoritarian climate that generates conformity (McKinley et al. 1995). Companies have targeted surviving managers with salary cuts, performance-related pay, stringent output targets, and early retirement. Collinson and Collinson (1997) have looked at the informal ways in which managers are assessed and monitored in an insurance company. The culture in this insurance company changed so those managers worked longer hours. The CEO told managers that he did not expect them to be home 'in time to bath the baby' (1997: 388). Individuals started to compete to see how late they could be there in the evenings. There was an unquestioning enthusiasm for working long hours at the weekend, as well as during the week, and for minimizing holiday time and sick leave. The women took less time off on maternity leave, so the informal culture dictated that if women in management were going to insist on having children, then they must do so with the minimum impact on the smooth running of management. A more ruthless, macho, aggressive, and coercive management style was used. Managers were encouraged to look confident, in control, and optimistic. Clocks were banned to encourage everyone to work hard and stop clock watching.

Junior managers tried to resist this change in the culture. They could make it appear that they worked even longer hours and that they were always there at work. For example they left jackets on chairs during the day and overnight or left their car keys on the desk (either taking public transport home or using a spare set of keys). They left the lights and computer on in their office and, if actually seen going home, would have a large pile of work to take with them for the evening (but might not do it). Of course it is possible to reject a macho aggressive culture; Marshall (1995) documents how many women managers have decided to move on, having experienced these pressures, and built a more balanced life between work and home.

Research by Howard Khan has shown how there needs to be a change of culture in many businesses in Scotland. The culture needs to change from a macho culture epitomized by the 'blame' and 'just do as you are told' culture, as this is leading to high levels of labour turnover, stress, and poor organizational performance. The biggest problem is getting macho managers to admit they have faults. Women make better bosses than men because they are less inclined to be confrontational (*The Scotsman*, 24 November 1997, p. 24).

Culture and Gender

Organizations differ according to their gender regimes. They are both constrained by and constitute the practices that occur within them. Despite claims of gender neutrality, organizations are structured according to the symbolism of gender. Their culture is gendered (Gherardi 1995). Organizational cultures express values and mark out places that belong to only one gender (Gherardi 1994). People weave together the symbolic order of gender in an organizational culture as they construct their understanding of a shared world or of difference. All cultures possess systems with which to signify sexual difference. Culture refers to the symbols, beliefs, and patterns of behaviour learnt, produced, and created by people in an organization. This includes something as banal as appearance and the symbolic message it transmits. Gherardi asks, 'Have you ever met a woman manager with long hair worn loose to the waist?' She argues that a woman manager having loose long hair would be inappropriate, would be seen as having a 'sexiness' that clashes with the role of woman manager and the authority this confers; it would be 'out of tune' (1995: 13).

Gherardi (1996) looked at women who are the first to enter a male culture, in particular women pioneers in male occupations. She looked at the stories these women told and realized that most of them shared the same plot—the outsider who enters an alien culture. These were women travellers in a male world. An organization's culture positions the male and female in reciprocal relation. The positioning acquired different meaning depending on whether the host culture was hostile or friendly. The female may, for example find herself in a friendly culture in a position of the guest, while the men play host extending a friendly and solicitous welcome, but maintaining a structure of their superior rights. An alternative might be a hostile culture where the female is in a position of marginality. Six different organizational cultures are identified.

Occupational segregation is a manifestation of the symbolic order of gender which opposes the male to the female (Gherardi 1994). Occupational segregation expresses a coherence: women do women's tasks (e.g. caring, cleaning), they occupy female jobs (nursing, cleaning, secretarial), they perpetuate the symbolic system of subordination and subservience. Occupational segregation protects women from male competition and men from competition from women. Sometimes the 'rules' change. There was, for example, a time when there were no full-time postwomen. (My spell check on the word processor does not recognize this word but it does recognize postman and postmen!) They were not recruited in urban areas because they were thought not to be able physically to carry the normal load. But when no man could be obtained to perform the work in rural areas, they were employed (see Grint 1995: 198).

STOP

What Jobs Do Women Do?

Grave digging is normally a job that men do. A woman won the job of gravedigger at a cemetery in Italy after all ten male candidates failed the practical test—exhuming a body—by fainting (*Guardian*, 30 August 1997, p. 5). Until recently women in Britain were not allowed to work on the front line in the army. Yet research from the USA has shown that women can make better fighters than men and women are twice as likely as their male colleagues to fire at the enemy. Female terrorists are far more dangerous and deadly as they are more likely to kill bystanders without remorse (*The Scotsman*, 14 November 1997, p. 15). Some of the Chechen terrorists who took hostages in the Moscow theatre in October 2002 were female (K. Myers 2002). Released hostages claimed the female terrorists were the cruellest (*Scotland on Sunday*, 27 October 2002). In 2002 seven women were selected for assassination by other women in a Mafia shooting incident (*Guardian*, 28 May 2002).

Masculine culture still dominates the British forces. Recently research has found that in the British army many of 'our boys' would like to keep the girls out (Utley 2003). Women are stereotyped as being gutsy types who would never be good enough to be real soldiers. They are characterized as sexy, tomboyish, and a disruptive influence. These attitudes are to be found in policies and promotional literature. Women are seen as so different, they are incompatible with military life.

The attributes of femininity are ingrained in the subordination relationship: caring, compassion, willingness to please others, generosity, sensitivity. These are attributes that other marginalized or dependent groups of people possess. In order to be assimilated into the dominant group (male) certain groups of women in the professions and in politics have adopted strategies. They use deeper voices; they swear and use taboo language; they adopt a more assertive style in groups; they address themselves in public to traditionally male topics—business, politics, economics (see Coates 1993).

Workplace cultures affect fathers as well as mothers and their ability to meet both their home and work commitments. Some fathers report a tension between the demands of work and home, and feel under pressure not to take time off work if a child is ill. If a father works in a culture in which family commitments are acknowledged and accepted, this can make the task of balancing work and family life much easier (Hatten et al. 2002). While some fathers accept the long hours culture as an inevitable part of their job, a change in culture could be invaluable for many to enable them to balance work and home life. If cultures could be developed where it is the norm to work only your contracted hours, rather than extra hours too, this would take pressure off working fathers (Hatten et al. 2002).

Culture and Hierarchy

The BBC had a pecking order of presenters, according to a letter in a newspaper from an assistant editor of the *Today* programme on Radio 4 between 1978 and 1983. Brian Redhead was first in the pecking order, followed by John Timpson and Libby Purves, despite the fact that Purves appeared four times a week and the other two, three times (*Daily Telegraph*, 2 October 1997).

Not all organizations are the same, nor are all female conditions the same (Alvesson and Billing 1992). Women are likely, though, to occupy management positions in less prestigious organizations. In order to gain insight into the working of an organization look at where the power and reputation in an organization or industry are; men will be found in those areas and there will be few, if any, women.

Few women make it to the top of universities. Despite the fact that nearly half of all undergraduates are women, their representation at the senior levels of academia remains low (Ward 2001). Latest figures reveal just small increases in the numbers of women working as professors, senior lecturers, and researchers. Women, for example, make up just 12 per cent of the professorial staff and 24 per cent of senior lecturers (*Times Higher*, 26 October 2001, p. 3). Lisa Jardine, the Professor of English at London University's Queen

Mary College, advises women to 'behave badly', show a tendency towards feistiness. She admits, though, that she never did.

An interesting example of how culture operates in subtle ways is to be found in the unwritten rule that males dominate conversation in organizations. Men command a dominating role within conversation and gain for themselves a disproportionate amount of floor space or speaking time. Zimmerman and West (1975) found, in a study of thirty-one two-party conversations between a man and a woman, that virtually all the interruptions and overlaps in speaking were made by the male speakers. This, they say, leads to disproportionate female silence within male–female interaction that does not occur in same-sex conversation, so men deny equal status to women as conversational partners. Some have tried to suggest (e.g. O'Barr and Atkins 1980) that this is because males, on average, hold higher-status positions than women do. Woods (1993) put this idea to the test by examining gender and occupational status and their relative influence of patterns of speaking time in a work setting. She found that gender tended to exert the greater influence on speaking time. While speakers in high occupational positions spent more time holding the floor than their subordinates, nevertheless even when women held high-status occupational positions, male subordinates still dominated by, for example, interrupting more and giving less assent to women.

Culture and Masculinity

Using company materials to examine corporate culture, Mills (1995) looked at the images projected by British Airways in their newsletters over time. He was struck by the centrality of men and masculinities in the images. The company first consciously constructed an image of the 'heroic pilot'. Around 1919–29 air travel was associated with danger and adventure. To counter that perception and to win new passengers the airlines used the image of the heroic First World War pilot. With changing times and 'normalization' of flying, the emphasis shifted from safety to service, provided by the male pilot and steward (and eventually the stewardess). The male (and white) association of the pilot's image did not change over time; this reflected recruitment practices and served to exclude and discourage female commercial pilots. BA did not recruit women flying crews until 1987, well after legislation against sex discrimination had been introduced.

Images of women did change over time. The first images, around 1945, were of the hard-working wife and mother who stepped into the breach to do her part for the war effort. Later a new image of the hard-working girl-next-door appeared as female flight attendants were employed. Throughout the decade ending in the mid-1950s there was an increasing focus on female bodily attractiveness and an eroticized female form.

Mills is able to show, through his research, that corporate images can sanction and encourage certain types of male/female behaviour and implicitly prohibit others. Corporate images can encourage the exclusion of women from positions of power, authority, and prestige. Where does this come from? Boys, at a young age, feel they have to identify with men and so tend to reject any semblance of femininity and adhere instead to a rigid notion of masculinity. As men's achievements and activities are more valued in our society, the rules of membership in the masculine 'club' and even people's notions of maleness are more stereotypically framed and enforced than those relating to femaleness (Hort et al. 1990).

Schools help form gendered identities, marking out 'correct' or 'appropriate' behaviour for males and females; they act as 'masculinity making devices'. Masculinity is not one-dimensional though; it has to be seen in the context of class, and sexual and ethnic relations, so for example there are white working-class gays and Asian middle-class heterosexuals. Masculinity is negotiated, rejected, and accepted. The different masculinities will have differential access to power, practices of power, and differential effects (Haywood and Mac an Ghaill 1996). Particular styles of masculinity will become dominant in certain situations; those in power will be able to define what is normal or ordinary male behaviour. For example, Willis (1977) found that the working-class 'lads' he studied thought that doing mental work or having girls as friends was effeminate. Manual work was the province of masculinity.

Activities seen conventionally as 'underachieving' or 'dropping out' are, in fact, a preparation for a life at work with few intrinsic satisfactions. Subversion at school and 'having a laff' is a preparation for a shop-floor job. In Haywood's (1993) study, a group of academic achievers were labelled as having an underdeveloped masculinity, and referred to as 'wankers'. The academic achievers in turn used terms such 'cripple', 'cabbage', and 'spanner' to describe the inadequacy of other male pupils. Masculinity is reinforced in schools through teacher behaviour too. Having power and authority as a teacher means being a 'proper man'. Good teachers were 'real men'. Incompetence was weakness or seen as being 'womanly'. Keeping a class quiet usually involved discipline and force like cuffing, shaking, and pushing.

Masculine culture in the police force is described very vividly in a study by Sharpe (1998; see also Brown 1998; Fielding 1994). Sharpe found that the 'cop culture' covered a multitude of sins. Much of the behaviour she could classify within specific locations. Van culture consisted largely of lavatorial humour, farting, and belching competitions. Patrol culture included making critical and judgemental assessments of individuals, invariably ordinary members of the public going about their daily business, coloured by racist and sexist remarks. In the office culture male and female officers would be picked out for their appearance and their sexual appetite. Custody room culture was mostly officer dependent. Pub culture was a combination of van, patrol, and office culture but heavily dominated by talk of the latest sexual conquests, sporting triumphs, and personal alcoholic consumption levels. As a researcher she reports that she was obliged to visit licensed premises with the vice squad and drink copious amounts of alcohol; failure to keep up with them was viewed with disdain and deep suspicion.

The topics of interest to the male officers were rugby, cricket, golf, horse racing, beer, cars, and women (in that order). Women were categorized and judged by their sexual habits and activity. Sharpe says 'To a policeman, sex was rather like a crime return—the more they could claim for, the better it looked to friends and colleagues' (1998: 15). The easiest target for gossip was the woman police officer. Official complaints about the behaviour of male officers were not common; sexism was just part of the culture. Policewomen had to 'tough it out' or go under.

Research has also looked at how masculinity is created and maintained in the police in the USA. Male police officers equate women with feminine moral virtue, the domestic realm, social service, formal rules, administration, cleanliness, and emotions. Men are equated with guns, crime fighting, a combative personality, fights, weapons, and a desire to work in high-crime areas. Many male police officers strongly believe that women are incapable of being good police officers. Male police officers cling to the image of police officers as crime fighters and downplay the femininely labelled aspects of the job such as paperwork. Prokos and Padavic (2002) looked at police training and found that women students were treated as outsiders through, for example, eliminating them from classroom examples. Gendered language was pervasive so the male pronoun and 'gentlemen' and 'guys' was used to refer to students or police officers. Women police officers were not shown how to search men though men were shown how to search men and women. In this culture men learned to disparage women by verbally denigrating and objectifying them as in the comment 'there oughtta be a law against bitches'.

Computing and Culture

The culture of computing is seen by many as a male domain. There is no inherent gender bias in the computer itself but the computer culture is not equally neutral (Turkle 1988). There is a legacy in the computer culture of images of competition, sport, and violence. There are still computer operating systems that use terms like 'killing' and 'aborting' programmes. Some, like Turkle (1988), would argue that women are expressing a computer reticence, wanting to stay away from computing, because it is a personal and cultural symbol of what a woman is not. Women look at computers and see more than machines; they see the culture that has grown up around computing. They see for example, a culture associated with dedicated and expert hackers, the heroes of the larger culture who take pride in being 'nerds' (their term), antisocial, and having no rules except mutual tolerance and respect for radical individualism, manipulation, and mastery of the computer. Women then ask if they belong to this culture.

Early studies of the computing culture suggested that males heavily dominate the adult world of computing; it is transmitted to children by males (Kiesler et al. 1985). The culture values technical rather than interpersonal skills, hardware over software, and engineering over business backgrounds (Turkle 1984, 1988). Both men and women hold stereotypes about computer professionals. Computing is seen as a 'man's job' both in computer classes, in popular computer magazines, and by students. It is perceived as a job for the antisocial, those low in social ease and frequency of social interaction. (For a fuller discussion see Wilson 1997; Wright 1996). As a result, applications to computer science have fallen (Lightbody and Durndell 1996). The most optimistic statistics, produced by the Higher Education Statistical Agency (Siann 1997), show that females make up only 19 per cent of students majoring in computer science at university. As a result, the number of female computer professionals is low. The new and rapidly expanding information technology occupations should be providing opportunities for women but women are under-represented in IT jobs (Panteli et al. 1997). Computer work is seen by women as a field for men and antisocial people (Newton 1991; Shade 1993). Females feel that taking too much interest in technology threatens their image of themselves as women (Lage 1991).

Culture and Race

Minority groups currently comprise 5.5 per cent of the UK's population; 11 per cent of undergraduates come from minority backgrounds. Yet the culture of most organizations is not only male, it is also white. Managers involved in the recruitment process reinforce this by having a hierarchy of criteria for acceptability (Jenkins 1985, 1988). The primary criteria involve appearance, manner, attitude, and maturity. Secondary criteria relate to 'gut feeling', employment history, experience, the ability to fit in, age, speech style, literacy, and marital status. Tertiary criteria are references and English-language competence. Minority workers are less likely to fit the stereotypical 'married with two kids and a mortgage' pattern recruiters seem to prefer; their accent may be regarded by white recruiters as inferior; and they are seen as less likely to fit in (Grint 1998: 251).

Employers' attitudes to race discrimination have been called lazy, benignly ignorant, and complacent by the Commission for Racial Equality (*Personnel Today*, 31 January 1995). While 88 per cent of organizations have equality policies on race, fewer than half put their words into action. Racism is not difficult to demonstrate. For example, the Head of the Department of General Practice at Manchester University showed that doctors with Asian names were less likely to be interviewed for jobs than those with English names. In a controversial research project, he sent off fake curricula vitae, identical in terms of sex, education, and training; all the doctors had trained in Britain. Half the names were Asian and half were English. Doctors with English names were twice as likely to be called for interview as those with Asian names (*Guardian*, 3 June 1997).

Several of the UK's leading corporations, however, are beginning to recognize the need to assemble a diverse staff team and have sought to devise recruitment strategies that reach out and attract qualified ethnic minority candidates (*Independent*, 13 November 1997, p. 22). This, they realize, will help them establish credibility and expertise to help access increasingly diverse consumer markets.

Other Aspects of Culture

There are many approaches to culture. One might be to look at the moral order, the ordering of expectations and moral imperatives in a work situation. A strand of the Chicago School in sociology (see Watson 1987) suggested we look at how an individual copes with or adapts to problems faced at work in maintaining their identity. Students were encouraged to look at the 'dirty' or deviant jobs in order to see factors of general relevance to work experience which might not be noticed in more conventional kinds of work where they might be taken for granted. We saw in an earlier chapter how, for example, prostitutes stress the extent to which they control their clients in order to maintain self-respect. This may also be happening when garage mechanics insist that they tell you what is wrong with your car and may resent it if you diagnose the fault when they are the experts. The taken-for-grantedness of organizational rules is quite hard to uncover. It is often only when the rules are broken that you see what they are. We will look at the rules and the learning of those rules in the Chapter 13 but meanwhile the next chapter looks at teams.

A Case of Company Culture

Schein (1990: 112) argues that it is possible for a group to hold conflicting values that manifest themselves in inconsistent behaviour while having complete consensus on underlying assumptions. Here is how that can happen in a company. The 'Action Company' is a rapidly growing high-technology manufacturing company. Its founder, who began the company thirty years ago, manages it; the founder has strongly held beliefs and values.

A visitor to the company would notice the open office layout, the high degree of informality, frenetic activity, a high degree of confrontation, conflict, and fighting in meetings. There is an obvious lack of status symbols such as parking spaces for senior managers or executive dining rooms. There is a sense of high energy and emotional involvement of people staying late in the office and expressing excitement about their work. The general view appears to be that hard work, innovation, and rapid solutions to problems are essential to this rapidly growing high-technology company. New employees are carefully screened. When an employee fails, he or she is assigned to another task, not fired or punished.

The company operates on several critical and coordinated assumptions:

1. Individuals are assumed to be the source of all innovation and productivity.

2. Truth can only be determined by pitting fully involved individuals against each other to debate ideas until only one idea survives. Ideas will not be implemented unless everyone involved in implementation has been convinced, through the debate, of the validity of the idea.

3. Every individual must think for themselves and will 'do the right thing' even if that means disobeying the boss of violating a company policy.

4. What makes it possible for people to live in this high-conflict environment is the assumption that the company members are one big family who will take care of one another and protect each other even if some members make mistakes or have bad ideas.

The organization appears then to tolerate extremely high degrees of conflict without destroying or demotivating its employees. (Adapted from Schein 1990.)

■ SUGGESTIONS FOR FURTHER READING

1. Sinclair, A. (1998), *Doing Leadership Differently: Gender, Power and Sexuality in a Changing Business Culture*, Melbourne: University of Melbourne Press. This helps us think about culture, leadership, and power.

2. Hatch, M. J. (1997), *Organization Theory: Modern, Symbolic and Postmodern Perspectives*, Oxford: Oxford University Press. Chapter 7 on Organizational culture is a good basic introduction on how culture is to be found amongst employees and how it may be researched.

3. Needle, D. (2000), 'Culture at the Level of the Firm: Organizational and Corporate Perspectives', ch. 7 in J. Barry et al. (eds.), *Organization and Management: A Critical Text*, London: Thompson Learning. This chapter provides a critical view of culture.

4. Alvesson, M. (2002), *Understanding Organizational Culture*, London: Sage; or Parker, M. (2000), *Organizational Culture and Identity: Unity and Division at Work*, London: Sage for a more in-depth look at culture.

5. Watson, T. (2002), *Organising and Managing Work*, Harlow: Pearson. Chapter 7 on structure, culture, and control and chapter 8 on choice and constraint in the shaping of structure and culture.

6. Fulop, L., and Linstead, S. (1999), *Management: A Critical Text*, Houndmills: Macmillan. Chapter 3 by Stephen Linstead on 'Managing Culture' provides a good critical view of the subject.

7. Grint, K. (1995), *Management: A Sociological Introduction*, Cambridge: Polity Press. Chapter 7 on the 'Culture of Management and the Management of Culture' provides a critical review. Or Grint, K. (2000) (ed.), *Work and Society: A Reader*, Cambridge: Polity Press. Chapter 6 on culture—'The Invention of Corporate Culture: A History of the Histories of Cadbury' by M. Rowlinson and J. Hassard provides a particular case.

■ WEB LINKS

www.mapnp.org/library/org_thry/culture/culture for some introductory notes on organizational culture or this site for Schein's view of culture: **www.tnellen.com/ted/tc/schein.html**

www.oise.utoronto.ca/~vsvede/culture.htm takes you on a 'web walk' on the topic.

■ QUESTIONS

1. Grint (1995) looks at the origins of the word 'culture' in agriculture and horticulture. Read Grint and describe how thinking about the origin of the word can help us think about culture.

2. Barley (1991) says that anything can be an expressive sign capable of signification. How is this the case with death and undertakers? Think of an occupation you have experienced and note the symbols that play an important part in creating the culture of that occupation.

3. Gherardi (1995) illustrates, through six cases of women entering all-male workplaces, how workplaces differ in how they receive a representative of the other sex. What did she find? Does what she found concur with any experience you have had?

4. Goffman (1961) gives us a detailed account of life in asylums. What insight can we gain from this work to help us understand the working and culture of organizations like universities?

5. Hopfl (1995) draws the analogy between acting and customer service. Read her paper and critically assess the similarities

6. What evidence is there to suggest that the culture within police forces is discriminatory (see Brown 1998; Fielding 1994; Sharpe 1998)?

7. There is an abundance of contradictions to be found in the culture of organizations. How does Aktouf (1996) describe the contradictions he found and what examples have you seen in your own experience?

■ **GROUP EXERCISE**

Does research by Woods (1993) on men dominating conversations in mixed-sex company concur with your personal experience? Read Woods's study. Try asking a mixed-sex group of friends if you can tape record a conversation and analyse the results for yourself. If men do dominate conversations in mixed sex company, what are the implications for organizational culture and management? Or
   Culture is just another form of social control. Discuss.

■ **REFERENCES**

Ackroyd, S., and Crowdy, P. A. (1990), 'Can Culture be Managed? Working with "Raw" Material: The Case of English Slaughtermen', *Personnel Review*, 19/5: 3–13.

Aktouf, O. (1996), 'Competence, Symbolic Activity and Promotability', in S. Linstead, R. Grafton Small, and P. Jeffcutt (eds.), *Understanding Management*, London: Sage.

Alvesson, M., and Billing, Y. D. (1992), 'Gender and Organization: Toward a Differentiated Understanding', *Organization Studies*, 13/2: 73–106.

Barley, S. R. (1991), 'Semiotics and the Study of Occupational and Organizational Culture', in P. J. Frost, L. F. Moore, M. R. Louis, C. C. Lundberg, and J. Martin (eds.), *Reframing Organizational Culture*, London: Sage.

Bates, B. (1988), *Communication and the Sexes*, New York: Harper & Row.

Beynon, H. (1984), *Working for Ford*, Harmondsworth: Penguin.

Brown, J. M. (1998), 'Aspects of Discriminatory Treatment of Women Police Officers Serving in Forces in England and Wales', *British Journal of Criminology*, 38/2: 265–81.

Burrell, G. (1992), 'The Organization of Pleasure', in M. Alvesson and H. Wilmott (eds.), *Critical Management Studies*, London: Sage, pp. 66–89.

Coates, J. (1993), *Women, Men and Language* (2nd edn.), London: Longman.

Collins, D. (1998), *Organizational Change: Sociological Perspectives*, London: Routledge.

Collinson, D. L. (1987), 'Picking Women: The Recruitment of Temporary Workers in the Mail Order Industry', *Work, Employment and Society*, 1/3: 371–87.

——(1992), *Managing the Shopfloor: Subjectivity, Masculinity and Workplace Culture*, Berlin: De Gruyter.

——and Collinson, M. (1997), 'Delayering Managers: Time–Space Surveillance and its Gendered Effects', *Organization*, 4/3: 357–407.

Dale, M. (1994), 'Learning Organizations', ch. 2 in C. Mabey and P. Iles (eds.), *Managing Learning*, Milton Keynes: Open University Press.

Deal, T. E., and Kennedy, A. A. (1982), *Corporate Cultures: The Rites and Rituals of Corporate Life*, Reading, Mass.: Addison Wesley.

——(1999), *The New Corporate Cultures: Revitalizing the Workplace after Down-sizing, Mergers and Reengineering*, London: Orion Books.

Denison, D. R. (1990), *Corporate Culture and Organizational Effectiveness*, New York: Wiley.

Detert, J. R., Schroeder, R. G., and Mauriel, J. J. (2000), 'A Framework for Linking Culture and Improvement Initiatives in Organizations', *Academy of Management Review*, 25/4: 850–63.

Du Gay, P. (1996), *Consumption and Identity at Work*, London: Sage.

Etzioni, A. (1961), *A Comparative Analysis of Complex Organizations*, New York: Free Press.

Eveline, J., and Booth, M. (2002), 'Gender and Sexuality in Discourses of Managerial Control: The Case of Women Miners', *Gender, Work and Organization*, 9/5: 556–78.

Fey, C. F, Nordahl, C., and Zalterstrom, H. T. (1999), 'Organizational Culture in Russia: The Secret to Success', *Business Horizons*, 42/6: 47–63.

Fielding, N. (1994), 'Cop Canteen Culture', in E. Stanko and T. Newburn (eds.), *Just Boys Doing Business: Men, Masculinity and Crime*, London: Routledge.

Fineman, S. (1993), 'Organizations as Emotional Arenas', ch. 1 in S. Fineman (ed.), *Emotions in Organizations*, London: Sage.

Geertz, G. A. (1973), *The Interpretation of Cultures*, New York: Basic Books.

Gherardi, S. (1994), 'The Gender We Think, the Gender We Do in our Everyday Organizational Lives', *Human Relations*, 47/6: 591–610.

——(1995), *Gender, Symbolism and Organizational Cultures*, London: Sage.

——(1996), 'Gendered Organizational Cultures: Narratives of Women Travellers in a Male World', *Gender, Work and Organization*, 3/4: 187–201.

Goffman, E. (1961), *Asylums*, Garden City, NY: Anchor.

Gordon, G. G., and DiTomaso, N. (1992), 'Predicting Corporate Performance from Organizational Culture', *Journal of Management Studies*, 29/6: 783–98.

Grint, K. (1995), *Management: A Sociological Introduction*, Cambridge: Polity.

——(1998), *The Sociology of Work* (2nd edn.), Cambridge: Polity.

Grugulis, I., Dundon, T., and Wilkinson, A. (2000), 'Cultural Control and the "Culture Manager": Employment Practices in a Consultancy', *Work, Employment and Society*, 14/1: 97–116.

Guardian (2002), 'The Rise of the Godmothers', 28 May, story found at www.guardian.co.uk/women/ story/0,3604,723327,00.html.

Guardian Higher (1997), 'Women Behaving Badly', 14 Oct., p. ii.

Guest, D. (1992), 'Right Enough to be Dangerously Wrong: An Analysis of the In Search of Excellence Phenomenon', in G. Salaman (ed.), *Human Resource Strategies*, London: Sage.

Harris, L. C., and Ogbonna, E. (1998), 'Employee Reactions to Organizational Culture Change Efforts', *Human Resource Management Journal*, 8/2: 78–92.

——(2002), 'The Unintended Consequences of Culture Interventions: A Study of Unexpected Outcomes', *British Journal of Management*, 13/1: 31–49.

Harrison, R. (1972), 'Understanding your Organization's Character', *Harvard Business Review*, 50 (May–June), 119–28.

Hatten, W., Vinter, L., and Williams, R. (2002), 'Dads on Dads: Needs and Expectations at Home and at Work', Mori Social Research Institute, Research Discussion Series, Manchester: Equal Opportunities Commission.

Hawkins, P. (1997), 'Organizational Culture: Sailing between Evangelism and Complexity', *Human Relations*, 50/4: 417–40.

Haywood, C. (1993), 'Using Sexuality: An Exploration into the Fixing of Sexuality to Make Male Identities in a Mixed Sex Sixth Form', unpublished MA dissertation, University of Warwick, cited in Mairtin Mac an Ghaill (ed.), *Understanding Masculinities*, Milton Keynes: Open University Press, ch. 3.

——and Mac an Ghaill, Mairtin (1996), 'Schooling Masculinities', in Mairtin Mac an Ghaill (ed.), *Understanding Masculinities*, Milton Keynes: Open University Press.

Hofstede, G. (1980), 'Motivation, Leadership and Organization: Do American Theories Apply Abroad?', *Organizational Dynamics* (Summer), 42–63.

——(1991), *Cultures and Organizations: Software of the Mind*, London: McGraw Hill.

——(1994), *Uncommon Sense about Organizations: Cases, Studies and Field Observations*, Thousand Oaks, Calif.: Sage.

——(1998), 'Attitudes, Values and Organizational Culture: Disentangling the Concepts', *Organization Studies*, 19/3: 477–92.

——(2002), 'Dimensions Do Not Exist: A Reply to Brendan McSweeney', *Human Relations*, 55/1: 1355–61.

Hopfl, H. (1995), 'Performance and Customer Service: The Cultivation of Contempt', *Studies in Culture, Organizations and Society*, 1: 47–62.

Hort, B. E., Fagot, B. I., and Leinback, M. D. (1990), 'Are People's Notions of Maleness More Stereotypically Framed than their Notions of Femaleness?' *Sex Roles*, 23/3–4: 197–212.

Jenkins, R. (1985), 'Black Workers in the Labour Market: The Price of Recession', in B. Roberts, R. Finnegan, and D. Gallie (eds.), *New Approaches to Economic Life*, Manchester: Manchester University Press.

——(1988), 'Discrimination and Equal Opportunity in Employment: Ethnicity and "Race" in the United Kingdom', in D. Gallie (ed.), *Employment in Britain*, Oxford: Blackwell.

Johnson, P., and Gill, J. (1993), *Management Control and Organizational Behaviour*, London: Paul Chapman.

Kanter, Rosabeth Moss (1985), *Change Masters: Corporate Entrepreneurs at Work*, London: Allen & Unwin.

——(1989), *When Giants Learn to Dance*, London: Simon & Schuster.

Kiesler, S., Sproull, L., and Eccles, J. S. (1985), 'Pool Halls, Chips and War Games: Women in the Culture of Computing', *Psychology of Women Quarterly*, 9: 451–62.

Kunda, G. (1992), *Engineering Culture: Control and Commitment in a High-Tech Corporation*, Philadelphia: Temple University Press.

Lage, E. (1991), 'Boys, Girls and Microcomputing', *European Journal of Psychology of Education*, 1: 29–44.

Legge, K. (1994), 'Managing Culture: Fact or Fiction', in K. Sisson (ed.), *Personnel Management: A Comprehensive Guide to Theory and Practice in Britain*, Oxford: Blackwell, pp. 397–433.

Leidner, R. (1993), *Fast Food, Fast Talk*, Berkeley, Calif.: University of California Press.

Lightbody, P., and Durndell, A. (1996), 'The Masculine Image of Careers in Science and Technology: Fact or Fantasy?', *British Journal of Educational Psychology*, 66: 231–46.

Lupton, T. (1963), *On the Shopfloor*, Oxford: Pergamon.

McIntyre, A. (1971), 'Is a Science of Comparative Politics Possible?', in A. McIntyre (ed.), *Against the Self Images of the Age: Essays in Ideology and Philosophy*, London: Duckworth.

McKinley, R., Sanchez, C. M., and Schick, A. G. (1995), 'Organizational Downsizing: Constraining, Cloning and Learning', *Academy of Management Executive*, 14/3: 32–44.

McSweeney, B. (2002), 'Hofstede's Model of National Cultural Differences and their Consequences: A Triumph of Faith—a Failure of Analysis', *Human Relations*, 55/1: 89–118.

Marshall, J. (1995), *Women Managers Moving On*, London: Routledge.

Mills, A. J. (1988), 'Organization, Gender and Culture', *Organization Studies*, 9/3: 351–69.

——(1995), 'Man/aging Subjectivity, Silencing Diversity: Organizational Imagery in the Airline Industry. The Case of British Airways', *Organization*, 2/2: 243–69.

Myers, K. (2002), 'The Terrible Sight of a Female Terrorist', *Daily Telegraph*, 27 Oct.

Myers, P. (2002), 'Customers, Boardrooms and Gossip: Theme Repetition and Metapatterns in the Texture of Organizing', *Human Relations*, 55/6: 669–90.

Newton, P. (1991), 'Computing: An Ideal Occupation for Women?', in J. Firth-Cozens and M. A. West (eds.), *Women at Work: Psychological and Organizational Perspectives*, Buckingham: Open University Press, pp. 143–53.

Newton, T., and Findlay, P. (1996), 'Playing God? The Performance of Appraisal', *Human Resource Management Journal*, 6/3: 42–58.

O'Barr, W., and Atkins, B. (1980), ' "Women's Language" or "Powerless Language"?', in S. McConnell-Ginet, R. Baker, and N. Furman (eds.), *Women and Language in Literature and Society*, New York: Praeger.

Ogbonna, E., and Harris, L. C. (1998*a*), 'Managing Organizational Culture: Compliance or Genuine Change?', *British Journal of Management*, 9: 273–88.

——(1998*b*), 'Organizational Culture: It's Not What You Think . . .', *Journal of General Management*, 9: 273–88.

——and Wilkinson, B. (1990), 'Corporate Strategy and Corporate Culture: The View from the Checkout', *Personnel Review*, 19/4: 9–15.

Ouchi, W. (1981), *Theory Z*. Reading, Mass.: Addison-Wesley.

Panteli, A., Ramsey, H., and Beirne, M. (1997), 'Engendered Systems Development: Ghettoization and Agency', paper published in Proceedings of the 6th International IFIP Conference, 'Women, Work and Computerization: Spinning a Web from Past to Future, Bonn', 24–7 May.

Pascale, R. T., and Athos, A. G. (1982), *The Art of Japanese Management*, Harmondsworth: Penguin.

Peters, T., and Waterman, R. (1982), *In Search of Excellence*, New York: Warner Communications.

Prokos, A., and Padavic, I. (2002), 'There Oughtta Be a Law against Bitches: Masculinity Lessons in Police Academy Training', *Gender, Work and Organization*, 9/4: 439–59.

Rafaeli, A., and Sutton, R. I. (1987), 'Expression of Emotion as Part of the Work Role, *Academy of Management* Review, 12/1: 23–37.

——(1989), 'The Expression of Emotion in Organizational Life', *Research in Organizational Behaviour*, 11: 1–42.

Roberts, K. H., and Porter, L. W. (eds.), *Handbook of Organizational Communication*, Newbury, Calif.: Sage.

Roy, D. (1960), 'Banana Time: Job Satisfaction and Informal Interaction', *Human Organization*, 18/2: 156–68.

Schein, E. (1985), *Organizational Culture and Leadership*, San Francisco: Jossey Bass.

——(1990), 'Organizational Culture', *American Psychologist* (Feb.), 109–119.

Schneider, W. E. (1994), *The Reengineering Alternative: A Plan for Making your Current Culture Work*, New York: Irwin.

Scotland on Sunday (2002), 'Can you hear me? We are all going to be blown up', 27 Oct.

Shade, L. R. (1993), 'Gender Issues in Computer Networking', paper presented at 'Community Networking: The International Fee-Net Conference', Ottawa, Aug.

Sharpe, K. (1998), *Red Light, Blue Light: Prostitutes, Punters and the Police*, Aldershot: Ashgate Publishing.

Siann, G. (1997), 'We Can, We Don't Want to: Factors Influencing Women's Participation in Computing', *Women in Computing*, Exeter: Intellect Books.

Silvester, J., Anderson, N. R., and Patterson, F. (1999), 'Organizational Culture Change: An Intergroup Attributional Analysis', *Journal of Occupational and Organizational Psychology*, 72: 1–23.

Smelser, N. J. (1992), 'Culture: Coherent or Incoherent', in R. Munch and N. J. Smelser (eds.), *Theory of Culture*, Berkeley: University of California Press, pp. 3–28.

Smircich, L. (1983a), 'Concepts of Culture and Organizational Analysis', *Administrative Science Quarterly*, 28: 339–58.

——(1983b), 'Studying Organizations as Cultures', in G. Morgan (ed.), *Beyond Method: Strategies for Social Research*, London: Sage.

Smith, P. B. (2002), 'Review Article and Response: Culture's Consequences. Something Old and Something New', *Human Relations*, 55/1: 119–35.

Thompson, W. E. (1983), 'Hanging Tongues: A Sociological Encounter with the Assembly Line', *Qualitative Sociology*, 6: 215–37.

Trice, H. M. (1993), *Occupational Subcultures in the Workplace*. Ithaca, NY: ILR Press.

Turkle, S. (1984), *The Second Self: Computers and the Human Spirit*, New York: Simon & Schuster.

——(1988), 'Computational Reticence: Why Women Fear the Intimate Machine', in C. Kramarae (ed.), *Technology and Women's Voices: Keeping in Touch*, New York: Routledge & Kegan Paul.

Utley, A. (2003), 'Army Struggles to Integrate Women', *Times Higher*, 7 Feb., p. 4.

Ward, M. (2001), 'Gender and Promotion in the Academic Profession', *Scottish Journal of Political Economy*, 48/3: 283–302.

Watson, R. J. (1987), *Sociology, Work and Industry* (2nd edn.), London: RKP.

Wilkinson, M., Fogarty, M., and Melville, D. (1996), 'Organizational Culture Change through Training and Cultural Transmission', *Journal of Organizational Change Management*, 9/4: 69–81.

Williamson, D. (2002), 'Forward from a Critique of Hofstede's Model of National Culture', *Human Relations*, 55/11: 1373–95.

Willis, P. (1977), *Learning to Labour: How Working Class Kids Get Working Class Jobs*, Aldershot: Saxon House.

Wilmott, H. (1993), 'Strength is Ignorance: Slavery is Freedom. Managing Culture in Modern Organizations', *Journal of Management Studies*, 30/4: 515–51.

Wilmott, R. (2000), 'The Place of Culture in Organization Theory: Introducing the Morphogenetic Approach', *Organization*, 7/1: 95–128.

Wilson, F. M. (1992), 'Language, Technology, Gender and Power', *Human Relations*, 45/9: 883–904 (Sept.).

——(1997), 'Computing, Computer Science and Computer Scientists: How they are Perceived', in R. Lander and A. Adam (eds.), *Women in Computing*, Exeter: Insight Books.

Woods, N. (1993), 'Talking Shop: Sex and Status as Determinants of Floor Apportionment in a Work Setting', in J. Coates and D. Cameron (eds.), *Women in their Speech Communities* (4th edn.), Harlow: Longman.

Wright, R. (1996), 'The Occupational Masculinity of Computing', in *Masculinities in Organizations*, London: Sage.

Zimmerman, D., and West, C. (1975), 'Sex Roles, Interruptions and Silences in Conversation', in B. Thorne and N. Henley (eds.), *Language and Sex: Difference and Dominance*, Newbury, Mass.: Rowley House.

12 | Teams and Teamworking

We have seen how managers may attempt to manage through improving organizational culture. Teams and teambuilding is another way that managers may manage. Teams may offer empowerment, job enrichment, and a vehicle for delivering better results.

Teamworking

Teamworking can offer a benign alternative to repetitive Tayloristic or Fordist work routines through the process of job enrichment and self-management (Buchanan 1993; Carr 1994). Workers in teams could be multi-skilled, routinely rotate tasks, organize and allocate their own work, prioritize tasks, select team members, and assume responsibility for product or service output and quality. It can represent an extension to employee involvement by offering a degree of influence and control over day-to-day working. Teamworking can replace inflexible, dehumanizing work methods with more humanistic, involving ones. Teamwork has been advocated by sociotechnical systems ideas, by the quality of working life movement during the 1960s and 1970s, as well as from advocates of Total Quality Management in the 1980s, business process re-engineering (BPR), and popular management thinkers like Drucker (1988) and Peters (1989). The performance of teams within organizations is important to managers when considering the performance of the organization as a whole. Teamworking is found in cellular manufacturing, in high involvement or high performance work systems (Lawler 1992) as well as in human resource management rhetoric (Beer et al. 1984). Teamworking has been advocated with almost religious zeal by management consultants and academics (Proctor and Mueller 2000). For example Katzenbach and Smith (1993) then partners in the New York office of McKinsey and Company, talk of the wisdom of teams and see them as a means to deliver results well beyond what individuals acting alone in a non-teamworking environment could do. Let's look first at popular views of teamworking.

Popular Views of Teamworking

Katzenbach and Smith and the Wisdom Of Teams

These consultants claim to have talked with hundreds of people in more than fifty teams in thirty companies and beyond to discover what differentiates various levels of team performance, where and how teams work best, and what management can do to enhance their effectiveness. Companies included Motorola, Hewlett-Packard, and the Girl Scouts.

They point out that a team is not just any group working together. To understand how teams deliver extra performance, it is necessary to distinguish between teams and other forms of working groups. A group's performance is a function of what its members do as individuals. A team's performance includes both individual results and 'collective work products' (Katzenbach and Smith 1993: 112). 'A team is a small number of people with complementary skills who are committed to a common purpose, set of performance goals, and approach for which they hold themselves mutually accountable' (1993: 113). The essence of the team is common commitment. Teams develop direction, commitment, and momentum by working to shape a meaningful purpose. Most successful teams do this in response to a demand from higher management. Management is responsible for clarifying the charter, rationale, and performance challenge for the team but management must leave enough flexibility for the team to develop its own specific goals, timing, and approach. The best teams invest effort in exploring, shaping, and agreeing a purpose that belongs to them both collectively and individually. They encourage open-ended discussion and active problem-solving meetings. There is mutual accountability. The best teams also translate their common purpose into specific performance goals like reducing poor quality work or responding to customer demand within a shorter time period. Performance goals are symbols of accomplishment that motivate and energize. They challenge the people on the team to commit; drama, urgency, and a healthy fear of failure combine to drive them to an attainable but challenging goal.

Size matters; effective teams can range between 2 and 25 people. Small size, less than 10, is a guide to success. Large numbers have trouble interacting effectively and face problems such as finding enough space and time to meet in.

Teams must also develop the right mix of skills—technical or functional expertise, problem solving, decision-making skills, and interpersonal skills. Teams, they believe will become the primary unit of performance in high-performance organizations. Teams will enhance existing structures without replacing them.

It is acknowledged that with teams comes organizational and personal risk. For example there may be personal career risks. Management has to share control and accept a measure of unaccustomed trust. For cultures with an inherent orientation toward individualism, the team approach may require a leap of faith.

Critique of Katzenbach and Smith

These authors do not claim to have researched team performance. Like other consultants, for example Tom Peters, they are talking from their experience and their personal point of view. They say they used interviews for gathering data but beyond this admission little is known of the interview process or how the interview data was analysed. They adopt a utilitarian or 'hard' Human Resource Management (HRM) approach (Storey 1995). They present a unitarist view of management where workers and managers are in pursuit of a common aim—higher productivity. While team-based approaches are being criticized, downsized, and abandoned, these authors appear undaunted by the growing evidence that results of team efforts often fall short. They are also inclined to ignore public sector or third sector examples.

They play down the intrinsic qualities and dimensions of teamworking such as job motivation and job satisfaction, or the social benefits. Little attention is paid to team member's feelings and personal reflections (Metcalf and Linstead 2003). Metcalf and Linstead (2003) argue that this approach to teams is 'masculinist'. It adopts a masculinist discourse that emphasizes managing control and performance, with the 'soft' components of teams, the sensitivities and intimacies of team members (traditionally linked to feminine qualities) being marginalized and subordinated. Katzenbach and Smith favour and privilege masculinist conceptions of teamwork behaviours and actions.

Belbin and Team Roles

As a great deal of work in organizations is now carried out in teams it could be important to consider whether the members of the team work well together so it is effective. One way in which effective team performance has been promoted is through looking at team roles and the work of Meredith Belbin, an early proponent of team roles. Team roles are described as 'a pattern of behaviour that characterizes one person's behaviour in relationship to another in facilitating the progress of the team' (Belbin 2000: xv). These team roles are distinguished from functional roles. Functional roles are those roles that relate to a person's job role and function in the organization, for example marketing manger. They are the role of the employee in terms of the job's technical demands, the experience and knowledge that it requires. Most people know the functional demands of a job and often people are chosen to be members of teams on the basis of their functional roles. However a team made up of functional roles might not be effective and may benefit from learning about the importance of team roles. Team roles focus on the interface of your technical or professional job with other people; they enable people to adjust their jobs and each other. For a team to be high performing it needs a balance or spread of naturally occurring functional and team roles. The ideal blend depends on the goals and tasks the team faces. The focus is then on the process through which a team of people makes decisions and implements them. A number of team roles can be identified.

Others, apart from Belbin, have identified team roles in their research. The largest number identified by Davis et al. (1992) is fifteen and the least four (Parker 1990). There is some overlap between different sets of roles these authors describe, but some roles seem to be unique to a certain writer.

For Belbin the development of the team role concept arose from observing, over a period of nine years, teams of managers on training courses playing management games where team performance was measured in terms of winning or losing. Belbin originally described, from his research, eight team roles (Belbin 1981) but later identified nine (Belbin 1993). He believes that there are only a limited number of ways in which people can usefully contribute in teamwork. The essential contributions are coordinating the team's efforts, imparting drive, creating ideas, exploring resources, evaluating options, organizing the work, following up on detail, supporting others and providing expertise; these contributions are translated into roles. Individuals outstanding in one role are often weak in another, hence the allowable weaknesses. To identify each person's natural team roles Belbin created the Self-Perception Inventory (SPI). Team members' colleagues who know their team member well may also use observer checklists. The names given to the types of contribution, their description, and allowable weaknesses are as in Table 12.1.

You may contribute more than one role to a team; each team member can be described in terms of their team role contribution pattern. The most competent managers seem to be able to function well in both a primary and a secondary team role (Belbin 1981). Individuals vary greatly in their patterns of team role. Who is combined with whom to make an effective team is then of central importance. Complementary combinations of people prove to be far more effective in their work performance than people with similar profiles competing with each other. Some combinations are unlikely to be found in the same person. For example a shaper and teamworker are an unlikely combination (Belbin 1981).

Belbin has claimed to be able to predict the performance of teams through knowledge

Table 12.1 Belbin's team roles

Description of team role	Allowable weaknesses
Plant: creative, imaginative, serious minded, knowledgeable, solves difficult problems, unorthodox	Inclined to ignore practical details, too preoccupied to communicate effectively
Resource investigator: extrovert, enthusiastic, curious, explores possibilities, develops contacts, responds to challenge	Over-optimistic; loses interest once initial enthusiasm has passed
Coordinator: mature, confident, good chair, calm, controlled, clarifies goals, promotes decision making, delegates	Can be seen as manipulative; no more than ordinary in terms of intellect or creative ability
Shaper: challenging, thrives on pressure, has the drive to overcome obstacles, outgoing, dynamic	Prone to provocation; can be highly strung; offends people
Monitor Evaluator: strategic and discerning, sober, prudent, sees all options and judges accurately	Lacks drive and ability to inspire or motivate others
Teamworker: cooperative, mild, perceptive, diplomatic, listens, builds, sensitive	Indecisive in difficult situations
Implementer: disciplined, reliable, hard-working, conservative, and efficient	Can be inflexible and slow to respond to new possibilities
Completer/finisher: painstaking, conscientious, searches out errors and omissions, follows through, delivers on time	Inclined to worry unduly, reluctant to delegate
Specialist: single-minded, dedicated, can provide rare and specialized skills.	Contributes in narrow way; dwells on technicalities

of each team members' team role. Given team role profiles for each team member where all team roles were strongly represented across the profiles, the team being 'balanced', the team was predicted to be high performing. Where team roles were absent, the team would have lower success.

A Critique of Belbin

One of the criticisms of his work is that what constitutes success or high performance in real teams in real organizations, rather than in artificially constituted management games, may be more complex (Senior 1997). Winning or losing can rarely be measured in real organizational settings. What usually counts is data such as customer complaints. There are also more concepts associated with high-performing teams than just team roles. At least 35 concepts have been associated with high-performing teams (Senior 1997). There is little evidence to support Belbin's original premiss; there is a paucity of research that attempts in a systematic way to test team role theories in real teams in real organizations. What evidence there is tends to concentrate on the psychometric properties of different ways of measuring individual's team roles (Furnham et al. 1993) and the relationship between self-perception measures and those used by observers who know the participants (Parkinson 1995). There is a lack of published research on the psychometric properties of the current nine-role version of the Self-Perception Inventory.

Fisher and Hunter (1998) have found that the team roles could be seen to fall into just two groups, two general categories—'task' and 'relationship' roles. Relationship roles include chairman, teamworker investigators who are good communicators, the chairman knowing how to use the team's combined human resources, the teamworker having a strong interest in people and the resource investigator developing wide networks of external contacts. The company worker works for the company rather than in pursuit of self-interest; they work well with a broad cross-section of people. The task roles include plant, monitor evaluator, completer finisher, and shaper. For example the clever individualistic and solitary plant produces ideas and suggestions that fill a role which allows the team's work to proceed. The disinterested monitor evaluation who specializes in evaluating alternate courses of action is especially useful when the team is facing crucial decisions. The completer finisher attends to details while the shaper galvanizes the team into goal directed activity.

These then are the popular views of teams. It is important to have an appreciation of what those who promote teams have to gain. It is also important to look at the critique of these popularist views to gain a balanced view. Let's turn now to the broader picture to see where interest in teams has come from.

A Historical View of Teamworking

Team-based work, as an approach to organizing work, has a long pedigree (Benders and Van Hootegem 1999; Buchanan 2000). Teams, you could say, were used to build pyramids and row galleys across oceans. In the management literature the benefits of teamworking, to reduce boredom and increase output, were recognized in the 1920s by researchers looking at industrial fatigue. Group work was seen as affecting morale and productivity in the Hawthorne studies. Particularly in at least the last two decades teamwork has become increasingly popular in organizations. By 1990 almost half of the largest companies in the USA said they were using self-managed work teams for at least some employees (Cohen et al. 1996). In the UK team-based working was found to be used for most of their employees in 65 per cent of workplaces (Cully et al. 1998). This current wave of interest in teamworking draws on two main traditions—sociotechnical theory and Japanese industry (Proctor and Mueller 2000).

Teamworking in Sociotechnical Theory

Sociotechnical theory evolved from the work of the London-based Tavistock Institute in the 1950s. Trist and Bamforth's (1951) study of coal-mining methods showed how automation displaced the autonomous multi-skilled groups that had operated under the old 'hand-got' method. Trist and Bamforth reintroduced multi-skilled self-selecting group working. Trist and Bamforth recognized, documented, and publicized the approach (but did not, as Buchanan (2000) notes, invent it—workers seem to have created autonomous group work in response to adverse working conditions). These ideas about autonomous groups were picked up particularly in Scandinavia (Benders and Van Hootegem 1999). The most well-known and controversial example of this autonomous group working is found at Volvo plants at Kalmar and Uddevalla (Berggren 1993a; Sandberg 1995). Here team-based manufacturing was introduced to alleviate recruitment and retention difficulties (Buchanan 2000).

Teamwork has been seen to 'empower' workers by providing them with the opportunity for increased control over their work (Harley 1999; Sewell 1998). Empowered employees are more positively disposed to workplace management, more committed to their organizations, and able to make greater use of their skills and problem-solving capabilities, all of which contribute to superior organizational performance (Dunphy and Bryant 1996; Harley 2001). Drawing on the logic of socio-technical systems theory, as teams involve self-regulation or self-control team members can utilize their knowledge skills and judgement to solve production problems as they arise and devise more effective work processes, enhancing productivity and efficiency (Cohen et al. 1996). Teams enhance employee discretion, which in turn feeds into motivation, satisfaction, and commitment. Similar arguments are to be found in relation to empowerment and high-performance work systems (Ramsey et al. 2000). This is the logic but how much autonomy do teams have in practice?

If you want to look at just how autonomous a team really is, you will have to see how full the trust of management is in the team. There should be no input from management in any decision making. Teams truly autonomous of management are accepted by management as full and equal partners (Murakami 1997). You might consider looking at nine task areas of teamworking to judge how autonomous a team is (see Gulowsen 1979; Murakami 1997).

STOP

To look at how autonomous a team is you could ask these questions:

1. Who selects the team leader?
2. Who decides on new members of the team?
3. Who decides on the distribution of work within the team?
4. How flexibly can the team's time be used?
5. Who accepts additional work for the team to complete?
6. How is the team represented in the wider organization?
7. Who decides on methods of production?
8. Who decides and sets production goals in terms of output?
9. Who decides and sets production goals in terms of quality?

Murakami (1997) used similar questions to look at levels of team autonomy in 'lean' production systems in fourteen car plants across the world. He found that full autonomy was not found in any of the teams studied but teams can influence management's decisions to some degree. Teams are given considerable autonomy about production (work distribution and quality) and in self-organization (team leader selection and representation outside the team). Management's power in prime task areas of production within the car industry however remains unchallenged by the introduction of teamwork.

Rosabeth Moss Kanter (1994) also discusses these kinds of issues when she discusses the dilemmas of teamwork. There are four kinds of inequalities that can drive a wedge between individuals and the team. Teams can be pulled together with people who have different status. They have the awareness that the individuals will be returning to their roles, so may slip into deference patterns that give those with higher status more airtime, give their opinions more weight, and generally provide a privileged position in the group. The seductiveness of the hierarchy has emotional roots. The emotions that make it easy to reproduce hierarchy are principally fear and comfort. Crossing a powerful figure in a group can make individuals afraid of later retribution. The comfort factor says that it is easy to maintain familiar patterns of relationships and interaction. Knowledge and information make some members of the team more powerful and effective in the team. Unequal distributions of skill and personal resources like verbal skill or access to information-bearing networks and levels of interest divide people. Further outsiders or newcomers may feel more uncomfortable about participating and speaking up in teams. Declaring people a team then does not automatically make them one just as seeking decisions in which many people have a voice does not ensure democratic procedures prevail.

Teamwork is often seen as a way of achieving the desired work attitudes. British and US managers were keen to adopt this feature of how they perceived successful Japanese companies to be working, in companies such as Disney and IBM. In fact the word 'team' was not used in Japan itself until teams became fashionable in Western countries (Benders and Van Hootegem 2000). The next section looks at the roles teams play in Japanese style manufacturing in order to distinguish it from what teams mean in the sociotechnical tradition.

Teams in Japanese Industry

Teamworking in the Japanese context in 'Western' countries appears to take three forms (Benders and Van Houtegem 2000). First it is the idea that the company or organization is the team; each individual has a responsibility for this. It refers to a collective spirit, and conveys the necessity of desired cooperative spirit when establishing Japanese companies in the West. The term 'Team Toyota' was used to describe the various methods used to socialize employees into the Japanese organizational culture of 'community of fate' that Toyota wished to create in Kentucky (Besser 1996).

The second form is 'off-line' teams, for example quality control circles. These would usually be small regular meeting groups of volunteers who discussed, proposed, and helped implement improvements to the production or service process. Quality circles became very popular in the USA and some European countries in the 1980s as they were believed to be the key to Japan's economic success.

The third type embodies the principle of waste elimination in labour time, important for 'lean production'. Here the basic work group is the team. Proponents of Japanese working practices would argue that the removal of 'slack', all human and material 'waste', from the manufacturing operation is enabled by the dynamic work team (Kenney and Florida 1993). The dynamic work team is at the heart of the lean factory (Womack et al. 1990). Team members need to acquire additional skills like simple machine repair, quality checking, housekeeping, and materials ordering. They need to think actively to contribute to superior performance. It must be noted though that the term 'team' particularly in the Toyota context, should not be equated with autonomy; nor does the team have the right to determine membership.

Japanese teamworking is based on the Toyota model that is little different from classic scientific management. Here there is minimum staffing, multitasking, multi-machine operation, repetitive short-cycle work, powerful first-line supervision, and a conventional hierarchy (Buchanan 1994: 219). British workers at the Toyota assembly line in Derby, England, for example, perform narrowly, specified individual tasks designed in the best scientific management tradition, supported by shelves of thick instruction manuals, continually improved and updated by the workers themselves (Buchanan 2000).

Group and individual autonomy is one of the key characteristics of sociotechnical thinking. Japanese and sociotechnical traditions differ with respect to autonomy and hierarchy (Benders and Van Hootegem 1999). Not all teamworking will empower workers. There will be real variations in the distribution of power, resulting from how work is structured and the context in which teamworking takes place. It is possible that teamworking can lead to disempowerment and deskilling in lean production settings characterized by direct management control, repetitive task routines, and heightened labour discipline (Danford 1998). Others have warned about the coercive and potentially totalitarian features of 'devotional' team culture and ideology (e.g. Barley and Kunda 1992). There appears to be a small but growing number of critical in-depth studies of teamworking (see, for example, McKinlay and Taylor 1996; Pollert 1996; Procter and Mueller 2000; Knights and McCabe 2000).

AN EXAMPLE OF WHEN SORRY IS THE HARDEST WORD

Manchester United manager Sir Alex Ferguson refused to apologize publicly to David Beckham for gashing his eyebrow with a football boot he had kicked in a fit of temper. The wound was bad enough that it was reported as still bleeding two hours later. It is thought that Sir Alex believed apologizing would undermine his authority over the team. Would it? (*Daily Telegraph*, 29 February 2003, Opinion Telegraph.co.uk)

Teamworking is not though simply a new and more sophisticated form of managerial oppression of labour. There are likely to be positive and negative effects. Employees can derive substantial benefits as well as suffer the work intensification pressures of teamworking (Berggren 1993*b*). Batt et al. (2002) report that self-directed teams and employee participation in off-line problem-solving groups is linked to low quit rates from the telecommunications industry.

Making Claims about Teamworking

Should we be wary of the positive claims made about teamwork? Many researchers are sceptical about the claims for a number of reasons. Teams have been implemented overwhelmingly by management explicitly as a means to enhance performance (Proctor and Mueller 2000). Teamwork can be fundamental to competitive advantage, particularly with respect to quality of product and of customer service, front-line problem solving, and time to market for product and service innovations (Buchanan 2000). The managerial agenda is that satisfied and committed employees will contribute to organizational success (Applebaum et al. 2000). Teamwork is not a manifestation of concern with employee quality of working life (Proctor and Mueller 2000). Job enrichment or job motivation are not necessarily enhanced for all members of a team (Buchanan 2000). Employees may see enhanced discretion, negatively. The autonomy offered by teamworking is very much on management's terms. There has been however very little research on teamwork from the point of view of employees. Could the experience of teamwork be negative for employees?

Critical accounts of teamwork discuss both positive and negative effects arguing that while teamwork might empower employees, it also generates new forms of control which assist management in extracting labour from employees through work intensification (Marchington 2000). If work is intensified then you would expect to find heightened stress levels (Findlay et al. 2000*a*, 2000*b*). A combination of high demands and high production responsibility can have negative effects on employees' well-being. Teams which monitor their own, and others, behaviour do so more effectively than traditional or managerial control may. Sewell (1998) says this is done through vertical and horizontal surveillance. Any employee discretion associated with teamwork is illusory and may well mask increased managerial control of production, even if that control comes from the team (Harley 2001). For example, first a team may decide to negotiate a consensus on how to shape their own behaviour to achieve organizational goals. This consensus is translated into rules and procedures by and for the team. Rules like 'We all need to be at work at the same time' move to 'And if you are more than five minutes late you will be docked a day's pay' (Sewell 1998: 410). We need to be alert then to the petty tyranny that can arise in teams, tyranny in the name of self-exploitation. Coercion and conflict can be camouflaged with the appearance of consultation and cohesion (Sinclair 1992). Managerial prerogative is likely to remain intact (Thompson and McHugh 2002).

Ezzamel and Wilmott (1998) have looked at the introduction of teamworking to a company they call StitchCo. Not all employees shared the same reaction to teamworking. The young, inexperienced, and least skilled who had no family responsibilities and therefore less pressure to make up their wages through bonuses were seen to reap the advantages of a team bonus level while working at below a minimum level of efficiency. This 'free riding' created resentment among those who were working harder. Further, while teamwork appeared to deliver universal benefits like cost effectiveness and enhanced profitability for the company, it also concealed a variety of unsavoury features of work reorganization, including coercion masquerading as empowerment and the camouflaging of managerial expediency in the rhetoric of 'clannism' and humanization (Knights and Willmott 1987).

Knights and McCabe (2000) looked at the results of teamworking in an automobile manufacturing company. Supporting Ezzamel and Wilmott (1998) they found that there is no single experience of teamworking. They build on these findings to identify three reactions of employees to teamworking—bewitched, bothered, or bewildered. Some are bewitched by the discourse of teamworking and internalize its norms and values. Some are bothered and disturbed by its incessant intrusion into their lives and by the reactions of colleagues who seem enthralled by the team discourse. They are particularly bothered by the psychological warfare waged by management through an ideology of teamworking. There was distrust in management and cynicism towards teamworking. It was generally felt that management was trying to change their way of thinking in order to secure more output from employees for less return. Finally there are those who are bewildered due to teamworking's attack on established ways of doing things—working practices and trade demarcations that reflect and reinforce their own sense of themselves.

Ezzamel et al. (2001) found a case where the workforce actively resisted the introduction of teamworking. The workforce were 'unreasonably reasonable' (2001: 1067), arguing that teamworking was unworkable for many employees due to age and personality-related problems. The stamina of younger workers would put undue stress on older workers in the team, which was unfair. 'Lazy bastards' would be 'carried ' by other team members. This would be unfair as it would impede team performance and diminish rewards. Further due to 'management's inability to manager properly', hard-working team members would be labelled 'lazy' by management. Some workers declared themselves 'loners'. Others simply questioned the need for change. These workers revelled in the fact that they felt they knew better than management what teamwork really involved; they sought to expose an inadequate management who were supposed to be in control.

To test whether or not teamwork produced more positive or negative results, Harley (2001) analysed the British Workplace Industrial Survey. He found that while teamwork did not herald a transformation of work in which employees regained the discretion denied to them by Taylorist work organization, neither did it appear to involve reductions in discretion, increased work intensification, or stress. Put bluntly team membership did not seem to matter much. Anderson-Connolly et al. (2002) found however that team-work reduced satisfaction and contributed to worsening health of non-managers. If we accept that teamwork is introduced to enhance performance and not to improve quality of working life for employees it seems fanciful to expect major gains for employees to be found. Also teamwork is unlikely to present any challenge to existing hierarchical struc-tures in which power and influence are exercised by virtue of your position. Unless teams bring about a fundamental change in dominant patterns of work organization, they are unlikely to make a difference to employee discretion or orientations to work.

What does teamworking cost an organization? While organizations are eager to reap the benefits of teamworking, they may be less eager to count the cost (Dunphy and Bryant 1996). There is a tendency to underestimate the implications teamwork has for training, in particular the short-term negative impact on performance that may be necessary for the benefits of teamworking to be fully exploited.

The issue of management of teams is an interesting one. The team is supposed to be self-managing so why do they need external management? The role of the team leader has emerged as one of the most important issues for organizations introducing teamworking (Proctor and Mueller 2000) but what leadership behaviour should they adopt? The encouragement of self-evaluation may be appropriate leadership behaviour in a team environment. There are difficulties involved in recruiting team leaders. One of these is the fact that the obvious candidate is a previous supervisor but they may not have the appro-priate behaviour for managing a team. If a team leader is brought in from the outside, this can cause resentment.

Management more generally is affected by teamworking; it would seem necessary to move away from command and control management and towards a more participative style if teamworking is introduced (Industrial Society 1995). However this does not seem to happen in practice. For example Proctor et al. (1995) found that the introduction of team-based cellular working brought with it a closed and uncommunicative style of management.

Why is Teamworking so Enduring?

Despite sustained criticism of teamworking, however, the concept appears to have sur-vived. Buchanan (2000) argues that there are a number of reasons why. First the concept of teamwork in Western societies has connotations of collaboration, mutual support, and commitment. Who wants to be accused of not being a team player? It has an irresistible appeal to our social and individual imperatives that are difficult to challenge or deny. Secondly it has connotations of shared skill, solving problems, and making decisions together. It provides opportunities to use and share our creativity, initiative, skill, and knowledge with others. Organizations rely on employees to provide quality of service to customers. Thirdly the team concept is very flexible; it could involve three or more than thirty-three people. For example the Italian car company, Fiat, created an international team of 300 to design a new vehicle for the Brazilian market. The creation of 'virtual teams' linked together through computer-supported cooperation remains to be researched.

It should be clear that the word 'team' can be used in many different ways; it assumes different meanings even within the context of Japanese style management. The meaning of the word varies over time and between settings. We need to continue to ask how teams are used in particular situations and whose interests they serve.

■ **SUGGESTIONS FOR FURTHER READING**

1. Proctor, S., and Mueller, F. (2000) (eds.), *Teamworking*, London: Macmillan. This edited book has a selection of excellent and varied readings about teamworking; it gives an in-depth coverage of the subject.
2. Thompson, P., and McHugh, D. (2002), *Work Organizations* (3rd edn.), Houndmills: Palgrave. Pages 324–33 on teamworking provides a short critical perspective on teams.
3. Fulop, L., and Linstead, S. (1999), *Management: A Critical Text*, Houndmills: Macmillan. Chapter 6 on Managing Teams. This chapter is particularly useful for making links between Taylorism and teamworking.
4. Belbin, R. M. (2000), *Beyond the Team*, Oxford: Butterworth Heinemann. It is useful to know more about the prescriptive view of teams. Davies et al. (1992) is a book in a similar vein.
5. Anderson-Connolly, R., Grunberg, L., Greenberg, E. S., and Moore, S. (2002), 'Is Lean Mean? Workplace Transformation and Employee Well Being', *Work, Employment and Society*, 16/3: 389–413. This research provides some interesting findings on the effects of teamwork on non-managers and managers.
6. Findlay, P., McKinlay, A., Marks, A., and Thompson, P. (2000), 'In Search of Perfect People: Teamwork and Team Players in the Scottish Spirits Industry', *Human Relations*, 53/12: 1549–74, for research on teamworking.
7. Jones, O. (1997), Changing the Balance? Taylorism, TQM and the Work Organization', *New Technology, Work and Employment*, 12/1: 13–23, for the argument that Japanese style teamworking is more than a passing fad.

■ **WEB LINKS**

All the web links on teams seem to lead to advertisements for consultants who will offer tips or training. They are not recommended.

■ **QUESTIONS**

1. What, in your view, are the strengths of Belbin's work on teams? What are the weaknesses?
2. Katzenbach and Smith (1993) talk about the wisdom of teams. How wise are they? What needs and whose needs do they serve?
3. Should we be wary of the 'tyranny' of teams (Sinclair 1992; Barker 1993)? How much support is there for this rather negative view?

4. 'Teamworking today is characterised by its strategic nature' (Proctor and Mueller 2000: 20). Discuss.

5. Wheelan (1999) describes the stages that teams go through in development. She says that you know when you are in the final stage of development when being on the team makes you feel better than Prozac. How much research evidence is there to support this very positive view?

6. 'There is no simple relationship between what management do and the attitude employees take' (Proctor and Mueller 2000: 19). Discuss this statement with regard to teamworking.

7. Why would there be resistance to the introduction of teamworking? Whose interests does teamworking serve?

■ GROUP EXERCISE

How were teams used at Volvo; what was the purpose? (See Berggren 1993*a*; Thompson and Wallace 1995, 1996; and others.)

■ CASE STUDY: THE CASE OF STITCHCO

StitchCo was a family-owned single brand company manufacturing garments for retail stores. Under a traditional Tayloristic management system there was a clear division between the conception and execution of work; management planned the work while labour did it. Employees were paid by a piecework payment system (you were paid according to the number of 'pieces' of work you made) which identified each person as the producer of the product. Each individual was responsible for maximizing their output and was rewarded accordingly.

A financial crisis in the company led to half the company's manufacturing facilities being closed. StitchCo management thought that teamwork could provide a cost-effective, continuously improving way of enhancing profitability of the company, helping it respond more rapidly to shifting market demands, competitive pressure, and opportunities. Management saw teamwork as a way of improving flexibility and speeds in response to fluctuating demand. It was planned to replace line work with teamwork. The change was announced without prior warning. It was introduced into parts of the manufacturing operations immediately then gradually phased into other sites over a few years. It led to a 30 per cent increase in productivity.

The new teamwork method put machinists into self-managing teams. Teams typically comprised six machinists with mixed skill levels. With the introduction of teamwork the division of conception from execution became blurred as employees were expected to assume a degree of self-managed responsibility for organizing the work process collaboratively. They were rewarded for modifying work practices in ways that improve profitability. Now the first targets they were expected to meet were delivery, performance, and quality; the third was output.

There were a number of elements of the new working practices. Workers were paid a flat-rate payment supplemented by a team-based bonus system. Your flat rate depended on your skill band. You would be labelled high, medium, or low skilled; the higher your skills, the higher you were paid. Any machinist who attained a minimum of 80 per cent efficiency in time and motion calculation tests of the minutes required to perform a particular task was allocated to one of three bands. Skill bands could be lowered as well as increased. The team-based bonus was designed to establish a clear link between performance and rewards. Teams were rewarded on the basis of quality and delivery then on output and the cost/profit implications of their activities. The quality of teamwork was measured each week. The efficiency of teams was posted up half-daily to stimulate motivation of teams to outperform others.

The machinists in the high skill band had misgivings about the change as they felt they might lose by being in a team with less skilled machinists. A style change, a change in the garment being produced by a team, meant lower levels of efficiency and reduction in pay. They happened every three or four weeks. Management thought that it was in the interests of the higher-skilled workers to help the lower-skilled improve their performance. Many machinists however were reluctant to manage themselves in ways intended by management. Team members were not necessarily committed to improving or maximizing output especially if that meant having to compensate for poor performance of other team members. Machinists accused supervisors and managers of looking to the harder-working and more productive machinists to set the pace. However they were unrecognized and unpaid for this. Harder-working and more highly skilled machinists felt under pressure to get the team as a whole to earn an acceptable bonus.

For some earning the bonus was comparatively unimportant. The flat-rate payment for 'just turning up' had been intended to signal a new ethos of trust but allowed those who were least concerned about reaping the bonus to reap the benefit of others' efforts. Those who did want to maximize bonus were not willing to accept the responsibility of resolving any tensions and conflicts within teams. (Adapted from Ezzamel and Wilmott 1998.)

Why was there resistance to teamworking at StitchCo (see Ezzamel and Wilmott 1998)? Teamworking can have the unintended effect of fermenting hostility towards management, Ezzamel and Wilmott argue. How? What could management have done differently?

■ REFERENCES

Anderson-Connolly, R., Grunberg, L., Greenberg, E. S., and Moore, S. (2002), 'Is Lean Mean? Workplace Transformation and Employee Well-Being', *Work, Employment and Society*, 16/3: 389–413.

Applebaum, E., Bailey, T., Berg, P., and Kalleberg, A. (2000), *Manufacturing Advantage: Why High-Performance Work Systems Pay Off*, Ithaca, NY: Cornell University Press.

Barker, J. (1993), 'Tightening the Iron Cage: Concertive Control in Self-Managing Teams', *Administrative Science Quarterly*, 38: 408–37.

Barley, S., and Kunda, G. (1992), 'Design and Devotion: Surges of Rational and Normative Ideologies of Control in Managerial Discourse', *Administrative Science Quarterly*, 37: 363–99.

Batt, R., Covin, A. J., and Keefe, J. (2002), 'Employee Voice, Human Resource Practices, and Quit Rates: Evidence from the Telecommunications Industry', *Industrial and Labor Relations Review*, 55/4: 573–94.

Beer, M., Spector, B., Lawrence, P., Quinn Mills, P., and Walton, R. (1984), *Managing Human Assets*, New York: Free Press.

Belbin, R. M. (1981), *Management Teams: Why They Succeed or Fail*, London: Butterworth-Heinemann.

——(1993), *Team Roles at Work*, Oxford: Butterworth-Heinemann.

——(2000), *Beyond the Team*, Oxford: Butterworth-Heinemann.

Benders, J., and Van Hootegem, G. (1999), Teams and the Context: Moving the Team Discussion beyond Existing Dichotomies, *Journal of Management Studies*, 36/5: 609–28.

——and Van Hootegem, G. (2000), 'How the Japanese Got Teams', ch. 3 in S. Proctor and F. Mueller (eds.), *Teamworking*, London: Macmillan.

Berggren, C. (1993a), *The Volvo Experience: Alternatives to Lean Production in the Swedish Auto Industry*, Basingstoke: Macmillan.

——(1993b), 'Lean Production: The End of History', *Work, Employment and Society*, 7/2: 163–88.

Besser, T. L. (1996), *Team Toyota: Transplanting the Toyota Culture to the Camry Plant in Kentucky*, Albany: University of New York Press.

Buchanan, D. (1993), 'Principles and Practice in Work Design', in K. Sisson (ed.), *Personnel Management in Britain*, Oxford: Blackwell.

——(1994), 'Cellular Manufacture and the Role of Teams', in J. Storey (ed.), *New Wave Manufacturing Strategies*, Liverpool: Paul Chapman.

——(2000), 'An Eager and Enduring Embrace: The Ongoing Rediscovery of Teamworking as a Management Idea', ch. 2 in S. Proctor and F. Mueller (eds.), *Teamworking*, London: Macmillan.

Carr, F. (1994), 'Introducing Teamworking: 'A Motor Industry Case Study', *Industrial Relations Journal*, 25/3: 199–209.

Cohen, S., Ledford, G., and Spreitzer, G. (1996), 'A Predictive Model of Self-Managing Work Team Effectiveness', *Human Relations*, 49/5: 643–76.

Cully, M., Woodland, S., O'Reilly, A., Dix, G., Millward, N., Bryson, A., Forth, J. (1998), *The 1998 Workplace Employee Relations Survey: First Findings*, London: DTI.

Danford, A. (1998), 'Teamworking and Labour Relations in the Autocomponents Industry', *Work, Employment and Society*, 12/3: 409–31.

Davies, J., Millburn, P., Murphy, T., and Woodhouse, M. (1992), *Successful Team Building: How to Create Teams that really Work*, London: Kogan Page.

Drucker, P. (1988), 'The Coming of the New Organization', *Harvard Business Review* (Jan.–Feb.), 45–53.

Dunphy, D., and Bryant, B. (1996), 'Teams: Panaceas or Prescriptions for Improved Performance?', *Human Relations*, 49/5: 677–99.

Ezzamel, M., and Wilmott, H. (1998), 'Accounting for Teamwork: A Critical Study of Group-Based Systems of Organizational Control', *Administrative Science Quarterly*, 43: 358–96.

————and Worthington, F. (2001), 'Power, Control and Resistance in "The Factory that Time Forgot"', *Journal of Management Studies*, 38/8: 1053–79.

Findlay, P., McKinlay, A., Marks, A., and Thompson, P. (2000a), 'Flexible when it Suits Them: The Use and Abuse of Teamwork Skills' in S. Proctor and F. Mueller (eds.), *Teamworking*, London: Macmillan.

——————(2000b), 'In Search of Perfect People: Teamwork and Team Players in the Scottish Spirits Industry', *Human Relations*, 53/12: 1549–74.

Fisher, S. G., and Hunter, T. A. (1998), 'The Structure of Belbin's Team Roles', *Journal of Occupational and Organizational Psychology*, 71/3: 283–8.

Furnham, S., Steele, H., and Pendleton, D. (1993), 'A Psychometric Assessment of the Belbin Team-Role Self-Perception Inventory', *Journal of Occupational and Organizational Psychology*, 66: 245–57.

Gulowsen, J. (1979), 'A Measure of Work-Group Autonomy', in L. E. Davis and J. C. Taylor (ed.), *Design of Jobs* (2nd edn.), Santa Monica: Goodyear, pp. 206–18.

Harley, B. (1999), 'The Myth of Empowerment: Work Organization, Hierarchy and Employee Autonomy in Contemporary Australian Workplaces', *Work, Employment and Society*, 13/1: 41–66.

——(2001), 'Team Membership and the Experience of Work in Britain: An Analysis of the WERS98 Data', *Work, Employment and Society*, 15/4: 721–42.

Industrial Society (1995), *Self-Managed Teams*, London: Industrial Society.

Kanter, R. M. (1994), 'Dilemmas of Teamwork', ch. 16 in C. Mabey and P. Iles (eds.), *Managing Learning*, Milton Keynes: Open University Press.

Katzenbach, J. R., and Smith, D. K. (1993), *The Wisdom of Teams: Creating the High Performance Organization*, Boston: Harvard Business School Press.

——and Douglas, K. (1993), 'The Discipline of Teams', *Harvard Business Review*, 71/2: 111–25.

Kenney, M., and Florida, R. (1993), *Beyond Mass Production: The Japanese System and its Transfer to the US*, Oxford: Oxford University Press.

Knights, D., and McCabe, D. (2000), 'Bewitched, Bothered and Bewildered: The Meaning and Experience of Teamworking for Employees in an Automobile Company', *Human Relations*, 53/11: 1481–517.

——and Willmott, H. (1987), 'Organizational Culture as Corporate Strategy', *International Studies of Management and Organization*, 17/3: 40–63.

Lawler, E. (1992), *The Ultimate Advantage: Creating the High Involvement Organization*, San Francisco: Jossey-Bass.

McKinlay, A., and Taylor, P. (1996), 'Power, Surveillance and Resistance', in P. Ackers, C. Smith, and P. Smith (eds.), *The New Workplace and Trade Unionism*, London: Routledge, pp. 279–300.

Marchington, M. (2000), 'Teamworking and Employee Involvement: Terminology, Evaluation and Context', in S. Procter and F. Mueller (eds.), *Teamworking*, London: Macmillan.

Metcalf, B., and Linstead, A. (2003), 'Gendering Teamwork: Rewriting the Feminine', *Gender, Work and Employment*, 10/1: 94–119.

Murakami, T. (1997), 'The Autonomy of Teams in the Car Industry: A Cross National Comparison', *Work, Employment and Society*, 11/4: 749–57.

Parker, G. M. (1990), *Team Players and Teamwork: The New Competitive Business Strategy*, Oxford: Jossey Bass.

Parkinson, R. (1995), 'A Silk Purse out of a Sow's Ear', *Organizations and People*, 2: 25–31.

Peters, T. (1989), *Thriving on Chaos: Handbook for a Management Revolution*, New York: Harper & Row.

Pollert, A. (1996), ' "Teamwork" on the Assembly Line', in P. Ackers, C. Smith, and P. Smith (eds.), *The New Workplace and Trade Unionism*, London: Routledge, pp. 178–209.

Proctor, S., and Mueller, F. (2000), 'Teamworking: Strategy, Structure, Systems and Culture', ch. 1 in S. Proctor and F. Mueller (eds.), *Teamworking*, London: Macmillan.

——Hassard, J., and Rowlinson, M. (1995), 'Introducing Cellular Manufacturing Operations, Human Resources and High-Trust Dynamics,' *Human Resource Management Journal*, 5/2: 46–64.

Ramsey, H., Scholarios, D., and Harley, B. (2000), 'Employees and High Performance Work Systems: Testing inside the Black Box', *British Journal of Industrial Relations*, 38/4: 501–33.

Sandberg, A. (1995), (ed.), *Enriching Production: Perspectives on Volvo's Uddevalla Plant as an Alternative to Lean Production*, Aldershot: Avebury.

Senior, B. (1997), 'Team Roles and Team Performance: Is there really a Link?', *Journal of Occupational and Organizational Psychology*, 70: 241–58.

Sewell, G. (1998), 'The Discipline of Teams: The Control of Team-Based Industrial Work through Electronic and Peer Surveillance', *Administrative Science Quarterly*, 43: 397–428.

Sinclair, A. (1992), 'The Tyranny of a Team Ideology', *Organization Studies*, 13/4: 611–26.

Storey, J (1995) (ed.), *Human Resource Management: A Critical Text*, London: Routledge.

Thompson, P., and McHugh, D. (2002), *Work Organization: A Critical Introduction* (3rd edn.), Houndmills: Palgrave.

——and Wallace, T. (1995), 'Teamworking: Lean Machine or Dream Machine?' 13th International Labour Process Conference, University of Central Lancashire: Blackpool.

———— (1996), 'Redesigning Production through Teamworking: Case Studies from the Volvo Truck Corporation,' *International Journal of Operations and Production Management*, special issue on Lean Production and Work Organization, 16/2: 103–18.

Trist, E., and Bamforth, K. (1951), 'Some Social and Psychological Consequences of the Longwall Method of Coal Getting', *Human Relations*, 4/1: 3–38.

Wheelan, S. A. (1999), *Creating Effective Teams: A Guide for Members and Leaders*, Thousand Oaks, Calif.: Sage.

Womack, J. P., Jones, D. T., and Roos, D. (1990), *The Machine that Changed the World*, New York: Rawson Associates.

13 | Organizational Learning

How do organizations learn? It could be said that organizational learning is done through individuals, groups, and organizations. Early work on the learning organization was concerned to find examples of good practice so that the learning organization might be replicated (Dale 1994). What happened was that some of the organizations held up as role models were subsequently found to be flawed. There is no perfect organization and all organizations are peopled by fallible human beings. Mistakes and setbacks are features of development and learning. Learning is 'a purposeful activity aimed at the acquisition and development of skills and knowledge and their application' (Dale 1994: 24).

The literature in this area is mainly prescriptive and aims to help individuals, groups, and organizations learn more effectively. As Mumford (1994) notes much of the literature on organizational learning has a flavour of the Organizational Development (OD) movement of the 1970s. Yet there is little learning from the OD movement to be found in current managerial thinking. Most managers are unwilling to accept, for example, the values usually held by OD practitioners—openness, trust, confrontation.

The View of the Individual Learning

One way of learning about organizations is to watch what goes on, or how a job is done. This used to be, or is, called 'Sitting by Nelly'. Nelly would show you how to do the job. You watch and learn, then you can do the job yourself. Charles Handy, the management writer, was, in his first job as a manager, asked to sit and watch the general manager of his office, called Ian. Charles Handy was asked to sit in the manager's room, in a corner, and be as inconspicuous as possible. He was told not to speak when anyone else was in the room and never to leave the room, no matter what was going on. The manager explained, 'You will learn more about this business from watching me for a month than by sitting by some other Nelly, and I will learn too from having to explain to you what is going on and why I did what I did' (Handy 2000: 116). Handy says he learned some important lessons in management, the biggest of which was the thrill of being trusted.

Psychology has traditionally focused on the individual when considering learning. The Golden Age of Learning theory dominated experimental psychology from about 1940 to

1960. Texts on organizational behaviour usually acknowledge individual theories of learning—the behaviourist approach, personified in the work of B. F. Skinner and J. B. Watson. The behaviourists focused on the smallest unit of behaviour the learned stimulus-response link. Behaviourism sees animals and people as black boxes. Behaviourists can observe what goes into the box, input in the form of stimulus, and output in the form of behaviour. It was not the job of the behaviourist to speculate about what was going on inside, for example thinking or reasoning. Direct observation of behaviour was seen as rigorous and objective. Anything else was unknowable and irrelevant.

Skinner and Pavlov saw behaviour as learned, acquired through the learning mechanism of classical and operant conditioning. Classical conditioning is where a learned link, an association between a stimulus and a response, could be forged simply by repeating the two together often enough. Pavlov found that a response could become conditioned. He believed that all learning was no more than a result of conditioning, conditioned reflex. Classical conditioning is usually discussed in relation to salivation and dogs but can be found in an experiment with humans. If a person's hand is plunged into ice cold water, vasoconstriction (the contracting and withdrawing of blood vessels from the skin's surface) occurs (Menzies 1937). If this is done at the same time as the person hears a buzzer, after a few trials, it is found that the sound of the buzzer itself elicits the response of vasoconstriction. It is important to bear in mind that this is the autonomic nature of learning; you don't have to think about it. As such it is not easy to break a conditioned response by thinking or reasoning. Classical conditioning tends to be associated with automatic responses like emotional reactions or reflexes.

Operant conditioning, in contrast, is mainly concerned with voluntary behaviour, acts which can be deliberately controlled. It is used to create new forms of behaviours or to shape behaviour. Reward or punishment shapes behaviour. Skinner believed that learning could become a conditioned response through positive or negative feedback. Behaviour is modified by its consequences. An example of positive feedback or positive reinforcement is the IBM manager (discussed in Chapter 11) who rewarded achievement he observed by writing out cheques as he wandered around the organization.

Organizations use positive reinforcement regularly when they reward attendance, accident prevention, productivity, and other goals. Negative reinforcement is not generally recommended. This does not mean that managers don't use it.

AN EXAMPLE OF A CONDITIONED RESPONSE

Many jobs require a conditioned response. Driving for example requires reflexive behaviour, knowing how hard to brake in various situations. If you normally drive a car with manual transmission and change to an automatic, you will find your left foot stomping on a non-existent clutch pedal—this is your conditioned response.

AN EXAMPLE OF NEGATIVE REINFORCEMENT

A manager called Richard Grote was faced with a disgruntled worker who had written a vulgar message on a corn chip that was discovered by a customer. Grote gave the employee a day off with pay and called it positive discipline. He found this had a positive effect on morale and cut down on labour turnover. Others have adopted the idea when they tell an employee to take the day off and decide if they want their job. After the day off, the employee has to agree, in writing, that they will not repeat the behaviour.

There are other theories of learning. E. L. Thorndike believed that learning might be achieved on the basis of trial and error. Wolfgang Kohler argued that there is insight learning, that you can learn by gaining an understanding of important elements within a problem and the relationship between them.

Texts usually go on to look at the cognitive approach. The assumption is that many of the laws of learning are common to a wide variety of species including humans. The use of animals leads to a relatively 'mechanistic' view of conditioning in humans and 'a crude slot machine model of behavior' (Koestler 1967: 3–18). Yet animal behaviour is not the same as human (Davey 1988). Even when principles that govern the behaviour are discovered, they may be specific to both the situation and the species under investigation (Schwartz and Lacey 1988).

Researchers have examined the relevance of animal-based experiments for human operant conditioning. They have found for example that it is useful to tell human subjects what to do to receive reward or avoid punishment (Perone et al. 1988). (This of course cannot and is not done in conventional experiments with animals.) Ayllon and Azrin (1964) arranged for psychiatric patients to receive treats contingent upon appropriate behaviour at mealtime. After twenty meals with no improvement, the problem was solved by instructing the patients about the contingency, about the fact they would receive a treat if they demonstrated the right behaviour.

STOP

It Makes You Think

This is the best story I know that makes you think twice about what behaviour modification can achieve. Don Bannister, a psychologist who worked at a psychiatric hospital near Leeds, told me how staff at the hospital had tried to use behaviour modification on psychiatric patients. Their behaviour was very bad (too much shouting, swearing, and disagreeing with staff's requests). The staff decided to reward good behaviour with tokens that could be 'spent' in the hospital shop on sweets, newspapers, cigarettes, and other goods. The result was that all the patients bar one behaved worse than ever. When the staff asked what was happening they found that the one well-behaved patient (an old man) was being rewarded with all the tokens. He was rewarding the other patients for their bad behaviour with the same tokens.

The principles of Taylorism and Scientific Management are virtually identical to those of behaviour theory. Traditional practices were suppressed and workplaces became describable and explicable in informative detail in terms of principles of reinforcement. Taylor and his present-day followers reward positive behaviour with wages.

Individual learning may be recognizing new ways of doing things or new possibilities; these may be based on prior experiences or images (Crossan et al. 1999; Weick 1995).

Group Learning

Individuals bring to the group their own thinking and learning and share that, engaging in individual and collective interpreting or sensemaking (Weick 1995). During the interpretation process existing views are revised and new ways of learning develop (Huff 1990). It may be that this results in new rules, routines, information systems, or strategy for the organization (Crossan et al. 1999).

The Organization Learning

Organizational learning has been seen as the aggregation of individual learning in an organizational context. This view now appears to have been superseded by organizations being seen as collective entities. Some see organizations as exhibiting similar learning characteristics to those of individuals. Learning is seen as an integral part of successful organizational functioning. Organizations need to learn in order to transform in response to rapidly changing environmental conditions. This model of the learning organization is popular with practitioners as well as business school academics and has a problem-solving orientation using specific diagnostic tools to identify, promote, and evaluate the quality of the learning processes within an organization (Easterby-Smith and Araujo 1999).

Peter Senge (1990) provides a broad theory of organizational learning. Senge separates organizational learning into five types or disciplines. The first is personal mastery that includes education, training, and development but also how that knowledge is brought to organizations to keep individuals and organizations responsive to the changing environment. The second discipline is the formation and examination of the mindsets we use to analyse our organizations, the competition, and ourselves. The third type involves the creation of a shared vision while the fourth is team learning; the fifth is systems thinking which it is suggested is the element that makes the other types work in harmony. This view then is very different from the typical approach to learning that would emphasize the individual learning done, not the organizational or its units.

Sociotechnical systems theory has a concept of a learning organization that focuses on the idea of collective participation by teams of individuals, especially workers, in developing new patterns of work, career paths, and arrangements for combining family and work. Work must be redesigned by workers and supervisors and managers must learn to create the context in which this can be done (Argyris 1999). The sociotechnical theorists and others like Peter Senge and Edgar Schein offer prescriptions to the kinds of structures, processes, and conditions that may function as enablers of productive organizational learning. These prescriptions would include creating a flat decentralized structure, information systems that provide fast public feedback on performance of the organization, measures of organizational performance, systems of incentives to promote learning, and ideologies such as total quality, continuous learning, and excellence.

One of the best-known writers in this area is Argyris, who believes that organizational learning is a competence that all organizations should develop. He defines significant learning in organizations as the ability to detect and correct errors (Argyris 1999). An error (technical, administrative, or human) is any mismatch between plan or intention and what actually happened when either is implemented. He and Donald Schon (1974, 1978) distinguish between single- and double-loop learning. Single-loop learning produces behavioural changes that are adaptive but do not produce significant value changes. For example you may want to deal with a person who is angry when a topic is raised by avoiding the topic or manipulating the way it is discussed. Double-loop learning produces a value change from which behaviour changes flow; for this to happen in the example just given, you would need to explore the reasons for the angers and design suitable behaviours. It is argued (Argyris 1993) that double-loop learning is more powerful than single-loop learning and that double-loop learning can be taught to individuals. There needs to be a strong motivation on the part of the individual to change.

The process of becoming a learning organization has been described as an 'evolutionary journey' (Pedler et al. 1997). Commitment to organizational learning is evident through formal and informal learning opportunities where people are encouraged to take responsibility for their own learning and development. The learning organization facilitates the learning of all its members (Pedler et al. 1997). It is assumed in most cases that there is some notion of consensus and unitarism (Fox 1974). The 'learning organization' (Pedler et al. 1997) assumes a shared vision and shared values (Handy 1995). Researchers are however beginning to document situations where identities are not shared and where conceptions and ideologies are diverse and possibly in conflict. Power and politics and diversity influence organizational learning (Easterby-Smith et al. 2000; Huzzard and Ostergren 2002).

Some researchers have distinguished between 'hard' learning which is formalized, prescriptive development and training and 'softer' process-based learning that is based on language development, relationships with others, memory, and identity. If learning is limited to training and self-development just to fulfil organizational goals, then the soft learning, through which individuals make sense of their world, is not utilized (Jones and Hendry 1994).

Self-development and continuous development has been acknowledged as important for organizational success (London and Smither 1999). There are thought to be three essential elements—the availability of choices, informational non-threatening feedback, and empathy (London and Smither 1999). Organizations then would have to shift from a control model of management to facilitate self-development.

Some academics have questioned whether or not organizations learn; it could be argued that individuals within organizations learn not organizations themselves. The counter-argument is that organizations learn in the sense that they 'encode inferences from history into routines that guide behaviour' (Leavitt and March 1988). An organization has learned if any of its units have acquired information and have this information to use on behalf of the organization (Huber 1989). Argyris (1999) would argue that thought and action carried out by individuals in interaction with one another, on behalf of the organization, can change that organization and become embedded in organizational artefacts like maps, memories, and programmes. It is possible for individuals to think and act on behalf of the organization because organizations are political entities that make collective decisions. On behalf of organizations individuals can undertake learning that in turn yields outcomes reflected in changes in action and artefacts.

There are factors that predict successful learning (Findlay et al. 2000). Managerial and organizational justice was found to be one of the predominant predictors of a positive attitude towards organizational learning. Where management is seen to be fair and employees have trust in the leadership, they feel more positive about learning. Further, individuals tend to perceive greater procedural justice when they believe that they have had the chance to participate in decision making.

Older employees have been found to have more negative perceptions of learning than their younger counterparts. This may be because older employees do not believe that training will bring them any benefit (Schuller and Bostyn 1992; Findlay et al. 2000). This could be true or it may be that companies decide it is not worthwhile investing in older workers. If older workers are seen as not as flexible as younger employees, they may not be given the same opportunities for learning (Findlay et al. 1999).

Organizational learning is not always beneficial. The term should not then be treated as if it is neutral. For example in the Nazi period bureaucracy became more efficient at extermination. The organization learned to be more efficient. Less dramatically it could be said that those who have power and use the term organizational learning as a vehicle of rhetoric, as a vehicle of normative control to gain compliance and commitment of subordinates, are doing so for their own good, but not for those subordinated. As Kunda (1992) notes, under normative control members act in the best interests of the company as they are driven by commitment, strong identification with company goals, managerial appeals, and exhortations. But it is the employee's self that is claimed in the name of corporate interest. We cannot escape the need then to declare what kinds of organizational learning we will take to be desirable or undesirable and why (Argyris 1999).

Organizational learning also implies rationality, being able to remember past events, analyse alternatives, evaluate the results of action. Some authors would argue that organizations are political systems made up of subgroups with their own interest and powers, engaged in battle for control, or avoidance of control, and incapable of acting as agents of learning (Crozier 1963). Maybe organizations are inherently chaotic, at best organized anarchies (March and Olsen 1976). March has also cast doubt on the ability of organizations to learn in his concept of 'competence traps' where organizations falsely project into the future the strategies of action that have worked for them in the past. He describes 'superstitious learning' (Leavitt and March 1988: 325) that happens when the experience of learning appears compelling but the connections between actions and outcomes are mis-specified. Further, learning does not always lead to intelligent behaviour. The behavioural theory of the firm (Cyert and March 1963; Simon 1976) notes that threats to effective action exist, for example dysfunctional patterns of behaviour undermine learning.

Organizations depend on control systems that set up conflicts between rule setter and rule followers which lead to cheating so that everyone appears to be rational and no one can be trusted.

Organizations, groups, and individuals can fail to learn. The learning process is neither systematic nor effective. While a majority of managers might have considered their organization to be a learning organization, Doyle et al. (2000) found that repeat mistakes were made, as there was no time to learn from what happened in the past. Managers do not have the luxury of time to pause and reflect on change. The principle of the learning organization finds fragile support in the findings of this research.

What we learn is not always obvious and it does not always appear to be common sense. For example firefighters dealing with forest fires have learned that it is not sensible for a fresh crew to replace a tired crew when a blaze is at its height—in the heat of the day when a strong wind is blowing. You would think that fresh resources would be expected to produce redoubled effort and faster fire suppression. However a change of command when a fire is at its most dynamic and volatile makes it harder for the incoming crew to catch up with its rapidly changing character. The incoming crew will always be behind. The crew never learns what it faces, its idea of what is happening tends to lag behind what is actually happening, and if it fails to get on top of the situation, the level of danger increases significantly (Weick 2002).

Some organizations, groups, or individuals may refuse to learn. An interesting example comes from learning in the London fire brigade (Salaman and Butler 1994). Seminars were designed to identify and, when necessary, modify attitudes towards the introduction of non-white and non-male firefighters. Resistance was evident. The station officers were markedly unsympathetic to the messages and refused to accept the validity of arguments presented to them. They were refusing to learn. One explanation may lie in the conservatism, racism, or sexism of the officers. A more plausible explanation, it is argued by Salaman and Butler, is that the refusal to learn was developed for another reason. The implementation of equality of opportunity would mean having a formalized open system. But this would bring about a significant reduction in the traditional authority of fire-station personnel to intervene in the recruitment and selection of new officers and to allocate advantage in these processes to applicants from among their own family and friends. (One wonders why their family and friends did not include women and those of ethnic origin.) The context was one of 'insiders' and 'outsiders' or 'them' and 'us'. Firefighters—the station offices and crews (us, the insiders) worked shifts. They were separate and distinct from the next layer of management who worked office hours and were based in regional offices, perceived to be far from the realities of fire-fighting. Close relationships developed with members of their own watch. They had a shared world composed of danger and boredom, jokes, memories, and myths. This loyalty and resistance got in the way of learning.

For some occupations, like fire-fighting, security work, and the armed forces we have learned that men are the norm. Our assumption that this is the case is sometimes challenged. For example recently a war photograph was published in the international newspapers; it outraged everyone who saw it. The photo was of an American soldier searching an Afghan woman. 'To most Pakistanis and Afghans, this photo is hyper-offensive, showing a demure Islamic beauty disrespected by an American brute' (McGirk 2002). If you look closely at the photo though you can see that the soldier is female and has her long hair bunched at the neck, under her helmet. However, the photo was published in Pakistan without the original caption identifying the soldier as Sergeant Nicola Hall.

Learning about Language in Organizations

The language people have learned to use in an organization tells us a good deal about the views held by organizational members about what goes on both within the organization and outside. For example if a logging company portrays environmentalists as 'deviant', 'lying' 'stinking', and 'zealots' while the environmentalists regard logging as the equivalent of forest rape and forest companies as 'greedy corporate pigs' (Wilson 1998), you know there is little meeting of minds between the two groups.

Research has shown how actions, like organizational change, can be legitimized through language. Language helps one learn about the change. Organizational change can be made rationally accountable and help define 'in' and 'out' groups. The language of warfare has been noted in the literature on takeovers and introduction of new technology (Wilson 1992). The language of religion can help define the 'saints' and the 'sinners'. It helps highlight and make coherent aspects of change and 'good practice' which may lead to improved systems. One commentator goes as far as to say that the language of the apocalyptic vision, missions, and doom scenarios is far more prevalent in business thinking than in most churches (Pattison 1991).

Language used in organizations is also sexist. The ridicule in the media of the concerns about sexism in language is one form of evidence that words are not neutral but deeply ideological. Rules about language and standards of correct speech reveal information about pattern of power and privilege in the wider society (Cameron 1995) and the organization. Language transmits social information (that we have learned) about discrimination against women.

For example organizations ask for titles. The titles Miss or Mrs supply information about a woman's sexual availability and lump single women with the young and inexperienced (Miller and Swift 1975). The title Ms is not an attractive option and provides more information about women. Ms is associated with feminism and widowhood (Wood 1997). Pauwels (1998) has suggested the only way to address the gender imbalance might be to introduce new titles for men that would provide information about marital status. The trouble around the use of Mr, Miss, or Ms can be understood as another demonstration of the dominant social order.

One of the ways in which gender is marked is by the use of suffix or adjuncts. One suffix in common use to indicate a female is '-ess' (stewardess, hostess, waitress). This marks women as being different or less important than men who do the same job. Adjuncts are found in terms like women doctor or female surgeon. The world is male unless proven otherwise (Weatherall 2002).

Masculine forms of words tend to have more positive connotations than feminine ones. For example bachelor is more positive than spinster. When being referred to in terms of the opposite gender, tomboy has positive connotations while sissy is used as an

---

AN EXAMPLE WITH QUESTIONS: DOES AN ORGANIZATION LEARN?

Annabel Brown, an academic, was passed over for promotion in favour of a far less qualified male whom she had recently helped recruit. The post had not been advertised nor had selection criteria been drawn up. She complained to the line manager, asked how the appointment could have been made in that way, and said that she felt her qualifications, work experience, and current performance made her the best qualified for the role. He suddenly proposed a U-turn solution. The original offer to the male colleague would be withdrawn and she and the man would be left to decide who should have the job. Annabel turned this offer down saying that she wanted an assurance from her department and the human resource department that in future all jobs would be properly advertised. The line manager referred Annabel to his manager who made it clear that she believed the case was clearly discrimination. She agreed that the appointment procedure had not been carried out properly. Annabel then asked the management to back down and advertise the post. By this time the male colleague had a potential case for grievance but agreed not to pursue it.

As no acceptable solution could be reached, the post was withdrawn. Annabel was assured that all future posts would be advertised. The main lesson that Annabel learned was that while her efforts were time consuming and stressful, they did achieve a positive result. She would now recommend others challenge similar unjust appointments. She also learned that you should keep matters completely confidential. In her case she only spoke to the union, to those colleagues who were directly concerned with the situation, and to her partner. By acting in this way she ensured that no damaging gossip was spread around her institution. During the experience she was better able to remain looking calm, professional, and rational though she may not have felt it. She managed to maintain good relations with her managers and her male colleague.

We have seen what Annabel learned. Do you think the organization has learned or can you only say that key individuals might have learned some lessons from the experience? How would you decide whether or not organizational learning had taken place; what would need to happen?

Case adapted from real case published in *AUTLOOK*, 223 (Jan. 2003), 30–1.

---

insult. A woman might feel complimented if it is said that she thinks like a man but it would be an insult if a man was likened to an old woman. Language use then demonstrates the social and moral order where men and masculinity are valued more than women and femininity.

Case Study: The Memory Skills of Cocktail Waitresses

Learning and memory are very important in some jobs. Memory, coupled with speed, can be particularly useful in service industries if staff are to provide a 'good' service. For the cocktail waitress, accurate drink memory increases both tipping and customer satisfaction. Bennet (1983/4) believed that cocktail waitresses could remember far greater amounts of information than theories of memory would predict. The waitresses did not write down drink orders but relied on their skill of remembering—this is a learned skill.

On a busy night a waitress would collect up to twenty orders, rearrange the sequence of the order for the bartender (who wanted the order to start with beers, then wines, and then combination drinks). She returned to the floor for more orders, paused for brief conversations, loaded her tray with the drinks the bartender had prepared, then returned to the floor to place the drinks in front of the customers who ordered them. The waitresses did not like to be seen to be 'auctioning' drinks, asking who had what drink, when they reached the table with the drinks order.

A study compared the learning skills of students with forty cocktail waitresses. While the waitresses could remember 84 per cent of 11 drinks and 86 per cent of 15 drinks, the students correctly placed 70 per cent of 11 and 68 per cent of 15. The study also found that the waitresses reported that their memories were more accurate during busy times when there was pressure on the number of drinks to remember and the number of customers to serve.

What strategies have you found yourself using to increase your memory?
What strategies would you use to help you remember the orders?
What strategies did these cocktail waitressses use? Would this help you remember?

■ SUGGESTIONS FOR FURTHER READING

1. Gabriel, Y., Fineman, S., and Sims, D. (2000), *Organizing and Organizations*, London: Sage. Chapter 8 on 'Learning the Ropes' challenges us to think about the nature of knowledge and learning; or chapter 2 gets you thinking about the learning involved in entering and leaving an organization.
2. Fulop, L., and Rifkin, W. D. (1999), 'Management Knowledge and Learning', ch. 1 in L. Fulop and S. Linstead (eds.), *Management: A Critical Text*, Houndmills: Macmillan. This chapter adopts a critical stance on learning and knowledge.
3. Noon, M., and Blyton, P. (2002), *The Realities of Work*, Houndmills: Palgrave Macmillan. Chapter 8 discusses knowledge and work.
4. Beardwell, I., and Holden, L. (2001) (eds.), *Human Resource Management: A Contemporary Approach*, Harlow: Pearson. Chapter 7 by Audrey Collin on learning and development is a useful summary of learning and includes a section on older workers.
5. Thompson, P., and McHugh, D. (2002), *Work Organizations* (3rd edn.), Houndmills: Palgrave. Chapter 16 on learning, change, and innovation; the first half is particularly strong on learning and socialization.
6. Fincham, R., and Rhodes, P. (1999), *Principles of Organizational Behaviour* (3rd edn.), Oxford: Oxford University Press. Chapter 1 on learning gives a good review of the history of learning.

Watson, T. (2002), *Organizing and Managing Work*, Harlow: Pearson. Pages 196–7 on the learning organization and knowledge.

■ WEB LINKS

www.mapnp.org/library/org_perf/org_lrng.htm for notes and links on the learning organization and **www.brint.com/papers/orglrng.htm** for definitions and discussion of various perspectives on organizational learning.

■ QUESTIONS

1. The issue of trust came up in Chapter 4. It arises again here where we have seen that research (Findlay et al. 2000) links trust with learning. Is trust a significant feature of organizational life, according to research?

2. Sambrook and Stewart (2000) have looked at twenty-eight European case studies and a further twenty organizations to understand the factors that effect the level of organizational learning and strategies to support it. What are their main findings? In the light of what you have learned here, how would you critique their work?

3. 'Learning organization initiatives are essentially technologies of regulation aimed at facilitating change processes' (Thompson and McHugh 2002: 240). Discuss.

4. How may behaviour modification be a useful approach to encouraging employee learning and to develop appropriate behaviour in organizations? What drawbacks might you anticipate if you used it?

5. How do managers learn about management? (See Fulop and Rifkin 1999.)

6. What is a knowledge worker? (See Noon and Blyton 2002: ch. 8.)

7. Our culture and socialization dictates that boys don't cry but it is OK for girls to weep. Research has found that before the age of 12 boys and girls cry as frequently as each other but after 12, boys cry four times less. Boys are discouraged from crying as part of a larger programme of socialization into masculinity. This socialization involves teaching boys to 'tough it out' and refrain from expressing their feelings—except for anger. However footballers cry when they miss a penalty, and penitential presidents cry on TV (see Witchalls 2003). What then are the 'rules' we have been required to learn about crying in organizations?

■ GROUP EXERCISE WITH SOME EXAMPLES OF LEARNING THE RULES

As a student, one summer, I worked in a hotel in a small community on the west coast of Scotland. The hotel was owned and run by an ex-army colonel. He enforced strict rules that he told you about verbally. For example, you may not entertain guests in your room, may not have visitors, receive phone calls, or use the public phone in the hotel. The only ways to keep in touch with friends and family were by public phone (using a phone box in the village in the afternoon break or after 9 p.m.), by letter, or by arranging to meet them away from the hotel. This way he ensured that you defined yourself as a lowly servant and less than a guest, and noted the superiority of the guest. The culture and rules he created operated as a 'boundary device' (see Grint 1995: 167), marking the privileged from the unprivileged. But there were also some rules that you only learned about when you broke them. For example I discovered that you might not sing in the empty dining room while setting the tables. What rules have you learned, in a work setting, only by having broken them?

A friend of mine noticed, in a café, if you ordered two teas, the waiter or waitress would write down 2T (always in the singular). Intrigued by this she asked for 'two tea' and found the waiter or waitress always corrected her. It would appear that the waiter/waitress has a rule that they can use the singular and shorthand but you cannot. The friend was also witnessed asking for a pound of satsuma in a fruit shop.

Can you think of an example of an organizational rule where there is one unwritten rule for you and another for the person enforcing the rule?

■ REFERENCES

Argyris, C. (1993), *Knowledge for Action: A Guide to Overcoming Barriers to Organizational Change*, San Francisco: Jossey Bass.

—— (1999), *On Organizational Learning* (2nd edn.), Oxford: Blackwell.

—— and Schon, D. A. (1974), *Theory in Practice*, San Francisco: Jossey Bass.

—— —— (1978), *Organizational Learning*, Reading, Mass: Addison-Wesley.

Ayllon, T., and Azrin, N. H. (1964), 'Reinforcement and Instructions with Mental Patients', *Journal of the Experimental Analysis of Behavior*, 7: 327–31.

Bennett, H. L. (1983/4), 'Remembering Drink Orders: The Memory Skills of Cocktail Waitresses', *Human Learning*, 2: 157–69 or in 1984 ch. 2.4 in P. Barnes, J. Oakes, J. Chapman, V. Lee and P. Czerniewska (eds.), *Personality, Development and Learning: A Reader*. Milton Keynes: Open University Press.

Cameron, D. (1995), *Verbal Hygiene*, London: Routledge.

Crossan, M. M., Lane, H. W., and White, R. E. (1999), 'An Organizational Learning Framework: From Intuition to Institutionalisation', *Academy of Management Review*, 24: 522–37.

Crozier, M. (1963), *The Bureaucratic Phenomenon*, Chicago: Chicago University Press.

Cyert, R. M., and March, J. G. (1963), *A Behavioral Theory of the Firm*, Englewood Cliffs, NJ: Prentice Hall.

Dale, M. (1994), 'Learning Organizations', ch. 2 in C. Mabey and P. Iles (eds.), *Managing Learning*, Milton Keynes: Open University Press.

Davey, G. C. (1988), 'Trends in Human Operant Theory', ch. 1 in G. Davey and C. Cullen (eds.), *Human Operant Conditioning and Behavior Modification*, Chichester: John Wiley & Sons Ltd.

Doyle, M., Claydon, T., and Buchanan, D. (2000), 'Mixed Results, Lousy Process: The Management Experience of Organizational Change', *British Journal of Management*, 11, Special issue, S59–S80.

Easterby-Smith, M., and Araujo, L. (1999), 'Organizational Learning: Current Debates and Opportunities', in M. Easterby-Smith, J. Burgoyne, and L. Arujo (eds.), *Organizational Learning and the Learning Organization*, London: Sage.

—— Crossan, M., and Nicolini, D. (2000), 'Organizational Learning: Debates, Past, Present and Future', *Journal of Management Studies*, 37/6: 783–96.

Findlay, P., McKinlay, A., Marks, A., and Thompson, P. (1999), 'Flexible when it Suits Them: The Use and Abuse of Teamwork Skills', in S. Proctor and F. Mueller (eds.), *Teamworking*, London: Macmillan.

—— —— —— —— (2000), 'Labouring to Learn: Organizational Learning and Mutual Gains', *Employee Relations*, 22/5: 485–502.

Fox, A. (1974), *Beyond Contract: Power, Work and Trust Relations*, London: Faber and Faber.

Fulop, L., and Rifkin, W. D. (1999), 'Management Knowledge and Learning', ch. 1 in L. Fulop and S. Linstead (eds.), *Management: A Critical Text*, Houndmills: Macmillan.

Grint, K. (1995), *Management: A Sociological Introduction*, Cambridge: Polity.

Handy, C. (1995), 'Managing the Dream', in S. Chawla and J. Renesch (eds.), *Learning Organizations: Developing Cultures for Tomorrow's Workplace*, Portland: Productivity Press.

—— (2000), *21 Ideas for Managers*, San Francisco: Jossey Bass.

Huber, G. P. (1989), 'Organizational Learning: An Examination of the Contributing Processes and a Review of the Literature', prepared for the NSF sponsored conference on Organizational Learning, Carnegie-Mellon University, 18–20 May, cited in Argyris (1999).

Huff, A. S. (1990), *Mapping Strategic Thought*, Chichester: John Wiley.

Huzzard, T., and Ostergren, K. (2002), 'When Norms Collide: Learning under Organizational Hypocrisy', *British Journal of Management*, Special Issue, 13: S47–S59.

Jones, A. M., and Hendry, C. (1994), 'The Learning Organization: Adult Learning and Organizational Transformation', *British Journal of Management*, 5: 153–62.

Koestler, A. (1967), *The Ghost in the Machine*, London: Hutchinson.

Kunda, G. (1992), *Engineering Culture*, Philadelphia: Temple University Press.

Leavitt, B., and March, J. (1988), 'Organizational Learning', *Annual Review of Sociology*, 14: 319–40.

London, M., and Smither, J. W. (1999), 'Empowered Self-Development and Continuous Learning', *Human Resource Management* (USA) 38/1: 3–16.

McGirk, J. (2002), 'GI Janes Flaunt their Sports Bras as Body Search Arrives in Cultural Minefield of Afghan Frontier', *Independent*, 14 Dec.

March, J., and Olsen, J. (1976), *Ambiguity and Choice in Organizations*, Bergen: Universitetsforlaget.

Menzies, R. (1937), 'Conditioned Vasomotor Responses in Human Subjects', *Journal of Psychology*, 4: 75–120.

Miller, C., and Swift, K. (1975), *Words and Women*, New York: Anchor Books.

Mumford, A. (1994), 'Individual and Organizational Learning: The Pursuit of Change', ch. 7 in C. Mabey and P. Iles (eds.), *Managing Learning*, Milton Keynes: Open University Press.

Noon, M., and Blyton, P. (2002), *The Realities of Work*, Houndmills: Palgrave Macmillan.

Pattison, S. (1991), 'Strange Theology of Management', *Guardian*, 27 May, p. 27.

Pauwels, A. (1998), *Women Changing Language*, London: Addison Wesley.

Pedler, M., Burgoyne, J., and Boydell, T. (1997), *The Learning Company: A Strategy for Sustainable Development*, Maidenhead: McGraw Hill.

Perone, M., Galisio, M., and Baron, A. (1988), 'The Relevance of Animal-Based Principles in the Laboratory Study of Human Operant Conditioning', ch. 5 in G. Davey and C. Cullen (eds.), *Human Operant Conditioning and Behavior Modification*, Chichester: John Wiley and Sons Ltd.

Salaman, G., and Butler, J. (1994), 'Why Managers Won't Learn', ch. 3 in C. Mabey and P. Iles (eds.), *Managing Learning*, Milton Keynes: Open University Press.

Sambrook, S., and Stewart, J. (2000), 'Factors Influencing Learning in European Learning Oriented Organizations: Issues for Management', *Journal of European Industrial Training* (UK) 24/2–4: 209–20.

Schuller, T., and Bostyn, A. M. (1992), 'Education, Training and Information in the Third Age', The Carnegie Inquiry into the Third Age, Research Paper no. 3, Centurion Press, London.

Schwartz, B., and Lacey, H. (1988), 'What Applied Studies of Human Operant Conditioning Tell us about Humans and Operant Conditioning', ch. 3 in G. Davey and C. Cullen (eds.), *Human Operant Conditioning and Behavior Modification*, Chichester: John Wiley & Sons Ltd.

Senge, P. (1990), *The Fifth Discipline: The Art and Practice of the Learning Organization*, New York: Doubleday.

Simon, H. (1976), *The Sciences of the Artificial*, Cambridge, Mass: MIT Press.

Thompson, P., and McHugh, D. (2002), *Work Organizations* (3rd edn.), Basingstoke: Plagrave.

Weatherall, A. (2002), *Gender, Language and Discourse*, London: Psychology Press.

Weick, K. E. (1995), *Sensemaking*, Thousand Oaks, Calif.: Sage.

—— (2002), 'Puzzles in Organizational Learning: An Exercise in Disciplined Imagination', *British Journal of Management*, 13, Special Issue, S7–S16.

Wilson, F. M. (1992), 'Language, Technology, Gender and Power', *Human Relations*, 45/9: 883–904.

Wilson, J. (1998), *Talk and Log: Wilderness Politics in British Columbia, 1965–1996*, Vancouver: UBC Press.

Witchalls, C. (2003), 'Parents: Boys don't Cry. It's OK for Girls to Weep, but Boys still have to Hold Back the Tears. How Unfair is that?', *Guardian*, 5 Feb.

Wood, J. (1997), *Gendered Lives: Communication, Gender and Culture* (2nd edn.), Belmont, Calif: Wadsworth.

14 | Leadership

Most of us start thinking about the topic of leadership with the assumption that leaders are necessary for the effective functioning of an organization. This thought is encapsulated in a quote from the beginning of Locke's (1991) book on leadership: 'There probably has never been a society, country, or organisation that did not have a leader; if there has, it probably did not survive for long.' Belief in hierarchy and the necessity of leaders is often an unrecognized ideology. Perhaps we should question if leaders are really necessary? Perhaps leaders are only necessary because, when we are faced with uncertainty and ambiguity in organizations, we project them onto 'leadership' or the 'leader' role. We do this in order to avoid directly confronting our own emotions like anxiety, discomfort, or fear of failure. Some writers (e.g. Gemmill and Oakley 1992) believe then that concepts of leader and leadership have become psychic prisons for us. Leadership is a process whereby 'followers' give up their mindfulness to a 'leader' (Smircich and Morgan 1982). The necessity of leadership is a social myth that induces helplessness, an inability to imagine or perceive viable options for us, with accompanying feelings of despair and resistance to any form of action. It is this social myth that maintains the status quo (Bennis 1989).

Another factor that maintains the status quo is individual's implicit theories of leadership. When describing leaders people apply 'information simplification heuristics' (Bryman 1987) or implicit leadership theories which influence their perceptions of leaders' behaviour and inform their descriptions of real leaders. This is particularly damaging to the questionnaire-based approaches to leadership as implicit leadership theories underpin individuals' descriptions of leaders when answering batteries of questions. Questionnaire-based representations of leader behaviour will only partially capture actual behaviour. The validity and meaning of questionnaires is then a matter of concern. It has also been shown that people's views about the behaviour of leaders are influenced by knowledge of their performance (Bryman 1987).

> **STOP** **Meindl (1990) would argue that leadership is more a creation in the minds of followers than a characteristic of those who occupy leadership roles. Is Meindl right?**

Some, like Grint (2000), would argue that research on leadership has been too scientific for this highly interpretative subject matter. Allegedly objective conditions and situations surrounding leaders are contestable and open to interpretation. Traditional scientific approaches to the study of leadership may then be inappropriate. Leadership might better be considered as an art rather than a science.

Another weakness of the research on leadership is that experimental subjects have tended to be North American. There is then the possibility that the findings have less applicability outside the United States. We would have good reason to doubt the generalizability of findings outside the USA. There is evidence to suggest that there are differences between Britain and the USA in connection with issues relating to leadership. For example Bass and Franke's (1972) research suggested that British university students are more likely than their American counterparts to believe that a manipulative approach to management is conducive to organizational success. Bass et al. (1979) found that British managers were more likely than American managers to prefer the use of authority rather than persuasion.

The controversy created by the subject of leadership is reflected in the research literature. Bass's (1990) *Handbook of Leadership* lists several thousand references to research on leadership. Most leadership research has been directed at the question of determinants of effective leadership behaviour (Bryman 1986). Leaders clearly believe in effective leadership skills to ensure business success. In a relatively recent survey (Smith 1997) of 250 British chief executives asked to identify the most important management skills for ensuring business success, leadership emerged as the top item. It might be useful, as a starting point, to know what characteristics leaders should have.

A Trait Theory of Leadership

The earliest research looked at the traits of leaders, the characteristics of effective leaders. If leaders are endowed with superior qualities that differentiate them from followers, it should be possible to identify these qualities. A 'great man' theory of leadership depicts great leaders such as Ghandi, Martin Luther King, or Churchill centre stage and looks for the heroic characteristics that marks them out as having the ability to transform societies or organizations. The great man theory is controversial for a number of reasons. Rarely are women such as Joan of Arc, Elizabeth I, Catherine the Great, Mother Theresa, or business leaders like Anita Roddick (of the Body Shop) or Oprah Winfrey (who owns her own production and media company) used as the basis of the analysis. It has also been argued (for example by Tolstoy 1957) that although leaders are commonly believed to command events and appear to be the causes of them, they are in fact merely 'labels' used to explain outcomes that otherwise seem inexplicable.

A classic survey by Stogdill (1948) looked at all the studies of traits and personal factors associated with leadership where factors had been studied by three or more investigators. He offers the following conclusions that are supported by positive evidence from fifteen or more of the studies surveyed: 'The average person who occupies a position of leadership exceeds the average member of his [sic] group in the following respects' (1948: 63): intelligence, scholarship, and dependability in exercising responsibilities, activity, and social participation and socio-economic status. As you might expect, the qualities, characteristics, and skills required in a leader are determined to a large extent by the demands of the situation in which the person functions as a leader. A person does not become a leader by virtue of the possession of some combination of traits but the pattern of personal characteristics of the leader must bear some relevance to the characteristics, activities, and goals of the followers. These will be in constant flux. It will then not be very difficult to find leaders but it is difficult to place these people in different situations where they will be able to function as leaders. The study of leadership should involve not only a study of leaders but of situations. Before looking at leaders in different situations, let's look at leadership style and inclusiveness.

Democratic Leadership Style

One of the major dilemmas facing leaders is how can you balance the advantages of a democratic approach which contributes better to the commitment, loyalty, involvement, and satisfaction of followers with a more authoritative approach which contributes to order, consistency, and the resolution of conflict? Should managers give directions and tell subordinates how to do the work or should they share with subordinates the need for solving problems or handling situations and involve them in working out what needs to be done and how? Most managers do both, depending on the circumstances, but in different amounts (Bass 1990).

Kurt Lewin and his associates were very keen to demonstrate the advantages of democratic decision making (see the class exercise at the end of this chapter). Lewin and his associates—Ronald Lippitt and Ralph White (Lewin et al. 1939; Lippitt and White 1959) explored the extent to which various aspects of leadership behaviour affect group behaviour. Using four clubs of 11-year-old children over a six month period they tried three styles of leadership—democratic, authoritarian, and laissez-faire. Four adults were selected as leaders and all of them took two or three different leadership roles with different groups during the course of the experiment. The groups of boys and types of activities remained constant while the form of leadership changed. The authoritarian leader was told to determine practically all club activities and procedures. The techniques and activity steps should be communicated one at a time and assigned. 'The dominator should keeps his standards of praise and criticism to himself in evaluating individual group activities. He should also remain fairly aloof from active group participation except in demonstrating' (Lippitt and White 1959: 498).

The democratic leader was instructed to discuss and decide policies with the group. Wherever technical advice is needed the leader should try to suggest two or more alternatives from which group members could make a choice. Everyone should be free to work with whoever they chose and divisions of responsibility should be left to the group. The bases of praise and criticism of individual and group activities should be communicated in an objective fact-minded way. They should try to be a 'regular' group member but not do much of the work.

The laissez-faire leader was asked to play a passive role and leave complete freedom to the group for decisions. They should make it clear that various materials were available and they would supply information and help when asked. They should take a minimum of initiatives in making suggestions. No attempt should be made to evaluate the behaviour of individuals or the group. They should be friendly rather than 'stand-offish'.

About 60 per cent of the behaviour of the average authoritarian leader could be described in the following way. The authoritarian leader usually initiated individual or group activity with an order. They often disrupted ongoing activity by an order that started activity off in another direction. They fairly frequently criticized work in a manner that carried the meaning 'It is a bad job because I say it is a bad job' rather than 'It is a poor job because those nails are bent over instead of driven in'.

The democratic leader took the initiative where they felt it was needed in making guiding suggestions. They did not take initiative for action away from the group. They stimulated child independence eight times as often as the authoritarian leader. They also had about eight times more social interaction than the authoritarian leader, where they discussed personal matters about home or school, or joked with the children. The laissez-faire leader concentrated on giving out information when it was asked for, stimulating child independence half as much as the democratic leaders.

Two types of reaction were found to the authoritarian leadership style. Three of the four clubs responded with dependent leaning on the adult leader, relatively low levels of frustration tension, and practically no capacity for initiating group action. For example if the leader arrived late, no group initiative to start new work or to continue work underway was found. The fourth club demonstrated considerable frustration and some aggression toward the leader. This was interpreted as a 'frustrated hopelessness in the face of overwhelming power' (Lippitt and White 1959: 510). The group average of inter-member aggressiveness under the autocracy is either very high or low; in democracy it is at a more medium level (Lippitt 1940; Lippitt and White 1943). It was thought that the 'we feeling' which tends to decrease inter-member aggression is diminished in autocracy (Lewin 1947: 20).

Demands for attention from the adult were greater than in the democratic and laissez-faire groups. In the democratic and laissez-faire groups there was less discontent in relations with the adult leader and conversation was less restricted. Members of the democratic and laissez-faire clubs initiated more personal and friendly approaches to their leaders and there was more spontaneous exchanging of confidences about life outside the club.

What about differences between the democratic and laissez-faire groups? Members in the democratic group felt much freer and more inclined to make suggestions on matters of group policy than in other groups. The absence or presence of a leader had practically no effect; groups were already active in production if a leader arrived late. The lower level of suggestions in the laissez-faire situation was thought not to be caused by any feeling of restricted freedom but due to lack of cooperative working relationships between the adult and the group members. The need for the laissez-faire club to get their own information meant that about 37 per cent of their behaviour consisted of asking for information as compared to about 15 per cent in the other three clubs. The groups under laissez-faire leaders were active but not productive.

The relationships between the club members also developed along different lines in the different groups. Expressions of irritability and aggressiveness toward fellow members occurred more frequently in both the authoritarian and laissez-faire groups than in the democratic. Further the child members depended more on each other for social recognition and were more ready to give recognition to each other in the democratic and laissez-faire situations.

It is interesting to find that all but one boy preferred the democratic leader to the other two types but there was disagreement about whether they preferred the laissez-faire or authoritarian type as a second choice. No attempt is made by Lippitt and White to discuss the implications of this research for behaviour amongst adults or the lessons for management of people.

Despite the weaknesses of these conclusions, other researchers went on to advocate the democratic approach. These included Likert (1961, 1967, 1977) and the whole Human Relations movement (for example Argyris 1957; McGregor 1960). Borrowing heavily from the original experimental concepts and results of Lewin and Lipitt (1938), Likert (1961) conceived of four systems of interpersonal relationships in large organizations. These were exploitative autocratic, benevolent autocratic, consultative, and democratic. In more than 500 studies completed, positive associations were generally found between measures of the organization's performance and whether they were closer to the democratic systems than the autocratic (Likert 1977). This demonstrated the efficacy of democratic as opposed to autocratic systems of management. (For more detail on these studies see Bass 1990: 430–2). The more positive results are to be found in the large-scale field studies rather than on small group laboratory experiments. Generally the patterns of leadership behaviour included in democratic leadership are more satisfying than those associated with autocratic leadership (Bass 1990). But autocratic leadership may enhance productivity in the short term, particularly if democratic leadership ignores the task and concern for production goals.

Task Versus Relations-Oriented Leadership

Looking at more distinctive components of democratic leadership, such as consideration for subordinates and relations orientation, produces a sharper picture of leadership. Leaders differ in the extent to which they pursue a human relations approach and try to maintain friendly supportive relations with their followers. Those with a strong concern are identified as relations oriented, or people centred. Here the leaders will have a sense of trust in subordinates, less felt need to control them, and more general rather than close supervision. Those with a strong concern for group goals and the means to achieve them will be considered task oriented or production oriented. The leader's assumptions about their roles, purposes, and behaviour reflect their interest in completing assignments and getting the work done. The most effective managers are those who can be both (Bass 1990).

The best-known model builders who prescribe the integration of both task and relations orientations are Blake and Mouton (1964). Managers and leaders vary from 1 to 9 in their concern for people and from 1 to 9 in their concern for production. The measurement of these concerns is based on a manager's endorsement of statements about assumptions and beliefs. Team leadership (9,9) is prescribed. It is attained by participation, openness, trust and respect, involvement and commitment, open confrontation to resolve conflicts, consensus, mutually determined management by objectives, mutual support, and change through feedback.

Blake and Mouton did not leave much room for exceptions (Bass 1990). Investigations of the success of the impact of the idea have been mixed or negative. Situations may impact on the satisfaction and productivity of the followers. We will look more closely at situational factors in a later section. Meanwhile let's look at a behavioural model.

Consideration Versus Initiating Structure

An attempt is made with this approach to describe individuals' behaviour while they act as leaders or groups or organizations. A Leader Behaviour Description Questionnaire was developed at Ohio State University using 150 statements that described different aspects of the behaviour of leaders. Two factors were produced—consideration and the initiation of structure.

Here are some of the kinds of statements you might ask people to agree or disagree with (on a five-point scale) if you were looking at consideration versus initiating structure in a male leader.

Initiating structure

He asks that group members follow standard rules and regulations

He decides what shall be done and how it shall be done

He assigns group members to tasks

He lets group members know what is expected of them

(See Bryman 1987)

Consideration

He is friendly and approachable

He treats all members as his equals

He looks out for the personal welfare of group members

He puts suggestions made by the group into operation

Consideration, as you could guess from the above and as the label implies, describes the extent to which a leader exhibits concern for the welfare of the other members of the group. The considerate leaders express appreciation for good work, stress the importance of job satisfaction, maintain self-esteem, or subordinate and put their suggestions into action. Initiation of structure shows the extent to which a leader initiates activity in the group, organizes it, and defines the way work is to be done. The initiation of structure includes leaders insisting on maintaining standards and meeting deadlines, deciding in detail what will be done and how it should be done (Bass 1990).

We noted earlier how people's views about the behaviour of leaders are influenced by knowledge of their performance. Performance cues have a clear effect on ratings of both consideration and initiating structure irrespective of the behaviour of leaders as implied by behavioural manipulations in experiments (Bryman 1987). Findings such as these prompt a questioning of the meaning of research that shows that leaders who score high on both consideration and initiating structure are more effective or successful.

Transactional versus Transformational Leadership

Transactional and transformational leadership were first conceptualized by Burns (1978) and later developed by Bass (1985). Transactional leadership happens where goods, services, and other rewards are exchanged so that various parties achieve their goals. It is a bargain to aid the individual interests of persons or groups going their separate ways (Burns 1978) where the emphasis is on exchange relationships between followers and leaders. The culture that results is likely to be one characterized by dissent that may be more or less tolerated.

In transformational leadership the leader changes the goals of followers or subordinates. New goals are assumed to be of a higher level and represent the collective good or pooled interests of leaders and followers (Burns 1978). A 'vision' combines the members into a collective whole with a shared set of aspirations capable of guiding their behaviour. The transformational leader inspires, intellectually stimulates, and is individually considerate to followers (Bass 1999). Charisma is needed to communicate the vision.

We know however that most managers do not exude charisma; indeed quite a few have a reputation for being boring (Tourish and Pinnington 2002). Maccoby (2000) suggests than many charismatic leaders are likely to be narcissists (people with a well-developed self-image in which they take great pride and on which they reflect frequently). They are also likely to have a strong need for power, high self-confidence, and strong convictions (De Vries et al. 1999). As Yukl (1999) has argued, expressing strong convictions, acting confident, and taking decisive action may create an impression of exceptional expertise, but it can also discourage feedback from followers. Charismatic leadership is an indispensable ingredient of cults and has been observed in the Jonestown cult of the 1970s (Layton 1999), the suicidal Heavens Gate cult in California (Booth and Claiborne 1997), and more recently in the Aum cult in Japan (Lifton 1999).

The assumption of 'greater' goals requires a leap of faith on behalf of the followers. By definition the transformation leader needs more power than constraints in order to restrain the power of potential dissidents. The transformational leader may have to take unpopular decisions, reject conventional wisdom, and take reasonable risk (Bass 1990). The dangers are considerable. For example research has shown that new group members, or those with low status, only acquire influence within a group by over-conforming to the norms (Brown 2000). If they don't, they risk being penalized, usually through the withdrawal of valued social rewards.

Rosener (1990) argues that men are more likely than women to describe themselves in ways that characterize transactional leadership; they exchange rewards for services rendered or punishment for inadequate performance. The men are also more likely to use power that comes from their organization and formal authority. She puts the case that women describe themselves in ways that characterize transformational leadership, getting subordinates to transform their own self-interest into the interest of the group through concern for a broader goal. They ascribe their power to personal characteristics like charisma, interpersonal skills, hard work, or personal contacts rather than to organizational stature. Women actively work to make their interactions with subordinates positive for everyone involved. They encourage participation, share power, and get others excited about their work. This reflects the belief that allowing employees to contribute makes them feel powerful and important.

It may be that, on average, women leaders are more democratic and participative than their male counterparts, or at least are perceived to be so (Bass et al. 1996). It may be that this is only how women describe their style and they have stereotyped their behaviour according to cultural views of gender-appropriate behaviour. Few women want to indicate that they are 'masculine' (Epstein 1991). However the magnitude of the differences between male and female leaders has generally been small (Eagly 1987). Organizational factors may make a difference. For example an operating room female nurse, seen in a job 'appropriate' for her gender, may be very task oriented while men are more task oriented in roles consistent with their gender such as coaching men's football teams (Bass 1967). Situations may then make a difference.

Situational Leadership

The situation may have some effect on the preferred leadership style. Contingency theories of leadership allow then for the situation to effect leadership. Situational leadership theory states that effective leadership depends on the ability of the leader to accurately diagnose situational conditions and to respond with the appropriate combination of behaviours. Hersey and Blanchard (1988) believe that leadership is contingent on the amount of guidance and direction a leader gives, the amount of socio-emotional support a leader provides, and the readiness level that followers exhibit. The critical situational factor that determines preferred leadership style is the task-related readiness of followers, labelled employee maturity in early descriptions. Readiness is the extent to which a follower has the ability and willingness to accomplish a specific task (1988: 174). This will depend on the ability and technical skills needed to do a task and the self-confidence in their ability.

Using four leadership styles and four readiness levels, several recommendations are made for leaders. Appropriate leader styles are summarized in terms of a leader primarily telling, selling, participating, or delegating in relations with subordinates. If for example subordinates are at the lowest level of readiness (for example in the case of a newly appointed employee), telling is the best leadership style; delegating is the least effective. For subordinates at the highest level of readiness, delegating is the best style.

Hersey and Blanchard are criticized for providing little evidence in support of their theory (Yukl 1981). They are also criticized for their lack of conceptual clarity and lack of theoretical justification (Bass 1990). Vecchio (1987) tested the theory. His results strongly supported the theory's prescriptions at low levels of follower readiness but the recommended matches were not confirmed for high-readiness subordinates. Goodson et al. (1989) also failed to support the theories use as a prescriptive tool. The most valuable contribution to evolve from the theory is its emphasis on leader flexibility or adaptability (Yukl 1981; Goodson et al. 1989). Training leaders to develop adaptive skills is a more promising approach than training leaders to adopt one particular style. Blake and

Mouton (1978) who add that the leader must assess the nature of the task, the task environment as well as subordinate characteristics, also advocate this conclusion.

However, are leaders free agents that can choose their style to suit the situation? Enmeshed in the organization the individual leader is constrained. They are expected to conform to the expectations of peers, subordinates, and superiors (Pfeffer 1978; Fulop et al. 1999). If you believe that leaders can and should change their style, can you imagine a narcissistic leader doing so?

Emotion and Leadership

These are two terms that are rarely seen together. Emotionality has been cast in opposition to and lesser than rationality (Blackmore 1996). In daily life rationality is seen to be a virtue and revered while emotionality is seen to be an encumbrance and reviled. Yet those in leadership positions are constantly being assailed by emotional demands placed on them by their peers and others (Sachs and Blackmore 1998). Emotional investment and emotion management is going to be found particularly in organizations where there is the uncertainty and ambiguity inherent in a changing environment. Disappointment with lack of promotion, conflict over work tasks and matters of policy and practice, for example, are going to be features of almost all organizations at times. As a result individuals typically talk about controlling emotions, handling emotional situations, as well as emotional feelings, and dealing with people, situations, and emotions. The effective and efficient functioning of organizations necessitates emotional control. Carefully regulated and tempered emotions like warmth, patience, strength, calm, caring, concern, and expressing vulnerability are likely to be privileged over anger, rage, and passion (Hargreaves 1995).

Managers and leaders have to assess feelings. Every time they handle an office quarrel, an interdepartmental rivalry, a family emergency they function as a mini judge, assessing who is under too much stress or feels angry or jealous (Hochschild 1993). They decide which feelings seem 'healthy' and which are 'sick' (Parkin 1993). Company culture sets the social boundaries between the right and wrong thing to do.

Charisma appears to be important for some when considering leadership (Conger and Kanungo 1998; Lindholm 1990). Charisma and emotion, it could be argued, are linked. If we are making judgements about how charismatic a leader is, we are articulating our emotional response to the leader.

Mood and leader's feelings may play an important role in leadership. George and Bettenhausen (1990) found that the extent to which leaders of work groups experienced positive moods was positively related to levels of pro-social behaviour performed by group members and negatively related to group labour turnover rates. George (1995) found that work groups led by sales managers who tended to experience positive moods at work provided higher-quality customer service than groups led by managers who did not tend to experience positive moods at work. Mood and emotion capabilities are addressed by emotion intelligence theory and research (George 2000) (See also Chapter 2 above).

Views of emotion tend to be highly gendered. The expression of anger has been seen as culturally acceptable for men but not for women. Negative terms like dragon, spitfire, bitch, and nag are applied to women but not to men. Women's anger is associated with characteristics of being sharp tongued, cruel, nasty, whining, and unpleasant while expressing her anger with tears will lead to her being described as emotional or manipulative (Court 1995).

Gender and Leadership

Until recently women were extremely rare in major positions of public leadership. In history only forty-two women have ever served as presidents or prime ministers and twenty-five of those have come to office in the 1990s (Adler 1999). Almost all the women who have attained top positions in corporations around the world have done so in the 1990s. The *Wall Street Journal* (1986) is credited with being the first to use the term 'glass ceiling' to acknowledge the invisible, but powerful barrier, that allows women to advance only to a certain level. Evidence supports the glass ceiling metaphor. In the USA in Fortune 500 companies women constitute only 4 per cent of top officers, 3 per cent of the most highly paid officers, and 0.4 per cent of the Chief Executive Officers (Catalyst 2000). The glass ceiling is a metaphor for prejudice and discrimination that takes a number of forms.

The traits that are characteristic of leaders and followers are similar to those that have been found to characterize men and women. Leaders are expected to be assertive and influential while followers are expected to be accommodating and responsive (Bass 1973; Stogdill 1950). The research on male–female leadership styles concludes that women are generally viewed as more nurturing, understanding, helpful, collaborative, empathetic, socially sensitive, cooperative, and expressive than their male counterparts (Eagly 1987; Eagly and Johnson 1990). In contrast men are expected to be more independent, masterful, assertive, and competent. These differences are thought to arise from socialization patterns rather than genetics. Females demonstrate more transformational leadership behaviour (individual consideration) than males (Bass et al. 1996). It has been argued that men and women seek work roles most appropriate and consistent with their gender, resulting in gender differences in leadership styles that may be, to some extent, self-fulfilling (Eagly 1987). Managerial positions may still be described as requiring characteristics like assertiveness, competitiveness, and tough mindedness which are associated primarily with men (Powell and Butterfield 1989). Female personality traits and behaviour patterns may make females appear less suited for leadership roles involving dominance and assertiveness (Morrison and Von Glinow 1990).

STOP

Offering Advice to Women in Leadership

Women are advised in books about women and leadership to maintain their sense of humour. This can be demonstrated in one-liners like 'Better to be big in the backside than have bullshit for brains', which is the retort attributed to a female Australian government minister after a male opponent made some unflattering comments about her appearance (Stewart 2002). More examples are to be found in Kirner and Rayner (1999).

However, evidence on leadership style offers a number of different conclusions. This subject is confusing as contradictory research findings exist. There is a large volume of research that has shown that men and women do not actually differ in leadership style (Eagly and Johnson 1990; Eagly and Karu 1991; Bass et al. 1996). The paradox is that men and women have been perceived as possessing different strengths but whether those differences result in either perceived or actual differences in leadership styles remains a point of contention in the literature.

These perceived differences between men and women come to the forefront again in research on discipline and leadership. If as individuals we have beliefs about the behaviour women and men should exhibit and they violate those beliefs, they may be negatively regarded. For example if women are expected to be warm, sensitive, passive, and supportive, then you might expect that it is more difficult for them to discipline. Females delivering discipline are perceived to be less effective and less fair than males (Atwater et al. 2001). It is more difficult for women to discipline if they are getting cues from subordinates that discipline from them is unwelcome; this could serve to reduce their confidence at discipline delivery, which in turn impacts on their behaviour and the way discipline from them is perceived. Further males may perceive women in positions of power as a threat (Hale 1996).

■ SUGGESTIONS FOR FURTHER READING

1. Fulop, L., Linstead, S., and Dunford, R. (1999), 'Leading and Managing', ch. 5 in *Management: A Critical Text*, Houndmills: Macmillan Press. This chapter asks some uncomfortable questions like, can leaders change their styles or behaviours and do we need leaders? It also provides some answers.

2. Billing, Y. D., and Alvesson, M. (2000), 'Questioning the Notion of Feminine Leadership: A Critical Perspective on the Gender Labelling of Leadership', *Gender, Work and Organization*, 7/3: 144–57. This article asks us to be aware of the unfortunate consequences of using gender labels when discussing leadership. For more on gender, management, and style, see Wajcman, J. (2000), 'Gender: It's Hard to be Soft. Is Management Style Gendered?', ch. 10 in K. Grint, *Work and Society: A Reader*, Cambridge: Polity Press.

3. Thomas, A. B. (2003), *Controversies in Management: Issues, Debates, Answers*, (2nd edn.), London: Routledge. ch. 8, 'Organizational Leadership: Does It Make a Difference? While much of the research on leadership can appear prescriptive (e.g. participative and democratic managers are best) this chapter throws into sharp relief a more confused picture with contradictory findings. The chapter is particularly useful as it is not at all prescriptive and invites us to ask all the interesting questions like: does leadership make a difference and does effective leadership exist?

4. Sinclair, A. (1999), *Doing Leadership Differently: Gender, Power and Sexuality in a Changing Business Culture*, Melbourne: Melbourne University Press. This book critically assesses the concept of leadership. It particularly questions the traditional tough heterosexual male form of leadership and why our faith in it is so misplaced. Wilson, F. M. (2003), *Organizational Behaviour and Gender*, Abingdon: Ashgate. This book has a chapter on leadership and gender for those who want to know more. A particularly good and recent article, which deals with leadership, gender and discipline, is Atwater et al. (2001).

5. Bass, B. M. (1990), *Bass and Stogdill's Handbook of Leadership: Theory, Research and Managerial Applications* (3rd edn.), London: Collier Macmillan. This is a 'bible' for students of leadership, though women are relegated to a chapter of their own.

6. Schein, V., Mueller, R., Lituchy, R., and Liu, J. (1996), 'Think Manager—Think Male: A Global Phenomenon?', *Journal of Organizational Behavior*, 17: 33–41. Schein and her colleagues argue that not only are men and women thought to manage or lead differently, they are perceived as different. Effectiveness as a manager is attributed more readily to men by men and women. This work makes you think about, and hopefully question, the inevitability of, 'think manager—think male'.

7. Thompson, P., and McHugh, D. (2002), *Work Organizations* (3rd edn.), Houndmills: Palgrave, ch. 12, 'Open to Persuasion: Communication and Leadership'. This chapter critically discusses how managers buy into ideologies of control and how that is more or less taken for granted.

■ **WEB LINKS**

www.questia.com/Index.jsp?CRID=leadership&OFFID=se1 will take you to a library page of books on leadership. There is however much rubbish on the web on leadership—for example 'big dog's' leadership page. My advice when searching the web is 'get your crap detector out'!

■ **QUESTIONS**

1. How generalizable are findings of experiments on leadership based on subjects in the USA?

2. Tourish and Pinnington (2002) draw on the similarities between the components of transformational leadership and the characteristics of leadership found in cults. How do they do this? To what effect?

3. Most models of leadership and power generally work on a crucial missing variable—tyranny (Bies and Tripp 1998). Discuss.

4. Is it time to stop talking about gender differences between men and women in leadership? (See Epstein's and others 1991 debate in *Harvard Business Review* and suggested readings).

■ **GROUP EXERCISE/CASE STUDY**

Kurt Lewin and his associates were keen to demonstrate the advantages of democratic decision making. They set up an experiment to compare the effects of a lecture and a group decision on behaviour. They wanted to change the food habits of housewives in order to help the war effort.

Six groups, ranging in size from 13 to 17, of Red Cross volunteers, were used. The objective was to increase the use in cooking of cow's hearts, sweetbreads (pancreas or thymus gland), and kidneys. In three groups 'attractive' (Lewin 1959: 202) lectures were given which likened the problem of nutrition with the war effort, emphasized the vitamin and mineral value of the three meats, and gave detailed explanations with the aid of charts. Both the health and economic aspects were stressed. The preparation of these meats was discussed in detail and included techniques for avoiding aversion to odour, texture, and appearance. Recipes were distributed; the lecturer gave hints on her own methods for preparing these 'delicious dishes' and mentioned her success with her own family (Lewin 1959: 202).

In the other three groups the problem of nutrition was linked with that of the war effort and general health in a discussion. Could the housewives be induced to participate in a programme of change without attempting any 'high pressure salesmanship' (Lewin 1959: 202)? The group discussion about 'housewives like themselves' led to an elaboration of the obstacles this change would encounter like the dislike, or smell during cooking. The nutrition expert offered the same remedies and recipes for preparation that had been presented in the lectures to the other groups. However in these groups preparation techniques were offered after the groups had become sufficiently involved to be interested in knowing whether certain obstacles could be removed.

Near the start of the meeting a show of hands demonstrated how many women had served any of these foods in the past. At the end of the meeting the women were asked who was willing to try one of these meats in the next week. Only 3 per cent of those who heard the lectures served one of the meats never served before. After the group decision, 32 per cent served one of them.

Lewin (1959) explained why the group discussion produced these results. First lecturing is a procedure in which the audience is chiefly passive. The discussion is likely to lead to a much higher degree of involvement. Further it is easier to change the ideology and social practice of a small group handled together than of single individuals. An individual in a small group is more likely to change if the group changes. (This is the practice adopted by those involved with alcoholics.)

It is interesting that Lewin himself notes that the difference between the results of the lectures and the group decision may be due to the fact that only after the group decision did the discussion leader mention that an inquiry would be made later as to whether a new food was introduced into the family diet. The 'threat' of follow-up in itself may therefore have influenced the results. It is also interesting that no mention is made of the gender of the nutrition 'expert'. However the discussion group appears to have been run by a male called Mr Bavelas who was an experienced group worker ('and doubtless of unusual ability in this field'—Lewin 1959: 204) and the lecture by a female, a 'housewife'. This too may have influenced the results but Lewin does not consider the effect of this variable.

What are the main lessons of Lewin's experiment for leaders and managers trying to influence groups in organizations? What are the flaws with Lewin's food experiment?

■ REFERENCES

Adler, N. J. (1999), 'Global Leaders: Women of Influence', in G. Powell (ed.), *Handbook of Gender and Work*, Thousand Oaks, Calif.: Sage, pp. 239–61.

Argyris, C. (1957), *Personality and Organization*, New York: Harper.

Atwater, L. E., Carey, J. A., and Waldman, D. A. (2001), 'Gender and Discipline in the Workplace: Wait until your Father Gets Home', *Journal of Management*, 27: 537–61.

Bass, B. M. (1967), 'Social Behaviour and the Orientation Inventory: A Review', *Psychological Bulletin*, 68: 260–92.

——(1973), *Leadership, Psychology and Organizational Behaviour*, Westport, Conn.: Greenwood Press.

——(1985), *Leadership and Performance: Beyond Expectations*, New York: Free Press.

——(1990), *Bass and Stogdill's Handbook of Leadership: Theory, Research and Managerial Applications*, New York: Free Press.

——(1999), 'Two Decades of Research and Development in Transformational Leadership', *European Journal of Work and Organizational Psychology*, 8: 9–26.

——and Franke, R. H. (1972), 'Societal Influences on Student Perceptions of how to Succeed in Organizations', *Journal of Applied Psychology*, 56: 312–18.

——Burger, P. C., Doktor, R., and Barrett, G. V. (1979), *Assessment of Managers: An International Comparison*, New York: Free Press.

——Alvio, B. J., and Atwater, L. (1996), 'Transformational and Transactional Leadership of Men and Women', *Applied Psychology: An International Review*, 45/1: 5–34.

Bennis, W. (1989), *Why Leaders can't Lead: The Unconscious Conspiracy Continues*, San Francisco: Jossey Bass.

Bies, R., and Tripp, T. (1998), 'Two Faces of the Powerless: Coping with Tyranny in Organizations', in R. Kramer and M. Neale (eds.), *Power and Influence in Organizations*, London: Sage.

Blackmore, J. (1996), 'Doing Emotional "Labour" in the Education Market Place: Stories from the Field of Women in Management', *Discourse*, 17: 337–50.

Blake, R. R., and Mouton, J. S. (1964), *The Managerial Grid*, Houston, Tex.: Gulf.

——— (1978), *The New Managerial Grid*, Houston, Tex.: Gulf.

Booth, W., and Claiborne, W. (1997), 'Cult Group's Leader among Suicides', *Washington Post*, 29 Mar.

Brown, R. (2000), *Group Processes* (2nd edn.), Oxford: Blackwell.

Bryman, A. (1986), *Leadership and Organizations*, London: Routledge & Kegan Paul.

—— (1987), 'The Generalizability of Implicit Leadership Theory', *Journal of Social Psychology*, 127/2: 129–41.

Burns, J. M. (1978), *Leadership*, New York: Academic Press and Harper & Row.

Catalyst (2000), *Census of Women Corporate Officers and Top Earners*, New York: Catalyst.

Conger, J. A., and Kanugo, R. N. (1998), *Charismatic Leadership in Organizations*, Thousand Oaks, Calif.: Sage.

Court, M. (1995), 'Good Girls and Naughty Girls: Rewriting the Scripts for Women's Anger', in B. Limerick and R. Lingard (eds.), *Gender and Changing Educational Management*, Sydney: Hodder & Stoughton.

De Vries, R., Roe, R., and Thaillieu, T. (1999), 'On Charisma and Need for Leadership', *European Journal of Work and Organizational Psychology*, 8: 109–26.

Eagly, A. H. (1987), *Sex Differences in Social Behavior: A Social Role Interpretation*, Hillsdale, NJ: Lawrence Erlbaum Associates Inc.

—— and Johnson, B. T. (1990), 'Gender and Leadership Style: A Meta-analysis', *Psychological Bulletin*, 108: 233–56.

—— and Karu, S. S. (1991), 'Gender and the Emergence of Leaders: A Meta-analysis', *Journal of Personality and Social Psychology*, 60: 685–710.

Epstein, C. F. (1991), 'Ways Men and Women Lead', *Harvard Business Review* (Jan.–Feb.), 150–1.

Fulop, L., Linstead, S., and Dunford, R. (1999), 'Leading and Managing', ch. 5 in *Management: A Critical Text*, Houndmills: Macmillan Press.

Gemmill, G., and Oakley, J. (1992), 'Leadership: An Alienating Social Myth?', *Human Relations*, 45/2: 113–29.

George, J. M. (1995), 'Leader Positive Mood and Group Performance: The Case of Customer Service', *Journal of Applied Social Psychology*, 25: 778–94.

—— (2000), 'Emotions and Leadership: The Role of Emotional Intelligence', *Human Relations*, 8: 1027–55.

—— and Bettenhausen, K. (1990), 'Understanding Prosocial Behaviour, Sales Performance and Turnover: A Group Level Analysis in a Service Context', *Journal of Applied Psychology*, 75: 698–709.

Goodson, J. R., McGee, G. W., and Cashman, J. F. (1989), 'Situational Leadership Theory: A Test of Leadership Prescriptions', *Group and Organization Studies*, 14/4: 446–61.

Grint, K. (2000), *The Arts of Leadership*, Oxford: Oxford University Press.

Hale, M. (1996), 'Gender Equality in Organizations', *Review of Public Personnel Administration* (Winter), 7–18.

Hargreaves, A. (1995), 'Development and Desire: A Postmodern Perspective', in T. Guskey and H. Huberman (eds.), *Professional Development in Education*, New York: Teachers College Press.

Hersey, P., and Blanchard, K. H. (1988), *Management of Organizational Behavior: Utilising Human Resources* (4th edn.), Englewood Cliffs, NJ: Prentice Hall.

Hochschild, A. (1993), *Preface to Emotion in Organizations*, ed. S. Fineman, London: Sage.

Kirner, J., and Rayner, M. (1999), *The Women's Power Handbook*, Melbourne: Viking.

Layton, D. (1999), *Seductive Poison: A Jonestown Survivor's Story of Life and Death in the People's Temple*, London: Aurum Press.

Lewin, K. (1947), 'Frontiers in Group Dynamics: Concept, Method and Reality in Social Science: Social Equilibria and Social Change', *Human Relations*, 1/1: 5–41.

——(1959), 'Group Decision and Social Change', in E. Maccoby, T. M. Newcomb, and E. L. Hartley (eds.), *Readings in Social Psychology* (3rd edn.), London: Methuen & Co. Ltd. pp. 197–211.

——and Lippitt, R. (1938), 'An Experimental Approach to the Study of Autocracy and Democracy: A Preliminary Note', *Sociometry*, 1: 292–300.

————and White, R. K. (1939), 'Patterns of Aggressive Behavior in Experimentally Created "Social Climates"', *Journal of Social Psychology*, 10: 271–99.

Lifton, R. (1999), *Destroying the World to Save it: Aum Shinrikyo, Apocalyptic Violence and the New Global Terrorism*, New York: Holt.

Likert, R. (1961), *New Patterns of Management*, New York: McGraw Hill.

——(1967), *The Human Organization*, New York: McGraw Hill.

——(1977), 'Past and Future Perspectives on System 4', paper, Academy of Management, Orlando, Fla.

Lindholm, C. (1990), *Charisma*, Cambridge, Mass.: Basil Blackwell.

Lippitt, R. (1940), *An Experimental Study of Authoritarian and Democratic Group Atmospheres*, Studies in topological and vector psychology I, Iowa: University of Iowa Press.

——and White, R. (1943), 'The "social climate" of children's groups' in R. Barker, J. Kounin, and B. Wright (eds.), *Child Behaviour and Development*, New York: McGraw Hill.

————(1959), 'An Experimental Study of Leadership and Group Life', in E. Maccoby, T. M. Newcomb, and E. L. Hartley (eds.), *Readings in Social Psychology* (3rd edn.), London: Methuen.

Locke, E. A. (1991), *The Essence of Leadership: The Four Keys to Leading Successfully*, New York: Lexington Books.

Maccoby, M. (2000), 'Narcissistic Leaders: The Incredible Pros and the Inevitable Cons, *Harvard Business Review*, 78: 69–77.

McGregor, D. (1960), *The Human Side of Enterprise*, New York: McGraw Hill.

Meindl, J. R. (1990), On Leadership: An Alternative to the Conventional Wisdom' in B. M. Staw and L. L. Cummings (eds.), *Research in Organizational Behavior*, vol. xii, Greenwich, Conn.: JAI Press, pp. 159–203.

Morrison, A., and Von Glinow, M. (1990), 'Women and Minorities in Management', *American Psychologist*, 45: 200–8.

Parkin, W. (1993), 'The Public and the Private: Gender, Sexuality and Emotion', ch. 8 in S. Fineman (ed.), *Emotion in Organizations*, London: Sage.

Pfeffer, J (1978), 'The Ambiguity of Leadership', in M. W. McCall and M. M. Lombardo (eds.), *Leadership: Where else can we Go?*, Durham: Duke University Press.

Powell, G. N., and Butterfield, D. A. (1989), 'The "Good Manager" Did Androgyny Fare better in the 1980s?', *Group and Organization Studies*, 14: 216–33.

Rosener, J. B. (1990), 'Ways Women Lead', *Harvard Business Review* (Nov.–Dec.), 119–25.

Sachs, J., and Blackmore, J. (1998), 'You never show you can't cope: Women in School Leadership Roles Managing their Emotions', *Gender and Education*, 10/3: 265–79.

Smircich, L., and Morgan, G. (1982), 'Leadership: The Management of Meaning', *Journal of Applied Behavioral Science*, 18/3: 257–73.

Smith, D. (1997), 'Managers Lack Proper Skills', *Sunday Times* (Business Section), 14 Sept.

Stewart, C. (2002), 'It's Amanda's World', *Weekend Australian*, 1–2 July.

Stogdill, R. M. (1948), 'Personal Factors Associated with Leadership: A Survey of the Literature', *Journal of Psychology*, 25: 35–71.

——(1950), 'Leadership, Membership and Organization', *Psychological Bulletin*, 47: 1–14.

Tolstoy, L. N. (1957), *War and Peace*, 2 vols., trans. Rosemary Edmonds, Harmondsworth: Penguin, first published in 1869.

Tourish, D., and Pinnington, A. (2002), 'Transformational Leadership, Corporate Cultism and the Spirituality Paradigm: An Unholy Trinity in the Workplace?', *Human Relations*, 55/2: 147–72.

Vecchio, R. P. (1987), 'Situational Leadership Theory: An Examination of a Prescriptive Theory', *Journal of Applied Psychology*, 72/3: 444–51.

Wall Street Journal (1986), 'The Corporate Woman: A Special Report', 24 Mar., in a 32-page supplement, New York.

Yukl, G. A. (1981), *Leadership in Organizations*, Englewood Cliffs, NJ: Prentice Hall.

——(1999), 'An Evaluative Essay on Current Conceptions of Effective Leadership', *European Journal of Work and Organizational Psychology*, 8: 33–48.

15 HEALTH, WELL-BEING, AND STRESS

Health is not an issue dealt with in most texts on Organizational Behaviour (though stress usually is). Yet work-related illness incurs very large personal and organizational costs. A Health and Safety Executive survey of self-reported work-related illnesses in Great Britain found stress, depression, and anxiety to be the second most prevalent condition claimed to be caused or made worse by work (HSC 1997: 129–30). The incidence of self-reported work-related stress has risen nearly threefold recently, the Health and Safety Executive say (Masterton 2003). In December 2002 the Health and Safety Executive reported that over half a million individuals in Britain believe they are experiencing work-related stress at a level that is making them ill. A study by *Personnel Today* and *IRS Employment Review* found that more than 40 per cent of employees had reported an increase in stress in the last year (Hilpern 2003). An estimated 13.5 million working days a year are lost to companies in the UK through employees being signed off with stress, anxiety, or depression. A study by Work Stress Management found that 2002 saw a twelvefold increase in the number of firms forced to pay damages for workplace stress with 6,428 of them paying an average of £51,000 (Hilpern 2003). The UK economy loses £12bn every year due to sickness absence, representing an estimated cost of around £500 per employee (Masterton 2003). Yet because stress and other negative emotions are not seen as productive, they are rarely acknowledged to exist within organizations.

Violence and abuse from customers can lead to employees taking time off work. Occasionally we see a newspaper headline about violence at work if a flight attendant is attacked with a broken bottle or if it is found that there is a tripling of assaults on railway workers. One in five workers in the UK has been found to be subject to verbal abuse (like swearing, sarcasm, and insults) or physical violence each year (TUC 1999). For the period 1999/2000, 5,034 minor incidents and 686 major incidents were reported to the Health and Safety Executive (HSE 2001). Women between the age of 25 and 34 are most at risk of attack or abuse (Mayhew and Quinlan 1999). The very threat of violence or abuse, particularly if accepted as 'part of the job' and occurring on a daily basis, can increase job stress. Recent research by the Nuffield Foundation (Guardian 2003; Baty 2003) shows that lecturers in higher education are increasingly at risk of violent attack.

Boring repetitive jobs can lead to mental strain. As early as 1965 Kornhauser's research with Detroit car workers was showing that the higher the occupation level, the better the mental health of the worker; better jobs with greater work skill, variety, responsibility, and pay lead to better mental health. The lower the occupational level the more likely workers are to have little support or discretion in their jobs. Recent research too shows how low job control and high demand makes for stress (Bosma et al. 1997; Schnall and Landbergis 1994). Marmot et al. (1997), in the Whitehall Studies, found that stress associated with low control in the workplace is linked to coronary heart disease. In addition to low control Bosma et al. (1998) found that an imbalance between workers' effort and their rewards was linked to heart disease. The higher the status of the worker the more likely they are to admit or believe they have stress problems (see Fletcher 1990). This may be explained by the fact that many of those in white-collar jobs, not least in the public sector (e.g. university lecturers, schoolteachers, and social workers), have experienced a deterioration in their work conditions and that these people are more articulate than most (Nichols 1998). For example recently clinical researchers were reported as experiencing stress as an outcome of extensive work pressure, a lack of control over the work situation, and unsatisfactory interpersonal relationships (Styhre et al. 2002). Perhaps this is why most courses on stress management are aimed at professional employees.

> **STOP**
>
> Do you think technology can increase stress? A training company found that one in three people complained that technology at work contributes directly to rising stress levels. Referring to this as 'digital depression' the managing director noted how he had recently come across a person who had 19,400 emails in his inbox (Hilpern 2003).

You do not need to be employed to experience stress, though. Stressful events include moving house, getting married, having fights and conflicts, or the death of a loved one. When people are under high stress they tend to fail to sleep a full eight hours, fail to eat full meals, and tend to stay up late at night. Stressful events affect health by decreasing health-sustaining behaviours that in turn play a role in physical and psychological illnesses.

Stress has been a topic of interest to researchers since the Second World War. Newton (1995) notes how an interest in stress arose out of ideas within Social Darwinism eugenics and a concern for maintaining a healthy race, with writers like Walter Cannon and Graham Wallas. Cannon studied the effects of stress on animals and people, focusing on the 'fight or flight' reaction, whether they choose to stay and fight or try to escape when confronting extreme danger. Post-war laboratory research later reflected military concerns as stress was assumed to affect the performance of pilots, gunners, and others. In the 1970s, though, role stress gathered interest, with 200 articles being written on the topic between 1970 and 1983 (Jackson and Schuler 1985).

Hans Seyle, researching in 1946, described three stages to a person's response to stress: alarm, resistance, and exhaustion (see Seyle 1976). In the first stage the muscles tense, and the respiration, heart, and blood-pressure rates increase. Next the person experiences anxiety, anger, and fatigue as they resist stress; they may make poor decisions or experience illness at this stage. The person will not be able to sustain this resistance and, if the level of stress continues, they will experience exhaustion and stress-induced illness (like headaches and ulcers). Seyle claims that all individuals go through the same pattern of response and we can only tolerate so much stress before a serious debilitating condition is brought about. Critics of Seyle's work say it ignores both the psychological impact of stress upon an individual and the individual's ability to recognize stress and act in various ways to change his or her situation (Cooper et al. 1988; Cooper and Payne 1990). Later theories of stress emphasized the interaction between a person and their environment. Others have added to this by discussing the individual's reaction. For example, Lazarus (1976) has suggested that an individual's stress reaction 'depends on how the person interprets or appraises (consciously or unconsciously) the significance of a harmful, threatening or challenging event'. All is dependent then on whether the person feels they can cope with a threat.

Cooper and Cummings (see Cooper et al. 1988) believe that stress results from a misfit between individuals and their environment. This helps explain why one person seems to flourish in a setting while another suffers. Individuals, they say, for the most part, try to keep their thoughts, emotions, and relationships in a 'steady state'. They have a range of stability with which they feel comfortable. When forces disrupt the emotional and physical state, the individual must act or cope to restore a feeling of comfort. If they fail to cope, the stress will continue. Symptoms of stress can be manifested physically in, for example, lack of appetite or craving for food, headaches, skin problems, insomnia, fainting spells, and high blood pressure. Mental symptoms may include irritability, feeling unable to cope, difficulty in concentrating, and a lack of interest in life.

What are the causes of stress? The following is a list of some of the factors that have been shown to contribute towards stress and strain:

1. The physical environment, for example being exposed to hazardous and noxious substances, density and crowding, lack of privacy, high noise levels, high or low temperature, poor quality lighting.

2. Role conflict, when the individual is torn by conflict in job demands or doing things they do not want to do or believe are not part of the job. Or role ambiguity, when an individual does not have a clear picture about work objectives, co-workers' expectations, the scope and responsibilities of the job.

3. Characteristics of the job, for example, work overload, lack of career progression, lack of autonomy, underutilization, too many meetings, shift work, or long hours.

4. Relationships with others, e.g. poor relationships with supervisors, work/family conflict. (For a fuller list see Cartwright and Cooper 1997: ch. 1; Cooper et al. 1988, ch. 4.)

AN EXAMPLE OF JOB RAGE

Some have suggested that job rage is rapidly becoming a phenomenon to rival road rage. A receptionist was dismissed, having run foul of the temper of her superior, for not being able to make coffee as he liked it (*The Scotsman*, 4 April 1998, p. 11).

Shift work is a common stress factor affecting blood (temperature and sugar levels), metabolic rate, mental efficiency, work motivation, sleep patterns, family, and social life (Arnold et al. 1995). A study of offshore oil-rig workers showed work patterns, including shift work, physical conditions, and travel, to be the third most important source of stress (Sutherland and Cooper 1987). The longer the work shift (for example, twenty-eight days on, twenty-eight days off versus fourteen days on, fourteen days off) the greater the stress. The shift patterns were a predictor of mental and physical ill health, particularly when the oil-rig workers were married and had children.

Research on balancing the needs of work and family and stress shows that mothers who work outside the home have better mental and physical health than those who do not. However, if partners contribute little to domestic tasks, they will have poorer mental health. The vast majority of mothers had partners who contributed less than 20 per cent to the domestic tasks (Khan and Cuthbertson 1994).

The home is a source of stress for women as they try to balance the dual needs of work and domestic responsibilities (Ginn and Sandell 1997; Wheeler and Lyon 1992) but it would appear that work probably impacts on family more than family impacts on work. Interestingly, husbands' attitude towards wives working has been studied extensively but wives' attitudes towards husbands' employment has not been so extensively researched. Also, research on impact of children on job stress has focused more on women than on men. While mothers might experience stress due to role overload, fathers might experience some stress as they attempt to fulfil the role of good provider (Gutek et al. 1990).

STOP

Have you noticed that if you are under stress, you have more vivid dreams? Work stress is thought to contribute to nightmares about killing the boss. Stress at work is contributing to a regular nightmare for one in two adults (Womack 2003). Research in Britain found that 51 per cent of respondents suffered work-related nightmares at least once a week with the figure rising to 61 per cent among Londoners. A row with the boss was the most common dream followed by arriving late for a meeting. Worryingly 7 per cent confessed to dreams where they wanted to murder the boss.

Stress in the City

Nicola Horlick hit the headlines by losing a top city job. She had a very large salary, a high-pressured job, and five children, but gave up her job after being falsely accused by a colleague. The costs of holding highly paid but high-pressured jobs can be large. For example an increasing number of senior women are likely to be found in second or third marriages. Women in top jobs are more likely to suffer from stomach problems, reflecting their struggle with stress. Few women will have been mentored for top jobs. Some are beginning to wonder if they can 'have it all'—a high-powered job and a family. 'Miranda Lawson' (not her real name) says, 'I know that I could not do this job and have a family. I can't have it all, it would be completely impossible. But it would be possible for a man to do my job and have a family. Is that really equality?' (Interview with Lisa Buckingham, 'Room at the Top for Hard Choices', *Guardian*, 18 October 1997, p. 25.)

Individual differences are involved in the stress process. There may be collections of traits that protect people from stress, for example 'hardiness' (Maddi and Kobasa 1984), positive self-image or self-esteem, flexibility. Their personality, coping strategies, personal history, and social support may affect the individual's vulnerability to stress. Some jobs are more stressful than others. The uniformed professions (prison service, police force, or civil aviation) have the highest average stress ratings (Cooper et al. 1988). There is also concern about the psychological health of doctors; rates of suicide for doctors are approximately two to three times that of populations of comparable social class. In 1996 doctors hit headline news when the British Medical Association published a report showing how doctors were turning to drink and drugs to cope with increased stress. One in five doctors had thought about killing themselves (e.g. *Daily Mail*, 10 April, p. 21; *The Scotsman*, 13 April, p. 10). Substance abuse may be up to thirty times more common among doctors than the general population (King et al. 1992). There is also a relatively high suicide rate among nurses (*Observer*, 19 March 1995, p. 1) and other health service workers (Rees 1995).

It may be that some individuals have personalities that predispose them to the effects of stress. One such difference that has been examined is Type A coronary-prone behaviour. Type A behaviour is characterized by sustained drive towards poorly defined goals, preoccupation with deadlines, competitiveness, and a desire for advancement and achievement. Mental and behavioural alertness or aggressiveness, chronic haste, and impatience also characterize it. Typically more than 50 per cent of the workforce would be classified as Type As. (You can gain a rough idea of the degree to which you might be a Type A personality by completing the questionnaire in Cooper et al. 1988: 51 or Arnold et al. 1995: 376.) This type of behaviour has been shown to be an important risk factor in the development of coronary heart disease, a leading cause of death in Britain and North America. It kills more than 150,000 people a year, one person every three or four minutes (Arnold et al. 1995). Type B personality types, a more relaxed type, in contrast have a low risk of coronary heart disease. There are some studies, though, which show contradictory results (see Cooper et al. 1988: 48).

The Dilemma

Type A behaviour can lead to heart disease yet is consistently found to predict career success (Steffy et al. 1989). The individual thus faces a conflict: should they work hard (going beyond what is expected is a virtue) or should they take care not to suffer the psychological and physiological effects of overwork? The individual faces the dilemma, not the organization. The individual has to adjust to work.

We have, through the measure of Type A behaviour and other measures of stress, like the General Health Questionnaire, a view of normality that is operationally defined through reference to abnormality (see Newton 1995: 65). There are other ways of looking at stress, for example taking a sociological approach and looking at the subjective experience of the distress of dealing with the impending closure of a factory, as Anna Pollert did (see Handy 1995; Pollert 1981). Most current models of work stress fit firmly within a functionalist paradigm but this is not the only way the subject matter could have been treated.

If you find that you are suffering from stress, there are a number of ways of coping, to 'transform maladaptive behaviour' (Cooper et al. 1988). The techniques Cooper et al. (1988) would recommend include becoming assertive, identifying the incidents that cause distress by keeping a stress diary, and noting what action you took and how effective it proved. You need to attempt to eliminate or change the problem or stressor. If the problem or stressor cannot be changed, find ways of coping with the problem, then monitor and review the outcome (Arnold et al. 1995).

Using highly individualized methods, some organizations have tried to answer the negative effects of stress by pre-empting it. Companies such as Federal Express, Hewlett Packard, and Conoco have adopted Stephen Covey's programme, 'The Seven Habits of Highly Effective People' (Vecchio 1995). Stress can be managed in a number of different ways: employment assistance programmes (EAPs), stress management training, and stress reduction or intervention (Murphy 1988; Newton 1995). EAPs generally refer to the provision of employee counselling for problems like alcoholism, drug abuse, and mental health. Stress management training is designed to provide employees with improved coping skills and so includes techniques like meditation, biofeedback, and muscle relaxation to help the individual. Stress reduction or intervention would usually change a job to reduce job stressors. Most workplace initiatives focus on stress management training or counselling and health promotion, not changing jobs. Companies like Anglia Railways, Cummings Engineering, and Pfizer are amongst those in Britain who have been using techniques like EAPs and stress management training (see Hipern 2003 and Industrial Society report 2001 for more UK examples). The US Department of Health and Human Services found that more than 60 per cent of work-sites there offered some form of stress management or health promotion activity (Cooper and Cartwright 1994). For example, the New York Telephone Company introduced a wellness programme for cardiovascular fitness, while PepsiCo created a physical fitness programme. Evidence of the success of such schemes is generally confusing and imprecise, possibly reflecting the idiosyncratic nature of the form and content of courses (Arnold et al. 1995: 383). The growing evidence that individual and company performance is adversely affected by stress has had little effect on companies in Britain (Wheeler and Lyon 1992).

AN EXAMPLE OF HOW SCHOOLS HAVE COPED WITH STRESS

A pilot project across five schools in York claims to have reduced absence rates among teachers from 10.5 days to 8.9 days a year. An assessment of mental and physical health was completed and those with higher stress levels were give extra support like mentoring and counselling. The project also identified the main causes of stress and drew up a calendar of workload hotspots so that peak times could be planned for. The marking policy was changed to better stagger workload and an extra teacher was employed (Hilpern 2003).

Overwork can lead to death. There have been reports in the newspapers recently of deaths due to over-work in Japan. Deaths due to this rose to 317 in 2003 doubling the previous record of 147 set in 2002. Doctors, factory workers, and taxi drivers are the worst affected. See **www.heraldsun.news.com.au/ common/story_page/0,5478,6581122 %255E663,00.html**

Stress and burnout can be treated by organizations as everyday work life problems that the individual is expected to deal with (Kunda 1982). Martin et al. (1998) studied the use of personal counselling as a method of reducing the negative effects of stress. They conclude 'however helpful such a counsellor may be, the implicit message is that work stress is an abnormal response that must be controlled with the blame for the problem and the responsibility for fixing it resting primarily with the individual experiencing the stress' (Martin et al. 1998: 458). Being able to handle yourself and stressful situations is seen as the mark of the professional.

While programmes like EAP may have genuine benefits for employees, they may also represent an extension of corporate control over staff who are now expected not only to sell their skills and time but to ensure that their total lifestyle ensures maximum corporate gain (Handy 1988). Newton (1995) argues that stress management techniques are not impartial and are not applied by caring progressive management; in fact they may be 'nakedly coercive', a tool of a cunning management intent upon domination and control of their workforce. Fineman (1995) shows how managers at a nuclear research establishment treated the results of a study on employee role stress. The managers were so alarmed by the results that they immediately suppressed the findings and tried to discredit the analysis.

Stress, Fineman (1995) would argue, has much to do with the organization and social context of the job. Stress is an emotional product of the social and political features of work and organizational life. The individual is actively involved in reproducing the social structures and there may be little they can do to affect them, either because they are tacit, taken-for-granted features of organizational life, operating at a more or less preconscious level, or because the individual is relatively powerless to affect them. We learn feeling rules; we have learnt how much emotion to display, about how to appear, and appropriate demeanour for the workplace. Some of the rules will reflect our gender, age, or class. Others will reflect the nature of the business we work in. Crucially we privately labour with, and work in, our feelings in order to create the socially desired emotional expression and impression. Stress feelings, like anxiety, fear, and dread will have to be dressed up for managers, customers, clients, and colleagues. In doing the 'face work' (Goffman 1961) camouflaging our feelings, we create new tensions. The polite automatic smile from the waitress may be relatively stress free but the emotional labour cost rises when the waitress starts to hate her work and the people she serves. We have discussed the explicit feeling rules in Chapter 3 and when looking at Hochschild's (1983) work on emotions. There are also implicit feeling rules. These would include, for example, the rules on what should remain a private doubt and worry and what can be openly expressed. Fineman (1995) shows how social workers provide much illustration of this. The social workers did not share their concerns with their colleagues and 'played a charade' with each other's stresses. They did not admit to their own stresses and would fail to care for colleagues. What they did to cope was go sick or absent, as this was organizationally acceptable. These tacit assumptions and rules about emotion and stress are not going to fall out neatly from the questions and answers in interviews or questionnaires but can be the unintended product of a lengthy process of establishing a relationship with individuals in a study.

A discussion of emotion management can also be found in a study of The Body Shop (Martin et al. 1998). Here the constrained expression of emotions at work was encouraged as it facilitated a sense of community and personal well-being. Employees of The Body Shop frequently discuss intimate personal issues with co-workers; employees felt they could 'be themselves at work' (1998: 460). Most employees shared a strong sense of being part of The Body Shop community. Anita Roddick herself repeatedly and persuasively articulated values such as caring, sharing, and love. These values were enacted by employees in practices such as one intimate self-disclosure encouraging another, hugs and kisses as common ways of saying hello, thank you, and goodbye. These expressions of emotion were, however, constrained.

A Case

A Seattle-based computer consulting firm lost an important client and a project worth over $100,000 when an employee, who was managing the project, had a personal crisis and disappeared for three days. The job was not completed due to the disappearance (Solomon 1999). The article implies that the absence was caused by stress: 'He began showing signs of stress but no one really thought much about it because he was well regarded' (1999: 48). His sister rang the company three days later and 'explained that he had started drinking again'. Other examples of stress mentioned in this article include throwing food in the cafeteria, finding employees standing in the rubbish bin smoking pot, and crying in the hallways.

The figures are compelling. A 1998 article in the *Academy of Management Executive* shows that 75–90 per cent of doctor visits are stress related. Those who are victimized at work cost 5,000,000 employees about 3.5 days of work per crime (Bureau of Justice Statistics, July 1994). But are these events necessarily due to stress? What systems could organizations have in place to deal with them? How much of this behaviour is under management control? Who does the source of the problem lie with—the individual or the organization?

■ **SUGGESTIONS FOR FURTHER READING**

1. Thompson, P., and McHugh, D. (2002), *Work Organizations* (3rd edition), Houndmills: Palgrave. Chapter 18—'Putting the Pressure on: Stress, Work, and Emotion'—makes some interesting linkages.

2. Baty, P. (2003), 'Violent Students Terrorise Staff, *The Times Higher Education Supplement*, 28 February, p. 1. for a discussion of violence in universities.

3. Cooper, C. (1998), *Stress Management* (2nd edn.), London: Hodder & Stoughton, published in association with the Institute of Management. This is a book which describes when and why stress is harmful, what causes it, why some people cope better than others, and how it can be overcome.

4. Clark, H., Chandler, J., and Barry, J. (2000), 'Work, Stress and Gender: Conceptualization and Consequence', ch. 4 in J. Barry et al. *Organization and Management: A Critical Text*, London: Thompson Learning. This chapter provides a critical review of the research on stress.

5. Cooper, C. L., Dewe, P. J., and O'Driscoll, M. P. (2001), *Organizational Stress: A Review and Critique* of the Theory, Research and Applications, London: Sage. This book is a good introduction to the field of stress.

6. Newton, T. (1995), with J. Handy and S. Fineman, *Managing Stress: Emotions and Power at Work*, London: Sage, for another link between emotion and stress.

7. Watson, T. (2002), *Organizing and Managing Work*, Harlow: Pearson. Pages 148–54 are on stress and make connections between home and work.

■ WEB SITES

See **www.thebodyshop.com/web/tbsgl/values.jsp** for more on the Body Shop's espoused values or **www.ltbn.com/fame/Roddick.html** for more on Anita Roddick. There are lots of web sites on Anita Roddick and the Body Shop.

Similarly there are many sites about stress from around the world. See for example **www.ilo.org/public/english/protection/safework/stress/**

■ QUESTIONS

1. Take one occupational group, like doctors, and try to assess, through research and reading, how vulnerable they are to stress compared to another group, like nurses.

2. Newton (1995) asks us to challenge the way we look at stress. How does he recommend we do this?

3. According to some, women cope better with stress in demanding jobs than men. What evidence can you find to support or refute this statement?

4. Some believe that stress can be measured (e.g. Cohen et al. 1995). What would be the strengths and limitations of such an approach?

5. Anna Pollert's study of women workers' responses to the impending closure of the tobacco factory where they were employed provides a sociological study of distress. Describe the stresses created by this work environment and the dual burden of work and family responsibilities that she uncovered.

6. Customer abuse is perpetuated by a range of cost-rational and profit-centred policies (Boyd 2002). Discuss.

7. 700,000 people phone in sick on a Monday morning. One in three people are faking it (*UK Undercover*, 'Throwing a Sickie', Channel 5, 2002). These bare facts raise more questions. For

example what kind of people throw a 'sickie'? Is it mainly those who are in stressful, repetitive, routine work, or professional workers? Is it because they feel they are not given enough holiday entitlement? How would you investigate why individuals do this?

■ GROUP EXERCISE

If you were an employer, what steps would you take to (*a*) research stress, (*b*) act to reduce stress levels? See Industrial Society (2001) and assess how realistic you think companies are about managing stress. Who mainly benefits (Newton 1995)?

■ REFERENCES

Arnold, J., Cooper, C. L., and Robertson, I. T. (1995), *Work Psychology: Understanding Human Behaviour in the Workplace*, London: Pitman Publishing, chs. 17 and 18.

Baty, P. (2003), 'Violent Students Terrorise Staff', *Times Higher Education Supplement*, 28 Feb., p. 1.

Bosma, H., Marmot, M. G., Hemingway, H., Nicholson, A. C., Brunner, E., and Stansfield, S. A. (1997), 'Low Job Control and Risk of Coronary Heart Disease in Whitehall II (Prospective Cohort) Study', *British Medical Journal* (22 Feb.), 558–65.

——Peter, R., Siegrist, J., and Marmot, M. (1998), 'Two Alternative Job Stress Models of the Risk of Coronary Heart Disease', *American Journal of Public Health*, 88/1: 68–74.

Boyd, C. (2002), 'Customer Violence and Employee Health and Safety', *Work, Employment and Society*, 16/1: 151–69.

Cartwright, S., and Cooper, C. L. (1997), *Managing Workplace Stress*, London: Sage.

Cohen, S., Kessler, R. C., and Gordon, L. U. (1995) (eds.), *Measuring Stress: A Guide for Health and Social Scientists*, Oxford: Oxford University Press.

Cooper, C. L., and Cartwright, S. (1994), 'Healthy Mind; Healthy Organization. A Proactive Approach to Occupational Stress', *Human Relations*, 47/4: 455–71.

——and Payne, R. (1990), *Causes, Coping and Consequences of Stress at Work*, Chichester: Wiley.

——Cooper, R. D., and Eaker, L. H. (1988), *Living with Stress*, Harmondsworth: Penguin.

Fineman, S. (1995), 'Stress, Emotion and Intervention', in T. Newton, *Managing Stress: Emotion and Power at Work*, London: Sage.

Fletcher, B. (1990), 'The Epidemiology of Occupational Stress', ch. 1 in C. L. Cooper and R. Payne (eds.), *Causes, Coping and Consequences of Stress at Work*, Chichester: Wiley.

Ginn, J., and Sandell, J. (1997), 'Balancing Home and Employment: Stress Reported by Social Services Staff', *Work, Employment and Society*, 11/3: 413–34.

Goffman, E. (1961), *Asylums*, Harmondsworth: Penguin.

Guardian (2003), 'Student Violence on Increase', 28 Feb., story found at http://education.guardian.co.uk/higher/news/story/0,9830,904449,00.html

Gutek, B. A., Repetti, R. L., and Silver, D. L. (1990), 'Non-Work Roles and Stress at Work', ch. 5 in C. L. Cooper and R. Payne (eds.), *Causes, Coping and Consequences of Stress at Work*, Chichester: Wiley.

Handy, J. A. (1988), 'Theoretical and Methodological Problems with Occupational Stress and Burnout Research', *Human Relations*, 41/5: 351–69.

——(1995), 'Rethinking Stress: Seeing the Collective', ch. 4 in T. Newton, *Managing Stress: Emotion and Power at Work*, London: Sage.

Health and Safety Executive (2001), *Health and Safety Statistics*, London: HSE.

Hilpern, K. (2003), 'Office House: Boiling over', *Guardian*, 17 Mar. story found at infoweb.newsbank.com.

Hochschild, A. R. (1983), *The Managed Heart: Commercialization of Human Feeling*, Berkeley, Calif.: University of California Press.

HSC (1997), *Health and Safety Commission Annual Report and Accounts 1996/1997*, London: HSE Books.

Industrial Society (2001), 'Managing Best Practice', Report no. 83, Occupational Stress, London: Industrial Society.

Jackson, S. E., and Schuler, R. S. (1985), 'A Meta-analysis and Conceptual Critique of Research on Role Ambiguity and Role Conflict in Work Settings', *Organizational Behaviour and Human Decision Processes*, 36: 16–78.

Khan, H., and Cuthbertson, J. (1994), 'Mothers who Work and Mothers who "only" Stay at Home: Are the Stressors Different?', paper presented to the annual conference of the Scottish Branch of the British Psychological Society, Crieff Hydro, 25–7 Nov. 1994.

King, M. B., Cockcroft, A., and Gooch, C. (1992), 'Emotional Distress in Doctors: Sources, Effects and Help Sought', *Journal of the Royal Society of Medicine*, 85: 605–8.

Kunda, G. (1982), *Engineering Culture*, Philadelphia: Temple University Press.

Lazarus, R. S. (1976), *Patterns of Adjustment*, New York: McGraw Hill.

Maddi, S. R., and Kobasa, S. C. (1984), *The Hardy Executive: Health under Stress*, Homewood, Ill.: Dow Jones-Irwin.

Marmot, M. G., Bosma, H., Hemingway, H., Brunner, E., and Stansfeld, S. (1997), Contribution of Job Control and Other Risk Factors to Social Variations in Coronary Heart Disease Incidence', *Lancet*, 350/9073: 235–9.

Martin, J., Knopoff, K., and Beckman, C. (1998), 'An Alternative to Bureaucratic Impersonality and Emotional Labor: Bounded Rationality at The Body Shop', *Administrative Science Quarterly*, 429–69.

Masterton, V. (2003), ' "Stressed' staff should Face Sack', *Scotland on Sunday*, 23 Feb., p. 6.

Mayhew, C., and Quinlan, M. (1999), 'The Relationship between Precarious Employment and Patterns of Occupational Violence: Survey of Evidence from Thirteen Occupations', paper presented at the Health Hazards and Challenges in the New Working Life conference, 11–13 Jan., Stockholm (cited in Boyd 2002).

Murphy, L. R. (1988), 'Workplace Interventions for Stress Reduction and Prevention', in C. L. Cooper and R. Payne (eds.), *Causes and Coping and Consequences of Stress at Work*, Chichester: Wiley.

Newton, T. (1995), with J. Handy and S. Fineman, *Managing Stress: Emotions and Power at Work*, London: Sage.

Nichols, T. (1998), 'Health and Safety at Work', review article in *Work, Employment and Society*, 12/2: 367–74.

Pollert, A. (1981), *Girls, Wives, Factory Lives*, London: Macmillan.

Rees, D. W. (1995), 'Work-Related Stress in Health Service Employees', *Journal of Managerial Psychology*, 10/3: 4–11.

Schnall, P. L., and Landsbergis, P. A. (1994), 'Job Strain and Cardiovascular Disease', *Annual Review of Public Health*, 15: 381–411.

Seyle, H. (1976), *The Stress of Life*, New York: McGraw Hill.

Solomon, C. M. (1999), 'Stressed to the Limit', *Workforce*, 78/9: 48–54.

Steffy, B. D., Shaw, K., and Noe, A. W. (1989), 'Antecedents and Consequences of Job Search Behaviours', *Journal of Vocational Behavior*, 3: 254–69.

Styhre, A., Ingelgard, A., Beausang, P., Castenfors, M., Mulec, K., and Roth, J. (2002), 'Emotional Management and Stress: Managing Ambiguities', *Organization Studies*, 23/1: 83–103.

Sutherland, V., and Cooper, C. L. (1987), *Man and Accidents Offshore*, London: Lloyds.

TUC (1999), *Violent Times*, London: TUC.

Vecchio, R. P. (1995), *Organizational Behaviour* (3rd edn.), London: Dryden Press.

Wheeler, S., and Lyon, D. (1992), 'Employee Benefits for the Employer's Benefit: How Companies Respond to Employee Stress', *Personnel Review*, 21/7: 47–63.

Womack, S. (2003), 'Worried Staff Find that Work is a Nightmare', *Daily Telegraph*, 11 Feb.

16 Being Unemployed, Being a Volunteer, and Being 'on the Fiddle'

There are many links between the subjects of this chapter and other chapters. Learning more about what being unemployed means tells us about what being employed means, what work means. Being unemployed can, for some, be stressful and lead to a lack of feeling of well-being. Doing voluntary work may help overcome some of the negative effects of work or lack of it. Being on the fiddle may be viewed as another form of 'misbehaviour'.

Being Unemployed

The burden of unemployment is not evenly spread throughout the social classes but lies heavily with the semi- and unskilled group. Those who have become even more vulnerable to unemployment are also likely to have fewer resources with which to protect themselves and their families from their loss of earning power.

An integral part of the experience of unemployment is the task of actively seeking paid work. There is, for many, particularly those in employment, a moral imperative on the unemployed to seek work actively or be labelled a scrounger or undeserving. The logical corollary of this attitude is that the unemployed only have themselves to blame if they fail. This attitude ignores facts like there are far more registered unemployed than there are job vacancies.

The media are inclined to present unemployment as social disintegration occasioned by male job loss. Pit closures, for example, focused on male job loss, the loss of community pride in the wake of male redundancy, and the loss of the community's 'heart' with the closure of the colliery. Yet women in these communities suffered in parallel ways to men. What emerges from Dicks's (1996) study of pit closures in two communities was that women's ability to cope with the aftermath of pit closure was not decided so much by their spouses' employment fate as by the material, social, and emotional resources that they could draw on. Since the women remained largely responsible for household management and childcare, the tasks of budgeting and catering on a reduced income as well as the provision of emotional support to distressed partners, largely fell on their shoulders.

STOP

Effects of Unemployment

John Lennon is quoted as saying 'Work is life, you know, and without it, there's nothing but fear and insecurity' (Solt and Egan 1988: 75). Do you share this view? What would your reaction be to facing unemployment?

Responses to unemployment vary from depression, through stoic acceptance, to celebration (Ezzy 2001). The emphasis in the literature has tended to be on the negative effects. Research since the 1930s has very clearly shown the negative effects of unemployment on well-being (Fryer 1992; Warr 1987; Warr et al. 1988). For most individuals unemployment manifests itself in ill health, despair, and chronic lethargy (symptoms remarkably like those to be found in bereaved individuals: see Archer and Rhodes 1987). The effect may not be universal, as a small minority will show gains in mental health after job loss. These people will have been in stressful jobs or will be happy to tolerate unemployment, taking jobs as they come along; a small minority will see it as a challenge and an opportunity to develop skills or interests. The experience of the unemployed varies depending on factors such as a person's age, gender, income, social support, reason for job loss, commitment to employment, satisfaction with previous work, expectation of returning to work, and length of unemployment (Winefield 1995). For the majority, unemployment impairs mental health. The impairment can involve increased psychological distress, including anxiety and depression, lowered self-esteem, resigned apathy, helplessness, powerlessness, social isolation, and disintegration. These disorders have been confirmed in many countries (Fryer 1992).

Classic studies in the 1930s began to detail what it meant to people to be unemployed (Jahoda et al. 1933; Bakke 1934; Komarovsky 1940; Eisenberg and Lazarsfeld 1938). In the 1930s a group of researchers (see Jahoda et al. 1933) lived for some months in an Austrian village which had suffered from the demise of the textile industry. The research reported that, although the unemployed inhabitants of the village spent more time in bed to shorten the length of the day, they were unable to account for other ways in which their days had been spent. They reported that they were slower moving about and were unpunctual for fixed arrangements like meals. Weekends blended into weekdays and they lost 'structured meaning', their sense of time disintegrated (Jahoda 1982). Women's sense of time was less disrupted because they still had a domestic routine to follow but many wanted to return to work because they missed the social contact of the factory. Despite the economic stringencies caused by unemployment, the researchers reported that people chose to do 'irrational' acts, for example spending money on a cream cake or growing flowers instead of vegetables when there was a food shortage.

Jahoda (1982, 1987) provides five categories of psychological experience which she says are not only conducive to feelings of well-being but vital. As unemployed people are deprived of these experiences, so their well-being declines. These experiences are:

- time structure—work imposes a time structure on the waking day
- social contact—work compels contact and shared experiences with others outside the family
- collective effort or purpose—work demonstrates that there are goals and purposes which are beyond the purpose of the individual but require collectivity
- social identity or status—work imposes status or social identity through the division of labour
- regular activity—work enforces activity. (For a more detailed discussion of the categories see Haworth 1997: 25.)

The employed take these categories of experience for granted but the unemployed have to find experiences within these categories if they can or suffer if they cannot. 'What preoccupies them is not the category but the quality of experience within it' (Jahoda 1982: 39). She recognizes that the quality of experience in some jobs can be very poor and stresses the importance of improving and humanizing employment.

Jahoda has been criticized for missing the fact that lack of money and contending with bureaucracy are two of the features of unemployment which contribute to feelings of lack of well-being. Also, the unemployed can gain access to the five categories of experience. Those unemployed with better access will have better well-being. But she concludes that the employed have better access to the categories of experience than the unemployed. Unemployment destroys the very structures that the employed take for granted—

structures of time, routine, status, social networks—as Bostyn and Wright (1987) also suggest. Given the excessive amount of time the unemployed have on their hands, they ought not to be late for interviews, but they are (Miles 1983); they ought to have more time for leisure activities but retreat from such social interaction (Grint 1998). Warr (1987) has built on the categories of experience by proposing a model of mental health. This model incorporates the five categories of experience advocated by Jahoda. He emphasizes nine principal environmental influences:

- opportunity for control—the opportunity for a person to control activities and events
- environmental clarity—feedback about the consequences of your actions, certainty about the future, and clarity of understanding about what is expected of you in the job
- opportunity for skill use
- externally generated goals
- variety
- opportunity for interpersonal contact
- valued social position
- availability of money
- physical security

These nine principal environmental influences or environmental categories of experience are seen as acting together in conjunction with personal factors to help or hinder psychological well-being or mental health. Warr likens these influences to vitamins; some will improve mental health up to a certain point and have no further effect, others producing benefits up to a certain level beyond which increases would be detrimental. He argues that there can be good and bad jobs and good and bad unemployment depending on how much of these influences are present in the individual's experience.

The nine-factor framework tells us a good deal of what work means to people in a psychological sense. There is also a widespread view amongst the unemployed that they should not be seen as lazy, even if this means taking a job which pays only marginally more than unemployment benefit (Turner et al. 1985). Being a breadwinner is also important to men for a sense of masculine identity (McKee and Bell 1986; Yankelovich 1973).

Becoming unemployed typically changes a person's life story (Ezzy 2001). Different people tell different types of stories and the type of story someone tells about their experiences shapes whether they become depressed as a consequence of becoming unemployed. Ezzy (2001) argues that there are three types of job loss narratives to identify. They are romances, tragedies, and more complex stories. Fourteen of the thirty-three people he interviewed described their job loss as romance, as a clearly positive experience. Unemployment brings both release from an oppressive job and the freedom to pursue alternative highly valued goals. Twenty-four were tragic stories where the experience of unemployment is painful and unerring. People describe the trauma of losing their job. The focus of the trauma is the loss of certainty about the future that secure employment provides. A sense of being unwanted and worthless when unable to find work leads into periods of depression and self-deprecation. For seven of the interviewees the situation was more complex as other events in their lives were at least as important as the consequences of their job loss. For example two were negotiation and marriage separation, two had chronic illness, and one was having a 'faith crisis'. This then provides us with a more complex analysis of the effect of unemployment on individuals.

One of the responses to massive rises in unemployment has been the growth of agencies, schemes, and initiatives designed to spread the gospel of enterprise and encourage new businesses (MacDonald and Coffield 1991). The new jobs tend to be in the service sector—clothes retailers, beauticians, car valets, sandwich deliverers, sign writers, car mechanics, private detectives. Yet we do not seem to be witnessing the birth of local enterprise culture. New small firms, even those which seem to do well initially, are unable to continue in the long term (MacDonald and Coffield 1991). The smallest and youngest firms are the least likely to survive and grow (Chittenden and Caley 1992). This is 'survival self employment' (MacDonald 1997) as individuals trade with skills informally learnt and experience from hobbies and pastimes. But competition is too fierce and the market place is saturated with similar businesses so the local economy cannot support all these new businesses.

Callender (1987) argues that women's experience of job search and job acquisition can be different from that of men. The demand and supply side of men's and women's labour are not the same. Her study of a group of married women who had experienced redundancy through the partial closure of a clothing factory showed that all the redundant women wanted to work again and were very flexible about the conditions and type of paid work they were prepared to accept. Many were willing to take a reduction in pay. The women had an astute view of the state of the labour market and of the way in which demand structured their choices and opportunities; they had little choice so were prepared to accept any job. They organized and marshalled resources, like assistance with childcare and dependent relatives, for coping with their paid and unpaid work, but paid work was not a moral imperative for them, unlike men. The most effective strategy for finding work was through informal social networks, such as family and friends, by word of mouth. Those women who succeeded in finding work were highly reliant upon other people in their social network for information about jobs and recommendations. These networks were closed, restricted, home and female centred; this then determined the type of jobs the women obtained and their opportunities. If the women got jobs, they were similar jobs to those their female contacts had, typical 'women's work'.

Those of us in work are in fear of becoming unemployed. Unemployment is not restricted to those at the bottom of the socio-economic hierarchy; the managerial and professional middle class also feel anxious and insecure about their jobs (Pahl 1996). Increases in managerial redundancy have followed in the wake of recession and fiercer competition. Managers may believe they are less vulnerable when it comes to redundancies, having invested a lifetime of service in return for job security (Hallier and Lyon 1996), so when job loss comes, it can be a fundamental shock to their personal identity and financial security (Kozlowski et al. 1993). Those with qualifications and job experience can, though, usually face redundancy with greater confidence than those without, as they have skills, competencies, and networks that others may lack. The highest rates of unemployment tend to be amongst those with no qualifications, from the working class, amongst the chronically sick and disabled, and from ethnic minorities.

Working Time

As those of us in jobs in the UK work longer hours, the numbers without jobs increase. Those who work have a decrease in their available free time. Research (Tyrell 1995) shows that available free time for full-time male workers declined by 4 per cent between 1985 and 1993 and for females the decline has been just over 10 per cent. In the USA the average American works the equivalent of an extra month each year compared to 1969 (Schor 1995). Yet many people do not want to work as long hours as they do. Survey research in Britain has shown, for example, that over 70 per cent of people working over forty hours a week wanted to work less (Mulgan and Wilkinson 1995). Schor (1995) shows how one-third of respondents wanted to work fewer hours even if this meant a 20 per cent reduction in household income. With this comes the admission that much of our spending is habitual, though; we are used to having our spending creep up with income.

Voluntary Work

Voluntary work has received little attention in the UK (Harris 1990; MacDonald 1997). Yet there has been a rapid growth in the number of charities and it is estimated that half a million people are employed in the sector (Halfpenny and Reid 2002). Levels of voluntary work have been high and can help give insight into the changing nature of what work and unemployment mean to people. In rural areas participation in voluntary groups is heavily skewed towards the relatively affluent who use them as vehicles for improving their social networks (Williams 2002). In economically depressed areas volunteering has been taken up increasingly by people not in employment. MacDonald's (1997) research on volunteer workers gives us some useful information. Volunteers are predominantly engaged in looking after the disadvantaged as carers or as fund-raisers. A minority work for only a few hours a week; most work virtually full-time. All are motivated by a moral concern for the disadvantaged in their communities. Some, particularly middle-aged and older women, rebuild their lives left empty through redundancy or bereavement (as husbands have died, children left home, or employment ceased) by volunteering. Volunteering gives them the opportunity to maintain self-identity in their socially ascribed roles as carers at home. Volunteering replaced many of the positive social psychological categories of experience (Jahoda 1982).

Voluntary work was also a semi-permanent response to being excluded from employment, particularly for the middle-aged men. They had realized that unemployment could be the norm for them. Volunteering provided new opportunities and challenges and the chance to give up images of worker and breadwinner. The new work had the potential to broaden their work aspirations and expectations. Volunteering could be a strategy for finding 'proper jobs' in the case of teenage and young adults. They were gaining work experience, skills, contacts, and references. It must be noted, however, that not all the responses were positive. The work could be hard, physically and emotionally, and they

> **AN EXAMPLE OF HOW VOLUNTARY WORK CAN PROVIDE A 'SPACE'**
>
> A different perspective on voluntary work is to be found in Gold and Fraser (2002). They describe how voluntary work can also provide a 'career space'. It provides an opportunity to balance working and non-work life; it can then provide an alternative career for those with employment. What would doing voluntary work mean to you?

could be treated like 'skivvies'; their treatment could come close to exploitation, as it is unpaid and often difficult and demanding.

Being 'on the Fiddle' or Working 'on the Side'

This is work carried out for pay by those who are also claiming social security or unemployment benefits to which they would not be wholly entitled if they declared this work to the benefit authorities. Some research (e.g. Bradshaw and Holmes 1989; Pahl 1984) shows that the unemployed are far less likely than the employed to engage in illicit work. Other work (e.g. Jordan et al. 1992) has found that around two-thirds of poor households benefit from undeclared work. In MacDonald's (1997) sample of non-standard employed (self-employed in very small businesses, those in voluntary work, 'on the fiddle', or in community enterprise and cooperatives) one-third had been 'on the fiddle'. These jobs were not preferred to 'proper' jobs; combining 'fiddly' work with unemployment benefits was a survival strategy initiated in the face of mass, structural unemployment and a system of benefits which failed to meet material needs. For the poor and long-term unemployed the fiddle is described by MacDonald as a necessary way of maintaining individual self-respect and household income. Fiddly work is better understood as representing a culture of enterprise rather than one of dependency. Those engaged in it fitted the model of entrepreneur showing high degrees of personal motivation, initiative, local knowledge, and risk taking.

Fiddly jobs tended to be short-lived, irregular, infrequent, and poorly rewarded. One young woman in the sample had just worked thirty hours in the week as a care assistant in a residential home on the 'fiddle'. Together with her Income Support she had netted the grand sum of £75. The jobs were most common in subcontracted labour at steelworks, in construction, as car mechanics, taxi driving, cleaning, and bar work. Some contractors cut their costs and won tenders by offering low pay to people they knew to be in receipt of benefit and therefore able to 'afford' to work cheaply. For those involved in fiddly work the material experience of unemployment was ameliorated. The social psychological impact of unemployment was softened and it helped tie the individuals back into work culture. The majority of those on the fiddle were white working-class males in their twenties and thirties in neighbourhoods of high and long-term unemployment with tradable skills and/or a reliable record of manual work experience. The work was distributed through local, pub-centred social networks.

The picture painted by MacDonald's (1997) work is not one of a dangerous parasitical underclass. There was an incipient culture of survival, resilience, and getting by. Reorganization of work in the late twentieth century is forcing an increasingly large proportion of people to seek the means for their economic and social survival through various types of disorganized, insecure, risky, and casualized work. Jones's (1997) research does not support the assumption that homeless youth represent a distinct and dangerous underclass. On the contrary they indicate a desire to achieve conventional goals such as a home, a family, and a job.

Research on homeless youth finds that the overwhelming majority would be interested in finding paid employment (Gaetz and O'Grady 2002). The homeless do not avoid legitimate paid employment. To make ends meet they have very varied ways of making money in the informal economy. Some are paid 'under the table' for child minding or for short-term casual jobs, but this paid employment is unlikely to be taxed or regulated. They also beg (which they regard as work activity), wash car windscreens, and are involved in the sex trade (street prostitution, escort services, exotic dancing, Internet sex, and phone sex). About 18 per cent are involved in criminal activity, like selling drugs or stolen property. Those who are windscreen washers and beggers are the most likely to be without adequate shelter while ironically those involved in crime and employment are most likely to be staying in temporary hostels and shelters.

Williams and Windebank (2003) critically evaluate women's paid informal work. Following 400 interviews, in low-income neighbourhoods, they conclude that the vast majority of this work is conducted for family, friends, and neighbours for motives more associated with redistribution, to help people out and cement or forge social networks, than economic gain. The work includes cleaning, shopping, ironing, hairdressing, making and repairing clothes, and baby sitting.

Non-Work?

It can be interesting to look at the work of anthropologists and studies of identity and labour. Gypsies have consciously rejected wage labour. Judith Okley (1983) lived alongside a group of gypsies, in a trailer caravan, for about two years. She went out to work with them, calling for scrap metal, and joined a potato-picking gang. She found that the identity of gypsies served as a political weapon for non-gypsies. Gypsies could be rejected as 'counterfeit' in contrast to a mythically 'real Romany'; through this discrimination, harassment, and oppression could be legitimated. They had a huge variety of occupations but spoke of wage labour with contempt. They could not be 'trained' for 'ordinary' employment.

■ SUGGESTIONS FOR FURTHER READING

1. Brown, R. (1997) (ed.), *The Changing Shape of Work*, Basingstoke: Macmillan. This book has some interesting chapters in it including one on informal working by Robert MacDonald and another by Sheila Allen on the right to be idle.

2. Haworth, J. (1997), *Work, Leisure and Well-Being*, London: Routledge. There are sections in the introduction on unemployment and well-being and unemployment and leisure.

3. Noon, M., and Blyton, P. (2002), *The Realities of Work*, (2nd edn.), Houndmills: Palgrave. Chapter 12 on hidden work includes voluntary work.

4. Strandh, M. (2000), 'Different Exit Routes from Unemployment and their Impact on Mental Well-Being: The Role of the Economic Situation and the Predictability of the Life Course', *Work, Employment and Society*, 14/3: 459–79. This article discusses the earlier research on unemployment and effects on mental health but goes on to look at different outcomes of exiting unemployment for different groups. For example exit to permanent employment is better for mental well-being than exit to temporary or self-employment.

5. Grint, K. (1998), *The Sociology of Work* (2nd edn.), Cambridge: Polity Press. Pages 36–44 are on unemployment.

6. Beatty, C., and Fothergill, S. (2002), 'Hidden Unemployment among Men: A Case Study', *Regional Studies: The Journal of the Regional Studies Association*, 36/8: 811–23. This paper provides a detailed case study of one area—Barrow-in-Furness—where major industrial job losses have coexisted with falling claimant unemployment among men. It argues that extensive hidden unemployment levels exist, especially among men on sickness-related benefits.

7. Bjarnason, T., and Sigurdardottir, T. J. (2003), 'Psychological Distress during Unemployment and Beyond: Social Support and Material Deprivation among Youth in Six Northern European Countries', *Social Science & Medicine*, 56/5 (Mar. 2003) 973–85. Psychological distress is a serious problem among unemployed youth, and may lead to various social and psychological problems. In this study, patterns of distress among previously unemployed youth in Denmark, Finland, Iceland, Norway, Scotland and, Sweden are examined.

WEB LINKS

For figures on unemployment see **www.bls.gov/news.release/empsit.nr0.htm**

For a web site on research on unemployment and mental health in Europe see **www.umhp.org/menu.html**

QUESTIONS

1. What are the personal and social consequences of unemployment? Are the consequences different for different groups of individuals? How?

2. Unemployment is associated with a psychologically distressing experience of time. Discuss. (See Fryer and McKenna 1987 and other references found in this chapter.)

3. How is a manager's reaction to lay-off the same as or different from other workers? (See Hallier and Lyon 1996.)

4. How might unemployment figures be 'massaged' by governments?

5. What do we know about the 'underclass' (MacDonald 1997)?

■ CASE STUDY: PAYBACK FOR COMPANIES THAT ENCOURAGE STAFF TO DO VOLUNTARY WORK

Encouraging staff to do voluntary work appears to make them better, more rounded, and capable individuals and so better employees. Also employees like to think they are working for a company that cares about the local community. The Royal Bank of Scotland employs a 'head of community investment'. Staff in the bank are supported in giving to the community in a number of ways. For every pound the employee gives to a charity though a direct payroll deduction, the bank will add two. Staff who give time to causes are supported by cash grants from the bank. For example if you choose to run in a marathon to fund-raise for a charity, the bank will match what you raise to a maximum of £1,000. If you act as a treasurer to a local charity, you will be supported through a grant from the bank worth £250.

Marks & Spencer has a Corporate and Social Responsibility unit. The company places employees in secondment roles with community organizations. Secondment can encourage employees to think for themselves, listen to and get along with a broader range of people than they meet at work, and develop a different perspective. Skills of dealing with people and successful negotiation may be improved.

KPMG has a corporate social responsibility group that identifies and develops partnerships with organizations that provide education, social inclusion, and conservation; they then provide staff with the appropriate training. Each employee has the opportunity to dedicate half a working day each month to volunteer programmes. They might help primary school children with literacy or numeracy.

■ GROUP EXERCISE

A cynic might argue that the benefits to the companies, in terms of good publicity and employee and public relations, are greater than the costs. Would this be fair? How big are the benefits to the communities compared to the benefits the companies reap in profits? Is that fair in your view? How would you make an evaluation of costs and benefits?

(Case adapted from a story by Harrington 2003.)

■ REFERENCES

Archer, J., and Rhodes, V. (1987), 'Bereavement and Reactions to Job Loss: A Comparative Review', *British Journal of Social Psychology*, 26/3: 211–24.

Bakke, E. (1934), *The Unemployed Man*, New York: E. P. Dutton & Co.

Bhavnani, R. (1994), *Black Women in the Labour Market: A Research Review*, Manchester: Equal Opportunities Commission.

Bostyn, A., and Wright, D. (1987), 'Inside a Community: Values Associated with Money and Time', in Fineman, S. (ed.), *Unemployment: Personal and Social Consequences*. London: Tavistock.

Bradshaw, A., and Holmes, H. (1989), *Living on the Edge*, Tyneside: Tyneside Child Poverty Action Group.

Callender, C. (1987), 'Women Seeking Work', ch. 3 in S. Fineman (ed.), *Unemployment: Personal and Social Consequences*, London: Tavistock.

Chittenden, F., and Caley, K. (1992), 'Current Policy Issues and Recommendations', in K. Caley et al. (eds.), *Small Enterprise Development*, London: Paul Chapman Publishing.

Dicks, B. (1996), 'Coping with Pit Closure in the 1990s: Women's Perspectives', ch. 2 in *Gender and Qualitative Research*, Aldershot: Avebury.

Eisenberg, P., and Lazerfield, P. F. (1938), 'The Psychological Effects of Unemployment', *Psychological Bulletin*, 35: 358–90.

Ezzy, D. (2001), *Narrating Unemployment*, Aldershot: Ashgate.

Fryer, D. (1992), 'Psychological or Material Deprivation: Why Does Unemployment have Mental Health Consequences?', in E. McLaughlin (ed.), *Understanding Unemployment*, London: Routledge.

——and McKenna, S. (1987), 'The Laying off of Hands: Unemployment and the Experience of Time', ch. 4 in S. Fineman, *Unemployment: Personal and Social Consequences*, London: Tavistock.

Gaetz, S., and O'Grady, B. (2002), Making Money: Exploring the Economy of Young Homeless Workers', *Work, Employment and Society*, 16/3: 433–56.

Gold, M., and Fraser, J. (2002), 'Managing Self-Management: Successful Transitions to Portfolio Careers', *Work, Employment and Society*, 16/4: 579–97.

Grint, K. (1998), *The Sociology of Work: An Introduction* (2nd edn.), Cambridge: Polity.

Halfpenny, P., and Reid, M. (2002), 'Research on the Voluntary Sector: An Overview', *Policy and Politics*, 30/4: 533–50.

Hallier, J., and Lyon, P. (1996), 'Job Insecurity and Employee Commitment: Managers' Reactions to Threat and Outcomes of Redundancy Selection', *British Journal of Management*, 7/1: 107–23.

Harrington, A. (2003), 'Big Benefits of Involving Staff in Community Activities', Business and Society, *Scotland on Sunday*, 30 Mar., pp. 14–15.

Harris, M. (1990), 'Working the UK Voluntary Sector', *Work Employment and Society*, 4/1: 125–40.

Haworth, J. (1997), *Work, Leisure and Well-Being*, London: Routledge.

Jahoda, M. (1982), *Employment and Unemployment: A Social Psychological Analysis*, Cambridge: Cambridge University Press.

——(1987), 'Unemployed Men at Work', in D. M. Fryer and P. Ullah (eds.), *Unemployed People: Social and Psychological Perspectives*, Milton Keynes: Open University Press.

——Lazarsfeld, P., and Zeisel, H. (1933) and (1971), *Marienthal: The Sociography of an Unemployed Community*, London: Tavistock.

Jones, G. (1997), 'Youth Homelessness and the Underclass', in R. McDonald (ed.), *Youth, the Underclass and Social Exclusion*, London: Routledge.

Jordan, B., et al. (1992), *Trapped in Poverty? Labour-Market Decisions in Low-Income Households*, London: Routledge.

Komarovsky, M. (1940), *The Unemployed Man and his Family*, New York: Dryden press (repr. by Arno Press, 1971)

Kozlowski, S. W., Chao, G. T., Smith, E. M., and Dedlund, J. (1993), 'Organizational Downsizing: Strategies, Interventions and Research Implications', in C. L. Cooper and I. T. Robertson (eds.), *International Review of Industrial and Organizational Psychology*, London: John Wiley, pp. 263–332.

MacDonald, R. (1997), 'Informal Working, Survival Strategies and the Idea of an "Underclass"', ch. 6 in R. Brown (ed.), *The Changing Shape of Work*, Basingstoke: Macmillan.

——and Coffield, F. (1991), *Risky Business? Youth and the Enterprise Culture*, Basingstoke: Falmer Press.

McKee, L., and Bell, C. (1986), 'His Unemployment, her Problem: The Domestic and Marital Consequences of Male Unemployment', in S. Allen, A. Waton, K. Purcell, and S. Wood (eds.), *The Experience of Unemployment*, Basingstoke: Macmillan.

Miles, I. (1983), *Adaptation to Unemployment?* Occasional Paper no. 20. Brighton: Science Policy Review Unit.

Mulgan, G., and Wilkinson, H. (1995), 'Well-Being and Time', *Demos*, 5: 2–11.

Okley, J. (1983), *The Traveller-Gypsies*, Cambridge: Cambridge University Press.

Pahl, R. (1984), *Divisions of Labour*, Oxford: Blackwell.

——(1996), 'Reflections and Perspectives', in C. H. A. Verhaar et al. (eds.), *On Challenges of Unemployment in Regional Europe*, Aldershot: Avebury Press.

Schor, J. (1995), 'The New American Dream', *Demos*, 5: 30.

Solt, A., and Egan, S. (1988), *Imagine: John Lennon*, London: Bloomsbury.

Turner, R., Bostyn, A. M., and Wight, D. (1985), 'The Work Ethic in a Scottish Town with Declining Employment', in B. Roberts, R. Finnegan, and D. Gallie (eds.), *New Approaches to Economic Life*, Manchester: Manchester University Press, pp. 476–89.

Tyrell, B. (1995), 'Time of our Lives: Facts and Analysis on the 1990s', *Demos*, 5: 23–5.

Warr, P. (1987), *Work, Unemployment and Mental Health*, Oxford: Clarendon Press.

——Jackson, P., and Banks, M. (1988), 'Unemployment and Mental Health: Some British Studies', *Journal of Social Issues*, 44: 37–68.

Williams, C. C. (2002), 'Harnessing Voluntary Work: A Fourth Sector Approach', *Public Studies*, 23/3–4: 247–60.

——and Windebank, J. (2003), 'Reconceptualizing Women's Paid Informal Work: Some Lessons from Lower-Income Urban Neighbourhoods', *Gender, Work and Society*, 10/3: 281–300.

Winefield, A. (1995), 'Unemployment: Its Psychological Costs', *International Review of Industrial and Organizational Psychology*, 10: 169–212.

Yankelovich, D. (1973), 'The Meaning of Work', in R. Rosnow (ed.), *The Worker and the Job*, New York: Columbia University Press/Prentice Hall, pp. 19–47.

17 | All Change?

This chapter begins by looking at whether or not it can be claimed that new forms of work organization have emerged in the last decades. It looks at different forms of working, managing change and technology. But how much change has really happened; is it change or just continuity?

Bureaucracy was a theme that dominated organization studies throughout the 1950s and represented the most common form of organizational design. Bureaucracy is as relevant today but some would say that new forms of organization have emerged. Now there is talk of clusters, networks, and strategic alliances among organizations. Within organizations some claim that the 'new work structures' (Geary 1995) are flatter, more flexible, places where employees can feel 'empowered'. Many writers in management talk of radical change and discontinuity. They speak of a 'revolution' (Kanter 1989; Peters 1989) and a 'transformation of industrial relations (Kochan et al. 1986), 'new industrial relations' (Kelly and Kelly 1991) and the 'new workplace' (Ackers et al. 1996). For some writers (for example, Clegg 1990) the new organizational forms are sufficiently different from bureaucracy to suggest they are called 'postmodern' or 'postbureaucratic' (Hecksher and Donnellon 1994). A counter-argument is rehearsed by Hales (2002) who says that organizational restructuring often entails changes within the basic bureaucratic model rather than paradigmatic shifts to radically new organizational forms. Before looking at the counter-argument, let's look at how the new structures and arrangements are described. They appear to be arranged as new organizational forms, to be found in both the external and internal environment.

New Organizational Forms—External

Clusters are where usually small and medium-sized enterprises cooperate at a local level; each will have its own specialism in a part of a production cycle. For example, in the knitwear industry, one company may specialize in dyeing, another in sewing, and so on. Some clusters have developed as a result of state interventions, in Northern Italy (Weiss 1988) and Germany (Herrigel 1993). Technology parks are also an example of a cluster, where university research laboratories and new enterprises are grouped together in the hope of creating a synergy and new collaborations. Networks can function to exchange information, share risk, or avoid duplication of effort. Strategic alliances are mechanisms to help firms enter new markets by, for example, sharing costs of development of new technology. In order to meet the needs of these new external relations, internal arrangements within organizations may have to change.

New Organizational Forms—Internal

Postmodern organizations are said to be decentralized and networked. The internal network organization is conceived as a loose federation of informally constituted self-managing, often temporary work units of teams within which there is a fluid division of labour. Leadership has to be team based, which means that team-building, conflict-resolution, and problem-solving skills are needed. What sets the post-bureaucratic internal network organization apart from bureaucracy is the absence of a rigid division of labour, hierarchy, and rules. Openness, trust, empowerment, and commitment characterize these organizations (Clegg and Hardy 1996). Once in motion 'virtuous circles' mean collaborative, open decision making that eliminates traditional hierarchical styles of secrecy, sycophancy, and sabotage. Decisions are sought from those with the expertise and accepted.

Clegg and Hardy's view is a very positive one. Examples of six organizations who have introduced network technology, computer networks, are found in Boddy and Gunson (1996). The networked computer systems link different organizational units, such as branches or subsidiaries. They give a vivid account of the practical difficulties, failures, and successes of the process of implementation. The process of change is not necessarily easy. The next section looks at some of the history of change and critically assesses it.

Change in Organizations

Organizational change is a very popular topic in management. A search of one of the electronic databases for the period 1999–2003 creates 726 references. Change is influenced by and influences behaviour in organizations. It is a highly complex business, difficult to understand and almost impossible to deal with systematically (Bate 1995).

One of the perennial problems faced by management in organizations is how to bring about change. Changes may be needed as products change, as we saw in the case of Stitch-Co. With this often comes a change in working methods in jobs. Workers resist change in a number of ways, through grievances about new piece-rates that go with new methods, high labour turnover, low efficiency, restriction of output, and marked aggression against management (Coch and French 1947; Coch and French 1959). Managers wish to know why people resist change so strongly and what can be done to overcome this resistance.

Mainstream approaches to managing change are dominated by concerns for prescription, linearity, and the maintenance of order (Jeffcutt 1996). The literature tends, then, to be very functionalist and prescriptive.

Research on implementing change, as a process, has its roots in the early work of Kurt Lewin (1947). Lewin is probably best known for his 'force field analysis', a method for analysing the dynamics in change processes through identifying the drivers for and resistances to change. He proposed that change progressed though successive phases of unfreezing, moving, and freezing. Lewin worked in the 1930s with White and Lippitt on the experiments in leadership style we saw in the leadership chapter. He also worked with Coch and French.

Coch and French (1947, 1959) looked at resistance to change in the Harwood Manufacturing company in Virginia, USA. Both Coch and French had been employed at the Harwood Manufacturing Company where John French was the Director of Research and Labour Relations and Lester Coch was the Director of Personnel (Biographical notes, 1947). The main plant where the research was done produced pyjamas and employed mostly women. The workers were recruited from rural mountainous areas surrounding the town and usually did not have previous industrial experience. The company appeared to care about workers' views and held plant-wide votes where possible to resolve problems affecting the whole working population.

Employees worked on an individual incentive system, on piece-rates set by time study. One unit was one minute of standard work and 60 units the standard efficiency rating. If a particular operation was rated at one dozen pieces equal to 10 units, the operator would have to produce 6 dozen pieces per hour to achieve the standard rating of 60 units per hour. The skill required was quite high; in some jobs the average trainee could take 34 weeks to reach the skill level necessary to perform at 60 units per hour. The amount of pay was directly proportional to the weekly average efficiency rating achieved. If you worked at an average efficiency rating of 75 units per hour (25 per cent higher than the standard) then you would receive 25 per cent more than the base pay. There was also a minimum wage. The operators saw their daily record of production each day when the supervisor spoke to them. When an operator changed from one type of work, a transfer bonus was given to that operator who relearned at an average rate so that they suffered no loss in earnings. Despite this allowance the general attitude toward job changes was negative. Many operators were refusing to change, preferring to leave the plant. Analysis showed that 38 per cent of operators who transferred jobs recovered to standard efficiency rating, but the other 62 per cent either became chronically substandard operators or quit during the relearning period.

Coch and French saw this slow relearning after transfer to a new job as resistance to change, and primarily a motivational problem. Interviews with transferred operators revealed a common pattern of feelings and attitudes—resentment against management for transferring them, feelings of frustration, loss of hope of ever regaining the former level of production and status in the factors, and a low level of aspiration. The frustration led to high turnover and absenteeism. Operators with more difficult jobs quit more frequently than those on easy jobs. It was also found that employees were aspiring to the standard production level of 60 units per hour; those who fell below it lost status in the eyes of their fellow employees. Relatively few operators set a goal appreciably above 60.

One reason for this was group pressure. For example the production record of a presser was recorded over forty days. For the first twenty days she was working in a group who were producing at about 50 units per hour. When she exceeded the production level of the other workers she became a scapegoat for the group. Her production decreased then toward the level of the group. After twenty days the group was broken up and members transferred leaving only the scapegoat operator. Her productivity shot up to 96 units per hour in a period of four days. It is possible to conclude that the motivational forces of the group are more powerful than those from management.

Resistance to change (change due to management's wishes, not those of the workers) comes about then due to individual reaction to frustration and strong group pressure. It would seem appropriate, Coch and French reason, that a way of overcoming resistance to change would be through group methods. An experiment was designed by Coch and French (1947) to employ three degrees of participation in handling groups to be transferred. The first group involved no participation by employees in planning the changes though the change was explained to them. They were asked to stack finished shirts in boxes rather than on sheets of cardboard and were told that the change was necessary because of competitive conditions. The second group involved participation through representation of the workers in designing the changes to be made in the jobs. They were shown two identical garments, one produced the year earlier and selling for 100 per cent more than its twin one year later. The group was asked to identify the cheaper one and could not do it. This demonstration effectively shared the problem with the group and demonstrated the necessity of cost reduction. A general agreement was reached that savings could be effected by removing the 'frills' of the work from the garment without affecting the opportunity to achieve a high efficiency rating. Management then used Taylorism to set a plan for the new job—check study of the job as it was being done, eliminate the unnecessary work, train operatives in correct methods, set piece-rates on these specially trained operators, explain and train all operators in the new method so they could reach a high rate of production within a short time. The group approved this plan and operators were chosen to be specially trained. 'They displayed a co-operative and interested attitude and immediately presented many good suggestions' (1959: 240). The 'special' operators referred to the new job and piece-rates as 'our job' and 'our rate'. These special operators trained the other operators in the new job.

The third group consisted of total participation of all members of the group. The groups were smaller and all operators were chosen as 'special' operators as they were all to participate directly in the designing of new jobs and all studied by time study. In these meetings it is reported that suggestions were made in such quantity that there was difficulty in recording them all. The group approved the plans.

The no participation group improved little beyond their early efficiency ratings. Resistance developed almost immediately after the change. Marked expressions of aggression against management included conflict with the methods engineer, expressions of hostility with the supervisors, and 'deliberate restriction of production' (1959: 240) and lack of cooperation with the supervisor. Seventeen people left in the first forty days. Grievances were filed about the piece-rate but checking found it to be a little 'loose'.

The group with representation showed an unusually good relearning curve. At the end of fourteen days they averaged 61 units per hour. The attitude was 'cooperative and permissive'. They worked well with supervisors and others and there were no quits in the first 40 days.

The total participation groups recovered faster than the other groups. After a slight drop on the first day of change the efficiency ratings returned to a pre-change level and showed sustained progress to a level about 14 per cent higher than the pre-change level. They worked well with supervisors and there were no quits in those forty days.

While Coch and French (1959) do not discuss the weakness of their research design you assume that they realized that it lay in the fact that the three different groups had different jobs, and were therefore not really comparable. A second experiment was subsequently designed which used the total participation technique again with some members of the earlier no participation group, who were transferred to a new job. This group's levels of productivity too recovered rapidly to previous efficiency ratings and continued to a new high level of production. There was no aggression or turnover for nineteen days. (You are left to question why not forty?) Coch and French were able to conclude that the rate of recovery is directly proportional to the amount of participation and that the rates of turnover and aggression are inversely proportional to the amount of participation. The second experiment showed that the results depended on the experimental treatment rather than on personality factors like skill or aggression. Total participation produces a stronger influence than participation through representation. It is possible for management to greatly modify or remove group resistance to changes in methods of work and piece-rates. This can be done through group meetings in which management communicates the need for change and stimulates group participation in planning the changes. Participation results in higher production, higher morale, and better labour-management relations.

> **STOP**
>
> What emotions do you think might be associated with a change process? Here are some found at ICL (Clarke 1994). 'Don't think the company realize how frightened people are.' 'We feel very battered.' 'In the past we worked hard and played hard and people laughed. They don't anymore.'

In a very functionalist 'how to do it' management style, and building on Lewin's early work, Kotter (1995) draws lessons from watching more than 100 companies who have tried to make fundamental changes in how business is conducted in order to help cope with a new, more challenging market environment. A few change efforts have been very successful while a few have been utter failures. Most fall in between with a distinct tilt toward the lower end of the scale. The general lesson to be learned from the more successful cases is that the change process goes through a series of phases over a considerable length of time. He says there are mistakes companies make. They do not establish a great enough sense of urgency. There needs to be a frank discussion of the unpleasant facts and employees have to be motivated to act to improve the situation. About 75 per cent of the management have to be convinced that business as usual is no longer acceptable. There needs to be a powerful guiding coalition that develops a picture of the future that is relatively easy to communicate. That vision needs to be successfully communicated and obstacles to achieving it need to be removed. For example the narrow job categories can seriously undermine efforts to increase productivity. There need to be short-term improvements to keep the level of urgency up and force detailed analysis to clarify or revise visions. Changes need to be anchored into the company structure.

There are many models of change for the practitioner to follow but similarities can be drawn. Basic lessons underscore implementation models of change (Armenakis and Bedeian 1999). The change process is seen to occur in multiple steps that take a considerable amount of time to unfold. Efforts to bypass steps seldom yield a satisfactory result. Mistakes made in any step can slow implementation as well as negate hard-won progress. Managing change is not then an easy process.

It is interesting to note, as Cooke (1999) does, that Lewin demonstrated a belief in egalitarianism, democracy, and an opposition to hierarchy. Coch and French were working colleagues of Lewin's and heavily influenced by him. But Lewin and the managing change literature seem to have been located in a sociology of regulation, not radical change. The behaviour of the workforce can be changed for managerial ends. It has been argued by Cooke (1999) that there is a willingness within the change management literature to adopt a position where the social, political, and ideological circumstances in which the change is made are assumed to be uncontested and as objectively given. I would go one stage further and argue that it is only the interests of management that seem to be represented in much of the change management literature. In Lewin's, and his follower's, work there appears to be no acknowledgement of how change represents the interests of the workforce.

Technology and Change

Some believe that there is a radical transformation of society going on due to changes in technology and organization. With the widespread use of information and communication technologies comes a convergence of ways of life as we, for example, log on to exchange goods, communicate with others, and find information. In the information society or knowledge economy the dominant form of work becomes information and knowledge based (Wajcman 2002). In the networked society the compression of space and time made possible by new communication technology alters the scope and speed of decisions. Organizations can decentralize and disperse. High-level decision making remains in world cities so that lower-level operations linked to the centre by communication networks can take place virtually anywhere (Castells 1996). The impression is that information and communication technology is the most important cause of social change. But as Wajcman (2002) notes this stance verges on technological determinism—where technology is seen as the driver. This argument is too simplistic as technological change is shaped by the social circumstances in which it takes place. Technology is not simply the product of rational technical imperatives; a particular technology will not triumph simply because it is the best.

We need to look at the social decisions behind technological development, for example why a technological change was seen to be compelling, when the decision making could have been challenged, and what counts as superior. Options are available. Technology is a sociotechnical product. A technological system is never merely technical. It is organizational, economic, and political elements. For example history tells us that once there was a choice between an electric and a gas refrigerator, both equally effective. General Electric had the financial resources to develop the electric model while the manufacturers of gas refrigerators lacked the resources to develop and market their machine (Cowen 1983). History also tells us that in the development of automatically controlled machine tools two options existed—the record playback where the machine replicated the manual operations of a skilled machinist or numerical control in which tool movements were controlled by a mathematical program produced by a technician. The machine tool suppliers, technologists, and managers in aerospace companies deliberately suppressed record playback in favour of numerical control in order to reduce their reliance on the unionized craft workers. However management found it needed to retain skilled machinists to operate new machines effectively, so the shift of power from the shop floor was not realized (Noble 1984).

How technology is used is crucial to our understanding of consequences. When thinking about information technology it is interesting to note that it appears to have two faces. On the one, for example, the Internet is seen as an environment of individual freedom, consumer convenience, shared knowledge, virtual community, and free markets. On the other, it can represent Orwellian control, computer-enabled surveillance, a world inhabited by pornographers, hackers, unscrupulous fraudsters, and paedophiles. Can it present two faces at the same time. Does it represent change or continuity?

Change or Continuity?

There are some writers who would say that researchers and theorists have paid more attention to change than to continuity. Roy Jacques, for example, notes that many of the characteristics of 'post industrial management' proposed for the 1990s were actually observed and reported sixty or more years ago. 'It appears to be a condition of modernity for every generation to believe it is in the midst of revolutionary change' (Jacques 1996: 18–19). In a different vein Blyton and Turnbull (1994), in discussing employee relations, say that we should consider both continuity and change, thinking of time as moving along a 'spiral' (Burrell 1992). 'Nothing changes yet everything is different: as we twist around the spiral of capitalist economic development we experience progression and return, never a return to exactly the same point but always to a point that is familiar' (Blyton and Turnbull 1994: 298). Legge (1995) would argue that all periods are characterized by both change and continuity. One of the new developments is e-business.

E–business

E-business is a combination of technologies, applications, processes, business strategies, and practices necessary to do business electronically (Taylor and Berg 1995). Some (for example Tapscott 1995) believe that e-business marks the beginning of a significant revolution as we move from using the computer as a tool for information to using it as a tool for communications. Others believe it may be just a management fad (McCalman and Anderson 2002). Whether fad or not, e-business has placed significant attention on the concept of the non-physical workplace. However OB and HRM specialists have pointed out that e-business still needs organizational form and this needs to be carefully considered. Key organizational behaviours come to the fore in a teleworking environment (Sparrow 2000). Design issues include how to manage knowledge and labour and the interaction between people in numerous workplaces.

E-business technologies like the Internet have had a significant effect on business to consumer trading but there appears to be an even bigger potential for business-to-business transactions (McCalman and Anderson 2002). It is expected that e-business will enhance the concept of teamworking as the technology demands multi-skilled teamworking. New forms of working are required—forms that are more flexible, in both work methods and structure.

New Organizations?

There have been other management critics who have cast doubt on the extent and true character of postmodern or network organizations (Alvesson 1995; Ezzamel et al. 1994; Thompson and O'Connell Davidson 1995; Warhurst and Thompson 1998; Whittington and Mayer 2000). It is argued that there are few examples of different organizational forms to be found and there are only a few recurring and celebrated cases. Indeed managers are guilty of using misleading rhetoric in their claims about the adoption of new organizational forms. Many forms of organizational change have entailed an extension or intensification of, rather than a departure from, bureaucratic control.

Hales (2002) suggests that organizational change may be far less radical than is claimed and may occur within bureaucratic forms. His research in organizations that claimed to have moved away from bureaucracy and towards decentralized or empowered organizations where hierarchy and rules are banished proved that the claims were illusory. Neither the forms of organization nor the work that managers did was all that 'new'. The units were firmly located within a system of hierarchical control. Responsibility for unit performance continued to be vested in individual managers who were accountable to more senior managers, and were judged on the basis of conformance with centrally imposed rules about appropriate levels of performance. Only one or two layers of management had been reduced. As a result the organizations were a little more bureaucracy 'lite', but as, if not more, consistent with the ethos of bureaucratic control. In addition, senior managers were very reluctant to relinquish control. Other researchers have noted that public sector organizations have actually become more bureaucratic as control by professionals has given way to tighter managerial control (Warhurst and Thompson 1998). This has often been done in response to external audit (Power 1997).

But what about the fundamental shifts in organization and management of manufacturing operations that have been witnessed, like autonomous group working, and 'flexible' and 'lean' production (Piore and Sabel 1984; Womack et al. 1990) just-in-time (JIT),

---

AN EXAMPLE OF CHANGE: SONY AND SPEED

Sony has been under great pressure to improve its ability to respond flexibly and speedily to market demand. The product has to be adjusted to market demand and the time taken to get the product to the consumer needs to be reduced. A step towards this goal for Sony was the introduction of cell-based manufacturing in the production of camcorders; lots of small groups or cells were introduced. Mass production factory lines are difficult to stop once started but cell-based manufacturing makes it possible to shift quickly for making one model of camcorder (there are 200–300 models of camcorder) to another which is selling better (Nakamoto 2003). How much change does this represent?

---

quality circles, Total Quality Management (TQM), and the Japanese model of manufacturing management?

Autonomous Work Groups

In autonomous work groups there is a team of workers who organize their own labour and how that is deployed; they enjoy discretion over work methods and time (Buchanan 1994: 204). In the Swedish model of autonomous group working, employees have enjoyed sufficient freedom to influence such matters as goal formation, performance monitoring, production methods, labour allocation, and choice of group leaders (Ramsay 1992). This system has allowed group control over work pace through the presence of buffers and the absence of supervision (Berggren 1993; Thompson and Sederblad 1994).

Quality Circles

Quality circles or problem-solving groups normally consist of small groups of employees from the same work area who meet together regularly and voluntarily. Their chair may be a supervisor, a 'facilitator', or another employee; they may have received training in statistical analysis and group dynamics. As well as quality issues, groups can deal with work flow, productivity, safety, and other problems. The concept was originally developed in the USA but quality circles were first widely adopted in Japan (Cole 1989). Quality circles are more common in Japan than the USA and more common in the USA than Britain (Heller et al. 1998). Quality circles can formalize the process of workplace innovation. Employees can frequently think of ways of making their job more efficient and problem-solving teams can encourage them to reveal their innovations. Most employees can see good reasons to want to improve the quality of work from a company. However in some circumstances quality circle meetings may be little more than managerial pep talks, with little opportunity for employee input. Alternatively, employees can find their ideas are ignored (Wilson 1989). They may feel they deserve some reward for their participation. Sometimes, however, quality circles evolve into work teams or TQM.

Total Quality Management

Total Quality Management goes beyond quality circles in that it is usually an organization-wide effort involving teams of employees and managers. TQM focuses on satisfying the needs of customers who are both internal and external to the company. TQM teams typically follow a procedure whereby they start by tracking the number and timing of problems, then analyse the source of the error, generate alternative solutions, and evaluate one solution, implement it, and check it. Thus it can contribute to organizational learning and increase participation. On the other hand, in practice TQM often permits little real participation (Tuckerman 1994).

Japan: The Post-Fordist Future?

Japanese management practices have evoked a good deal of interest in the last two decades. During the 1960s and 1970s there was a dramatic increase in Japanese manufacturing exports. In 1980 Ford Europe began an 'After Japan' programme, following a fact-finding visit to Japan, to tighten labour discipline, increase output, and enhance worker flexibility at Ford plants. In the 1980s attention shifted to the role of Japanese firms in Europe and North America as auto, auto components, and electrical manufacturing plants were set up.

It was argued that innovative and competitive Japanese car manufacturers had developed a distinctive form of production organization or 'lean production' (Womack et al. 1990). This was characterized by minimization of stocks and work in progress by 'just-in-time' (JIT) production (producing and delivering finished goods just in time to be sold, sub-assemblies just in time to be assembled, and so on) and by an emphasis on the continuous improvement of production procedures. This was the dominant form of production used by vehicle producers in Japan (particularly Toyota) and the methods were apparently transferable to locations outside Japan. Writers such as Schonberger (1982, 1986) popularized the approach to the management of stocks and material flow. The fundamental doctrine of the Toyota production system is the elimination of waste (Ohno 1988). Under the JIT system production is driven by market requirements as information regarding demand pulls production through the processes. In contrast, the traditional mass production model pushes production scheduling as output plans are developed on the basis of historic information and production is decoupled from demand. The intention with JIT is to reduce costs through reducing stock, labour, and time. This in turn reduces the amount of 'buffering' between processes. TQM was developed in the USA but implemented in Japan. Here the focus is on quality design and conformance to specification, using statistical process control to monitor quality and control standards. It can also involve employees with customer responsiveness and service. Kenney and Florida (1993) too identified the leading Japanese firms as the innovators of a new model of organization of work and production they called 'innovation-mediated production', a symbiosis between research and development and continuous improvement in the production process aided by the knowledge and intelligence of all employees.

Few people have not heard of the four 'sacred treasures' of Japanese management: lifetime employment (where employees are hired fresh out of education on a lifetime basis), seniority-based wage systems and promotions (provided according to seniority as the employee accumulates skills and experience with the company), consensus decision making, and enterprise unions (all the clerks, engineers, and labourers of a company join together, facilitating labour/management compromises). It has been argued, for example, that offering lifetime employment secures a loyal and secure workforce in Japan. The organization is viewed as a collectivity to which employees belong; there is considerable emphasis on interdependence, shared concerns, and mutual help. Once employees have joined an organization they are guaranteed continuing employment; in turn the employees make a lifelong commitment to the organization which they see as an extension of their family.

How real was this Japanese dream? How easy would it be to transfer Japanese management practices into British organizations? These were the questions raised by researchers in the late 1980s. Ackroyd et al. (1988) believed that there were major constraints on the implementation of Japanese forms of work organization and employment relations in British-based organizations, as Britain and Japan had different economic and social structures with contrasting employment systems, labour markets, different organization of finance, and investment policies.

Oliver and Wilkinson (1992) also emphasized how the new production methods required very specific social conditions, of the sort provided by Japanese social structures, for them to work. They found that the success of major Japanese corporations could not be readily assigned to a specific set of practices, like manufacturing methods or personnel policies. What appeared to be crucial was the goodness of fit between a set of business strategies and a set of wider supporting conditions. They studied British companies who tried to emulate Japanese practices. They concluded that the companies faced substantial obstacles. The problems were related to the heightened dependencies of companies on their employees, suppliers, markets, and key political and economic agencies. In the case of suppliers, they must be trusted to deliver goods of the right quality, in the right quantity, and 'just in time'. Buyers have to nurture long-term relations with their suppliers and exert influence over their operations. The supplier should find the buyers constantly 'on the doorstep', be dependent on the customer financially, and be under intense pressure to deliver the goods.

In terms of employees, many Japanese-style manufacturing practices require willing cooperation, not merely compliance, on the part of a workforce. For example they require a willingness to perform a range of tasks, a commitment to engage in activities of continuous improvement, and a preparedness to do what is required to satisfy both internal and external customers. For the workforce this means, on the one hand, that work is likely to be more varied and higher in involvement and 'ownership'. On the other hand, accountability and responsibility are increased, performance is more closely monitored, and the visibility of failings (and successes) heightened. Some Japanese companies reinforce this visibility through public displays of group or individual output and quality levels. No wonder there are mixed opinions on these methods. Advocates claim that the Japanese style of work organization is humanistic, while the critics see it as being manipulative and coercive.

There are some other interesting 'realities' about Japanese human resource strategies. The practice of lifelong employment is for an elite, favoured group of employees. It applies almost exclusively to regular, male employees and is not as widespread as was once believed. It has been estimated that no more than 30 per cent of the Japanese labour force work for the same company throughout their career (Smith and Misumi 1994) and rather more Americans than Japanese continue to work for their first employer. One reason that there is so little lifetime employment is that there is widespread subcontracting (for example, 70 per cent of a Nissan car is produced by subcontractors) and subcontracting workers do not enjoy job security in time of cutbacks. 'Rings of defence' are built around the core workers and their activities. Employees who find themselves in the outer rings, peripheral workers employed on temporary contract or employees of firms subcontracted to the main subcontractors, are likely to have a rather different experience of work (Oliver and Wilkinson 1992). Close attention is given to hiring new permanent employees who will fit into the company culture. Careful screening ensures that candidates likely to endorse the company's values and philosophy are selected. Private investigators are routinely used to check a candidate's background, families, neighbours, and friends (Oliver and Wilkinson 1992).

The adult Japanese male identifies with the immediate work group of peers and his superior; this is very intense (Dore 1973). Comparative studies reveal that Japanese employees see work as more central to their lives than employees in ten other countries (Meaning of Working 1987). They also spend substantial time eating and drinking with their workmates after work. Employees are also more likely to participate in company-organized sports, holidays, and outings. Companies in Japan spend twice as much on social and recreational facilities for their employees than US companies (Smith and Misumi 1994). You are obliged to develop and maintain harmonious relations with your work colleagues. National service through industry, fairness, harmony and cooperation, struggle for betterment, courtesy and humility, adjustment and assimilation, and gratitude are the values employees should adopt. New recruits share overall responsibility for their team's work; commitment to the company is fostered through extensive training programmes for new recruits.

The society is not only collective but has a hierarchical status system, the bases being education, age, gender, and the firm you work for. Authority relations are often paternalistic and highly traditional and deferential. Prospects for promotion are strongly dependent upon a senior mentor within the company. (A very detailed study of Japanese management practices can be found in Whitehill 1991.) As Morgan (1986: 116) has noted, some of the more distasteful aspects of work experience have been ignored in many accounts of Japanese organization. The emphasis has been on how Japanese workers arrive at work early or stay late to find ways of improving efficiency through working in quality circles or how the dedicated Honda workman straightens the windshield wiper blade on all Honda cars he passes on his way home in the evening. Less attention is given to the disgruntled workers like Satoshi Kamata (1982) who describes how he lived in a camp rigidly policed by company guards. There were constant pressures to achieve demanding work targets and fulfil the requirements of company values and norms. Day-to-day life was gruelling.

Distasteful Work?

'Faced with the choice of going on the dole or working like the Japanese, the men so far would prefer the dole. It's as simple as that' (Turnbull 1988: 44).Williams et al. (1994) describe the more than intense nature of work in a car plant press shop in Japan. The shift runs for nine hours, including one hour of unpaid meal breaks. After nine hours on shift, the workers are required to work overtime as necessary; the overtime requirement is only put up on a board halfway through the shift. Two hours of overtime are routinely required so an eleven-hour day is the expected norm. The scheduled meal breaks are often taken up with company business like quality circle meetings. Workers have been obliged to work six days a week. Their one day off may not be completely free as loyal workers are expected to join in company sports and social events. Car plant managers decided the plant should work over weekends because the local electricity board charged a lower tariff at weekends; the result was that workers could not take their day off over the weekend. How would you feel about working for a Japanese company?

The apparent harmony in Japanese society may be overstated (Wagatsuma 1982). There is clear evidence of conflict within and between organizations. The harmony of the work group may be being sustained by a sense of obligation; this obligation may be relaxed when employees are having a few drinks together. There is also evidence to suggest that Japanese workers are less satisfied than Western workers. Many Japanese workers work extremely long hours for what they regard as inadequate pay (Smith and Misumi 1994). When viewed in the Western cultural and socio-political context, many aspects of Japanese business and management systems are socially and politically unacceptable and even illegal (Sethi et al. 1984). The views of 100 British executives who had experience of working for Japanese companies is explored in depth by Jones (1991), who also is able to question many of the beliefs about Japanese companies, especially those fuelled by articles in the popular press.

Disciplined Selves?

Kondo (1990) gives a vivid account of everyday life on the shop floor of a small family-owned sweet factory in Tokyo, where she worked for a year. At one stage in her story she is sent to an ethics school with two other employees. At this school they were organized in groups or squads. Each squad slept in the same room, ate at the same table, exercised together, and sat together in class. The position of squad leader changed daily, giving each the opportunity to be leader and share responsibility.

EXAMPLE OF WORKING IN A JAPANESE COMPANY

Here is a brief description of Kondo's (1990) activities before breakfast each day. The day started at 5 a.m. with a call to rise. Waking up late was regarded as unnatural, indulgent, selfish, slovenly. Cleaning came next and was a standard ingredient of spiritual education. Each cleaning task was to be performed with a glad heart. The counsellors would lead the group in chants of 'Fight!' as they hosed down the toilets, emptied the tins of sanitary napkins, and scrubbed the floors. After cleaning they jogged to the statue of the founder and after a rousing shout of 'Good Morning' would be briefly lectured on an inspirational theme. A tape recorder played the national anthem as the flags were raised. They then had shouting practice where they were required to scream greetings at the tops of their voices or shout 'I am the sun of x company. I will make x company number one in Japan.' Every word was rewarded by shouts of encouragement from the others and applause. The idea was to inculcate receptiveness and a willingness to greet and appreciate others and eliminate resistance toward responding positively towards authority. They ran for at least 2.5 kilometres as a rehearsal for the 7.5 kilometre run scheduled for the end of the programme. Shouting and chanting was required during running. Speed was not the issue; it was important to finish and not give up. Neglect of the body was seen as lack of appreciation of the gift of life. Ritual ablution ceremonies with cold water, in order to give thanks to water, followed. The morning classes were for reciting in unison phrases like 'Hardship is the gateway to happiness' and 'Other people are our mirrors'. Students would be given instructions on how to bow at the proper angle, have a pleasant facial expression, and use the appropriate language level. Read the account yourself and answer the question: how successful was the ethics centre in crafting disciplined selves?

Graham (1994) was a participant observer for six months in a Japanese car plant in the USA. She documents both the compliance and resistance to management's technical and social control strategies. Managers had attempted to gain compliance through lengthy pre-employment and selection procedures, careful handling of training of new recruits, the team concept of working, the philosophy of continuous improvement, the shaping of shop-floor culture, and technical pacing and discipline of computerized assembly lines coupled with JIT. They used techniques like the company song, celebrations, and team meetings. But there was worker resistance, which emerged as sabotage when the workers surreptitiously stopped the assembly line. They protested and refused to participate in company rituals and confronted management in team and departmental meetings. Workers were seldom allowed to make even inconsequential decisions on their own. The company was not totally successful in instituting a spirit of cooperation and a culture of egalitarianism.

More recently Delbridge (1998) reports his findings from two periods of study as a participant observer working on the shop-floor in a European-owned automotive components supplier and a Japanese-owned consumer electronics plant. The European company was seeking to introduce cellular manufacturing, TQM, JIT inventory control, and teamworking during the time of his study while the Japanese company had many characteristics of lean production and has been cited as an exemplar of 'world class manufacturing'. He found that management at the Japanese-owned company had successfully marginalized the effects of uncertainty and shop-floor relations were clearly and explicitly founded upon a 'negotiated order' between management and labour. Workers faced very strict coercive controls and felt they had to comply. There was no heightened sense of commitment from the workforce; they remained opposed to many of management's goals and mistrustful of the rhetoric of teamworking and mutuality. At the European-owned plant the managers relied on informally negotiated solutions to problems, due to the uncertainty inherent at the plant. Workers at both plants were sceptical of management intentions and clearly favoured an oppositional stance, so needed the protection of trade unions (see also Knights and McCabe 1998; Wilkinson et al. 1997, 1998).

An example of a company that has 'creatively' imitated the Japanese model is the car company Fiat in Italy. The production system was reorganized and initiatives launched aimed at enhancing the involvement of the workforce (Bonazzi 1998). Traditional bureaucratic management, with its rigid division of responsibility and unwieldy linkages between various bodies, was abandoned. The new system encouraged supervisors to assume managerial responsibilities in order to ensure maximum reactivity as and when process and product anomalies arose. Fiat appears to have taken some elements of the Japanese methods and used them for their own benefit.

There are then some clear lessons to draw from the research on Japanese manufacturing methods. The main conclusion is that we need to be sceptical about claims of the unitarist management writers who present Japanese management practices only in a positive light and paint organizations as unitarist, where workers and managers simply work happily together to fulfil mutual goals. There need to be serious questions asked about the ease with which Japanese management practices can be appropriated and used in both Japanese and other organizations.

■ SUGGESTIONS FOR FURTHER READING

1. Elger, T., and Smith, C. (1994), *Global Japanization? The Transnational Transformation of the Labour Process*, London: Routledge. This book brings together a collection of articles exploring the impact of Japanese manufacturing investment and the adoption of Japanese working practices.

2. Jones, S. (1991), *Working for the Japanese: Myths and Realities, British Perceptions*, Basingstoke: Macmillan. This book is based on research with over 100 British executives with Japanese companies.

3. Carnell, C. A. (1999), *Managing Change in Organizations* (3rd edn.), Harlow: Pearson. This is a standard text in the managing change literature. It makes the links between learning, leadership, and change.

4. Mabey, C., and Mayon-White, B. (1993), (eds.), *Managing Change* (2nd edn.), London: Paul Chapman. This edited book contains some interesting chapters that question for example why change programmes do not produce change. There are also linkages made between change and middle management, teams, and power.

5. Buchanan, D., and Badham, R. (1999), *Power, Politics and Organizational Change*, London: Sage. This book focuses on the shaping role of political behaviour in situations of organizational change.

6. Itzin, C., and Newman, J. (1995), *Gender, Culture and Organizational Change: Putting Theory into Practice*, London: Routledge. A study representing a decade of experience of change and the public sector.

7. Dawson, P. (2002), *Understanding Organizational Change: The Contemporary Experience of People at Work*, London: Sage. This is a new book on change.

■ WEB LINKS

For a description of research on working for a Japanese company see **www.thejapanpage.com/ html/book_directory/Detailed/327.shtml**

Or **www.gate39.com/business/jpncompany.aspx** for a description of the daily routine in a Japanese company.

www.change-management.com/ provides a list of books on managing change, mainly 'how to do it' books.

■ QUESTIONS

1. Japanese managers transfer as little or as much as they wish of their management practices to the new environment (Dedoussis and Littler 1994). How much evidence is there to suggest this is the case? (See Delbridge 1998: ch. 10, for sources.)

2. To its advocates, TQM is unequivocally good. To some management researchers, it produces some bad outcomes. What are the realities? See Wilkinson et al. 1997, 1998; Knights and McCabe 1998; and related sources.

3. What are the similarities and differences between Taylor's, the Hawthorne study's, and Coch and French's findings on production norms?

4. How would you design a study of restriction of output?

5. What methods have you witnessed for trying to bring about change in organizations. Was group participation used? If not, why not?

■ CLASS EXERCISE

Taking the sources cited here, weigh and balance the pros and cons, from the workforce point of view, of working under Japanese methods.

■ REFERENCES

Ackers, P., Smith, C., and Smith, P. (1996), (eds.), *The New Workplace and Trade Unionism*, London: Routledge.

Ackroyd, S., Burrell, G., Hughes, M., and Whitacker, A. (1988), 'The Japanization of British Industry?', *Industrial Relations Journal*, 19/1: 11–23.

Alvesson, M. (1995), 'The Meaning and Meaningless of Postmodernism: Some Ironic Remarks', *Organizational Studies*, 16/6: 1047–75.

Armenakis, A. A., and Bedeian, A. G. (1999), 'Organizational Change: A Review of Theory and Research in the 1990s', *Journal of Management*, 25/3: 293–315.

Bate, P. (1995), *Strategies for Cultural Change*, Oxford: Butterworth Heinemann.

Berggren, C. (1993), *The Volvo Experience: Alternatives to Lean Production in the Swedish Auto Industry*, London: Macmillan.

Biographical notes on Coch and French in *Human Relations*, 1/4: 512–32.

Blyton, P., and Turnbull, P. (1994), *The Dynamics of Employee Relations*, London: Macmillan.

Boddy, D., and Gunson, N. (1996), *Organizations in the Network Age*, London: Routledge.

Bonazzi, G. (1998), 'Between Shock Absorption and Continuous Improvement: Supervisors and Technicians in a Fiat "Integrated Factory"', *Work, Employment and Society*, 12/2: 219–43.

Buchanan, D. (1994), 'Cellular Manufacture and the Role of Teams', in J. Storey (ed.), *New Wave Manufacturing Strategies*, Liverpool: Paul Chapman.

Burrell, G. (1992), 'Back to the Future: Time and Organization', in M. Reed and M. Hughes (eds.), *Rethinking Organization*, London: Sage, pp. 165–83.

Castells, M. (1996), *The Rise of the Network Society*, Oxford: Blackwell.

Clarke, L. (1994), *The Essence of Change*, Hemel Hempstead: Prentice Hall.

Clegg, S. R. (1990), *Modern Organizations: Organizational Studies in the Post-modern World*, London: Sage.

——and Hardy, C. (1996), 'Organizations, Organization and Organizing', Introduction to S. R. Clegg, C. Hardy, and W. R. Nord (eds.), *Handbook of Organization Studies*, London: Sage.

Coch, L., and French, J. R. (1947), 'Overcoming Resistance to Change', *Human Relations*, 1/4: 512–32.

————(1959), 'Overcoming Resistance to Change', in E. Maccoby, T. M. Newcomb, and E. L. Hartley (eds.), *Readings in Social Psychology* (3rd edn.), London: Methuen, pp. 233–50.

Cole, R. (1989), *Strategies for Learning: Small Group Activities. America, Japan and Sweden*, Berkeley, Calif.: University of California Press.

Cooke, B. (1999), 'Writing the Left out of Management Theory: The Historiography of the Management of Change', *Organization*, 6/1: 81–105.

Cowen, R. S. (1983), *More Work for Mother: The Ironies of Household Technology From the Open Hearth to the Microwave*, New York: Basic Books.

Dedoussis, V., and Littler, C. (1994), 'Understanding the Transfer of Japanese Management Practices: The Australian Case', in T. Elger and C. Smith (eds.), *Global Japanization? The Transnational Transformation of the Labour Process*, London: Routledge, pp. 175–95.

Delbridge, R. (1998), *Life on the Line in Contemporary Manufacturing: The Workplace Experience of Lean Production and the 'Japanese' Model*, Oxford: Oxford University Press.

Dore, R. P. (1973), *British Factory, Japanese Factory*, London: Allen & Unwin.

Ezzamel, M., Lilley, S., and Willmott, H. (1994), 'The "New Organization" and the "New Managerial Work"', *European Management Journal*, 12/4: 454–61.

Geary, J. (1995), 'Work Practices: The Structure of Work', in P. Edwards (ed.), *Industrial Relations: Theory and Practice in Britain*, Oxford: Blackwell, pp. 368–96.

Graham, L. (1994), 'How Does the Japanese Model Transfer to the United States: A View from the Line', ch. 4 in T. Elger and C. Smith (eds.), *Global Japanization? The Transnational Transformation of the Labour Process*, London: Routledge.

Hales, C. (2002), 'Bureaucracy-lite and Continuities in Managerial Work', *British Journal of Management*, 13: 51–66.

Hecksher, C., and Donnellon, A. (1994), *The Post Bureaucratic Organization: New Perspectives on Organizational Change*, Thousand Oaks, Calif.: Sage.

Heller, F., Pusic, E., Strauss, G., and Wilpert, B. (1998), *Organizational Participation: Myth and Reality*, Oxford: Oxford University Press.

Herrigel, G. B. (1993), 'Power and the Redefinition of Industrial Districts: The Case of Baden-Wurttemberg', in G. Graber (ed.), *The Embedded Firm: On the Socioeconomics of Industrial Networks*, London: Routledge, pp. 227–51.

Jacques, R. (1996), *Manufacturing the Employee: Management Knowledge from the Nineteenth to Twenty-First Centuries*, London: Sage.

Jeffcutt, P. (1996), 'Between Managers and the Managed: The Process of Organizational Transition', ch. 11 in S. Linstead, R. Grafton Small, and P. Jeffcutt (eds.), *Understanding Management*, London: Sage.

Jones, S. (1991), *Working for the Japanese: Myths and Realities, British Perceptions*, Basingstoke: Macmillan.

Kamata, S. (1982), *Japan in the Passing Lane*, New York: Pantheon.

Kanter, R. (1989), 'The New Managerial Work', *Harvard Business Review*, 67/6: 85–92.

Kenney, M., and Florida, R. (1993), *Beyond Mass Production: The Japanese System and its Transfer to the US*, Oxford: Oxford University Press.

Kelly, J., and Kelly, C. (1991), ' "Them and Us": Social Psychology and "The New Industrial Relations" ', *British Journal of Industrial Relations*, 29/1: 25–48.

Knights, D., and McCabe, D. (1998), 'Dreams and Designs on Strategy: A Critical Analysis of TQM and Management Control', *Work, Employment and Society*, 12/3: 433–56.

Kochan, T., Katz, H., and McKersie, R. (1986), *The Transformation of American Industrial Relations*, New York: Basic Books.

Kondo, D. K. (1990), *Crafting Selves: Power, Gender and Discourses of Identity in a Japanese Workplace*, Chicago: University of Chicago Press.

Kotter, J. P. (1995), 'Leading Change: Why Transformation Efforts Fail', *Harvard Business Review*, (Mar.–Apr.), 59–67.

Legge, K. (1995), *Human Resource Management: Rhetorics and Realities* London: Macmillan.

Lewin, K. (1947), 'Frontiers in Group Dynamics', *Human Relations*, 1: 5–41.

McCalman, J., and Anderson, C. (2002), 'Designing Oases for Corporate Nomads: The Impact of Facilities Management on Work Design and the Flexible Workforce', ch. 2 in P. Jackson and R. Suomi (eds.), *eBusiness and Workplace Redesign*, London: Routledge.

Meaning of Working, International Research Team (1987), *The Meaning of Working*, London: Academic Press.

Morgan, G. (1986), *Images of Organization*, London: Sage.

Nakamoto, Michoto (2003), 'A Speedier Route from Order to Camcorder', *Financial Times*, 12 Feb., p. 11.

Noble, D. F. (1984), *Forces of Production: A Social History of Industrial Automation*, New York: Knopf.

Ohno, T. (1988), *Just-In-Time: For Today and Tomorrow*, Cambridge, Mass.: Productivity Press.

Oliver, N., and Wilkinson, B. (1992), *The Japanization of British Industry*, Oxford: Basil Blackwell (originally published in 1988).

Peters, T. (1989), *Thriving on Chaos: Handbook for a Management Revolution*, New York: Harper & Row.

Piore, M., and Sabel, C. (1984), *The Second Industrial Divide*, New York: Basic Books.

Power, M. (1997), *The Audit Society: Rituals of Verification*, Oxford: Oxford University Press.

Ramsay, H. (1992), 'Swedish and Japanese Work Methods: Comparisons and Contrasts', *European Participation Monitor*, 3: 37–40.

Schonberger, R. (1982), *Japanese Manufacturing Techniques: Nine Hidden Lessons in Simplicity*, New York: Free Press.

——(1986), *World Class Manufacturing: The Lesson of Simplicity Applied*, New York: Free Press.

Sethi, S. P., Namiki, N., and Swanson, C. L. (1984), *The False Promise of the Japanese Miracle: Illusions and Realities of the Japanese Management System*, London: Pitman.

Smith, P. B., and Misumi, J. (1994), 'Japanese Management: A Sun Rising in the West?', ch. 4 in C. L. Cooper and I. T. Robertson (eds.), *Key Reviews in Managerial Psychology, Concepts and Research for Practice*, Chichester: John Wiley.

Sparrow, P. R. (2000), 'New Employee Behaviours, Work Design and Forms of Work Organization: What is in Store for the Future of Work?', *Journal of Managerial Psychology*, 15: 3.

Tapscott, D. (1995), *The Digital Economy: Promise and Peril in the Age of Networked Intelligence*, London: McGraw Hill.

Taylor, D., and Berg, T. (1995), 'The Business Value of Electronic Commerce', *Strategic Analysis Report*, Stanford, Conn.: Gartner Group.

Thompson, P., and O'Connell Davidson, J. (1995), 'The Continuity of Discontinuity: Managerial Rhetoric in Turbulent Times', *Personnel Review*, 24/4: 17–33.

——and Sederblad, P. (1994), 'The Swedish Model of Work Organization in Transition', in T. Elger and C. Smith (eds.), *Global Japanization? The Transformation of the Labor Process*, London: Routledge.

Tuckerman, A. (1994), 'The Yellow Brick Road: TQM and the Restructuring of Organizational Culture', *Organization Studies*, 15: 727–51.

Turnbull, P. (1988), 'The Limits to Japanization: Just-in-Time, Labour Relations and the UK Automotive Industry', *New Technology, Work and Employment*, 3/1: 7–20.

Wagatsuma, H. (1982), 'Internationalization of the Japanese: Group Model Reconsidered', in H. Mannari and H. Befu (eds.), *The Challenge of Japan's Internationalization: Organizations and Culture*, Tokyo: Kodansha, pp. 298–308.

Wajcman, J. (2002), 'Addressing Technological Change: The Challenge to Social Theory', *Current Sociology*, 50/3: 347–63.

Warhurst, C. and Thompson, P. (1998), 'Hands, Hearts and Minds: Changing Work and Workers at the End of the Century', in P. Thompson and C. Warhurst (eds.), *Workplaces of the Future*, Basingstoke: Macmillan pp. 1–24.

Weiss, L. (1988), *Creating Capitalism: The State and Small Business since 1945*, Oxford: Blackwell.

Whitehill, A. M. (1991), *Japanese Management: Tradition and Transition*, London: Routledge.

Whittington, R., and Mayer, M. (2000), *The European Corporation: Strategy, Structure and Social Science*, Oxford: Oxford University Press.

Wilkinson, A., Godfrey, G., and Marchington, M. (1997), 'Bouquets, Brickbats and Blinkers: Total Quality Management and Employee Involvement in Practice', *Organization Studies*, 18/5: 799–819.

——Redman, T., Snape, E., and Marchington, M. (1998), *Managing with Total Quality Management: Theory and Practice*, London: Macmillan Business.

Williams, K., Mitsui, I., and Haslam, C. (1994), 'How Far From Japan? A Case Study of Japanese Press Shop Practice and Management Calculation', ch. 2 in T. Elger and C. Smith (eds.), *Global Japanization? The Transnational Transformation of the Labour Process*, London: Routledge.

Wilson, F. M. (1989), 'Productive Efficiency and the Employment Relationship', *Employee Relations*, 11/1: 27–32.

Womack, J., Jones, D., and Roos, D. (1990), *The Machine that Changed the World*, New York: Rawson Associates.

18 Alternative Organizations

This book has discussed many of the problems associated with work design and how those problems could be overcome. It has looked at alienation, lack of control, boredom, theft, sabotage, and other organizational ills. Cooperatives could help solve a lot of the organizational ills discussed so far. They can potentially reduce levels of industrial conflict and enhance productivity by aligning the interests of workers with those of their firm. In principle cooperatives offer a model of a more humane and productive alternative to bureaucratic organization (Rothschild-Whitt 1982). Some may claim (e.g. Mellor et al. 1988) that, in cooperatives, the dispossessed seek to control the very existence of work itself. Ultimately it is a desire to change the whole basis of control and radically shift it towards those who have so little.

Cooperatives

A cooperative is a business that is wholly or substantially owned and controlled by those who work in it; it is run for their mutual benefit. Control is exercised on the basis of one person, one vote; membership is open as far as possible to all workers. Italy has the largest cooperative sector of any European country. Earle (1986) records that, following Mussolini's fall, 9,000 cooperatives were set up between 1944 and 1946, and the total reached 23,000 in 1949. Cooperation was also well established in France. Government legislative and financial support for cooperatives has continued in both France and Italy, in marked contrast to the experience of Britain. In West Germany a network of business projects was initiated in the alternative sector. These businesses did not necessarily adopt formal cooperative status but share many of their characteristics, such as collective ownership and democratic management. They also have a strong commitment to providing a socially useful product or service and aim to pay an income equivalent to the general level of wages. In the USA, as in Europe, the new wave of cooperative development was associated with the alternative movement (see Ehrenreich and Edelstein 1983; Lichtenstein 1986). An estimated 500,000 people are employed by producer cooperatives in Western Europe (Heller et al. 1998).

STOP

Cooperatives are based on values of self-help, self-responsibility, democracy, equality, equity, and solidarity. Here are the Rochdale Principles of Cooperation, established by the Rochdale pioneers of the cooperative movement in the 1840s. These are the basic principles you would expect to find in a cooperative.

1. *Open, voluntary membership.* Membership in a cooperative should be voluntary and available without restriction or discrimination to all persons who can make use of its services and are willing to accept the responsibilities of membership.

2. *Democratic control.* Cooperatives are democratic organizations. Their affairs should be administered by persons elected or appointed in a manner agreed to by the members and accountable to the members. Members should enjoy equal rights of voting and participation in decisions affecting the co-op. No member has greater control than any other. Members must 'cooperate' to effectively govern their business.

3. *Limited return, if any, on equity capital.* Share capital should receive a strictly limited rate of interest. This means that cooperatives do not seek speculative investments that care more about profits than people. Investments in the cooperative are for the good of the whole.

4. *Net surplus belongs to user-owners.* The net savings from the operations of a co-op belong to the members of that co-op and should be distributed in an equitable manner. This usually means one of three things: (*a*) setting aside money for the development of the co-op; (*b*) providing a service to the members; or (*c*) distributing money to the members in proportion to their transactions with the co-op.

5. *Education.* All cooperatives should make provision for the education of their members, officers, and employees and of the general public in the principles and techniques of cooperation, both economic and democratic. Members who understand the social vision of cooperatives, and who understand how their co-op works, can and do play a more active role in controlling their business.

6. *Cooperation among cooperatives.* All cooperative organizations, to best serve their members' interests and their communities, should actively cooperate in every practical way with other cooperatives at local, national, and international levels. The same way that co-ops seek to aid and protect their members through the implementation of these principles, co-ops can do the same for each other. Through helping one another, co-ops can strengthen the movement and broaden the social vision.

Do these principles hold any appeal to you?

Adapted from this source: www.foodcoop.com/linewaiters/rochdale.html

Interest in cooperatives has waxed and waned in Britain over the years. In 1945 there were just forty-four cooperatives (Mellor et al. 1988). Their numbers reached a low point in the early 1970s when there were about thirty-five registered in Britain. However, an alternative movement in the 1970s brought about a number of idealistic cooperatives. With growing unemployment in the late 1970s and early 1980s interest in cooperatives increased; by 1985 there were over 1,000 cooperatives in Britain. Local authorities and government agencies, like the Highlands and Islands Development Board in Scotland, promoted cooperatives as a means of job creation. The average size of cooperatives in Britain is, though, not large. The mean size is about seven workers and the median only four. They are concentrated in particular sectors like clothing, printing, catering, wholefoods, and bookshops (Cornforth et al. 1988).

What is the experience of cooperative working? In a study of sixteen British case studies Cornforth et al. (1988) found that cooperative working was intense and involving, whether for better or worse. The individuals felt a heightened emotional involvement with their work. The worries could be severe but when cooperative working was going well, it gave rise to feelings of great excitement and satisfaction that were far more stimulating than conventional employment had ever been. While instrumental benefits, like job security, were important and a powerful spur to founding or working in a cooperative, social benefits were also an advantage. It was a welcome luxury to work with people who were congenial, both politically and personally. Working in a cooperative is a way in which self-esteem and self-identity needs can be met within a work environment. Many of the members of the cooperatives had joined because they felt attracted to the radical products or services and egalitarian working practices. Many found it difficult to think of the things they liked least about their work but there were costs like low pay (especially at the start of the cooperative) and tiredness due to long hours. Workers in cooperatives were able to secure more control over organization and management of work on the shop floor than is usually the case, although there were limits imposed by the need for efficiency, the nature of technology, the workers themselves, knowledge, and experience. The cooperatives' achievements included less supervision, more flexible working arrangements, more variety of work, lower wage differentials, and more direct control over how workers carry out their jobs. Over time, however, the increasing complexity of some businesses and pressures for specialization and continuity have led to limits being placed on job rotation and the introduction of small differentials.

Cooperatives and the Labour Process

It cannot be assumed that ownership of a job bestows control over that job. The nature of the labour process in the particular industry or service will affect the control an individual has. The labour process can be defined as 'The means by which raw materials are transformed by human labour, acting on the objects with tools and machinery: first into products for use and, under capitalism, into commodities to be exchanged on the market' (Thompson 1983: p. xv). When it comes to technology in cooperatives there is often little choice about the technology that is purchased or hired. Inappropriate or outdated equipment might actually contribute to the demise of a cooperative (Wajcman 1983). A fledgling cooperative might be tied to previous production methods and even to previous suppliers or customers. Others will be constrained by the amount of money available. Machinery itself will impose its own limits. The workforce, will, though, within certain parameters have some choice about specific equipment and work design. They might choose less efficient machinery that is more safe; they may choose to situate workers facing each other in pairs to allow them to talk, allow workers discretion in unscheduled breaks, or flexibility in hours of work.

As cooperatives are unlikely to find themselves in a monopoly selling position or as a market leader, they are unlikely to be able to determine the type, quantity, or price of the product, particularly if linked to a single buyer. The speed and skill required to produce competitively conflicts with the ability of cooperatives to practise preferred forms of work organization such as job rotation. Worker cooperatives can, then, face stark choices in often very unfavourable circumstances and poor economic climates. A different set of problems based on ideological differences arose within the Israeli experience of worker cooperatives (see Russell 1995). Before a real note of pessimism sets in, let us look at an example of how cooperatives can succeed.

Mondragon

In 1956 Father Jose Maria Arizmendi-Arieta inspired workers in the Basque region of Spain to take over a redundant factory. (The ideas of egalitarianism and industrial democracy are an important constituent of Basque identity: Kasmir 1996.) By 1982 over 18,000 people were employed by the Mondragon group of cooperatives and they had created their own network of financial and welfare services; in 1986 the numbers employed were 19,500. In the 1980s the Spanish economy was more severely affected by recession than other Western industrialized nations yet the Mondragon cooperatives coped with the extreme economic adversity.

In Mondragon there are primary cooperatives that produce a variety of manufactured products including electrical goods, refrigerators, and machine tools. The difficulty of obtaining funding and the need to provide social and welfare services led to the establishment of secondary cooperatives of which the most important is the Caja Laboral Popular, a savings bank. The Caja lays down a democratic governing structure and a code of practice for each cooperative (Mellor et al. 1988) and provides about 60 per cent of the funding for new cooperatives. Workers, though, must make an investment; this provides incentive to workers' commitment to the cooperative's success. Successful cooperatives like Mondragon provide jobs, security, reduced labour-management strife, flexibility in hours, and work location. All profits return to workers or to community welfare (Hacker 1987).

Participation by workers is mediated though a committee system. Directors are elected on the basis of one person, one vote; directors are accountable to a general assembly. The general assembly meets at least annually and members of the firm have an obligation to vote there. The governing council is the top policy-making body which may call meetings. This governing council is elected by the members, who are all workers; non-members may attend but are not members. A works or social council effectively replicates

Is Mondragon an example of a utopian organization? The Mondragon cooperatives have achieved some of the principal goals utopia strives for. For a fuller discussion of Mondragon and how it matches up to a utopian ideal, see **www.ac.wwu.edu/~khoover/Mondragon.html**

the role of trade unions and could, for example, question abuses committed by management, make suggestions on safety and health, social security, systems of compensation, and social work activities or projects. Many of the cooperatives employ no non-members and by their own constitution and by-laws, no cooperative may employ more than 10 per cent of non-members.

Until the early 1970s worker participation was limited to governance. In the late 1970s this was extended to the organization and management of work. A manager was asked to look at personnel and human relations and concluded that:

• The personnel department should play a leading role in linking the economic and technological objectives of the firm with the social concerns of the members.

• The growing tensions in the workplace revealed the inherent contradiction between the democratic system of cooperative governance and the rigid authoritarian system for organizing work according to the scientific management principles of Taylor.

• Management should explore the possibility of creating new forms of work organization that would be economically efficient yet more in harmony with the social values on which the cooperative movement was based. Personnel should work with line managers to do this (see Whyte and Whyte 1988: 113–14).

Changes were made to work organization, for example an assembly line for the manufacture of thermostats was removed and work tables substituted. Workers could now set their own work rhythm and freely exchange information and ideas. All workers were expected to perform all the tasks and could rotate tasks as they themselves decided. As they gained skill and confidence they began to take over supervisory and staff functions, such as requisitioning tools and materials and recording their output. As a result of reorganization the workers could more readily visualize their contribution to the total product; they were better able to respond to customer needs and improve the planning process; the inventory of work in progress was reduced and the research and development process strengthened. Both managers and workers were in favour of the new ways of working. The monotony of work was relieved. The work groups increased workers' self-esteem and made individuals feel responsible to the group for their performance and workers welcomed the opportunity to learn new skills and improve relationships with supervisors. Improved productivity and quality reduced scrap and stock levels.

Mondragon is not without its critics. For example, Kasmir (1996) is disappointed that the more or less democratic entrepreneurial decisions are implemented through a hierarchy of managers, experts, and skilled workers. Hacker claims that empirical research on work democracy has tended to ignore issues of gender, with studies of Mondragon failing to note the situation of women or ask questions about gender before she arrived (1987). Yet Whyte and Whyte do look briefly at the situation of women and find that at the outset single women had been required to leave the firm when they married but by the mid-1960s this policy had been abandoned. They also note the efforts made to establish a women's cooperative within Mondragon.

Sally Hacker's (1987) study (which was aided by Clara Elcorobairutia) suggests that women fare somewhat better in Mondragon cooperatives than in private firms in the region, in employment, earnings, and job security. But the concentration of technical and scientific skill lay with the men in the cooperatives. Women workers are found clustered at the bottom of the pay and occupational hierarchies.

The Israeli Kibbutz

The kibbutz movement in Israel remains a viable attempt to provide an alternative to capitalism without managerial authority and worker subordination and exploitation (Warhurst 1998). The kibbutz movement was founded at the beginning of the twentieth century and grew rapidly in the two decades after 1931. The pioneers wished to create an economy and society that was free, working, and classless. The organizational design uses socialist principles where the means of production are owned by the community and all work is shared equally and rotated to give every member experience of every activity, including the most routine and demeaning work. In the kibbutz members live and work communally. This is a logical extension of cooperative working. A common 'household' and treasury exists. Nobody receives payment but all basic needs are met on an agreed basis with equality; all members receive a small, personal, and equitable allowance regardless of contribution. A general assembly is the source of power and every member has equal access to it. This assembly is supplemented by committees of work branches, work allocation, culture, services, economic planning, and others. The typical kibbutz will have as many as thirty different committees and between 30 and 50 per cent of members annually participate in them. General managers are elected and open to regular rotation approximately every five to seven years. In recent years the situation has become less favourable as support for socialist solutions has dwindled (Heller et al. 1998). Today there are 269 kibbutzim with a total population of 123,900 members (Yad Tabenkin 1997). The average size is just less than 500 members. Membership is voluntary but subject to the approval of the community.

Warhurst (1998) has produced a case study of a kibbutz through open participant observation, living and working there. In this kibbutz he found the managers had a coordination rather than a control function. There were no job descriptions, no direction, monitoring, or evaluation by managers of work or workers, no records of individual workers or work group performance or attendance. Workers decided their own specific tasks and how to do them. It was the antithesis of Taylorism. Labour discipline came about in part due to the commitment of individual members and their identification with the purposes of the kibbutz. There is a common framework of norms, values, and beliefs about the organization and the importance of work to which all members, as workers, consent and conform. At least one alternative form of organization and control is possible then, Warhurst concludes, in the workplace.

Imagine being able to say this to your boss. He asks you to do a particular job and you say, 'No, I prefer to do something else.' This is how a worker in Warhurst's (1998) case study factory explained his relationship with his line manager. The manager can only ask you to do something; he cannot tell you to do it.

Yugoslav Self-Management

Yugoslav workers enjoyed social ownership and worker self-management until that country's break-up. For about three decades social scientists studied the Yugoslav self-management system, which was based on the assumption that organizations could be run by their employees operating through elected Workers' Councils. These had the right to hire and fire management and make major decisions. Theoretically, all decisions were made by workers; the role of management was simply one of implementation of those decisions. Technically, managers should not be members of workers' councils though they were able to attend and speak.

Research showed, however, that top management were members of the works council and tended to dominate discussions on strategic issues; they had most of their proposals accepted (Heller et al. 1998). There was then a great gap between expectations of what self-management could achieve and what it did achieve. Much of this gap could be explained by differences in experience and knowledge of managers and workers. It may have been a mistake to expect all employees (most of whom came from peasant backgrounds) to take part in decisions on technology, marketing, and innovation, and to think that professional managers would carry out decisions without having a say. The Tayloristic scientific division of labour was widespread; democratic management was curbed. Self-management degenerated into little more than self-interest, a situation reinforced by the personal financial remuneration of workers within these enterprises (Warhurst 1998).

There were, however, some successes. Yugoslav industries were the most participative of the industries studied in eleven countries. Self-management educated the workers and created a feeling of collective ownership and responsibility. It did much to transform a traditional hierarchical society. Self-management also trained a generation of managers (Heller et al. 1998). Self-management disappeared when the Yugoslav state broke apart in 1990. Research by Pusic (see Heller et al. 1998) shows that Croatian managers feel quite positively about self-management and in Slovenia a new structure has emerged based in co-determination. While Yugoslav workers' self-management has now largely disappeared, its experience provides some important lessons.

Employee Involvement: Profit Sharing and Share Ownership

Interest in employee participation in organizational decision making peaked in the 1970s but continued interest in the subject is maintained by, for example, financial participation. One form of financial participation, which is thought to foster greater identification among employees with their employer and a means by which employees can bear some of the risks and rewards of the enterprise, is through profit sharing. In profit sharing employees are given the opportunity to take some of their income from employment in a form related to their employer's profits. Profit sharing was initially introduced in the mid-nineteenth century to prevent or inhibit union activity. Schemes were often withdrawn when profits declined along with the threat of union influence (Baddon et al.

1989). Further surges of interest in profit sharing emerged just before the First World War, the inter-war period, and post-war. The fluctuating history suggests that the schemes were introduced for two main purposes: as an act of faith by employers towards their employees or as a means of securing employee compliance (Baddon et al. 1989). Interest in profit sharing has grown again in recent years (Bhargara 1995; Gomez-Mejia and Balkin 1992; Morris and Pinnington 1998). It is now estimated that 24 per cent of private-sector employees in the UK (3.7 million) currently receive profit-related pay (Robinson and Perotin 1997).

Profit sharing can be effective in eroding the 'them and us' divide between owner and employees and in increasing commitment to enterprise goals and raising efficiency and profitability. There is very strong research evidence to show that profit sharing does act to increase company productivity (Robinson and Perotin 1997). With profit sharing there is the potential incentive effect of a payment system which links workers' productive performance with their remuneration; it can also be seen as offering an incentive to employees to increase profitability as a group. One disadvantage is that it loses the directness of the effort–pay relation which can create 'free rider' problems (Kim 1998) where workers do not put in the expected effort as they only receive a small part of the profits generated by their effort.

Share ownership means that employees are able to acquire a degree of ownership of the assets of the employer. The purpose is to allow employees to develop a sense of belonging to the company and to envisage a breaking down of the 'them and us' divide. In theory, employee ownership should generate more favourable attitudes towards the company and greater organizational commitment (Kelly and Kelly 1991). This in turn will lead to changes in behaviour, such as greater personal effort, a reduced propensity to quit, and greater scrutiny of colleagues' work behaviour (Pendleton et al. 1998). In time these changes should be reflected in improvements in collective performance as measured by productivity and profitability. Like profit sharing, employee share ownership schemes have become widespread in the UK (Millward et al. 1992), some parts of the European Union (Uvalic 1991), the USA (Blasi and Kruse 1991), the former Eastern bloc countries (Karsai and Wright 1994), and Japan (Jones and Kato 1995).

Although Robinson and Perotin (1997) say there is a link between profit sharing and productivity, others, like Baddon et al. (1989), have concluded that the evidence on increased profitability and productivity arising from profit sharing and share ownership schemes is mixed. Although employers and employees are potential beneficiaries of financial participation, there is surprisingly little hard evidence on what the benefits are or to whom they accrue (Baddon et al. 1989). Baddon et al. (1989) surveyed about 400 employee share ownership and profit-sharing schemes in companies. They found that companies commonly run more than one scheme of financial participation for more than one objective. The managers themselves had only a very general sense of what they were trying to achieve through these schemes. Case studies showed that there was a strong sense of unitary thinking in which share ownership (and to a lesser extent profit sharing) was seen as reinforcing employee loyalty and commitment, but there was no systematic attempt by the companies to measure the benefits of running these schemes. The conclusion is that the management objectives were not being achieved and that personal financial gain is a stronger motivating factor among employees than some of the loftier objectives. The benefits tended not to be seen by employees as an essential element of pay which would generate commitment, even where profit bonus benefits were quite substantial. They were 'just another kind of bonus' (1989: 275) which fell short of moving employees to a feeling of unity of purpose. No specific scheme held any significant advantage over others. Similarly Dunn et al. (1991) and more recently Keef (1998) have found that employee ownership does not result in expected improvements in attitudes. Two reasons are that employee equity stakes are too small in relation to total equity to bring about a pronounced sense of ownership and that few opportunities are provided for employees to translate ownership into increased control and participation in decision making (Pendleton 1997). It would appear that a 'sense of ownership' is important in bringing about attitudinal change. Opportunities for participation in decision making are more important than ownership per se in generating feelings of ownership. Feelings of ownership are significantly associated with higher levels of commitment and satisfaction (Pendleton et al. 1998).

There are, then, alternatives to highly bureaucratic, hierarchical organizations which involve greater democracy, wider decision making, ownership, and involvement. While Frederick Taylor, Henri Fayol, and Max Weber legitimated the managerial right to manage in the USA, Britain, and other parts of Europe, the managers' right to analyse the work situation scientifically and rationally, devising the most appropriate, efficient methods, this might not be the only way to organize. In Scandinavia, for example, there was a 'historic compromise' between capital and labour (Burnes 1996) with government-backed approaches to industrial democracy and extensions of workers' rights. Rules, divisions of labour, and some bureaucracy will not be eliminated, but organizations could be more democratic, less hierarchical, and more collectivist. There are circumstances under which workplace democracy is possible (Joseph 1989). As Joseph notes, what is striking about Britain is the extent to which alternatives to conventional management arrangements are non-issues. Greater moves could be made towards extending and renewing existing organizational forms. There are a variety of possible organizational forms of decision making, ownership, and involvement to choose from that could result in a minimal bureaucracy. Would task sharing, egalitarian rewards, democratic controls, cooperative cultures, and participation appeal to you? Alternative organizational forms could offer solutions to the problems created by Taylorism, bureaucracy, hierarchy, and social inequality. You decide.

■ SUGGESTIONS FOR FURTHER READING

1. Cornforth, C., Thomas, A., Lewis, J., and Spear, R. (1988), *Developing Successful Worker Cooperatives*, London: Sage. This book has been considered key in understanding cooperatives and describes how historically the formation of worker cooperatives has varied cyclically.

2. Mellor, M., Hannah, J., and Stirling, J. (1988), *Worker Cooperatives in Theory and Practice*, Milton Keynes: Open University Press. This book is a classic of its time.

3. Whyte, W. Foote, and Whyte, K. King (1988), *Making Mondragon: The Growth and Dynamics of the Worker Cooperative Complex*, Ithaca, NY: ILR Press, New York State School of Industrial and Labor Relations, Cornell University.

4. Hickson, D. J., and Pugh, D. (1995), *Management Worldwide*, London: Penguin. In chapter 5 there is a description of the kibbutz both in theory and in practice.

5. Oakshott, R. (1990), *A Case for Workers' Cooperatives*, (2nd edn.), Houndmills: Macmillan Press. This book provides an account of independent worker cooperatives in the UK and around other European countries, including Mondragon in Spain.

6. Lammers, C. J., and Szell, G. (1989) (eds.), *International Handbook of Participation in Organizations: For the Study of Organizational Democracy, Cooperation and Self Management*, Oxford: Oxford University Press. This book of readings covers organizational democracy, cooperatives, employee share ownership, job involvement, job design, semi-autonomous work groups and self-management in European, Scandinavian, and other countries.

7. Warhurst, C. (1999), *Between Market, State and Kibbutz: The Management and Transformation of Socialist Industry*, London: Mansell Publishing. This book is a 'before' and 'now' exposition and explanation of the kibbutz in Israel.

■ WEB LINKS

www.wisc.edu/uwcc/ University of Wisconsin site offering news of cooperative organizations around the world. A similar site is run from the University of California—**http://cooperatives. ucdavis.edu/**

http://ivo.uvt.nl/fulltext/03nrf_groot.pdf provides a research paper reporting a study of thirty cooperatives in India.

www.sfworlds.com/linkworld/mondragon.html for more references on Mondragon.

■ QUESTIONS

1. The impetus and motivation for cooperatives comes from a number of different sources, according to the research. What motivation for the establishment of alternative organizations can you find in your reading?

2. Why would firms adopt profit sharing and employee ownership plans (see Kruse 1996 and others).

3. If share schemes improve productivity, why don't the majority of firms use them? (See Drago and Turnbull 1996 and others).

4. There are examples from all over the world of people taking control of their own economic destiny. The Rochdale pioneers are one such example. Another is the Antigonish Movement in Nova Scotia (Coady 1967; Gherardi et al. 1989). What were the advantages for these people in being involved in owning and controlling their enterprises? What were the drawbacks?

5. Credit Unions help provide financial support to people in their local communities and are regulated by the Financial Services Authority in Britain. What advantages and disadvantages (apart from the obvious financial ones) do they offer their members?

■ GROUP EXERCISE

Is the cooperative movement dead? If you search on the BIDS system (a search system for finding articles and books) for 'cooperatives', it produces 119 references for the years 1999–2003 alone. Look for yourselves and decide if it is 'all history'. Would you want to work in a cooperative? Why or why not?

■ REFERENCES

Baddon, L., Hunter, L., Hyman, J., Leopold, J., and Ramsay, H. (1989), *People's Capitalism? A Critical Analysis of Profit-Sharing and Employee Share Ownership*, London: Routledge.

Bhargara, S. (1995), 'Profit Sharing and Financial Performance of Companies: Evidence from UK Panel Data', *Economic Journal*, 104: 1044–56.

Blasi, J., and Kruse, D. (1991), *The New Owners: The Mass Emergence of Employee Ownership in Public Companies and What it Means to American Business*, New York: Harper Business.

Burnes, B. (1996), *Managing Change: A Strategic Approach to Organizational Dynamics* (2nd edn.), London: Pitman.

Coady, M. M. (1967), *Masters of Their Own Destiny: The Story of the Antigonish Movement of Adult Educaton through Economic Cooperation*, New York: Harper & Row.

Cornforth, C., Thomas, A., Lewis, J., and Spear, R. (1988), *Developing Successful Worker Cooperatives*, London: Sage.

Drago, R., and Turnbull, G. K. (1996), 'On the Incidence of Profit Sharing', *Journal of Economic Behaviour and Organization*, 31: 129–38.

Dunn, S., Richardson, R., and Dewe, P. (1991), 'The Impact of Employee Share Ownership on Worker Attitudes: A Longitudinal Case Study', *Human Resource Management Journal*, 1/1: 1–17.

Earle, J. (1986), *The Italian Cooperative Movement*, London: Allen & Unwin.

Ehrenreich, R. C., and Edelstein, J. D. (1983), 'Consumers and Organizational Democracy: American New Wave Cooperatives', in C. Crouch and F. Heller (eds.), *Organizational Democracy and Political Processes*, New York: Wiley.

Gherardi, S., Strati, A., and Turner, B. (1989), 'Industrial Democracy and Organizational Symbolism', ch. 13 in C. J. Lammers and G. Szell (eds.), *International Handbook of Participation in Organizations*, vol. i, Oxford: Oxford University Press.

Gomez-Mejia, L., and Balkin, D. (1992), *Compensation, Organizational Strategy and Firm Performance*, Cincinnati: South Western Publishing.

Hacker, S. (1987), 'Women Workers in the Mondragon System of Industrial Cooperatives', *Gender and Society*, 1: 358–79.

Heller, F., Pusic, E., Strauss, G., and Wilpert, B. (1998), *Organizational Participation: Myth and Reality*, Oxford: Oxford University Press.

Jones, D., and Kato, T. (1995), 'The Productivity Effects of Japanese Employee Stock Ownership Plans: Evidence from Japanese Panel Data', *American Economic Review*, 85: 391–414.

Joseph, M. (1989), *Sociology for Business*. Cambridge: Polity in association with Basil Blackwell.

Karsai, J., and Wright, M. (1994), 'Accountability, Governance and Finance in Hungarian Buy-outs', *Europe-Asia Studies*, 46: 997–1016.

Kasmir, S. (1996), *The Myth of Mondragon: Cooperatives, Politics and Working Class Life in a Basque Town*, Albany, NY: SUNY Press.

Keef, S. P. (1998), 'The Causal Association between Employee Share Ownership and Attitudes: A Study Based in the Long Framework', *British Journal of Industrial Relations* (Mar.), 73–82.

Kelly, J., and Kelly, C. (1991), ' "Them and Us": Social Psychology and the New Industrial Relations', *British Journal of Industrial Relations*, 29: 25–48.

Kim, S. (1998), 'Does Profit Sharing Increase Firms' Profits?', *Journal of Labor Research*, 19/2: 351–70.

Kruse, D. L. (1996), 'Why Do Firms Adopt Profit Sharing and Employee Ownership Plans?', *British Journal of Industrial Relations*, 34/4: 515–38.

Lichtenstein, P. M. (1986), 'The Concept of the Firm in the Economic Theory of Alternative Organizations', in S. Jansson and A.-B. Hellmark (eds.), *Labour-Owned Firms and Workers' Cooperatives*, London: Gowe.

Mellor, M., Hannah, J., and Stirling, J. (1988), *Worker Cooperatives in Theory and Practice*, Milton Keynes: Open University Press.

Millward, N., Stevens, M., Smart, D., and Hawes, W. (1992), *Workplace Industrial Relations in Transition: The ED/ESRC/PSI/ACAS Surveys*, Aldershot: Dartmouth.

Morris, T., and Pinnington, A. (1998), 'Patterns of Profit-Sharing in Professional Firms', *British Journal of Management*, 9: 23–9.

Pendleton, A. (1997), 'Shareholders as Stakeholders', in A. Gamble, D. Kelly, and G. Kelly (eds.), *Stakeholder Capitalism*, Basingstoke: Macmillan.

——Wilson, N., and Wright, M. (1998), 'The Perception and Effects of Share Ownership: Empirical Evidence from Employee Buy-outs', *British Journal of Industrial Relations*, 36/1: 99–123.

Robinson, A., and Perotin, V. (1997), 'Is Profit Sharing the Answer?', *New Economy*, 4: 112–16.

Rothschild-Whitt, J. (1982), 'The Collectivist Organization', in F. Lindenfeld and J. Rothschild-Whitt (eds.), *Workplace Democracy and Social Change*, Boston: Porter Sargent.

Russell, R. (1995), *Utopia in Zion: The Israeli Experience with Worker Cooperatives*, Albany, NY: SUNY Press.

Thompson, P. (1983), *The Nature of Work*, London: Macmillan.

Uvalic, M. (1991), *Social Europe: The PEPPER Report*. Brussels: European Commission.

Wajcman, J. (1983), *Women in Control*, Milton Keynes: Open University Press.

Warhurst, C. (1998), 'Recognizing the Possible: The Organization and Control of a Socialist Labour Process', *Administrative Science Quarterly*, 43: 470–97.

Whyte, W. Foote, and Whyte, K. King (1988), *Making Mondragon: The Growth and Dynamics of the Worker Cooperative Complex*, New York: ILR Press, New York State School of Industrial and Labor Relations, Cornell University.

Yad Tabenkin (1997), *Kibbutz: Facts and Figures*. Efal: Yad Tabenkin.

■ INDEX